PORTFOLIO INSURANCE

PORTFOLIO INSURANCE
A GUIDE TO DYNAMIC HEDGING

EDITED BY DONALD L. LUSKIN

WILEY

JOHN WILEY & SONS
NEW YORK CHICHESTER BRISBANE TORONTO SINGAPORE

ISBN 0-471-85849-8

Printed in the United States of America

10 9 8 7 6 5 4 3 2 1

LIST OF CONTRIBUTORS

SUMNER ABRAMSON, a Managing Director of The Putnam Companies, has 25 years of investment experience as an income and growth portfolio manager. Mr. Abramson, a graduate of Harvard College, was the Chief Investment Officer at Colonial Management Associates before joining Putnam in 1983. He developed Colonial's option and corporate cash programs, programs that now constitute the bulk of assets managed. He was the first option income fund manager, having started that fund in 1977 and the first corporate cash fund manager, having started that fund in 1981.

Mr. Abramson joined Putnam as a Senior Vice President directing the firm's overall mutual fund and institutional option activities and is the originator and Portfolio Manager of the Putnam Corporate Cash Trusts. Mr. Abramson, as Chief Investment Officer of the Equity Derivative Products Group, currently oversees over $4 billion in assets directly using derivative investment instruments.

Mr. Abramson is a member of the Boston Society of Security Analysts, a Chartered Financial Analyst, and a past President of the Boston Institutional Options and Futures Society.

ROBERT D. ARNOTT is the author of 18 articles of original research published in professional journals, 3 of them required reading for the Chartered Financial Analyst program. Mr. Arnott has twice won the Financial Analyst Federation's Graham & Dodd Scroll. This award is given each year for the best published articles on investment theory. Scrolls were awarded for

Mr. Arnott's original research in the development of a Strategic Asset Allocation approach and for research on the relationship between the business cycle and security selection. He is a member of the editorial board of the *Journal of Portfolio Management*. Mr. Arnott is responsible for equity strategy and asset allocation strategy at Salomon Brothers, Inc. Prior to joining the firm he was President and Chief Investment Officer of TSA Capital Management, based in Los Angeles. TSA Capital Management and its parent company, Trust Services of America, rank among the most successful in the United States, with combined institutional and personal trust assets under management totaling $4.5 billion. TSA is widely known for active asset allocation and core equity management activities.

FISCHER BLACK is a Partner in the Trading and Arbitrage Division of Goldman, Sachs & Co. Mr. Black works on hedging, investment, and financing strategies for the firm and its clients, especially strategies that make use of analytical methods. Before joining Goldman, Sachs, Mr. Black was Professor of Finance at the Massachusetts Institute of Technology's Sloan School of Management and at the University of Chicago. Mr. Black developed, with Myron Scholes, the Black–Scholes option pricing formula. In 1985 he was President of the American Finance Association.

REN Y. CHENG is Vice President and Analyst of the Derivative/Equity Options Group at The Putnam Companies. Mr. Cheng joined Putnam in 1985 as an options and futures analyst. He has most recently played an important role in the development of Putnam's portfolio insurance product. Mr. Cheng holds a Bachelor of Economics degree from the National Taiwan University and an M.A. from Brown University, where he is currently a Ph.D. candidate.

ROBERT P. CLANCY is a Vice President in the Portfolio Strategies Group at the First Boston Corporation. He is responsible for marketing structured fixed income portfolio products and developing new products and portfolio strategies for insurance companies, investment advisors, and mutual funds. Before joining First Boston, Mr. Clancy was a portfolio manager and fixed income department head at State Street Bank and Trust Company. Prior to that, he served in both actuarial and financial officer roles at John Hancock Mutual Life Insurance Company, dealing with product pricing, portfolio management, and asset-liability management. He is a Fellow of the Society of Actuaries and a recipient of the Halmstad Prize for actuarial research for his paper on options on bonds.

ROGER G. CLARKE, Chief Investment Officer and Managing Director, joined TSA as a senior investment strategist in August 1985. He is primarily responsible for development of new investment strategies and products involving financial futures and options. Dr. Clarke also manages institutional portfolios employing these instruments. Dr. Clarke has extensive experience in investment research specializing in the areas of options theory and corporate finance. In 1986 he was named by the Financial Analysts Federation to receive the prestigious Graham & Dodd Scroll for his article "Problems in Evaluating the Performance of Portfolios with Options," which was written with Richard Bookstaber. In 1982 Dr. Clarke and Dr. Bookstaber were honored with the Roger F. Murray Award from the Institute for Quantitative Research inFinance for the year's best investment research. Prior to joining TSA, Dr.Clarke spent seven years on the faculty of Brigham Young University, serving most recently as associate professor of finance at the University's Graduate School of Management. His extensive research work has resulted in the publication of numerous articles in the *Financial Analysts Journal*, *Journal of Portfolio Management*, *Journal of Business*, *Journal of Finance*, and other periodicals. He is also co-author of the book *Options Strategies for the Institutional Investment Manager: A Guide for Improving Performance*. He holds a B.A. and M.B.A. from Brigham Young University and a Ph.D. in finance from Stanford University.

JOHN C. COX is the Nomura Professor of Finance at the Massachusetts Institute of Technology. Mr. Cox is the author or co-author of a number of articles on financial economics. Mr. Cox is also the co-author of a recently published book *Options Markets*. His current research interests include equilibrium asset pricing, dynamic portfolio theory, the term structure of interest rates, and corporate finance.

DON ELAN is Vice President and Senior Analyst of the Derivative/Equity Options Group. Mr. Elan joined Putnam in 1981 and has responsibility for the banking, savings and loan associations, insurance, media, entertainment, and other industries in the Derivative/Equity Options Group. Prior to working with Putnam, he was a retail stockbroker. Mr. Elan is a Chartered Financial Analyst. He holds a B.S. from Hebrew University, an M.S. from Tel Aviv University, and an M.B.A. (with honors) from Boston University, where he is currently a candidate for a doctorate in business administration and finance.

JEREMY EVNINE is a Senior Vice President at Wells Fargo Investment Advisors in San Francisco, California, where he is a co-manager of Arbitrage and Hedging. Previously he was Wells Fargo Investment Advisors' Manager of Product Development. Before joining Wells Fargo in 1984, he served as a consultant to Oakley Sutton Management Company and as a research associate at BARRA, where he was responsible for option-related products. Mr. Evnine has lectured graduate and undergraduate courses in finance and operations research at Stanford University, the University of California at Berkeley, and California State University. He has published several articles in financial journals. Mr. Evnine received his Ph.D. in operations research/finance from the University of California at Berkeley in 1983, an M.Sc. in pure mathematics from the Hebrew University of Jerusalem in 1977, and a B.Sc. in mathematics from Manchester University, England, in 1972.

ROBERT FERGUSON is an Executive Vice President at Leland O'Brien Rubenstein Associates and Associate Editor of the *Financial Analysts Journal*. He has written numerous articles on investments and is a three-time winner of the Graham and Dodd award for excellence in financial writing. Prior to joining LOR, Mr. Ferguson was a Vice President of College Retirement Equities Fund. There he developed an improved dividend discount model, created a theory of active and passive investing for tax-free and taxable investors, designed an improved risk model, and managed a $140 million equity portfolio. He also helped frame investment policy and met regularly with the Finance Committee of the Board of Trustees to discuss investment strategy. Mr. Ferguson has had extensive experience applying mathematics and computers to investing. He has worked with security analysts to develop more effective methods of analysis and has created the quantitative tools needed to implement them. He also has designed advanced portfolio management systems that combine the best of human judgment and quantitative techniques. His experience as a security analyst and portfolio manager has provided him with a valuable perspective for this work. Mr. Ferguson received a B.A. degree in physics from Columbia University and has completed a year of graduate work in physics at Cornell. He has a Ph.D. in finance from New York University.

MICHAEL R. GRANITO is a Managing Director of J.P. Morgan Investment Management Inc. He heads the Capital Market Research Group, which is responsible for Morgan's quantitative product research and pension finance efforts and is a member of the firm's investment policy committee. Prior to joining Morgan in 1979, Mr. Granito taught at the Wharton School while earning a Ph.D. in finance. He has written extensively on both the theory and practice of investment management and is a member of the finance faculty at Yale University.

SCOTT F. GRANNIS is Vice President, Client Services and Marketing at Leland O'Brien Rubinstein Associates Inc. (LOR), a Los Angeles-based investment management firm. LOR specializes in designing and managing dynamic hedging strategies for large corporations and pension funds. Prior to joining LOR, Mr. Grannis was Senior Economist at the Claremont Economics Institute (CEI). At CEI Mr. Grannis advised large corporations and institutional money managers on business and investment strategies and wrote numerous publications dealing with asset allocation, country risk analysis, interest rates, and foreign currency issues. He received his B.A. degree in philosophy from Pomona College and an M.B.A. in finance from Claremont Graduate School. Mr. Grannis is also a Registered Investment Advisor and member of the National Futures Association.

ANDREW HARMSTONE-RAKOWSKI is Vice President of J.P. Morgan Investment Management Inc. Mr. Harmstone-Rakowski is a member of the Equity and Balanced Accounts Group with account management responsibilities for futures and options strategies. He is also involved in coordinating futures and options trading activity. Prior to joining Morgan, Mr. Harmstone-Rakowski was a Vice President at Paine Webber Capital Markets as a stock index futures specialist servicing institutional investors. A graduate of the University of Wisconsin, Mr. Harmstone-Rakowski received his M.A. from the University of Pennsylvania and will receive a Ph.D. from the University of Pennsylvania on completion of his dissertation.

DOUGLAS HOLMES is Vice President and Department Head at State Street Bank and Trust of Boston. Mr. Holmes has extensive experience in hedging and arbitrage techniques, restructuring portfolios, and passive fund management. Besides managing separate core accounts and a South African free portfolio, Mr. Holmes also does research to help update existing products and create new ones. Previously, Mr. Holmes was a partner at Lovett, Ward & Bertelsen and before that was at Batterymarch Financial Management. He has a B.S. in mathematics from Northeastern University. In addition, he holds the CFA designation.

MARK P. KRITZMAN, CFA, is a General Partner of New Amsterdam Partners, an investment advisory firm located in New York City. Before co-founding New Amsterdam Partners. Mr. Kritzman was a Vice President in the Investment Management Group at Bankers Trust Company. He also held investment positions at AT&T and The Equitable Life Assurance Society. Mr. Kritzman is active in several industry groups, including the Investment Technology Association, the Institute for Quantitative Research in Finance, and the Institute of Chartered Financial Analysts, where he is a member of the Council of Examiners and the Candidate Curriculum Committee. Mr. Kritzman has published many articles on the application of financial theory to investment management, and he is the co-editor and co-author with Stephen Brown of *Quantitative Methods for Financial Analysis* (Dow Jones–Irwin). He holds a B.S. in economics from St. John's University and an M.B.A. from New York University.

HAYNE E. LELAND is Professor of Finance at the University of California at Berkeley. He has published numerous articles in finance and economics journals and served as editor of the *Journal of Economic Theory* and the *International Economic Review*. He is a Director of the American Finance Association. Mr. Leland has consulted for a number of private and public clients, including the RAND Corporation, the National Science Foundation, and the Department of Energy. In 1981, together with John O'Brien and Mark Rubinstein, he founded Leland O'Brien Rubinstein Associates Incorporated, a firm that provides portfolio risk management (also known as portfolio insurance). He is currently a Director of LOR. Mr. Leland received his B.A. and Ph.D. in economics from Harvard University and his M.Sc. from the London School of Economics.

LARRY MARTIN is Vice President and Department Head at State Street Bank and Trust of Boston. Mr. Martin is responsible for overseeing all international, active, and passively managed portfolios. Mr. Martin joined the Asset Management Division in 1982 and was instrumental in the development of the stock index futures funds, SPIFF and SPIFF-Plus. Specializing in quantitative analysis, Mr. Martin developed the CASH Plus product which engages in arbitrage trading between stocks and stock index futures. Prior to his position in the International Department, Mr. Martin was head of the Core Portfolio Services Department, overseeing all U.S. passive equity portfolios. Mr. Martin is a graduate of Cornell University with a degree in applied mathematics and holds an M.B.A. from Boston University. Additionally, he holds the designation of CFA.

BRUCE J. PULLMAN started his career in the City of London working for N.M. Rothschild and Sons in international corporate finance. He moved to County Bank in 1981 as a fund manager of short term multicurrency accounts. In late 1982 he started a Quant group as a team of one and six months later picked up one of the first UK passive management mandates. The group was an early user of BARRA's index software and rapidly became a major player in the UK index fund industry. It now manages in excess of $2 billion in a variety of passive and quasipassive strategies. Mr. Pullman's main focus of research work for the past two years has been enhancing and extending a portfolio insurance model that had been specially tailored for County by a software consultant. His studies have included detailed analysis of the varying return structures experienced across both markets and assets. Mr. Pullman is a frequent speaker at conferences around the world on portfolio insurance and on the practical aspects of trading non-U.S. stock index futures. He has written for a number of publications including *Intermarket* in the United States. Mr. Pullman is a director of County NatWest Investment Management in London and responsible for quantitative research and the marketing of quantitatively oriented investment products.

STEPHEN A. ROSS, Sterling Professor of Economics and Finance, is a specialist in financial economics. Professor Ross has been at Yale University, School of Management, since 1977. He received a B.S. in physics with honors from the California Institute of Technology in 1965 and a Ph.D. in economics from Harvard University in 1969. He has been Director at CREF since 1981 and was made President-Elect of the American Finance Association in 1987. Mr. Ross is Associate Editor of the *Journal of Finance* and the *Journal of Economic Theory*. He is a principal with Richard Roll in MRR, Inc. and in Ross and Roll Asset Management Corporation, Registered Investment Advisors, Gwynedd, Pennsylvania. Mr. Ross was awarded the Leo Malamed Prize for Best Research by a Business School Professor (1978–79) by the Graduate School of Business, University of Chicago. He also received the Pomerance Prize for Excellence in the Area of Options Research by the Chicago Board Options Exchange in 1978. Mr. Ross has held a Guggenheim Fellowship (1975–76), and he has been nominated three times for the University Lindback Award for Distinguished Teaching (1972–73, 1973–74, 1974–75). Professor Ross is the author of many journal articles, including "Arbitrage Pricing Theory Approach to Strategic Portfolio Planning."

MARK RUBINSTEIN is Professor of Finance at the University of California at Berkeley. He has published widely in academic journals and co-authored a book with John Cox titled *Options Markets* (Prentice-Hall, 1985). He was awarded the CBOE Pomerance Prize for excellence in options research, has twice received prizes for papers related to options from the Institute for Quantitative Research in Finance, and received the 1985 Graham & Dodd Plaque Award from the Financial Analysts Federation for excellence in financial writing. For the last decade he has been an associate editor of the two leading academic finance journals: *Journal of Finance* and *Journal of Financial Economics*. Recently he was appointed to the editorial advisory board of the *Journal of Portfolio Management*. He received his B.A., magna cum laude, from Harvard University, his M.B.A. from Stanford University, and his Ph.D. from the University of California at Los Angeles. In 1981, together with Hayne Leland (also from Berkeley) and John O'Brien, he formed the firm Leland O'Brien Rubinstein Associates Incorporated, which specializes in institutional portfolio risk management using Dynamic Asset Allocation.

ROGER SAYLOR, Managing Director of J.P. Morgan Investment Management Inc. Mr. Saylor is a member of the Equity and Balanced Accounts Group and is responsible for futures and options activities. Mr. Saylor manages portfolios that use futures and options strategies to control overall asset mix, enhance performance, or control risk. Mr. Saylor joined Morgan's Research Group in 1977 specializing in the application of financial theory to investment management. A graduate of Dartmouth College, Mr. Saylor earned his M.B.A. at the University of Chicago and is a Chartered Financial Analyst.

MYRON S. SCHOLES is Frank E. Buck Professor of Finance, Graduate School of Business, Stanford University, and Professor of Law, Stanford Law School, Stanford University. *Background*: Ph.D., Graduate School of Business, University of Chicago, 1969; M.B.A., Graduate School of Business, University of Chicago, 1964; B.A., McMaster University, 1962. Formerly, Edward Eagle Brown Professor of Finance and Banking, Graduate School of Business, University of Chicago, 1981–1983; Professor of Finance and Director of the Center for Research in Security Prices, 1976–1981; Associate Professor and Executive Director of the Center for Research in Security Prices, 1974–1976; Assistant and Associate Professor of Finance, Sloan School of Management, M.I.T., 1968–1973. *Selected Publications*: "The Capital Asset Pricing Model: Some Empirical Tests" (with Fischer Black and Michael Jensen); "The Market for Securities: Substitution Versus Price Pressure and the Effect of Information on Share Prices"; "The Valuation of Option Contracts and a Test of Market Efficiency" (with Fischer Black); "The Pricing of Options and Corporate Liabilities" (with Fischer Black); "The Effects of Dividend Yields and Dividend Policy on Common Stock Prices and Returns" (with Fischer Black); "Estimating Betas from Nonsynchronous Data" (with Joe Williams); "Dividends and Taxes" (with Merton Miller); "Executive Compensation, Taxes and Incentives" (with Merton Miller); "Dividends and Taxes: Some Empirical Results" (with Merton Miller); "Taxation and the Dynamics of Corporate Control: The Uneasy Case for Tax-Motivated Acquisitions" (with Ron Gilson and Mark Wolfson); "Issues in the Theory of Optimal Capital Structure" (with Mark Wolfson). *Other Positions*: Research Associate, National Bureau of Economic Research, Member of Econometric Society, past Member of Board of Directors of the American Finance Association.

STEVEN PAUL SOMES, Assistant Vice President and Manager, Risk Controlled Products, joined BEA in September, 1986. His responsibilities include the research and management of "engineered" portfolios employing dynamic hedging, structured fixed income, options and futures, and low risk arbitrage. Prior to joining BEA, Mr. Somes was a Director of the portfolio hedging group at Aetna Life & Casualty, responsible for the research and management of the firm's dynamic hedging programs. He also managed structured fixed income portfolios and provided fixed income research. A chartered financial analyst, Mr. Somes received a B.A. degree from Bates College and an M.S. from the Massachusetts Institute of Technology.

SCOTT STEWART is Vice President of Investments at Fidelity Management Trust Company in Boston, Massachusetts. He is currently responsible for developing and managing global index and index plus products, including both equities and derivative securities. Mr. Stewart was previously an Assistant Vice President at State Street Bank and Trust of Boston where he managed bond funds, global equity portfolios, and portfolio insurance and asset allocation strategies. Mr. Stewart completed his Ph.D. in finance from Cornell University in 1985, concentrating on the information in dealers' quotes and transaction prices. He has published papers in the *Financial Review* and the *Financial Analysts Journal* and is actively involved with research in finance.

RALPH S. TATE is the President of Aetna's Portfolio Hedging Group and as such manages the group responsible for all of Aetna's dynamic hedging operations. A native of Davenport, Iowa, Mr. Tate received his undergraduate education at Amherst College and his M.B.A. from Stanford University's Graduate School of Business. He has been involved with various aspects of asset management for pension clients since 1971 and has headed Aetna's highly successful portfolio insurance program since 1980.

OLDRICH VASICEK is Senior Research Associate at Gifford Fong Associates in Walnut Creek, California, and a Vice President and Partner at Dimensional Corporate Finance, Inc. in San Francisco, California. His experience includes eight years as a Vice President in the Management Science Department at Wells Fargo Bank in San Francisco, California, and four years of graduate teaching at the University of Rochester, Rochester, New York, and the University of California at Berkeley, California. A native of Czechoslovakia, he holds a Ph.D. in probability theory and statistics from Charles University in Prague and a M.S. degree in mathematics from Czech Technical University. He has received several honors, including the Graham & Dodd Award and the Institute for Quantitative Research in Finance Award. He has written some 20 articles in financial and mathematical journals.

WAYNE H. WAGNER provides conceptual direction and strategic product development to PLEXUS GROUP and also serves as Portfolio Manager. PLEXUS GROUP is a Registered Investment Advisor to institutional funds, organized as a partnership of Wayne Wagner, Larry Cuneo, and Edward Story. Plexus was formed July 1, 1986. Mr. Wagner previously served as Chief Investment Officer of Wilshire Associates' Asset Management Division where he managed $2.5 billion. Prior to that, Mr. Wagner created and operated the Trust Universe Comparison Service (TUCS) as well as the Index Fund Management Service and other departments at Wilshire. Mr. Wagner was a founder of Wilshire Associates. Prior to Wilshire, Mr. Wagner served with Wells Fargo Bank and helped operate the first index funds there. Mr. Wagner has written and spoken frequently on subjects such as equity risk measurement and diversification; index fund construction and applications; trading methods, costs, and cost assessment; bond risk measurement and passive bond portfolios; social divestment and social portfolio constraints; portfolio ethics; and futures and portfolio insurance. Mr. Wagner has received two prestigious Graham & Dodd Awards for excellence in financial writing. Four of his articles were featured as the cover article of the journal in which they appeared. Mr. Wagner has a M.S. in statistics from Stanford University as well as a B.B.A. from the University of Wisconsin.

AN IDEA WHOSE TIME HAS FINALLY COME

The institution of insurance is surely one of the most ancient and durable pillars in the foundation of human society. Without insurance as a means of pooling and transferring risk, it is difficult to imagine the development of the complex economic structures that define civilized culture. It is surprising, then, that mechanisms for insuring investments in stocks and bonds against depreciation have only evolved and become popular in the last decade. Perhaps "popular" is too mild a word—from virtual nonexistence 10 years ago, *portfolio insurance*, as it has come to be called, is currently in effect for institutional assets valued at more than $50 billion. Although a late starter, it is now by any measure the fastest growing investment strategy in the history of investment strategies.

Perhaps portfolio insurance did not evolve earlier because the nature of portfolio risk is unlike that of the risks insurance companies traditionally underwrite. For automobiles, insurance can be achieved through *risk pooling* in which each insured individual contributes a small fraction of total anticipated claims. Because only a few participants will experience collisions in any one period, the *more* participants in the pool, the *lower* the risk to the underwriter. Portfolios, however, are too highly correlated to be insured by risk-pooling. A depreciation in the value of one participant's portfolio suggests that there will be similar depreciation in the portfolios of all the other participants as well. Therefore, underwriters of portfolio insurance cannot hedge their risk through diversification across many customers—the *more* participants in the pool, the *greater* the risk for the underwriter.

For this reason portfolio insurance, despite its name, is not a creation of the insurance industry. Rather, it is the product of creative application by investment managers of leading-edge developments from the academic world of financial theory. Therefore, to implement a program of portfolio insurance an institutional investor cannot simply buy a policy from an insurance company. Instead, he must create, or hire an investment manager to create, an investment discipline that will replicate the pattern of returns afforded by a hypothetical insurance policy. Because such a discipline typically involves the ongoing reallocation of assets, the process of portfolio insurance is often called *dynamic hedging*. And since dynamic hedging is an ongoing customizable process rather than a rigid insurance policy, it can be used to shape patterns of return unlike those normally associated with the traditional notion of insurance.

This book is a collection of the best current thinking about the concept of portfolio insurance and the process of dynamic hedging. Its contributors, both academic and institutional, comprise a virtual who's who of portfolio insurance, including its originators and leading practitioners. The depth and diversity of their contributions demonstrate that portfolio insurance and dynamic hedging are among the most exciting issues in current investment theory and practice.

Part 1 of this book discusses the evolution and basic principles of portfolio insurance. In "The Evolution of Portfolio Insurance," Hayne E. Leland and Mark Rubinstein describe the path that led these two University of California professors to develop the concept that academic options pricing theory could be applied to create portfolio insurance, and how (with John O'Brien) they formed Leland O'Brien Rubinstein Associates, Inc., the investment management firm primarily responsible for the strategy's dramatic and sudden institutional acceptance. Next, in "Alternative Paths to Portfolio Insurance," Rubinstein describes and compares the strategy's basic processes. Finally, in "Patterns of Reward for Portfolio Insurance," Roger G. Clarke and Robert D. Arnott describe the costs and benefits of adopting programs of portfolio insurance.

Part 2 examines a wide spectrum of applications for portfolio insurance and dynamic hedging. In his introduction to this section called "Applications of Dynamic Strategies," Scott F. Grannis surveys some creative applications of dynamic hedging that extend well beyond mere insurance. Next, in "How to Beat the S&P 500 (Without Losing Sleep)," Robert Ferguson suggests that superior returns may be attainable by insuring a levered portfolio. In "Insuring the Asset/Liability Ratio," Mark P. Kritzman discusses how a corporate pension plan sponsor can use dynamic hedging to control the volatility of a pension surplus. In "Insuring International Portfolios," Bruce J. Pullman shows how dynamic hedging can be used to manage the constellation of capital and currency risks attendant to global investing. Finally, in "The Best-Return Strategy," Oldrich Vasicek discusses how dynamic hedging can be geared to provide an investor the best return from among a universe of multiple risky assets.

The practical application of dynamic hedging is discussed in Part 3. It begins with "Structuring a Portfolio Insurance Program," in which Steven Paul Somes discusses some of the concepts to be considered by an investor contemplating the use of dynamic hedging. In "The Many Dimensions of Risk," Wayne H. Wagner discusses the complex nature of the risks institutional investors may wish to insure. In "Stock Index and Financial Futures," Larry Martin details the mechanics of the most widely employed portfolio insurance instruments. In "Listed Stock Index Options," Sumner Abramson, Ren Y. Cheng, and Don Elan look at the benefits and pitfalls of exchange-traded options contracts. In "Integrating Listed Stock Index Options," Andrew Harmstone-Rakowski and Roger Saylor show that careful structuring of listed options positions can overcome their ostensible shortcomings for portfolio insurance. In "Estimating Volatility," Jeremy Evnine discusses the measurement and estimation of volatility, the proxy for the magnitude of expected risk required for most dynamic hedging processes. In "The Insurance Company Guarantee," Ralph S. Tate discusses Aetna Life Insurance Company's role as the only underwriter offering actual portfolio insurance. Finally, Robert Clancy, Douglas Holmes, Harry Martin, and Scott Stewart discuss "Constant Horizon Portfolio Insurance" in which a commingled index futures fund can be employed as the hedging instrument.

The book's final part traces the roots of portfolio insurance to their origins in academic financial theory. In his introduction titled, "The Intellectual Origins of Portfolio Insurance," Michael R. Granito compares and contrasts the seminal contributions of the papers collected in this part. "Individual Investment and Consumption under Uncertainty," a previously unpublished 1972 paper by Fischer Black, contains the seeds of the pattern of returns now called portfolio insurance. "The Pricing of Options and Corporate Liabilities" is the breakthrough 1973 paper by Fischer Black and Myron Scholes detailing the famous Black-Scholes options pricing model. In 1978's "Option Pricing: A Simplified Approach", John C. Cox, Stephan A. Ross, and Mark Rubinstein distill the Black-Scholes model into a form revealing its underpinnings in arbitrage pricing theory. In 1980's "Who Should Buy Portfolio Insurance," Hayne E. Leland links the patterns of returns associted with options contracts to those associated with insurance. Finally, in 1981's "Replicating Options with Positions in Stocks and Cash" Leland and Mark Rubinstein explicitly demonstrate that portfolio insurance, and other optionlike patterns of risk and return, can be practicably achieved by dynamic reallocation between asset classes.

Portfolio insurance has been a long time coming. But thanks to the creative contributions of the authors who have made this book possible, it is an idea whose time has, finally, come.

DONALD L. LUSKIN

Chicago, Illinois
January 1988

Contents

PART 4: ROOTS

PART 5: NEXT

BASICS

1. THE EVOLUTION OF PORTFOLIO INSURANCE

Hayne E. Leland and Mark Rubinstein

The financial product known as portfolio insurance was born the night of September 11, 1976. Hayne Leland had recently returned from France, and had been lamenting the weakness of the dollar. Ronald Reagan played a bit role: As governor of California, his administration saw a substantial reduction in the real income of academics. Lifestyles were in danger, and it was time for invention.

On September 11, Leland was wondering what product might have appeal to the financial community. He recalled conversations with his brother, a principal in an investment management firm. His brother mentioned that after the decline of 1973–74 many pension funds had withdrawn from the stock market, only to miss the subsequent rally in 1975. "If only insurance were available, those funds could be attracted back to the market," he had said.

So portfolio insurance seemed a product that would have considerable appeal. The only problem was how to provide it. Clearly, the parallels with regular insurance were limited. While the form of an insurance contract might look familiar—an assured value in return for a premium—the manner in which it would be provided would have to be quite different. In contrast with houses, when one portfolio burns down, virtually all others are likely to follow suit. So "risk pooling," the typical method of insurance, was not appropriate for portfolio insurance.

Although no expert in options theory at the time, Leland suddenly realized that insurance was equivalent to a put option—not on a stock, but on an entire portfolio. In 1976, however, exchange-traded put options did not exist. (When they were introduced the following year, they were limited to a few stocks, and had short maturities.)

At this point Leland's background as an academic provided an advantage. Three years earlier, Fischer Black and Myron Scholes had written a key paper on the pricing of options.[1] This paper used a local arbitrage argument to derive option prices in an environment where stock prices followed a logarithmic, continuous-time random walk. Over a very short time period, Black and Scholes showed that a call option could be perfectly hedged by a negative stock position. Since the resulting hedge position was riskless, it must return the riskless rate. This requirement produced a partial differential equation which had to be satisfied by the value of the option. The solution to the equation is the celebrated Black-Scholes formula.

In wrestling to understand fully the Black-Scholes approach, Leland had come to realize that the local arbitrage argument used by Black and Scholes to price options could be extended to actually create options. Rather than create a risk-free return by dynamically hedging an option with stock, as in Black-Scholes, why not reverse the process and create an option by dynamically hedging the stock with a risk-free asset?

Arbitrage means that there are two ways of doing the same thing. If an option were desired, either the option could be purchased, or it could be created by a dynamic strategy which involved just the underlying stock and a risk-free asset. And an option could be created on a portfolio of stocks as easily as on a single stock—for any desired striking price or time to expiration. At that moment, Leland realized portfolio insurance could be provided![2]

A sleepless night of excitement gave rise to a further revelation: Leland really didn't know much about options at all! Exactly what was the appropriate hedge ratio? Would short positions be needed? And how could the problem be put on a computer to implement easily the shifting of equities to Treasury bills and vice versa?

Fortunately, Leland knew he didn't have to look far. Mark Rubinstein, a colleague in the finance group at Berkeley, had recently become both an options expert and a computer nut. Recognizing the importance of the emerging field of options, Rubinstein had just published what proved to be an important paper in the development of option pricing theory. Moreover, carried away by his enthusiasm for the emerging possibilities for stand-alone computing, he had nervously just purchased a desktop IBM 5100 computer, containing a grand maximum of 64K of core memory with a 200K cassette tape drive for $20,000.

Rubinstein was convinced that Leland's ideas could be implemented, in part because he had used the same principles to hedge positions as a market

[1]Footnotes appear at end of chapter.

maker with a seat on the options floor of the Pacific Stock Exchange. However, he was concerned about two potential problems. First, he was worred that the transactions costs created by the frequent trading required by the dynamic strategy could prove excessive. Second, he was then in the process of preparing an economic justification for exchange-traded index options to be submitted to the SEC by the Philadelphia Stock Exchange.

If this proposal were approved, he feared that it would not be necessary to use dynamic trading strategies to manufacture portfolio insurance when this insurance could be purchased directly in the form of exchange-traded index puts. Nonetheless, Rubinstein's own SEC report demonstrated his belief that index options (exchange-traded or manufactured) would prove to be an invaluable tool for investors.

Thus, on September 12, a verbal agreement was made to form Leland-Rubinstein Associates. The objective was to develop the technique and appropriate software to provide portfolio insurance. It was clear to both that this was to be done as a part-time activity. While it was directly relevant to the field of finance, neither Leland nor Rubinstein wanted portfolio insurance to be the sole focus of their time or research interests.

Progress was not particularly rapid, as other academic responsibilities took their toll. The cloud of exchange-traded index options continued to cast its shadow. Also worrisome was the problem for insurance posed by random volatility.

But the concerns abated for two reasons. First, the Philadelphia Stock Exchange's proposal was turned down—ostensibly because of the new feature of cash settlement on exercise, but also, we believe, because the Securities and Exchange Commission and the Commodities Futures Trading Commission had not yet resolved which was to have regulatory power over such instruments.

Second, we came to realize that most institutional funds would prefer longer-term protection—and indeed, our programs increasingly are of three- to seven-year duration. Since exchanges only make money from turnover, it would only pay them to list options with high trading volume and these would likely have short maturities. (Subsequently, with some irony and luck, it turned out that the phenomenal success of these relatively short-lived index options has provided a useful set of instruments for the long-term insurance programs if carefully rolled-over in conjunction with other securities.)

Yet another reason to prefer the dynamic approach was the fact that most institutional portfolios were unique, and contained bonds and other securities besides stocks. Options on bonds and stocks separately would prove an inefficient way to protect such a portfolio.

A remaining problem was random volatility. The Black-Scholes formula assumes that the volatility of the underlying asset remains constant over an option's horizon. But even a cursory familiarity with the behavior of stocks, as well as stock indexes, suggests that this is not a realistic assumption. In the depression, the S&P 500 index had annual volatilities exceeding 30 percent. During most of the 1960s, the index had annual volatilities of less than 15 percent. Hedging based on a 15 percent volatility could be disastrous if the actual volatility turned out to be 30 percent. We felt this problem had to be solved before portfolio insurance could be marketed.

During the summer of 1978, while working in France, Leland saw a possible resolution to the volatility problem. The Black-Scholes formula had several arguments: the striking price, time to maturity, the interest rate, and the variance of the stock return. But time and variance always entered as a single term, multiplied together. This meant that if the variance were higher, all pricing and hedging would remain identical if the time period were shorter! With a little more math, Leland realized that exact insurance could be provided, if what was insured was a total volatility, which could be expressed as a predetermined number of moves of the underlying portfolio. At the same time, Rubinstein had been working on a binomial approach to option valuation and hedging, which could be interpreted in much the same way.

So Leland-Rubinstein Associates' first product was portfolio insurance for a given number of moves of the underlying portfolio. Our sales presentation contained an example in which protection was provided for five moves (any combination of ups and downs) of 5 percent. The protection was good until the maximum number of moves had occurred. By specifying the term of the insurance in this manner, we did not have to worry about excessive costs or mishedging. Increased volatility would simply result in quicker expiration, at which point (we hoped) the client would renew his policy.

When Rubinstein first programmed this new approach, the historical simulation results were disappointing. Errors often exceeded an unacceptable 5 percent. But a programming error was found, and suddenly, simulation errors dropped to less than 0.1 percent. Turnover was not excessive. We knew we were on our way!

To demonstrate that the system worked in the real world, Rubinstein actually used the system on his own account, shifting money between Vanguard's Index Fund and Money Market Fund. The experiment was a complete success and formed the basis for results later reported in *Fortune* magazine (June 1980).

Barr Rosenberg, a colleague at Berkeley and a pioneer in applying financial theory to portfolio selection, wrote a very supportive introductory letter to institutional money managers. It was now 1979. Leland made a swing to several major Eastern and Midwestern banks, giving seminars about the ideas behind portfolio insurance. Several expressed interest; scheduled 1-hour meetings turned into half-days.

Leland went home and eagerly waited for the phone to ring. It never did. In our quickly diminishing naiveté, it was difficult to understand why such an appealing idea as portfolio insurance would not be immediately picked up by someone. It seemed if we didn't run into the stone wall of disbelief that it was possible to create portfolio insurance, we ran aground on the old conservative argument: "If this is so good, why isn't someone already doing it?" Worst of all were the silent types who would nod with approval and apparent understanding during our whole presentation, but never tell us their reservations. As familiar as this response may be to many salespeople, this was new to us academics who never had to go far among our colleagues to find an argument.

It soon became evident that while we did not doubt our technical expertise or the viability of the product, we just weren't—either by temperament or by the time available—going to succeed at marketing. We needed an individual with the background to understand the technical aspects of portfolio insurance, while at the same time having the ability to market the product professionally. It was then, in late 1980, that we made our first "sale" to John O'Brien.

O'Brien had years earlier formed O'Brien Associates, the first firm to provide analytical services for portfolio managers based on MPT. Concerned by the shift to competitive commissions and its impact for soft-dollar-funded services, O'Brien moved to A. G. Becker, where he was vice president in their pension fund services research group. (O'Brien Associates continued under the name Wilshire Associates.)

Leland and Rubinstein met O'Brien at a seminar run by the Berkeley Program in Finance; a casual description of portfolio insurance led to more serious discussions about the possibility of a joint venture. Characteristically, standing on his faith in the power of a good idea and his ability to sell it, O'Brien was willing to give up his safe and comfortable position at Becker and throw in with us. An agreement was reached in the fall of 1980 and Leland O'Brien Rubinstein Associates, Inc. (now mercifully known as LOR) was incorporated in February 1981 with three principals, two part-time secretaries, one computer, and no clients.

Within a month, however, we had our first client. MidContinent Capital Management, headed by John Mabie, insured a $500,000 account for six moves of 4 percent. Funds were moved between Treasury bills and an actively managed portfolio. The account delivered as promised, and protection lasted almost exactly the planned six months.

O'Brien's marketing plan included an emphasis on fund sponsors, as contrasted with money managers. He felt that portfolio insurance allowed sponsors to regain the risk control of their entire portfolio. Managers typically held only a portion of a sponsor's funds. Insuring a small fraction made little sense; furthermore, it seemed a conflict of interest for managers to offer insurance when their product was often predicated on "beating the market."

O'Brien's plan for attracting sponsors worked well, and by the end of the first year our assets under management were up to $135 million. But simultaneously, we had our first major problem. MidContinent's second program, also for six moves of 4 percent, did not last the six months which average volatility would imply. The market fell with higher-than-average volatility. The program delivered as promised—but the moves had expired more quickly than projected—the program was completed after only four months. And, while providing protection against losses as we had expected, the program's early termination had unsettled the client.

The first of many research projects was launched: How to provide insurance for fixed time periods when volatility was random, without violating minimum returns and limiting the variability of upside costs. The resulting product clearly had more market appeal than the previous (and to us, more elegant) random-horizon model—the model that convinced us to offer the product in the first place. It was not the only lesson we've learned about the marketplace since 1976!

The business grew rapidly. Soon our success, our willingness to risk explanation of our procedures even to potential competitors, and publication of a pedagogic article in the *Financial Analysts Journal*[3] inevitably took its toll: We had our first competition from two well-established firms. Ironically, neither firm met with much success but inadvertently helped to legitimize the product in the minds of many firms who later became our customers.

Although the business continued to grow, we were always burdened by two major problems. First, the shifting of stock to Treasury bills, and vice versa, was in many cases opposed by money managers. It was disruptive to their investment process, they said. Second, it was difficult to coordinate the shifting of funds when there were many managers. All had to agree to work with the system, and a way of deciding how much each manager needed to sell needed to be worked out.

Both of these problems were solved with the development of the index futures markets. Shorting index futures is the equivalent of selling a portfolio of stocks, and investing the proceeds in a short-term Treasury bill. Thus hedge positions could be increased by shorting index futures, and decreased by removing these positions. Portfolio insurance based on futures does not interfere with money managers (indeed, they need not even know the program is in place). The liquidity of the futures markets, and low cost of transacting compared with stocks, made the protection of very large programs feasible for the first time.

Our first account using index futures was started in March 1984. As of the end of 1986, roughly 80 percent of the dollar value of LOR accounts was protected using futures. While offering many advantages, there are some subtleties to using futures, including proper attention to the basis, and the use of appropriate fixed-income futures for long-run programs.

In 1983, we began to attract large money managers as licensees. Because our software was soon transferred from the IBM 5100 to its successor, the IBM/PC, its portability meant that our product could be used in a truly distributed computing environment. Our software allows certain functions to be performed locally and others to be performed on a PC-based time-sharing system run out of our offices in Los Angeles (with a complete backup system in New York in case California falls into the sea).

Through the offerings of licensees, two of our original goals dating back to our 1976 discussions have been realized. One licensee, Wells Fargo Investment Advisors, uses the product to insure part of its extensive index fund. Another licensee, Aetna Life and Casualty, uses our service to guarantee minimum rates of return on equity investments, and backs this guarantee with their corporate assets.

Not least, the term "portfolio insurance"—which we coined but were at first reluctant to use in a commercial environment because of its potentially misleading implications—has become generic.

The sophistication of portfolio insurance users has grown as rapidly as the product itself. Currently, more than 75 percent of LOR accounts are not run with traditional Black-Scholes hedging. Rather, time-invariant or "perpetual" programs are used. These programs have the advantage that there is no fixed expiration date: The program can be left in force as long as the client wishes. And, in another development, sponsors are realizing the advantage of programs that protect a fund's surplus. Portfolio insurance is being applied to many different classes of assets besides equities; fixed-income and international investments are growing areas of application.

An early criticism of portfolio insurance was that it reduced return as well as reducing risk. But users are discovering that portfolio insurance can be used aggressively rather than simply to reduce risks. Long-run returns can actually be raised, with downside risks controlled, when insurance programs are applied to more aggressive active assets. Pension, endowment, and educational funds can actually enhance their expected returns by increasing their commitment to equities and other high-return sectors, while fulfilling their fiduciary responsibilities by insuring this more aggressive portfolio. Compared with current static allocation techniques, annual expected returns can be raised by as much as 200 basis points per year.

The future looks as exciting as the past. LOR has always maintained that it is in the Dynamic Asset Allocation business, of which portfolio insurance is but one product. Dynamics can be used to mold a set of returns to virtually any feasible investor objective. It can be used to manage the risks of corporate balance sheets as well as investment funds. As such, it may represent the most significant advance to date in the science of financial engineering.

FOOTNOTES

1. See Chapter 19: "The Pricing of Options and Corporate Liabilities." Robert Merton extended the Black-Scholes model in many important ways in his paper, "Theory of Rational Option

Pricing," *Bell Journal of Economics and Management Science*, Vol. 4 (Spring 1973), pp. 141–183.

2. At the same time a professor at the University of British Columbia, Michael Brennan, and his student, Eduardo Schwartz, published a related paper entitled, "The Pricing of Equity-Linked Life Insurance Policies with an Asset Value Guarantee," *Journal of Financial Economics*, Vol. 3 (June 1976), pp. 195–213.
3. See Chapter 22: Mark Rubinstein and Hayne Leland, "Replicating Options with Positions in Stocks and Cash."

2. ALTERNATIVE PATHS TO PORTFOLIO INSURANCE

Mark Rubinstein

Portfolio insurance, in its purest and simplest form, is equivalent to a securities position comprised of an underlying portfolio plus an insurance policy that guarantees the insured portfolio against loss through a specified policy expiration date. Should the underlying portfolio (including any income earned and reinvested in the portfolio but deducting the cost of buying the insurance) experience a loss by the policy expiration date, the insurance policy can be used to refund the amount of the loss. On the other hand, should the underlying portfolio show a profit, all profit net of the cost of the insurance is retained.

Consider a portfolio with the same composition as the Standard & Poor's 500 and suppose it is covered by an insurance policy that has one year until expiration. The S&P 500 is at 100 at the start of the policy, and the one-year insurance policy costs \$3.33. After buying the insurance, an investor with \$100 has \$96.67, which can buy 0.9667 "shares" of the S&P 500.

Table I shows the pattern of returns this investor will realize at the end of the year. The *minimum* value of the insured portfolio is \$100; there will be no loss, even after the cost of the insurance is deducted. On the upside, the value of the insured portfolio depends on the behavior of the full \$100 investment in the S&P 500. Because the insured portfolio owns 0.9667 shares of the S&P 500, its value on the upside will always be 0.9667 times the value of the S&P 500 with dividends reinvested (e.g., 125 × 0.9667 = 120.84). This number is sometimes referred to as the "upside capture."

Reprinted from *Financial Analysts Journal*, July–August 1985.

TABLE I. PATTERNS OF RETURNS FROM PORTFOLIO INSURANCE AFTER ONE YEAR

Value of S&P 500 with Dividends Reinvested	Value of Insured S&P 500 Portfolio
$ 75	$100
80	100
85	100
90	100
95	100
100	100
105	101.50
110	106.34
115	111.17
120	116
125	120.84
130	125.67

PROPERTIES OF INSURED PORTFOLIOS

The return pattern of the insured portfolio has several important properties:

(A) The probability of experiencing any losses is zero.
(B) The return on any profitable position will be a predictable percentage of the rate of return that would have been earned by investing all funds in the S&P 500.
(C) If the portfolio is restricted to investments in the S&P 500 and cash loans, if the expected rate of return on the S&P 500 exceeds the return on cash, and if the insurance is fairly priced, then among all investment strategies possessing properties (A) and (B), the insured portfolio strategy has the highest expected rate of return.

Stop-loss orders are perhaps the simplest examples of investment strategies that have property A (ignoring jumps through the stop-limit price) but lack property B. To implement a stop-loss order strategy, one invests the entire $100 in the S&P 500 and instructs the broker to sell out completely and convert to cash if the S&P 500 (with dividends reinvested) falls so low that a conversion to cash, given then current interest rates, would result in a value of exactly $100 at the end of the year.

Clearly, this strategy possesses property A. However, the value of the portfolio is not completely determined by the level of the S&P 500. If, midway through the year, the S&P 500 fell low enough to trigger the conversion into cash, then the return on the portfolio from then on would be entirely unrelated to the S&P 500.

It is easy to devise other strategies that have both properties A and B but lack C. Suppose an investor is restricted to "buy and hold" positions using only the S&P 500 and cash and wants to maximize expected rate of return while insuring against a loss. If the interest rate is 10 per cent, he can invest $90.91 in cash and $9.09 in the S&P 500. Now, even if the S&P 500 falls to zero, he would just break even (since $90.91 × 1.1 = $100). If the expected rate of return on the S&P 500 is 16 per cent, the overall expected rate of return from following this strategy would be 10.5 per cent (= (90.91 × 10%) + (9.09 × 16%)).

The proof that portfolio insurance satisfies property C, hence must have a higher expected rate of return than the buy and hold strategy, will not be reproduced here.[1] However, it will be demonstrated by example in the course of the discussion.

WHY PURCHASE PORTFOLIO INSURANCE?

Clearly, anyone who wants to insure against any losses while maximizing expected return is a candidate for the purchase of portfolio insurance.[2] Equally clearly, for every investor who purchases portfolio insurance there needs to be an investor who sells it.[3] We are thus led to conclude that intelligent buyers of portfolio insurance are typically more sensitive to downside risk than the average investor.

For either the buyer or seller of portfolio insurance, property B still holds: The return from the insured portfolio (S&P 500 plus insurance policy) will be fully determined by the return from the underlying portfolio (S&P 500) at the insurance expiration date. The path taken to reach this level of return will have no effect on the outcome.

Outcomes of "path-dependent" strategies are usually much more difficult to describe and evaluate than those of "path-independent" strategies.[4] That is, predicting returns from path-dependent strategies requires knowledge of many more factors. It is also difficult to see why an investor would want his return to be influenced by intermediate levels of the index, apart from their cumulative effect on the ending level of the index.

The remainder of this article focuses on the purchase of portfolio insurance —specifically, how is it done?

[1] Footnotes appear at end of chapter.

ALTERNATIVE PATHS

We assume that the investor wants to insure against losses in the S&P 500 with dividends reinvested. We further assume the economic environment that gives rise to the Black-Scholes option valuation formula.[5] In particular, the interest rate is known and constant, the dividend yield of the S&P 500 is known and constant, the volatility of the S&P 500 is known and constant, the value of the S&P 500 moves smoothly over time without jumps or gap openings, there are no opportunities for riskless arbitrage profits, and transaction costs are zero.

In the interest of comparability, we will assume that the interest rate is 10 per cent per year, the expected rate of return on the S&P 500 is 16 per cent, the dividend yield on the S&P 500 is 5 per cent, and the (arithmetic) volatility of the S&P 500 is 18 per cent.[6]

Each technique for creating portfolio insurance is designed to be 100 per cent reliable in preventing losses. Our comparison will focus on differences in path-independence and expected rate of return.

Stop-Loss Orders. The analysis of stop-loss orders as a method for approximating portfolio insurance is complicated by path-dependence. Suppose, for instance, that the investor executes a stop-loss order at the end of each quarter. To keep things as simple as possible without sacrificing the main elements of the problem, suppose that the S&P 500 (with dividends reinvested) moves either up or down by a fixed percentage over each quarter.

Figure A gives the S&P 500's pattern of movement over the year, given its assumed expected rate of return and volatility.[7] Both the S&P 500 and the value of the stop-loss portfolio (in parentheses) begin at $100. In each quarter, the probability of the index moving up by 8.02 per cent is 0.721, and the probability of the index moving down by 7.42 per cent is 0.279.

As the stop-loss portfolio starts out fully invested in the S&P 500, both the index and the portfolio are at either 108.02 or 92.58 after the first quarter. During the second quarter, however, path-dependence appears. If the index moved up in the first quarter, the portfolio remains fully invested in the S&P 500 during the second quarter; whether the index moves up or down, the portfolio tracks it to either 116.68 or 100.

If, on the other hand, the index moved down during the first quarter, the stop-loss order would be triggered. It is easy to see why. The interest rate must be 2.41 per cent during any quarter if it is to compound out to 10 per cent over the year while remaining at a constant level. If the portfolio is down to 92.58 at the end of the first quarter, it can only reach 99.45 $(= 92.58 \times 1.0241^3)$ by the end of the year, even if it is invested in cash over the remainder of the year. Because this ending level is less than 100, the stop-loss order is executed and the portfolio reverts for the remainder of the year to 100 per cent cash. At the end of the second quarter, the portfolio is thus

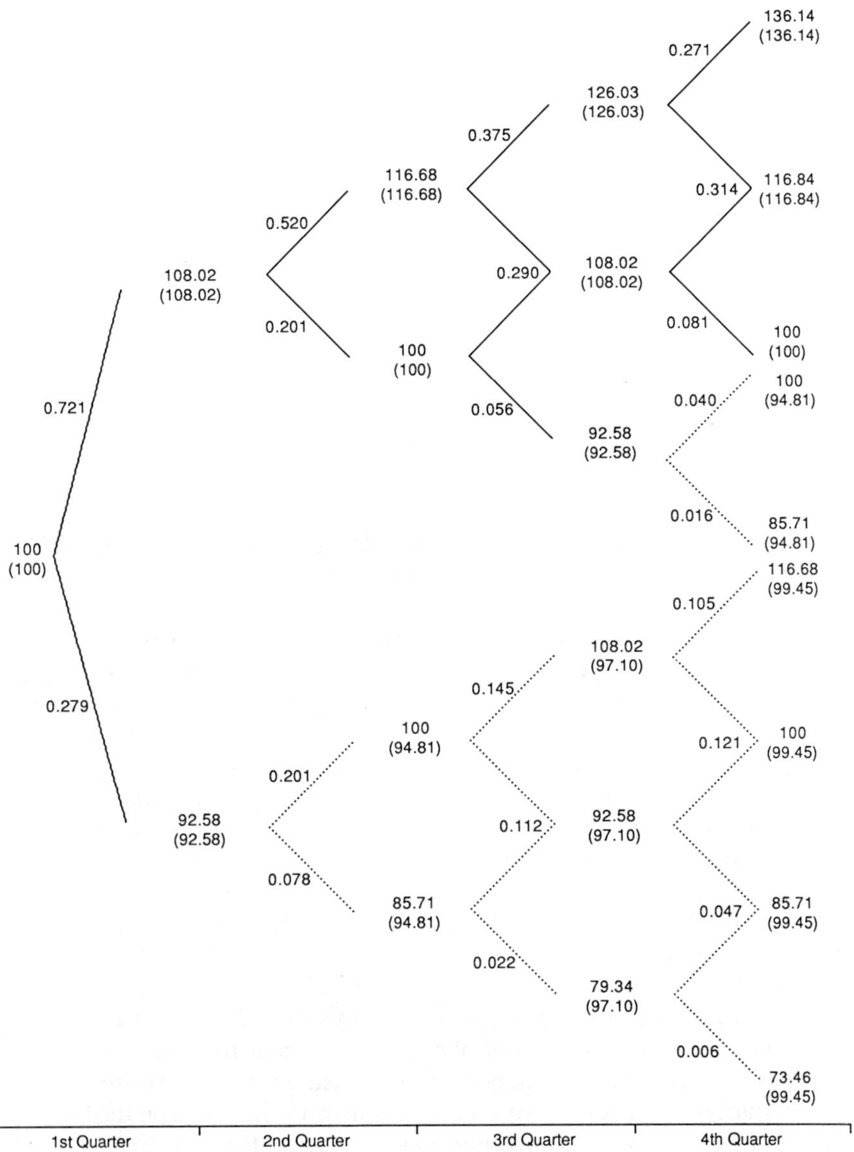

FIGURE A. Portfolio insurance with stop-loss orders

at 94.81 (= 92.58 × 1.0241). The dashed lines in Figure A indicate that the portfolio has been stopped out.

When the index is at 100, there is a 0.201 probability (0.721 × 0.279) that the portfolio will be at 100 and a 0.201 probability (0.279 × 0.721) that it will

TABLE II. POSSIBLE OUTCOMES OF STOP-LOSS STRATEGY

Value of S&P 500 with Dividends Reinvested	Stop-Loss Portfolio Return	Probability
$136.14	36.14%	0.270
116.68	16.68%	0.314
116.68	−0.56%	0.105
100.00	0.00%	0.081
100.00	−0.56%	0.121
100.00	−5.19%	0.040
85.71	−0.56%	0.047
85.71	−5.19%	0.016
73.46	−0.56%	0.006

be at 94.81. That is, although the index may reach the same level either by moving up and then down or by moving down and then up, the same is not true of the portfolio. The *path* by which the index reaches 100 leads to different values for the stop-loss portfolio.

To evaluate a stop-loss order as a method for creating portfolio insurance, it is necessary to measure its expected rate of return, given its degree of path-dependence. Path-dependence can be measured by the expected absolute deviation of the rate of return conditional on the level of the index; the appendix illustrates the calculation. Perfect portfolio insurance requires that path-dependence be zero; the stop-loss order has a path-dependence of 3.14 per cent. Table II lists the nine distinct possible outcomes from the stop-loss strategy considered above.

European Payout-Protected Puts. The stop-loss strategy is path-dependent, but it *is* a step in the right direction. It suggests that there may be a way to transfer systematically between the S&P 500 and cash to generate portfolio insurance. By moving *gradually* into stock from cash as the stock price goes up, and *gradually* out of stock into cash as the stock price falls, it is possible to generate the equivalent of an insured position in stock.[8]

Alternatively, if one-year European payout-protected puts on the S&P 500, were available, these instruments could provide perfect portfolio insurance. An investor would select a put option on the index with striking price K such that K satisfies the following equality:

$$P(K) = K - S.$$

Here, P is the price of the put (shown above as a function of its striking price) and S is the concurrent level of the S&P 500 index.[9] If the index, with dividends reinvested, were to fall below its initial level by the end of the year, it could be sold by exercising the put at price K; this would be just enough to make up for the index decline and the initial cost P of the put.

The strategy is 100 per cent reliable in preventing losses. In addition, because the payoff of such a put would be solely dependent on the year-end level of the S&P 500 (with dividends reinvested), the protective put position would be completely path-independent. Assuming, as before, that the S&P 500 has an arithmetic expected rate of return and a volatility of 16 and 18 per cent, respectively, the striking price of the put would need to be 103.45 to provide insurance against losses. The expected rate of return on the insured portfolio (S&P 500 plus put) is 14.30 per cent.[10] The payoff pattern given in Table I is from just this strategy.

Of course, the investor must pay for the index put out of his initial $100. The ratio of the initial S&P 500 level to the striking price of the put is 0.9667 (100/103.45). The investor then ends up with 0.9667 shares of the S&P 500 and 0.9667 puts, each at a striking price of 103.45. He must invest $3.33 ($3.45 × 0.9667) in puts and $96.67 in the S&P 500.

Several other types of instruments can be used to effect the same pattern of returns. From the European put-call parity relation, we know that a protective put is equivalent to a *fiduciary call* (purchased call plus cash), where the call has the same time to expiration and striking price as the put.[11] Moreover, with known rates of interest, a European put (or call) on the S&P 500 is equivalent to a European put (or call) on S&P 500 futures contracts, provided the expiration date of the option coincides with the delivery date of the underlying futures contracts.[12] Perfect portfolio insurance could be provided by either a *protective index futures put* or a *fiduciary index futures call.*

If a one-year European payout-protected option were available on each stock in the S&P 500, these instruments could be used to insure the S&P 500 by insuring each stock in the portfolio against loss for the year. However, use of conventional options on individual stocks leads to path-dependent outcomes with lower expected rates of return than index option strategies.[13]

Unfortunately, currently listed index options do not have the terms we have assumed. First, all listed options are *American.* American options can be exercised at any time before expiration, whereas European options can be exercised only at expiration. Because American options have every advantage of European options (they can be turned into European options by holding them to expiration) as well as the increased flexibility of early exercise, American options should be more expensive than otherwise identical European options. Second, listed options are not protected against dividends. As a result, they can be used to insure the capital appreciation component of stock returns, but not the dividend component. Third, all listed options have maturities of less than nine months. Because almost all trading volume is concentrated in the nearest maturities, the longest effective maturities are about three months for index futures options and two months for index spot options.[14] Finally, listed options have highly standardized striking prices that do not typically match the striking prices needed for portfolio insurance. This, combined with the advisability of early exercise of some American options, means that no American options of particular striking prices may survive in the market, even though European options of the same striking price would.

Sequential Short-Term Index Options. Although the listed markets do not offer options with the proper terms, there may still be some way of using these options to approximate portfolio insurance. In order to focus on the most significant feature of listed index options, we will assume that payout-protected European options are available in maturities of less than a year.

If six-month payout-protected European options were available, an investor could approximate portfolio insurance by rolling over a position in index puts every six months. He might start with a protective put that would insure the portfolio against loss over the first six months. If, at mid-year, the S&P 500 has declined so that it pays to exercise the put, the investor will buy another protective put to insure the portfolio over the next six months. At worst, by the end of the year, he should break even.

But suppose the S&P 500 rises over the first six months, so that the put is not exercised. In this case, the investor would buy a put that will insure the portfolio's mid-year value with a deductible equal to the profit earned over the first six months.

Figure B illustrates this strategy when the year is divided into four (binomial) intervals. Using the Block-Scholes formula, the striking price of the purchased six-month put at the beginning of the year is $103.86 (in brackets). After two quarters, the S&P 500 index is at 85.71, 100 or 116.68. In each case, the striking price of the six-month put purchased next is different.

When the index is at 85.71 or 100, the portfolio has just broken even over the first six months; the investor can't afford to lose money over the next six months. He must purchase a put with the same striking price relative to the stock price as the put he purchased at the beginning of the year.[15] When the index is at 116.68, however, such conservatism is not needed. Now, the investor can afford to lose $12.34 during the next six months and still break even at the end of the year. He can purchase a put with a striking price considerably below the current value of the portfolio.

This strategy is 100 per cent reliable in preventing losses, but it does suffer from path-dependence. Its expected rate of return, moreover, will usually fall short of the expected rate of return that could be achieved with a one-year protective European put, if one were available or could be created from a dynamic asset allocation strategy. Table III (which assumes the year is divided into 144 binomial intervals) provides estimates of the magnitudes of

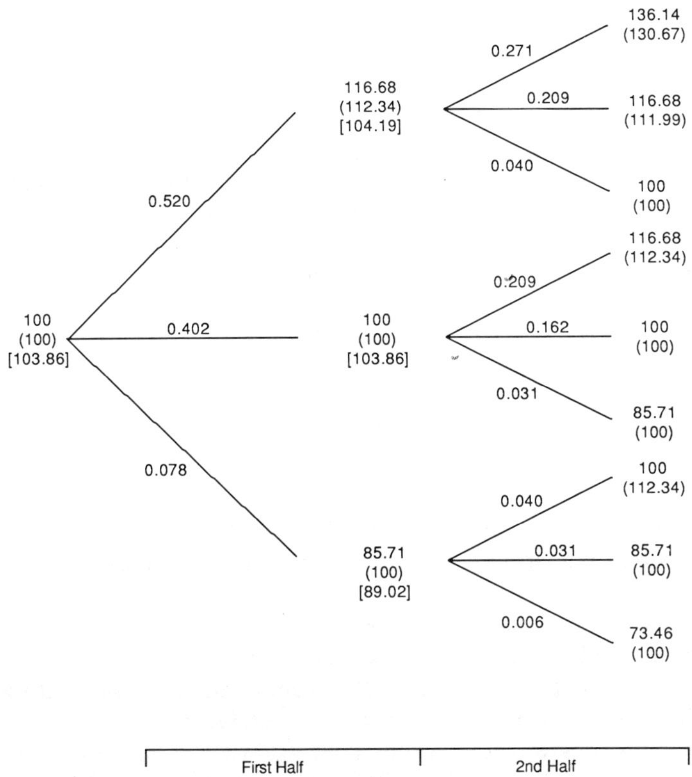

FIGURE B. Sequential short-term European index options

TABLE III. PATH-DEPENDENCE AND EXPECTED RATES OF RETURN FOR ROLL-OVER OF SHORT-TERM PROTECTIVE EUROPEAN PUTS*

Roll-Over Period	Path-Dependence	Expected Rate of Return
one year	0.00%	14.30%
six months	1.50 (1.67%)	14.04 (13.74%)
four months	2.12 (2.39)	13.96 (13.63)
three months	2.56 (2.90)	13.90 (13.53)
two months	2.97 (3.45)	13.86 (13.44)
stop-loss orders	3.73	14.70

*These results are particularly sensitive to the assumptions that volatility is known in advance and that there are no jump movements in the S&P 500 index.

path-dependence and rate of return for different roll-over periods. As the roll-over becomes more frequent, the path-dependence increases and the expected rate of return decreases.

The limited availability and liquidity of listed striking prices that are distant from the money, and the five-point intervals at which they are listed, force the investor to be more conservative in practice than he might want to be.[16] Suppose that striking prices are only available in three-point intervals and the deepest out-of-the-money put available is at most eight points out-of-the-money (relative to an S&P 500 level of 100). The numbers in parentheses in Table III show the degree to which this constraint increases path-dependence and reduces expected rate of return.

REAL-WORLD CONSIDERATIONS

The discussion so far has ignored complications created by American options, uncertain interest rates, uncertain volatility, jumps in security price movements, apparently mispriced securities, and transaction costs.

American Options. As building blocks for portfolio insurance, even long-term American index puts pose an unfortunate dilemma: It is either impossible to provide path-independence and 100 per cent reliability in preventing losses, or the insurance must be purchased at an excessive price!

As noted, if it is to insure a portfolio against loss, the index put must have a striking price K such that P(K) = K − S. Because of the possibility of early exercise, however, this is the lowest price an American option can have. Furthermore, if the option is priced properly, it would pay to exercise it immediately.

If the put were worth less than K − S, an investor could earn a riskless arbitrage profit by buying the put and the underlying stock and then immediately exercising the put to receive K > P + S. If the put were worth exactly K − S, the investor who exercised the option immediately would get the full benefit of the put and also be able to start earning interest on the net receipt of K − S. By pricing the put at its exercisable value, the market implies that the interest that can be received through early exercise of the put outweighs its time value.

Using American puts to generate portfolio insurance thus presents an awkward choice. On the one hand, buying a put priced higher than K − S can lead to a portfolio loss equal to the premium over parity (P − (K − S)) if the index falls. On the other hand, a put priced such that P = K − S will be overpriced, inasmuch as the insurance purchaser doesn't plan to exercise it immediately. The investor must steer between Scylla and Charybdis; as he avoids one difficulty, he approaches the other. In brief, the American put purchaser pays for something he doesn't want—the right to exercise the option early.

Uncertain Interest Rates. In all the strategies we have considered, except the use of long-term European payout-protected index options, uncertain interest rates increase the difficulty of predicting upside returns. The strategies' ability to protect against loss is unaffected, however, if care is taken to measure changes in interest rates and to factor these changes into the ongoing strategy.

In the case of the stop-loss strategies, for example, declining interest rates during the year translate into a shorter time to the stopout point. For the sequential option strategies (since option prices are partly determined by interest rates) uncertainty regarding interest rates increases the uncertainty regarding the prices that must be paid for options at future dates; nevertheless, changes in the option prices offset interest rate changes, preserving full loss protection.

Within the context of Black-Scholes assumptions, there is no reason to distinguish between options and their replicating dynamic asset allocation strategies; both produce identical results. With uncertain interest rates, however, dynamic strategies no longer have the power to replicate long-term European options exactly. Nonetheless, dynamic strategies that transfer holdings between stock and cash can hedge changes in interest rates over the year. Proper implementation using one-year Treasury bills as the hedging instrument (cash) should make conventional dynamic strategies less susceptible to shifts in shorter-term rates than either the stop-loss or sequential option strategies.

Dynamic option replication strategies can be implemented by using index futures. A purchased index futures contract, if held to the delivery date, implicitly embodies a long position in the index coupled with an equal amount of borrowing at a risk-free rate over the life of the contract. Instead of selling stock and lending the proceeds (as in conventional dynamic asset allocation), the investor can sell futures to accomplish similar ends by much simpler means. If the futures delivery date is less than a year, however, it will be necessary to roll over the futures hedge during the year. The strategy is thus more susceptible to uncertainty surrounding upside returns than conventional dynamic asset allocation utilizing one-year Treasury bills.

Uncertain Volatility. In practice, the source of the greatest difference between options and dynamic strategies is uncertain volatility. Not only does predicted volatility have an important effect on option prices but, of all their determinants, it is the most difficult to measure. Purchasing an index option amounts to insuring against fluctuations in the volatility of the index through the expiration date of the option. Proper implementation of the replicating dynamic asset allocation strategy retains full loss protection, but the upside capture now depends on the realized volatility over the year. The greater the volatility, the less the upside capture. This introduces a form of path-dependence into the outcome.

Sequential option strategies are exposed to a similar form of path-dependence. The prices of options to be purchased at future dates are dependent on the market's future predictions of volatility.

Security Price Jumps. As noted, stop-loss strategies may be threatened by jumps in security prices. For this reason, as contingent immunization (a form of stop-loss order applied to bond portfolio management) is practiced, the position remains 100 per cent invested in the actively managed bond portfolio as long as the stopout point is sufficiently distant. However, when the stopout point comes into view, the active portfolio is gradually transferred into the immunized portfolio.

In the case of dynamic asset allocation, this gradual transition to cash is an automatic and continuous feature. Because the portfolio will tend to be invested mostly in cash just before a jump that could create a loss, jumps will be less of a problem. The additional conservatism required of stop-loss orders to prevent losses from jumps will tend to equalize the expected rates of return from the stop-loss and dynamic asset allocation strategies.

Mispriced Securities. The investor who believes he can identify mispriced index futures, index options or even conventional options on common stocks may want to consider different approaches to portfolio insurance at different times. For example, when index calls are underpriced relative to index puts, he should give preference to fiduciary calls in place of protective puts as a means of creating portfolio insurance. If he thinks he can identify relatively underpriced calls on individual stocks, he may want to use a portfolio of fiduciary calls on individual stocks, despite the disadvantages of this strategy. If index futures appear to be underpriced, the preferred method may be to buy futures against a position in cash, rather than selling futures against a long position in the index.

Transaction Costs. By far the most liquid spot index option contracts are the S&P 100 options traded on the CBOE, which now comprise in total about 33 per cent of all CBOE options volume—typically representing trades to more than 20 million shares of the index per day (about $3 billion). The S&P 500 index futures traded on the CME are also highly liquid, representing trades to over 25 million shares per day (about $3.750 billion).

Currently, almost all trading volume for both index futures and options is concentrated in the nearest maturing contracts. As a result, it is necessary in the case of large trades to turn over option hedges about once every two months and futures hedges about once every four months to obtain sufficient liquidity. For options, we assume a 2 per cent one-way commission and a 1 per cent one-way spread give-up for a total one-way transaction cost of 3 per cent —about 12 cents on a $4 option, or about 0.08 per cent of the spot index. Additional costs from terminating index options at their expiration are ignored, because of their cash resettlement feature. For futures, we estimate a round-trip commission of $30 per contract and a $25 spread give-up for a total round-trip transaction cost of 0.07 per cent of the spot index price.

With a turnover of six times per year for a sequential options strategy, the total annual options transaction cost is 0.48 per cent of the spot index price. For dynamic asset allocation using index futures, turnover comes from two sources—from rolling the futures over three times per year (each time on an average of half the index portfolio) and from the requirements of dynamic asset allocation (which, based on simulation, is roughly 50 per cent per year). In total, futures would need to be bought or sold on 2.5 times the value of the index portfolio, which in turn implies a total annual futures transaction cost of 0.18 per cent of the spot index price.

Conventional dynamic asset allocation, which requires transferring assets between S&P 500 stocks and Treasury bills, is estimated from experience to cost 0.56 per cent of the spot index price.

In summary, conventional dynamic asset allocation is only slightly more expensive than a sequential index options strategy (0.56 per cent versus 0.48 per cent per annum). Dynamic asset allocation implemented with index futures is the cheapest, at about one-third this cost.

CONCLUSION

Long-term European payout-protected index options provide perfect portfolio insurance, but they do not currently exist in exchange-traded markets. Until they do, it will be necessary to use other instruments to approximate portfolio insurance on broad-based stock market indexes.

Stop-loss order strategies suffer from extreme path-dependence. Sequential index option strategies are also path-dependent and have a lower expected rate of return than perfect portfolio insurance. Of all the methods examined above, dynamic asset allocation, which attempts to replicate a long-term European protective put, seems to come closest to perfect portfolio insurance.

APPENDIX

CALCULATING PATH-DEPENDENCE

For each ending level of the index, make the best possible estimate of the portfolio rate of return. On average, as Table AI shows, the realized portfolio

TABLE AI. CALCULATION OF PATH-DEPENDENCE

Value of S&P 500 with Dividends Reinvested	Conditional Portfolio Expected Value	Expected Absolute Deviation	Probability
\$136.14	\$136.14	0.00	0.271
116.68	112.37	6.47	0.418
100.00	98.85	1.35	0.243
85.71	98.28	1.74	0.062
73.46	99.45	0.00	0.006

$$\text{Path Dependence} = (0.418 \times 6.47) + (0.243 \times 1.35) + (0.062) \times 1.74) = 3.14\%$$

Example: When S&P 500 = 116.68:

$$112.37 = \frac{(0.314 \times 116.68) + (0.105 \times 99.45)}{0.314 + 0.105}$$

$$6.47 = \frac{[0.314 \times |116.68 - 112.37|] + [0.105 \times |99.45 - 112.37|]}{0.314 + 0.105}$$

rate of return may be expected to err by 3.14 per cent. At worst—if the index ends at 116.68—the error may be expected to be 6.47 per cent.

The overall expected rate of return on the stop-loss strategy is calculated by summing the products of the second and third columns of Table II in the text. This results in 14.57 per cent.

For a very close approximation of the results from continuous S&P 500 movements, divide the year into 50 equally spaced intervals with binomial moves over each interval.[17] In this case, the path-dependence and expected rate of return are 3.73 and 14.70 per cent, respectively. With a continuous process, the stop-loss order could be executed at exactly 100; in that case, the stop-loss strategy would be 100 per cent reliable in preventing losses.

Also of interest for the stop loss strategy are the stopout probability, which is 40 per cent, and the expected time to stopout, which is 0.76 of a year (roughly, the beginning of the fourth quarter).

FOOTNOTES

1. The proof of this proposition is contained in an unpublished note by Hayne Leland.
2. For a more complete treatment, see Chapter 21: Hayne Leland, "Who Should Buy Portfolio Insurance?"

3. It is hypothesized that an investor who sells portfolio insurance wants to maximize the probability of obtaining a specified level of profit (the insurance premium in the case of a no-loss policy). In compensation for this, the investor must absorb all losses in the index.
4. For a proof that rational, risk-averse investors in a complete-markets, random-walk, time-additive utility environment should prefer path-independent to path-dependent strategies, see John C. Cox and Hayne Leland, "A Characterization of Path-Independent Policies." For the special case of investors who maximize the terminal value of their wealth at the end of a specified horizon, the intuition behind their proof is easily grasped. Suppose the only thing an investor cares about is the amount of wealth he will have at his horizon date and he has no reason to be concerned about the implications of past outcomes for future returns (the random-walk assumption). Then, if he can achieve path-independent outcomes for the pattern of returns that he desires at his horizon date, he will prefer these to path-dependent outcomes. The additional uncertainty from path-dependence is uncompensated risk. It is as though, in addition to his desired outcome of $120.84, the investor had to flip a coin to determine whether he receives $5 more or $5 less. No risk averter would willingly accept this gamble.
5. See Chapter 19: Fischer Black and Myron Scholes, "The Pricing of Options and Corporate Liabilities."
6. The Black-Scholes option pricing formula uses the logarithmic or continuous volatility (the standard deviation of the *natural logarithm* of one plus the rate of return) as in input, rather than the arithmetic or discrete volatility (the standard deviation of the rate of return). In our case, the S&P 500 is assumed to have an arithmetic mean and volatility of 16 and 18 per cent, respectively. Assuming lognormality of its rate of return, this translates into a logarithmic volatility of 15.5 per cent.
7. Formulas for transforming the mean and volatility of a lognormal security price process into the sizes and probabilities of the up and down moves of a discrete binomial process are given in Chapter 20: John C. Cox, Stephan A. Ross and Mark Rubinstein, "Option Pricing: A Simplified Approach."
8. See Chapter 22: M. Rubinstein and H. Leland, "Replicating Options with Positions in Stock and Cash."
9. Readers familiar with options may wonder if a striking price K can be chosen satisfying this equation. If the put were American (permitting early exercise), then the striking price would be so high that the put should be immediately exercised. But the put under consideration here is European (it cannot be exercised early), so its price must only satisfy $P > Kr^{-t} - S$, which permits its price to fall such that $P < K - S$ prior to expiration. Here, r is one plus the annual rate of interest and t is the time to expiration. Since a protective European put is always worth $S + P$, it follows that at no time in its life can the value of this position fall below Kr^{-t}. This implies that if, at any time during its life, the put were converted into cash, the investor could realize a minimum $Kr^{-t} \times r^{t} = K$ by the expiration date.
10. This technique for calculating the expected rates of return of European options is developed in Mark Rubinstein, "A Simple Formula for the Expected Rate of Return of an Option over a Finite Holding Period" (Working paper #119, Research Program in Finance, Institute of Business and Economic Research, University of California at Berkeley, March 1984).
11. If S is the stock price, C the call price, P the price of an otherwise similar put, r one plus the annual rate of interest, t the time to expiration of the options, and K their common striking price, according to the put-call parity relationship, at all times during the lives of the options:

$$P + S = C + Kr^{-t}.$$

The left-hand side of this equation is a protective put and the right-hand side is a fiduciary call.

12. Because neither the European spot call nor the European futures call can be exercised early, and because the spot and futures prices must be equal on the expiration date of the options, the cash flows received from either option must be identical.
13. See Mark Rubinstein, "Alternative Paths to Portfolio Insurance: A Detailed Analysis" (Expanded version of this article, May 1984).
14. The most active listed index options, the CBOE S&P 100 options, are not even listed with maturities beyond three months. A casual glance at the *Wall Street Journal* reveals that about 90 per cent of the volume in listed index puts is concentrated in puts with less than 40 days to expiration, with negligible volume in puts with more than 60 days to go.
15. Observe that when the index is at 85.71, the striking price of the next six-month put, relative to the index level is 103.86. (=89.02/85.71.)
16. To preserve reliability at three-point intervals, the investor must buy puts at slightly higher striking prices than optimal. Moreover, when the S&P 500 rises, the eight-point limitation will also force one to buy options at higher than optimal striking prices.
17. With 50 intervals, the minimum number of separate nodes at the end of the tree is 51 and the maximum number is 2^{50} or 123 trillion. In the stop-loss strategy, the number of different ending nodes turns out to be 638.

3. PATTERNS OF REWARD FOR PORTFOLIO INSURANCE

Roger G. Clarke and Robert D. Arnott

The investor using portfolio insurance has a broad array of choices which can be made in designing a protection strategy. Some of the factors that have a bearing on the performance of portfolio insurance can be directly controlled by the investor, while some cannot. It is important for the investor to have an understanding of the implications of those choices as well as the implications of factors which cannot be controlled. Studies of portfolio insurance usually summarize the impact insurance has on the expected return and standard deviation of a portfolio. While it is important to understand the impact of portfolio insurance on these two characteristics, an examination of the effects on the entire return distribution is also instructive because many other return attributes are also substantially affected by the insurance.

Many studies of portfolio insurance have explored the investment tradeoffs involved based on historical results.[1] These studies serve a very important role in suggesting the historic behavior of protection strategies. However, they may not offer an appropriate guide to the *costs* of portfolio insurance, since results are highly dependent on the specific time period covered by the research. Also, historic research usually provides inadequate precision in defining the *shape* of the return distribution.[2] For this kind of information, we turn to theoretic or stochastic modeling.

Forthcoming in *Financial Analysts Journal*.

[1] Footnotes appear at end of chapter.

THE BASIC SHAPE OF PORTFOLIO INSURANCE

To illustrate the impact of the various insurance choices we use an algorithm developed by Bookstaber and Clarke[3] to describe the ex ante return distribution of a combined portfolio of risky assets and option positions.[4]

Portfolio insurance can be created in several different ways.[5] In actual practice most use a dynamic hedging approach by changing the effective exposure to risky assets in the portfolio using the futures markets.[6] The dynamic strategy is usually designed to approximate the behavior of purchasing a put option directly on the portfolio. The dynamic hedging strategy, commonly called a *synthetic put option*, has become popular for creating insurance with longer time horizons since put options are usually not available with long maturities.

Not all portfolio insurance strategies are based on the creation of a synthetic put option.[7] However, in this discussion, we focus explicitly on the factors that affect the return characteristics of a synthetic put strategy. Even so, the factors that affect a synthetic put will have a similar effect on most other portfolio insurance strategies. Therefore, this discussion has relevance for nearly all of these approaches.

For our analysis, we assume that insurance is implemented through the purchase of a put option, with a floor equal to the current value of the portfolio and that the put option is priced consistent with a Black-Scholes model adjusted for dividends. We also assume that the investor begins with a portfolio composed of 100 percent equity invested in an index fund, that the riskless rate is equal to 8 percent and that the fund had a dividend yield of 3 percent.

With these assumptions, Figure 1 illustrates the impact of portfolio insurance on the probability distribution of returns. Curve A shows the return distribution for the uninsured portfolio. This distribution is based on an assumption that the returns for the underlying equity portfolio are log-normally distributed, with a mean return of 15 percent and a standard deviation of 18 percent.[8] Curve B shows the effect that a simple one-year portfolio insurance strategy has on the probability distribution. As would be expected, performance below the intended floor return is eliminated. Much of the upside performance of the portfolio is retained, although it is diminished somewhat by the cost of the put option.

Table 1 summarizes the statistical attributes of this insurance strategy. Most of the other tables are based on this format, so it is useful to review this material in some detail:

1. The *mean* return for an insured portfolio with a one-year horizon and a floor return of zero percent decreases by about 2.0 percent. This can be viewed as the long-term expected cost of portfolio insurance. In essence,

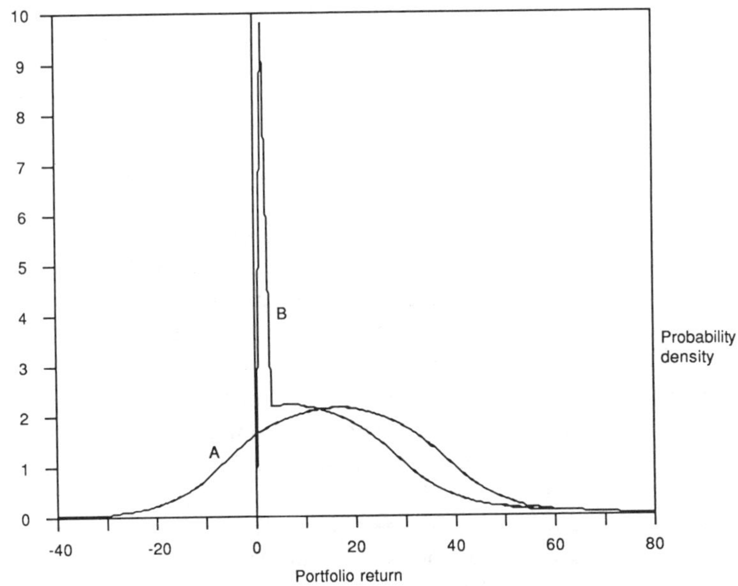

FIGURE 1. Return distribution

TABLE 1. INSURED FLOOR RETURN

	Uninsured	+5%	0%	−5%	−10%	−15%
Mean return	15.0	11.1	13.0	14.0	14.5	14.8
Median return	13.6	5.0	9.0	11.5	12.7	13.3
Average beta	1.00	0.49	0.75	0.88	0.95	0.98
Standard dev.	18.0	10.2	14.2	16.1	17.1	17.6
Skewness	0.47	2.1	1.24	0.88	0.69	0.57
Loss of upside capture	0.0	10.2	4.1	1.8	0.8	0.3
Expected insurance cost	0.0	3.9	2.0	1.0	0.5	0.2
Probability of Return Less Than:						
0%	20.7	0.0	0.0	24.2	22.2	21.2
8%	37.3	61.9	47.6	41.9	39.2	38.0

Assumptions

Dividend yield	=	3.0%
Expected market return	=	15.0%
Market volatility	=	18.0%
Riskless rate	=	8.0%
Percent of portfolio insured	=	100%

an insurance premium is paid in good years as the insured portfolio lags the uninsured portfolio. This loss in upside capture from just the put premium alone amounts to approximately 4.1 percent which is partially offset by the protection in bad years giving a net expected long-term cost of 2.0 percent per annum.

2. One of the unfortunate attributes of portfolio insurance, which has not been widely recognized by the investment community, is the impact of insurance on the *median* return. The median return declines by much more than the mean return. In this example, the median return declines from 13.6 percent to 9.0 percent. In essence, the insured portfolio is sacrificing 4.6 percent in years with a positive return in exchange for the benefit of a protected return in down markets.
3. Naturally, the average beta and the standard deviation decline by a substantial margin. By shifting exposure from the stock market into a "risk-free" investment in adverse market conditions, the average beta is decreased. At the margin, the beta of the insured portfolio will vary from 0.00 to 1.00 depending on the market conditions. But over time it will tend to average 0.75. The standard deviation is similarly reduced from 18.0 percent to 14.2 percent.
4. By eliminating the negative end of the return spectrum, the skewness of the portfolio is increased. In essence, this means that the distribution of returns is not symmetric, with a longer tail on the upside of the distribution than on the downside.
5. Finally, the probability of a return less than the 0 percent floor return is cut from 20.7 to 0 percent. *This is the entire purpose of portfolio insurance: To eliminate the risk of losses below the designated floor*. On the other hand, the investor pays for this by accepting an increased likelihood of modest returns. This is illustrated by the fact that the likelihood of returns below the risk-free rate rises from 37 percent to nearly 48 percent and that the median return declines by 4.6 percent as we noted previously. In essence, the investor cannot get "something for nothing." By eliminating the possibility of loss, the investor must accept an increased likelihood of modest gain. This shift in probabilities is underscored by looking at Table 2. Probability is shifted from returns at the extremes both above and below the floor to the range just above the floor.

CHANGING THE LEVEL OF PROTECTION

There are several alterations that the investor can make in the structure of portfolio insurance. These can be used to directly control the cost and return characteristics of an insured portfolio.

TABLE 2. PROBABILITY DISTRIBUTION OF RETURNS

Return (R)	Uninsured Portfolio	Insured Floor Return				
		+5%	0%	−5%	−10%	−15%
Below −40	0	0	0	0	0	0
−40 ⩽ R < −30	0.1	0	0	0	0	0
−30 ⩽ R < −20	1.1	0	0	0	0	0
−20 ⩽ R < −10	5.5	0	0	0	0	7.0
−10 ⩽ R < 0	13.9	0	0	24.2	22.1	14.2
0 ⩽ R < 10	21.3	66.3	52.3	22.3	21.7	21.4
10 ⩽ R < 20	21.9	17.4	20.8	21.6	21.8	21.9
20 ⩽ R < 30	16.9	9.6	14.0	15.6	16.4	16.7
30 ⩽ R < 40	10.3	4.3	7.5	9.1	9.8	10.1
40 ⩽ R < 50	5.3	1.6	3.4	4.3	4.9	5.1
50 +	3.7	0.8	2.0	2.9	3.3	3.6
	100.0	100.0	100.0	100.0	100.0	100.0

Assumptions

Dividend yield	=	3.0%
Expected market return	=	15.0%
Market volatility	=	18.0%
Riskless rate	=	8.0%
Percent of portfolio insured	=	100%

If a home owner wants to reduce the cost of an insurance policy, the easiest way to do so is by raising the deductible on the insurance. The analogy for portfolio insurance is to reduce the target floor return. If the investor seeks to assure that the return will not fall below −10 percent, the expected cost of the insurance will be much less than the cost with a 0 percent floor.

In Figure 2, we illustrate the tradeoffs available when the floor return is adjusted. As the floor return declines, less and less of the portfolio is protected but more upside potential is captured as indicated by a sharp increase in the median. As a result, the insurance costs less. With a very low insurance floor, such as −15 percent, the impact of protection on the return characteristics of the portfolio is very modest, but the worst case catastrophic loss is still averted. Curve A represents the uninsured portfolio. Curves B, C, D and E in Figure 2 represents floor returns of 0 percent, −5 percent, −10 percent, and −15 percent respectively.

Table 1 summarizes these results statistically. The expected cost of insurance decreases from 3.9 percent to 0.2 percent as the insurance floor decreases from +5 percent to −15 percent. The likelihood of returns below −15 percent on the uninsured portfolio in our example is comparatively

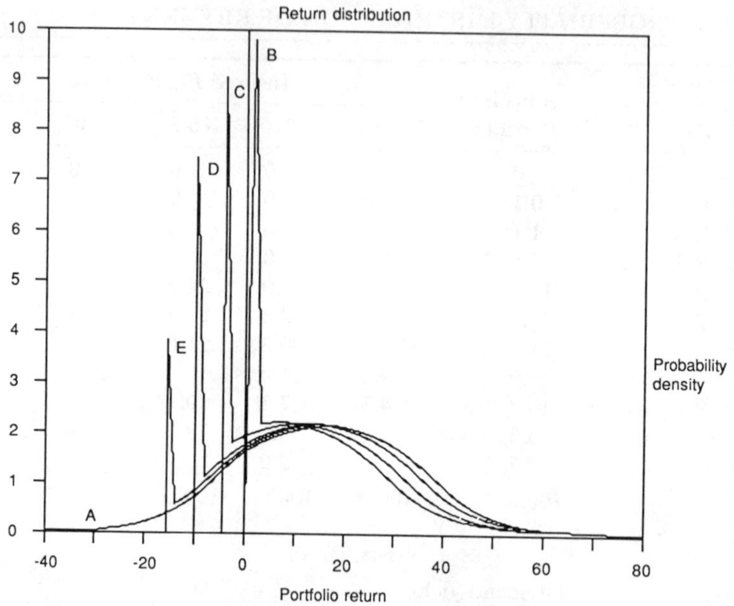

FIGURE 2. Return distribution

modest. As a result, the cost of the portfolio insurance is negligible if the floor return is set at or below this very low threshold. The impact of further decreases in the floor return beyond this level is minimal. The changes in the mean, median, upside loss, and expected cost for changes in the floor return are illustrated in Figure 3.

An alternative way to reduce the cost of insurance is by insuring only a portion of the assets. This is sometimes called "coinsurance." With this strategy, the investor chooses to bear some of the risk of loss by only applying an insurance strategy on a portion of the entire portfolio. As the investor bears more of the risk of the portfolio, less protection is provided but more upside potential is retained. This reduces the expected cost of a portfolio insurance strategy, but increases the likelihood of significant losses. Even so this strategy still reduces the likelihood of "catastrophic losses."

In a year like 1974, with the market down 26 percent, coinsurance in which protection with a 0 percent floor is applied to half of the portfolio would lose a far more tolerable 13 percent. The cost of coinsurance varies with the proportion of the portfolio which is insured. The expected cost increases from 0.5 percent to 2.0 percent as the insured proportion of the portfolio increases from 25 percent to 100 percent.

Table 3 describes the effects of coinsurance statistically for various levels of coverage. As is evident, the degree of coinsurance is directly correlated with

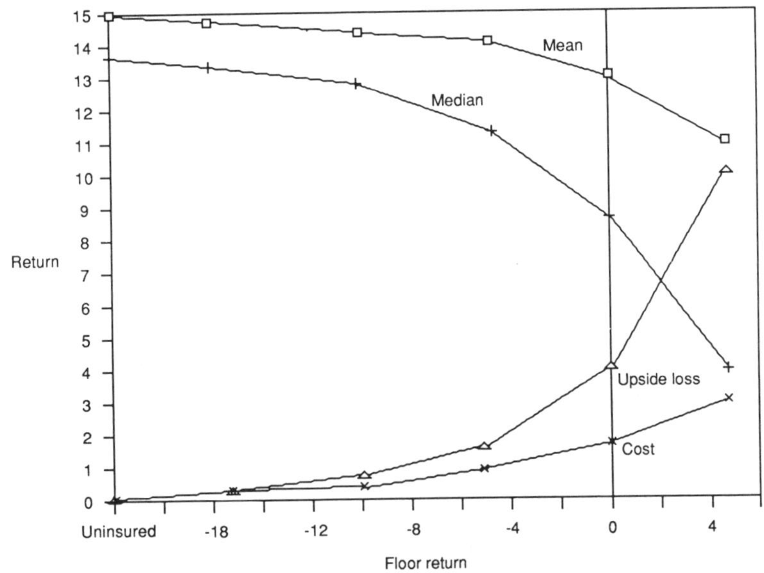

FIGURE 3. Change in floor return

TABLE 3. PERCENT OF PORTFOLIO INSURED

	0%	25%	50%	75%	100%
Mean return	15.0	14.5	14.0	13.5	13.0
Median return	13.6	12.5	11.4	10.2	9.0
Average beta	1.00	0.94	0.88	0.82	0.75
Standard dev.	18.0	16.9	15.9	15.0	14.2
Skewness	0.47	0.68	0.89	1.08	1.24
Loss of upside capture	0.0	1.0	2.1	3.1	4.1
Expected insurance cost	0.0	0.5	1.0	1.5	2.0
	Probability of Return Less Than:				
0%	20.7	20.7	20.7	20.7	0.0
8%	37.3	39.7	42.3	44.9	47.6

Assumptions

Dividend yield	=	3.0%
Expected market return	=	15.0%
Market volatility	=	18.0%
Riskless rate	=	8.0%
Insured floor return	=	0%

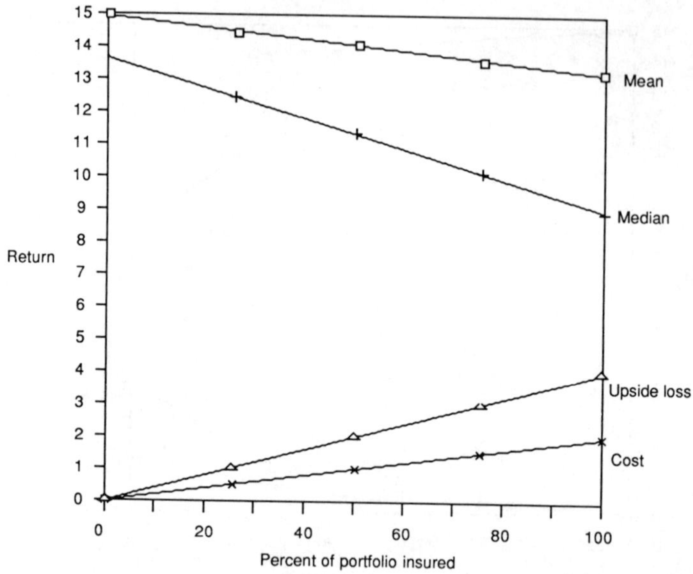

FIGURE 4. Effect of coinsurance

the changing rewards of a portfolio insurance process. Figure 4 illustrates the impact of coinsurance on the expected returns and costs of the insured portfolio.

Changing the Portfolio Beta. Many practitioners of insurance strategies have argued that the use of protection is ideally suited to a strategy where the protection is used as a safety net for a more aggressive exposure to the high-return (and high-risk) asset classes.[9] This rationale makes good sense *if* the increase in the rate of return is acceptable given the changes in the other dimensions of the portfolio return distribution.

The results for various increases in beta are given in Table 4. Notice particularly the contrast between the uninsured equity portfolio with a beta of 1.0 and an insured portfolio with an underlying beta of 1.75. Both portfolios have an average beta of approximately 1.0 but the risk profiles are quite different. Notice also the comparison with the portfolio of a beta of 1.50. Both the index fund and the insured leveraged portfolio have standard deviations of 18.0 percent, but again the probability distributions are quite different. Figure 5 illustrates the change in portfolio parameters caused by a change in the beta of the underlying portfolio.

The expected return of the insured portfolio rises with the increase in leverage. But, the investor contemplating this strategy should be fully cognizant of the changes in other attributes of the return distribution. The

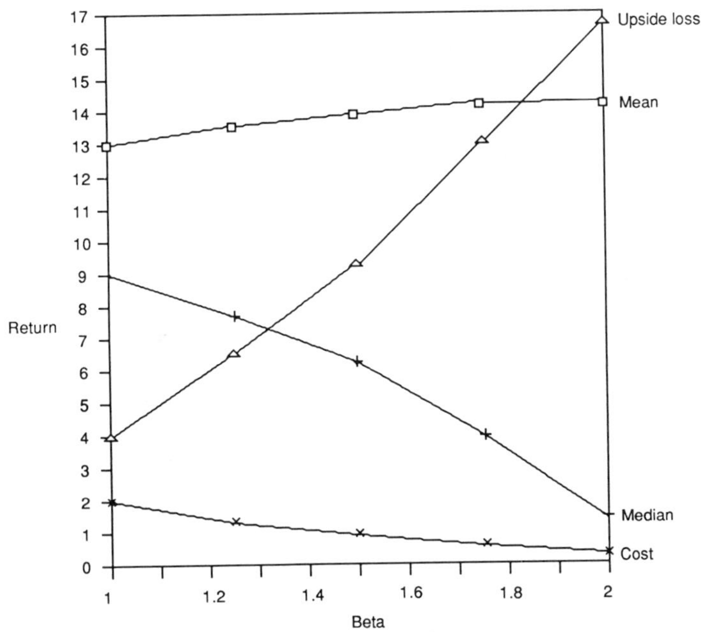

FIGURE 5. Effects of a change in beta

most noteworthy is the sharp decrease in the median return, reflecting the increased probability of returns below the riskless rate. For example, the median return for the insured portfolio with underlying beta of 2.0 declines all the way to 2.1 percent reflecting the fact that there is a 57.6 percent probability that the portfolio's return will be less than the riskless rate of 8 percent. *The effects of portfolio insurance on the median return are often neglected by investors.*

These comparisons illustrate an important point often overlooked by many in considering the use of portfolio insurance. As noted elsewhere, the traditional method of comparing risk and return by using just mean and standard deviation, or mean and average beta, is not well suited to return distributions altered by the use of options.[10] Option instruments can change the shape of the probability distribution in such drastic ways that other dimensions of the return distribution are also important. Since the probability distributions are not symmetric anymore, the simple measures of mean and standard deviation usually do not give a very complete description of the tradeoffs involved.

Changing the Protection Horizon. One indirect way to change the level of protection is to change the protection horizon. With a one-year floor return of 0 percent, it would require a return only 15 percent below expectations to

TABLE 4. LEVERAGE (BETA) OF UNDERLYING PORTFOLIO

	Uninsured	Insured				
	1.00	1.00	1.25	1.50	1.75	2.00
Mean return	15.0	13.0	13.6	14.0	14.3	14.4
Median	13.6	9.0	7.8	6.1	4.2	2.1
Average beta	1.00	0.75	0.86	0.94	1.01	1.06
Standard dev.	18.0	14.2	16.3	18.2	19.8	21.1
Skewness	0.47	1.24	1.42	1.56	1.69	1.81
Loss of upside capture	0.0	4.1	6.7	9.7	13.1	16.7
Expected insurance cost	0.0	2.0	1.4	1.0	0.7	0.6
Probability of Return Less Than:						
0%	20.7	0.0	0.0	0.0	0.0	0.0
8%	37.3	47.6	50.5	53.2	55.5	57.6

Assumptions

Dividend yield	=	3.0%
Expected market return	=	15.0%
Market volatility	=	18.0%
Riskless rate	=	8.0%
Percent of portfolio insured	=	100%
Insured floor return	=	0%

"hit the floor." If we extend this same level of protection over two or three years, it will require a cumulative shortfall of some 30 percent or 45 percent below expectations respectively to hit the floor. In short, extending the portfolio insurance horizon is an indirect way of reducing the degree of protection, and thereby reducing the cost.

The cost reduction associated with extending the protection horizon is fairly dramatic. To assure a three-year floor of at least 0 percent would require three separate 0 percent portfolio insurance programs. The expected cost would be 200 basis points annually. If the investor has a longer investment horizon than one year, this cost can be brought down to 20 basis points per annum for a three-year horizon. Yet the investor still achieves the same long-run objective. Table 5 illustrates the effects of extending the protection horizon and Figure 6 displays the change in portfolio parameters graphically.

If an investor has unusual circumstances which require a short protection horizon, this discussion may be noted. For example, if a pension executive has a board which expects positive returns each year, regardless of market movements, then a one-year insurance strategy may be the only prudent course.

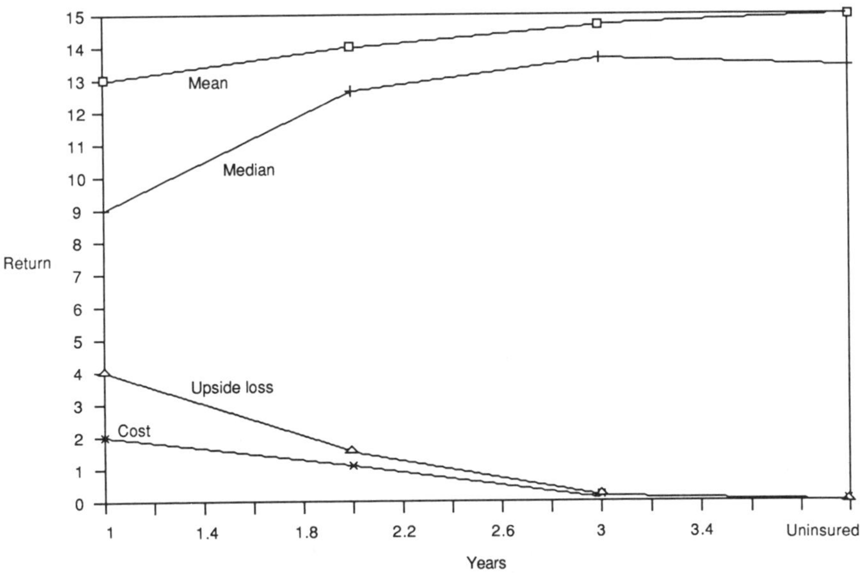

FIGURE 6. Change in protection horizon

On the other hand, if the horizon of the underlying portfolio is a long-term one, one-year insurance may help the investor to achieve a very costly objective (namely, positive returns each year), which is irrelevant for the long-term needs of the portfolio.

Effects of Changing Market Conditions. Several other factors affect the cost of portfolio insurance. We have reviewed four factors which the investor can directly control. Some factors are out of the control of the investor, but their effects should not be ignored. Conditions in the capital markets have a great deal of impact on the expected cost of portfolio insurance. This impact can come from:

1. *Changes in the Risk-Free Rate.* If the risk-free rate drops, then the implicit return available in the hedged portion of the portfolio similarly drops. This means that portfolio insurance will be more costly in an environment of low risk-free returns.
2. *The Equity Risk Premium.* The expected long-term cost of portfolio insurance is closely related to the expected long-term reward for bearing risk. The higher the expected reward for equities, vis-à-vis a free-risk asset, the more costly will be any strategy which avoids risk. This is true of portfolio insurance. The higher the market risk premium, the more costly the insurance will be.

TABLE 5. EFFECT OF INVESTMENT HORIZON

	Portfolio Insurance Horizon					
	1 Year		2 Year		3 Year	
	Uninsured	Insured	Uninsured	Insured	Uninsured	Insured
Mean annual return	15.0	13.0	15.0	14.3	15.0	14.8
Median annual return	13.6	9.0	14.0	12.9	14.2	14.0
Average beta	1.00	0.75	1.00	0.92	1.00	0.98
Standard dev.	18.0	14.2	12.7	11.8	10.4	10.22
Skewness	0.47	1.24	0.58	0.85	0.62	0.69
Loss of upside capture	0.0	4.1	0.0	1.0	0.0	0.2
Expected insurance cost	0.0	2.0	0.0	0.7	0.0	0.2
	Probability of Return Less Than:					
0%	20.7	0.0	8.6	0.0	2.5	0.0
8%	37.3	47.6	28.7	32.2	20.4	21.3

Assumptions

Dividend yield	=	3.0%
Riskless rate	=	8.0%
Expected market return	=	15.0%
Market volatility	=	18.0%
Percent of portfolio insured	=	100%
Insured floor return	=	0%

3. *Market Volatility*. The greater the volatility of the risky asset, the greater the cost of portfolio insurance.

Table 6 details the impact of changes in the riskless rate on the cost of portfolio insurance. An increase in the riskless rate sharply reduces the likelihood of achieving only the floor return. Part of this is due to the fact that the uninsured portfolio is expected to have a higher return. As such, it takes a greater shortfall vis-à-vis expectations, for the uninsured portfolio to fall below the target floor. Indeed the probability of negative return drops from 24.5 percent to 14.0 percent as the riskless rate rises from 6 percent to 12 percent. This means that a put option is further "out-of-the-money" at high-riskless rates than in an environment with low rates. Out-of-the-money options cost less than "at-the-money" options.

TABLE 6. EFFECT OF RISKLESS RATE

	Riskless Rate							
	6%		8%		10%		12%	
	Uninsured	Insured	Uninsured	Insured	Uninsured	Insured	Uninsured	Insured
Mean return	13.0	10.3	15.0	13.0	17.0	15.5	19.0	17.9
Median return	11.6	5.2	13.6	9.0	15.6	12.3	17.7	15.3
Average beta	1.0	0.67	1.0	0.75	1.0	0.81	1.0	0.86
Standard dev.	18.0	12.9	18.0	14.2	18.0	15.1	18.0	15.8
Skewness	0.48	1.49	0.47	1.24	0.47	1.06	0.46	0.92
Loss of upside capture	0.0	6.0	0.0	4.1	0.0	2.9	0.0	2.0
Expected insurance cost	0.0	2.7	0.0	2.0	0.0	1.5	0.0	1.1
Probability of Return Less Than:								
0%	24.5	0.0	20.7	0.0	17.1	0.0	14.0	0.0
Riskless rate	37.3	51.9	37.3	47.6	37.2	44.5	37.2	42.3

Assumptions

Dividend yield	=	3.0%
Expected market return	=	Riskless rate + 7%
Market volatility	=	18.0%
Percent of portfolio insured	=	100%
Insured floor return	=	0%

TABLE 7. EFFECT OF EQUITY RISK PREMIUM

	Equity Risk Premium					
	5%		7%		9%	
	Uninsured	Insured	Uninsured	Insured	Uninsured	Insured
Mean return	13.0	11.5	15.0	13.0	17.0	14.5
Median return	11.6	6.9	13.6	9.0	15.6	11.2
Average beta	1.00	0.71	1.00	0.75	1.00	0.79
Standard dev.	18.0	13.6	18.0	14.2	18.0	14.7
Skewness	0.48	1.38	0.47	1.24	0.47	1.12
Loss of upside capture	0.0	4.3	0.0	4.1	0.0	4.0
Expected insurance cost	0.0	1.5	0.0	2.0	0.0	2.5
	Probability of Return Less Than:					
0%	24.5	0.0	20.7	0.0	17.1	0.0
8%	41.8	52.5	37.3	47.6	32.8	42.6

Assumptions

Dividend yield	=	3.0%
Riskless rate	=	8.0%
Expected market return	=	8% + Equity risk premium
Market volatility	=	18.0%
Percent of portfolio insured	=	100%
Insured floor return	=	0%

As we have already seen, a lower floor return does reduce the cost of portfolio insurance by a substantial margin. So, part of this effect is simply a function of a lower floor vis-à-vis the uninsured expected return. The primary cause of this reduced cost is the increased return available for the risky asset, therefore greater room for adverse performance before a significant hedge position is required. *Even so, this relationship between the riskless rate and the cost of portfolio insurance is often overlooked.*

A change in the equity risk premium also affects the cost of insurance as is illustrated in Table 7. The equity risk premium was presumed to be 7 percent in all of our other exhibits. This is a figure which is commonly used in the investment industry, and is in line with long-term historical research.[11] However, this expected equity risk premium will change from time to time as investors' tolerance for risk changes. Therefore, this 7 percent equity risk premium can only be viewed as a ballpark estimate of the future risk premium.

As Table 7 clearly illustrates, the cost of portfolio insurance increases with an increase in the equity risk premium. If investors expect a higher return in order to bear risk, it is natural that insurance will cost more in order to avoid that risk. Table 7 indicates that for each 2 percent increase in risk premium, the expected cost of insurance will increase by approximately 0.5 percent.

Finally, it has often been observed (not entirely accurately) that portfolio insurance is a "buy high, sell low" strategy. It *is* a strategy which involves buying at the margin after market rises and selling after market declines. It is not necessarily buy high, sell low since a market increase or market decrease is not meaningfully correlated with subsequent movements in the market. Nonetheless, an increase in market volatility will mean that portfolio insurance will be subject to more "whipsaws." For example, as the market drops, portfolio insurance sells; when the market rebounds, portfolio insurance buys. This pattern will be more common, more pronounced, and more costly in an environment of increased market volatility. This cost is clearly demonstrated in Table 8. The expected cost of portfolio insurance increases from 1.3 percent to 3.0 percent with an increase in market volatility from 13 percent to 28 percent. The effect of increased market volatility on the median protected return is particularly striking, falling all the way from 12.1 percent to 1.3 percent.

The Role of Transaction Costs. Perhaps most important of all, the investor must watch transaction costs. To some extent these cannot always be controlled. However, carelessness on this score translates directly into reduced rewards for a portfolio insurance strategy. Portfolio insurance is a high turnover strategy. It can introduce from 40 to 100 percent annualized turnover on the insured assets. If these assets are actively managed, they will already be experiencing perhaps 50 percent turnover. So, every 100 basis point reduction in transaction costs translates into a 40 to 100 basis point increase in the long-term return of the portfolio. For a $1 billion portfolio, with compounding, a single basis point per annum will be worth well over $2 million after a decade. Careless trading can cost many times this amount.

One way to look at the impact of increased transaction costs is to treat transaction costs as a means of affecting the purchase price of the option. As is indicated in Table 9, each increase in transaction costs on insurance trades has the same effect as buying an option at an "unfair" price. A 50 basis point round-trip transaction cost has approximately the same impact as buying an option for 5 percent above fair value. The relationship is not linear. The larger the transaction cost, the larger the effective option mispricing; however, as the effective transaction costs rise, they force still greater turnover, leading to an accelerating increase in the magnitude of the effective options mispricing. Figure 7 displays these results graphically.

TABLE 8. EFFECT OF MARKET VOLATILITY

	Annualized Standard Deviation of Equity Results							
	13%		18%		23%		28%	
	Uninsured	Insured	Uninsured	Insured	Uninsured	Insured	Uninsured	Insured
Mean return	15.0	13.7	15.0	13.0	15.0	12.4	15.0	12.0
Median return	14.3	12.1	13.6	9.0	12.8	5.4	11.8	1.3
Average beta	1.0	0.86	1.0	0.75	1.0	0.67	1.0	0.60
Standard dev.	13.0	11.5	18.0	14.2	23.0	16.3	28.0	18.2
Skewness	0.34	0.80	0.47	1.24	0.61	1.64	0.74	2.01
Loss of upside capture	0.0	1.9	0.0	4.1	0.0	7.0	0.0	10.3
Expected insurance cost	0.0	1.3	0.0	2.0	0.0	2.6	0.0	3.0
Probability of Return Less Than:								
0%	11.9	0.0	20.7	0.0	27.3	0.0	32.2	0.0
8%	30.9	37.0	37.3	47.6	41.4	55.0	44.4	60.5

Assumptions

Dividend yield	=	3.0%
Expected market return	=	15.0%
Riskless rate	=	8.0%
Percent of portfolio insured	=	100%
Insured floor return	=	0%

TABLE 9. EFFECT OF OPTION MISPRICING

		Average Transaction Costs of Synthetic Put Trades					
		−50bp	0bp	50bp	70bp	100bp	200bp
		Equivalent Option Mispricing Percent					
	Uninsured	−5%	0%	+5%	+10%	+15%	+30%
Mean return	15.0	13.4	13.0	12.6	12.1	11.7	10.3
Median return	13.6	9.5	9.0	8.6	8.1	7.6	6.1
Average beta	1.00	0.76	0.75	0.75	0.74	0.73	0.71
Standard dev.	18.0	14.3	14.2	14.1	13.9	13.8	13.4
Skewness	0.47	1.23	1.24	1.25	1.27	1.28	1.33
Loss of upside capture	0.0	3.9	4.1	4.4	4.6	4.8	5.4
Expected insurance cost	0.0	1.6	2.0	2.4	2.9	3.3	4.7
Probability of Return Less Than:							
0%	20.7	0.0	0.0	29.8*	30.8*	31.8*	35.2*
8%	37.3	46.5	47.6	48.6	49.7	50.8	54.5

Assumptions

Dividend yield	=	3.0%
Expected market return	=	15.0%
Market volatility	=	18.0%
Riskless rate	=	8.0%
Insured floor return	=	0%
Percent of portfolio insured	=	100%

* Floor can be missed by .20, .40, .60, 1.19 percent respectively.

This mispricing can have two effects. First, it can lead to the possibility of "missing the floor." If an overpriced put option is purchased to protect against downside risk, the effect can be a slight shortfall vis-à-vis the intended floor return. It should be noted that these shortfalls are quite modest, and should not be viewed with alarm. The more pronounced impact is on the mean and median returns. The average return on a protected portfolio, with an overpriced option, drops markedly vis-à-vis the average return without transaction costs. If transaction costs are zero, the cost of a conventional portfolio insurance strategy is about 2.0 percent. If transaction costs are 50 basis points, the cost of the portfolio insurance rises to 2.4 percent. This 50 basis point figure is on the high side for those who advocate the use of futures for portfolio insurance strategies. Nonetheless, with the increased activity in portfolio insurance strategies, it is not implausible that futures might be adversely

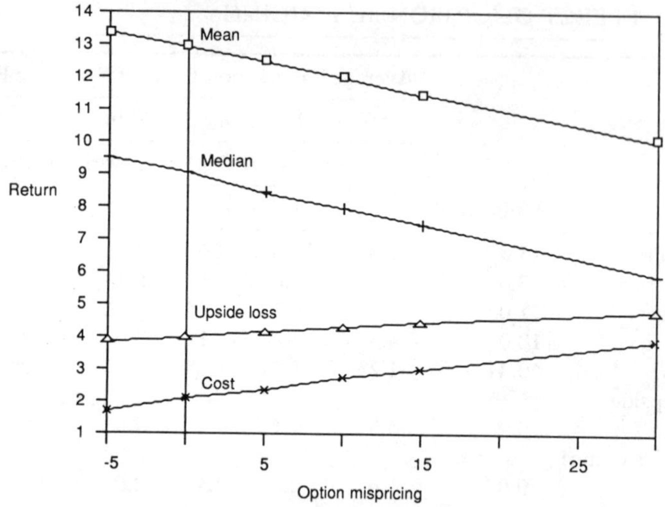

FIGURE 7. Effect of option mispricing

mispriced by an average of 25 basis points on each trade (leading to a 50 basis point round-trip transaction cost). It is conceivable that the round-trip cost on some trades could even rise to 100 basis points, or more.[12] If that were to happen, the cost of portfolio insurance would rise sharply.

The final example on Table 9 is based on a 200 basis point round-trip transaction cost. It is not unreasonable for us to expect a 200 basis point transaction cost for portfolio insurance implemented *without* futures. Here the cost is enormous. Instead of portfolio insurance depressing long-term performance by 200 basis points per annum, the long-term performance drops by 470 basis points per annum. Even more alarming, the median return actually falls below the risk-free rate.

Table 9 clearly illustrates the enormous importance of transaction costs in effective portfolio insurance management. If the manager of an insurance strategy is sloppy in effecting the futures trades, or if the futures markets systematically present adverse mispricing for portfolio insurance strategies, the cost will rise sharply. Fortunately, this is not the situation currently and does not represent an immediate risk. Nonetheless, it is a risk which the investor should recognize and should bear in mind in planning futures strategies.

HOW DO WE CONTROL THE COST?

The cost of portfolio insurance is sensitive to many factors, some of which are under the control of the investor, and some of which are not. The investor can control the following:

1. The intended floor return
2. The percentage of the portfolio subject to insurance
3. The risk of the underlying portfolio which is being insured (measured by its beta in our example)
4. The investment horizon covered by the insurance strategy

The investor *cannot* control:

5. The riskless rate
6. The expected equity risk premium
7. The volatility of the stock market

Finally, the investor has some control, but not complete control, over the transaction costs associated with the implementation of a portfolio insurance strategy.

If an investor wishes to reduce the cost of insurance, several steps can be taken:

1. Examine the need for portfolio insurance, with specific attention to the floor return. A lower floor return *costs less*. Can the investor tolerate a negative return? A loss of 10 percent. A loss of 20 percent. The floor return can be adjusted to reflect the maximum tolerance for loss. The long-term cost of the insurance is reduced if a larger deductible, hence a lower floor return, is employed.
2. The investor can choose to insure only part of the assets in a portfolio. This reduces the cost of the insurance, but at the risk of increased losses in a disastrous market.
3. Increasing the risk and expected long-term return of the underlying assets being insured can also decrease the expected cost of insurance. This decreased cost comes by substantially decreasing the medium return and increasing the upside loss.
4. The investor can extend the portfolio insurance horizon. How many investors really have a one-year horizon? If this is not the case, a longer horizon can sharply reduce the expected cost of portfolio insurance.

FOOTNOTES

1. See Chapter 5: R. Ferguson, "How to Beat the S&P 500 (without losing sleep)." See also D. Luskin, "The Surprising Performance of Portfolio Insurance, Historical Evidence: 1883 to 1985" (Jefferies and Company, Inc.), 1985.

2. A recent exception to this is a study by C. B. Garcia and F. J. Gould, "The Risks of Portfolio Insurance—Facts and Fallacies," Working Paper, Graduate School of Business, University of Chicago, August, 1986.
3. See R. Bookstaber and R. Clarke, "An Algorithm to Calculate the Return Distribution of Portfolios with Option Positions," *Management Science*, April 1983.
4. The algorithm has been adapted for the assumption that the underlying return distribution for the risky asset is lognormally distributed. Though this may not be a totally accurate assumption in practice, the algorithm is a means to illustrate the general impact of portfolio insurance parameters. Actual portfolios may deviate from this distribution but the qualitative results will generally not change.
5. For a discussion of other ways to create portfolio insurance see Chapter 2: M. Rubinstein, "Alternative Paths to Portfolio Insurance."
6. The dynamic approach to creating portfolio insurance is discussed by M. Rubinstein and H. Leland in Chapter 22: "Replicating Options with Positions in Stock and Cash."
7. See F. Black and J. Jones, "Simplifying Portfolio Insurance," Goldman Sachs Research, August 1986.
8. The assumed risk premium of 7 percent, equity volatility of 18 percent per annum, and dividend yield of 3 percent are in line with historical experience. The assumed riskless rate of 8 percent is arbitrary, but has only a minor impact on the shape of the return distribution. It does impact the expected cost of insurance, however.
9. See R. Ferguson, *op. cit.*
10. See R. Bookstaber and R. Clarke, "Problems in Evaluating the Performance of Portfolios with Options," *Financial Analysts Journal*, January–February 1985.
11. See R. Ibbotson and R. Sinquefield, *Stocks, Bonds, Bills and Inflation: 1926–1982* (Charlottesville, VA: Financial Analysts Research Foundation, 1983).
12. See R. Arnott and R. Boling, "Portfolio Insurance's Future Rides on Futures," *Pension and Investment Age*, September 1, 1986, p. 44.

USES

4. APPLICATIONS OF DYNAMIC STRATEGIES

Scott F. Grannis

Imagine the following situation: Two drivers are racing from Los Angeles to San Francisco via the Pacific Coast Highway. Both of their cars are the same, but the brakes on one are not very good. Who is most likely to win?

The driver of the car with poor brakes will have to keep his speed relatively slow and constant through most of the journey to avoid shooting off the edge of the Big Sur mountains. Yet the driver with brakes can speed up on the straightaways and slow down as he hits the curves. They both have about the same risk of taking a turn too fast, but the driver with good brakes will likely be the winner since he can average a faster speed than the driver with poor brakes.

The point of this chapter is that dynamic strategies are useful not only for hedging against downside risk, but for a variety of other strategies as well. *Portfolio insurance is only one application of this broad technology we call Dynamic Asset Allocation (DAA).* Dynamic protection strategies can beat fixed-allocation strategies, for example, because they react to rising markets by increasing a portfolio's exposure to equities, and do just the opposite in falling markets—just as the driver with good brakes can speed up on the straightaways and slow down on the curves.

For many people it is difficult to separate the *concept* of dynamic allocation strategies from their *application* to portfolio insurance. The two have become almost synonymous over the years due to the fact that they have grown up hand-in-hand, and portfolio insurance is the *only* application so far (of any significant size) to which dynamic allocation strategies have been put. The main difference between dynamic allocation strategies and portfolio insurance is that dynamic strategies can mimic the payoff patterns of *any kind of option*, whereas a portfolio insurance strategy is designed to mimic just the payoff pattern of owning a put option on your portfolio.

Dynamic allocation strategies can be used to create a pattern of investment payoffs which are *similar*, yet not identical, to those created by options—or any combination of options. What this means is that option-mimicking strategies can be applied to portfolios holding multiple assets, in multiple countries, whether they be in large or small amounts, as long as the assets are regularly traded and priced. There is no need for forecasts, no need for futures or forward markets, and no need for options. It is preferable to use futures markets if they are available, because they can make trading easier and reduce transactions costs. Regardless, a dynamic allocation strategy can be conducted perfectly well using simple cash transactions. Any time horizon can be accommodated, no matter how long. And the protection can be exactly tailored to the size of the exposure, however large or small.

Dynamic allocation techniques are in many cases better than using actual options to implement the previously mentioned strategies. For one, options have only limited strike prices available, and time horizons are typically limited to less than one year. Dynamic strategies, on the other hand, can be designed around any strike price and any time horizon. When very large portfolios are involved, dynamic strategies are often the *only* way to implement an option strategy, since the liquidity of many option contracts is limited and regulations often limit the size of option position held by an individual or institution. Some dynamic strategies, such as LOR's Perpetual Policies in particular, are structured to avoid the pitfalls of options-replicating strategies based on Black-Scholes options pricing models. Specifically, Perpetual Policies avoid the unpredictable upside capture, time dependence, and unpredictable trade sizes of standard option-replicating strategies. Dynamic strategies can be fine-tuned to tailor the payoff to exactly suit the manager's objectives—something that is difficult or impossible to do with options.

With its potential to manage a wide variety of risks around the globe, dynamic allocation strategies will eventually become one of the indispensable tools of both the domestic and the international portfolio manager and corporate treasurer. The next five sections expand upon the different uses to which dynamic allocation strategies can be put. The list is by no means exhaustive, since the potential applications of dynamic allocation strategies are theoretically unlimited.

Dynamic Strategies Can Increase Expected Returns. A dynamic strategy can increase the expected return of a portfolio when it is used to replace an inefficient fixed-allocation strategy. Prior to the development of dynamic strategies, there were only two ways to get "insurance" against loss. A manager either had to adopt a fixed-allocation policy (such as 60 percent equities and 40 percent bonds), or he had to run a dynamic strategy by informal rules (i.e., he had to sell equities if it looked like the market was going down). The problems with these procedures are obvious. The fixed-allocation is a poor way to get insurance, because it lacks the ability to fully participate in rising equity markets, where most of the action should be over the long haul. Moreover, if the equity market has a terrible year, the fixed-allocation portfolio may even be unable to deliver the protection it was designed to provide. The informal dynamic strategy is a poor one as well, because it is only as good as one's judgement or market timing.

Dynamic strategies which replace fixed-allocation strategies usually allow a portfolio to start with a high level of exposure to equities and, in most cases, to maintain a higher average level of equities over time. Since equities have the highest expected return, a dynamically run portfolio is expected to have a higher return than a fixed-allocation portfolio of similar downside risk exposure.

Consider this example of a fixed allocation portfolio vs. one using DAA:

OBJECTIVE:

Maximize expected return, limit losses to 5 percent.

ASSUMPTIONS:

Expected Return: Bills 10 percent, Stocks 18 percent
Volatility: Bills 2 percent, Stocks 20 percent
Correlation: 0.2

RESULTS:

	Initial Mix	Average Mix	Expected Return
Fixed Allocation	55/45	55/45	14.4
DAA	72/28	78/22	16.2

Gain from using DAA: 1.8 percent

Although both portfolios in this example are structured so that they are not *expected* to lose more than 5 percent over a 12-month period, there is nevertheless a 1-in-20 chance that the fixed allocation portfolio *will* (in the case of a terrible bear market, for example) lose this much. In contrast, the dynamic portfolio is virtually assured of not losing more than 5 percent in one year. Not only does the dynamic portfolio have better risk protection, it also has a higher expected return—180 basis points, as a matter of fact.

When comparing dynamically protected portfolios with fixed-allocation portfolios of comparable downside risk, the insured portfolio will *always* have a higher *expected* return. Is this a free lunch? No. In some market scenarios the fixed-allocation portfolio will produce a higher return than the dynamic allocation portfolio, but the expected return of the fixed-allocation portfolio is less. The big difference lies in the fact that portfolio insurance costs less than the "insurance" derived from a fixed-allocation strategy. Portfolio insurance only reduces equity exposure when necessary to ensure results; the fixed-allocation strategy reduces equity exposure permanently. The fixed-allocation strategy can be very costly in times of strong equity markets. Permanent diversification, in the case of a fixed-allocation strategy, does provide insurance against risk, but it is costly because *diversification is not always needed*.

Yet some will still argue that portfolio insurance is unattractive because it has a cost, namely, that a portfolio protected by a dynamic allocation strategy will underperform an all-equity portfolio in the long run. This is true, but it is not a relevant comparison. It is a fair comparison only if the portfolio would otherwise have remained 100 percent invested in equities. And this is certainly not the case for the majority of portfolios seeking some form of downside protection. It is only a fair comparison if you compare the expected return of the dynamically protected portfolio with the expected return of the fixed-allocation protected portfolio. Whenever a dynamically balanced portfolio has a higher equity mix, its expected return will be higher and it does not necessarily have a "cost" associated with it.

Dynamic Allocation Strategies Can "Sell" Insurance. Dynamic strategies are so often used in the context of *buying* portfolio insurance that most people overlook the fact that they can just as easily be used to *sell* portfolio insurance. What does "selling insurance" mean in a portfolio context?

First of all, let's go back to the case where a manager buys portfolio insurance. He wants insurance because he isn't comfortable with the idea of suffering losses, and he is willing to give up some of his gains should they occur, in "payment" for receiving protection against loss. He can create the payoff pattern he wishes by using dynamic strategies to effectively buy a put option on his portfolio. In practice, the buyer of portfolio insurance will buy equities as they rise, and sell equities as they decline.

Sellers of portfolio insurance must do essentially the opposite of what the buyers of portfolio insurance are doing, that is, sell as the market rises and buy when the market falls. Sellers of portfolio insurance also go by the name of *rebalancers*. They are the ones, for example, who want to use "dollar averaging" to lower their average cost of ownership: The more a stock falls in price, the more shares they buy.

Intuition suggests that there are more sellers of portfolio insurance than there are buyers. This is because most investors appear to be value-oriented; they are sellers of portfolio insurance because their appetite to hold stocks decreases as the stock prices increase, and vice versa. In effect, most investors are "closet" sellers of portfolio insurance because they are not consciously aware that their "buy low, sell high" strategy is actually a form of selling portfolio insurance. Yet a dynamic strategy would allow these closet sellers to accomplish their objectives more efficiently.

What sort of investor or money manager would make a *conscious* decision to become a seller of portfolio insurance? If an individual is not worried about a big market drop, and he doesn't think the market is going to soar, then he is a perfect candidate to sell portfolio insurance. Selling insurance means effectively collecting a premium by selling a call option on one's portfolio to someone who is buying portfolio insurance (i.e, to someone who is buying a put option on his portfolio). If the seller of portfolio insurance is right (in other words, if the market does not rise significantly), then his portfolio will outperform the market. His tradeoff, of course, is that his portfolio will decline in value by almost as much as the market in a bad year. *The seller of portfolio insurance has virtually no protection on the downside and his upside potential is limited.*

The mechanics of using a dynamic strategy to sell insurance are basically the opposite of running a strategy designed to buy insurance. The seller of portfolio insurance would establish short futures positions against his portfolio as the market rose, until at some level his portfolio would be completely hedged. At this point, he would earn only the risk-free rate of interest. If the market fell, he would reduce his short futures positions until he became fully invested. At this point, he would be fully exposed to further market declines. The premium he would receive from selling portfolio insurance would be equivalent to the premium paid by a buyer of portfolio insurance.

Dynamic Strategies Can Manage the Funded Status of a Pension Fund. Under Financial Accounting Standards Board Statement 87, the funded status of a pension fund becomes very important to a sponsoring corporation. Liabilities are now "marked to market" every year according to the prevailing level of long-term interest rates. If long-term interest rates (which are used to discount future liabilities) continue to be volatile, then the present value of pension fund liabilities could become extremely volatile in the future. If a corporation takes no steps to cope with the potential volatility of its liabilities, it risks having these liabilities impact its financial condition.

FASB 87 thus gives corporations an incentive to manage the "funded status" of their pension funds. If the pension fund can retain or generate a surplus (an excess of assets relative to the present value of future liabilities), then the fund can have an indirect impact on the corporation's profitability. Net pension fund liabilities will reflect as a liability on the sponsor's balance sheet, though a net surplus will not.

Since the funded status of the pension fund will now be spotlighted more prominently in the corporation's financial statements, it is very likely that *the focus of the pension fund will increasingly be on managing the relative performance of assets versus liabilities*. No longer is it sufficient to concentrate on maximizing asset performance in a prudent manner. Now, a pension sponsor must also concentrate on how his assets are performing relative to his liabilities in order to insure that market dynamics do not cause his fund to become underfunded, and thus turn into a burden on the corporation's balance sheet. The *relative* performance of assets and liabilities is the key, because both are now volatile elements as far as the corporate balance sheet is concerned.

Before dynamic strategies were available, pension funds had only one way to control their funded status, through the use of dedicated bond portfolios. By matching the duration of a pool of assets (typically government bonds) with the duration of a batch of future liabilities, the liabilities could be effectively hedged, and their potential impact on the funded status would be immunized. However, this sounds a lot like using a fixed allocation strategy to control risk, doesn't it? And we know dynamic allocation strategies offer a better way.

With dynamic hedging strategies, the funded status can be controlled without locking away money in a dedicated bond portfolio. Of course, there is a tradeoff which must be made. The pension sponsor must be willing to accept some loss (i.e., see the funded status erode to some extent) in order to maximize its expected gain. Of course, this is nothing but our old friend, the deductible.

The mechanics of a dynamic strategy which is designed to protect the funded status of a pension plan are somewhat different from that of a regular portfolio insurance program. In one type of funded status management program, the active asset is equities, just as with a regular protection plan. But the reserve asset (the one which will provide guaranteed income and which has a duration equivalent to the duration of the plan's liabilities) is a dedicated bond portfolio, not Treasury bills. The dynamic allocation program tracks the relative performance of equities versus the value of the dedicated bond portfolio; as equities do better, funds are shifted out of the bond portfolio and into stocks, and vice versa.

If equities outperform the bond portfolio, then the manager will have enhanced the value of his assets (i.e., they will have been put to better use than being permanently tied up in a dedicated bond portfolio), and the status of the pension fund will contribute to improving the financial condition of the corporation (to the extent that a surplus reduces the corporations future funding requirements). If equities underperform the bond portfolio, the pension fund status will be eroded by the premium cost of the dynamic protection program. Again, this is the potential cost of using a dynamic strategy to outperform a fixed (dedicated bond portfolio) strategy.

Dynamic Allocation Strategies Can Control Commodity Price Risk. Dynamic strategies can be used by a commodity producer to protect against the risk of falling prices, yet still allow gains should prices rise. Similarly, a commodity user can protect against price increases while still benefiting from price declines. He only has to be willing to give up some of his potential gains in exchange for the downside protection.

Dynamic Strategies Can Create "Caps" and "Collars." There are a variety of other options strategies which may be implemented using dynamic techniques. The number is limited only by the imagination (and regulatory restrictions). All of these strategies start with the basic desire to alter one's payoff pattern of returns. A few examples should suffice.

Suppose an oil company doesn't want to sell its oil for less than $10 a barrel, but is willing to forego some profits if oil goes over $20 a barrel in the next two years. In effect, the company is willing to gamble that the price of oil won't go over $20, yet is unwilling to risk it going below $10. In a situation like this, a dynamic strategy can be used to construct a "spread" to meet the company's desired payoff pattern. If oil sells for less than $20 per barrel, the company may end up getting slightly more than the market price for its oil, but not less than $10. However, if the price of oil goes above $20, the company will receive no more than $20 per barrel.

If a manager works for a savings and loan which makes capped mortgage loans, he can use dynamic strategies to cap the risk the institution is assuming by issuing these types of loans. By using dynamic strategies to control his risk, he will probably be better off than his associates who resort to swaps to reduce their risk exposure. Remember, dynamic strategies may be used to provide efficient risk management for any risk associated with actively traded securities or portfolios. The risk associated with holding securitized loan portfolios is another good example of a use for dynamic strategies, because there are no marketable options available to date for these securities. Again, the dynamic strategy effectively creates the exact option which a manager needs to provide the payoff patterns he prefers.

What sort of manager or investor would want to *sell* a cap? It might be someone who, for legal or contractual reasons, is unable to retain profits beyond a certain point. An example of this might be a defense contractor who passes pension fund contributions through to the government as part of his cost structure. If the contractor's pension fund should become overfunded beyond a certain amount—because of strong investment gains—the government might lay claim to those extra gains on the theory that it had been "overcharged" by the contractor initially. To take advantage of the fact that he was effectively unable to participate in market gains beyond a certain point, the contractor should manage his pension fund surplus with a dynamic strategy designed to mimic the payoffs he would receive had he sold a call against his portfolio. For any market return up to the government-imposed limit, his fund would outperform the market.

Dynamic Strategies Can Control Risk in International Markets. With dynamic hedging strategies, managers can cope with a wide variety of international risks and virtually unlimited time frames. Downside loss resulting from unfavorable currency, interest rate, or equity market moves can be limited, while still allowing for gains should markets move favorably. In fact, *any of the strategies described in the preceding sections may be applied in an international context. The only difference is that of foreign currency risk.*

Multinational corporations are exposed to substantial risk from currency exposure, interest rate exposure, and asset market exposure, both in their home countries and abroad. Traditionally, however, most international risk managers do not want to be exposed to these risks. They trust neither their own abilities to make consistently correct market timing decisions, nor the advice of forecasters. Consequently, they forego the opportunity to manage their exposure in favor of fully hedging their exposure. Of course, by eliminating risk, they also forego the opportunity to gain should the markets move favorably.

There exists a wide variety of instruments around the world to control risks in creative ways, but managers have typically been limited in their ability to use these because of the limited size and time horizons of most existing instruments, and the lack of adequate instruments in many cases. Currency risk, for example, can be controlled through the use of forward markets, futures, and options. Unfortunately, futures and options markets thin out when maturities approach one year or longer, and forward markets have limited flexibility. When exposures extend over a period of years, a manager must either hedge his exposure completely with forward markets, leave it open, or pay unreasonably high premiums or bid-ask spreads for customized, long-term options and forward contracts.

If a manager holds foreign assets, he is exposed to the risk that those assets will decline in value in terms of the foreign currency. In other words, he, like all other investors in that country, is exposed to market risk. Hedging this risk is as simple for the foreign asset owner as it is for domestic asset owners. Exposure to foreign interest rates presents the same problem, and is just as easily dealt with by setting up a standard dynamic strategy to buy insurance in the foreign country, whether it be to protect against losses in the equity market or against adverse moves in the interest rate market.

The added twist with using dynamic strategies to control international risk comes with exchange rates. Exchange rates effectively add another dimension to any risk-control problem. Fortunately, exchange rate risk is rather easy to deal with. To protect against adverse currency moves, a dynamic strategy can be set up with foreign Treasury-bills as the active asset and domestic Treasury-bills as the reserve asset. The value of foreign Treasury-bills must be tracked in domestic currency, which is where the exchange rate comes in. If the value of the foreign Treasury-bills falls, relative to the domestic bills, then the program would call for selling foreign Treasury-bills (in either the cash or futures markets) and buying domestic Treasury-bills. If the value of the foreign bills rise, then foreign bills would be purchased and domestic bills sold.

SUMMARY

Dynamic strategies have changed the face of finance forever. Even though options markets have been with us for years, and their applications have become widespread, options markets are still limited. Dynamic strategies open up a whole new array of alternatives to options, because they can be used to replicate the payoff patterns produced by any option or combination of options which one desires. There is no limit to the type of option or combination of options strategies, and virtually no limit on the size of portfolio involved.

With this greater freedom that dynamic strategies have brought, however, comes increased responsibility. Managers must learn more about options and payoffs, and more about their own tolerance and preference for risk if they are to optimize their investment performance. Dynamic strategies may look awesome and threatening to some, but they will eventually help the markets become more efficient and will ultimately provide investors and managers around the world with more and better tools.

5. HOW TO BEAT THE S&P 500 (WITHOUT LOSING SLEEP)

Robert Ferguson

Almost all professional investors believe they can beat the S&P 500 stock index. Yet there is not much evidence that they do. Perhaps this is to be expected. After all, professional investors as a group manage so much wealth that the aggregate of their portfolios cannot be much different from the S&P 500. To the extent they represent the market, it is impossible for them to beat the market. In the final analysis, the average must be the average. But this does not rule out the possibility that there are talented investors who are able to take advantage of less talented investors.

Talent can be thought of either as being assigned to investors for life (or at least for long periods) or as being assigned randomly over relatively short periods. In the first case, investors who outperform other investors in one period will be likely to outperform them in subsequent periods.[1] In the second case, there will be no correlation between relative performance from one period to another.

Studies so far suggest that talent does not persist. Put another way, relative advantage varies from one investor to another over time. It is thus unlikely that a particular professional investor will continue to outperform the S&P 500 over a long period of time, even if he has done so in the past.

According to both the Capital Asset Pricing Model (CAPM) and Arbitrage Pricing Theory (APT), however, it should be easy to beat the S&P 500 over

---

Reprinted from *The Financial Analysts Journal*, March–April 1986.

[1] Footnotes appear at end of chapter.

TABLE 1. THE S&P 500 AND THE LEVERED S&P 500 IN DOWN YEARS

Year	S&P 500 Return (β = 1.0)	Levered S&P 500 Return (β = 1.5)
1981	−4.90%	−13.70%
1977	−7.20	−13.00
1974	−26.50	−40.30
1973	−15.50	−25.10
1969	−8.50	−15.50
1966	−10.10	−17.10
1962	−8.00	−13.80
1957	−10.80	−17.60
1953	−1.00	−2.70
1946	−8.10	−13.60
1941	−11.60	−17.50
1940	−10.90	−17.40
1939	−0.40	−2.90
1937	−35.00	−49.60
1934	−1.60	−4.40
1932	−8.20	−21.20
1931	−43.30	−59.80
1930	−24.80	−37.70
1929	−8.50	−18.80

a long period.[2] Because expected return should be proportional to risk, all one needs to do is hold a portfolio that is riskier than the S&P 500. Over the 56 years from the end of 1927 to the end of 1983, for example, the S&P 500 achieved an annual return of about 9 percent. A levered investment in the S&P 500, with the leverage chosen to achieve a beta of 1.5, would have earned an annual return of about 10.5 per cent. One-hundred-fifty basis points annually is nothing to sneeze at.

This would seem to be an easy way to satisfy clients. But not everyone can do this, or would want to. In some of the years from 1927 to 1983 the S&P 500 declined substantially, and a levered investment in the index declined even more. Table I shows the S&P 500's returns in these loss years and compares them with the losses from the levered strategy. For most investors, both strategies are clearly untenable, but the levered strategy is downright scary.

An investor who uses traditional investment techniques will increase his downside exposure if he tries to increase his expected return. Table I illustrates this fact. Even the S&P 500 represents too much downside exposure for most investors. This is why they sacrifice long-term return by allocating a substantial proportion of their portfolios to relatively safe assets.

What is needed is an investment strategy that can provide good upside participation when the S&P 500 rises while limiting downside exposure when the S&P 500 declines. Traditionally investment techniques cannot achieve this goal. A relatively new investment technique, called Dynamic Asset Allocation (DAA), can.

LEVERAGE AND RISK

Think of leverage as the volume control on a phonograph. If the volume is set at neutral (no borrowing or lending), the portfolio's fluctuations will exactly mimic those of the S&P 500. Borrowing is equivalent to turning up the volume; the levered portfolio's fluctuations will exaggerate those of the S&P 500. Conversely, lending (negative borrowing) is equivalent to turning down the volume; the portfolio's fluctuations will be smaller than the S&P 500's.

Increasing volume control makes both low and high notes louder—there is no way of avoiding this. Similarly, if leverage is used to control risk and return, then the investor can achieve high long-term return only by exposing himself to occasional large losses.

Table I shows that from 1928 to 1983 an investment in the S&P 500 would have lost money in 19 years—about 33.9 per cent of the time. The loss would have exceeded 15 per cent in five of those years. The maximum loss would have been 43.3 per cent.

A levered investment in the S&P 500 would have lost money in 20 years. On 12 occasions, the loss would have exceeded 15 per cent. The worst loss would have been 59.8 per cent. Imagine what it's like to lose 60 per cent of your wealth—it makes horror movies seem tame.

Using leverage to beat the S&P 500 is likely to cause a heart attack. Investing all your money in the S&P 500 without leverage may cause a heart attack, too. The secret to achieving upside participation without commensurate downside exposure is to change the leverage over time, as the S&P 500 changes.

Adjusting the Volume

Suppose an investor allocates 50 per cent of his portfolio to the S&P 500 and the remaining 50 per cent to a one-year Treasury bill (leverage of 0.5) at the beginning of the year. Now suppose the market rises 30 per cent by the end of the year. If the interest rate is 10 per cent, the investor's 50-50 portfolio will earn a return of 20 per cent for the year, assuming his leverage remains static. To have achieved a higher return, the investor would have had to increase his equity investment beyond 50 per cent as the S&P 500 rose.

If the investor increases his equity allocation each time the S&P 500 outperforms the Treasury bill (even by a small amount), he will wind up with a high average exposure to the S&P 500 in any year in which the S&P 500 trends up relative to the bill. This will assure him good upside participation in an up year.

But suppose the S&P 500 has a bad year, declining by 30 per cent. In this case, leverage of 0.5 will result in a return of − 10 per cent, if the investor maintains the 50-50 portfolio mix over the entire year. By reducing his equity allocation each time the S&P underperforms the Treasury bill, however, the investor can achieve a low average exposure to the S&P 500 in years when the S&P 500 declines sharply. He will thus be able to avoid a loss in down years.

Of course, some investors may feel uncomfortable with the idea of buying the S&P 500 *after* a rise and selling *after* a decline; it sounds too much like "buy high, sell low." A more comfortable strategy might call for selling a little of the S&P 500 after it rises and buying more after it declines; this sounds more like "buy low, sell high." But buying after a rise and selling after a decline is the *only* way to assure both upside participation and downside protection. Any other approach will fail under some market scenarios. Buying after a decline will result in excessively poor returns in years when the market trends down, for example, while selling after a rise will result in a loss of upside participation in years when the market trends up.

The computation of when and by how much to change the portfolio's leverage in order to achieve a specified result is not easy. But it can be done. The computations are based on option pricing theory.

Changing the S&P 500 allocations in this manner is like continuously adjusting the phonograph's volume control. Suppose the listener turns the volume down slightly each time he detects a decrease in tone and turns it up slightly each time he detects an increase in tone. For a score that displays smooth oscillations in tone, the low tones will be almost filtered out and the high tones will remain almost as loud as before. A smoothly rising tone will be transformed into a smoothly rising tone that gets louder. A smoothly falling tone will be transformed to a smoothly falling tone that gets softer.

Similarly, a series of DAA programs, each with a time horizon of one year, will provide a return higher than the return on either of the assets in a two-asset portfolio over a period of years in which strong up and down markets predominate. When the S&P 500 trends up, DAA will provide a slightly lower return than the S&P 500 if the portfolio's stock component is the S&P 500. When the S&P 500 trends down, however, DAA will provide a specified minimum return.

BASIC DYNAMIC ASSET ALLOCATION

A DAA program involves shifting a portfolio's mix between two assets—a risky asset and a "safe" asset. If the two assets are the S&P 500 and a Treasury bill, then the expected return from the DAA program will be between the expected return on the S&P 500 and the interest rate. Whatever the two assets used, a DAA program's expected return will be between the expected returns of the two assets.

The specified minimum return must thus be no greater than the appropriate interest rate. If the investor has a one-year time horizon and the interest rate on one-year riskless investments is 10 per cent, then the investor's specified minimum return must not exceed 10 per cent. If the time horizon is three years, and the riskless interest rate on three-year investments (bullets or other instruments with a three-year duration) is 11 per cent, then the maximum possible specified minimum return is 11 per cent.

The higher the specified minimum return, the lower must be the proportion of the portfolio allocated to the risky asset. In the extreme case where the specified minimum return is the interest rate, the entire portfolio must be invested in the riskless asset. In the other extreme where the specified minimum return is −100 per cent, there is no need for a reverse; the entire portfolio can be allocated to the risky asset.

The expected return from a DAA program thus depends on the expected average allocation to the risky asset. Because more reserves are needed, the higher the specified minimum return, a DAA program with a high minimum return must have a lower expected return than one with a low minimum return.

The specific characteristics of a DAA program will also depend on the riskiness of the risky asset and on the investor's time horizon. Avoiding losses in a down year is like having insurance, or owning a put on the portfolio: the protection comes only at a cost. One measure of this cost is the shortfall between the return provided by the risky asset in an up year and the DAA program's return. If the risky asset—say, the S&P 500—returns 30 per cent and the DAA program returns 25 per cent, then the cost is 5 per cent.

The cost of a DAA program will thus be higher, the greater the risk of the risky asset. It will be lower, the greater the deductible—the difference between the interest rate and the specified minimum return. A longer time horizon will also reduce the cost of a DAA program.

An Example

Suppose a conservative investor is willing to invest in the S&P 500 and a one-year Treasury bill and wants to avoid a loss over one year. The one-year interest rate is 10 per cent; the volatility of the S&P 500 is 20 per cent annually; and the S&P 500's expected return is 16 per cent.

TABLE II. SUMMARY OF CHARACTERISTICS FOR VARIOUS DAA PROGRAMS

Min. Ret.	Exp. Ret.	Upside Capture	Likely Cost	Init. SP500 Alloc.	Exp. Avg. SP500 Alloc.	SP500 Vol.	Int. Rate	Time Horizon (Years)
5.0%	12.5%	90.0%	10.3%	36.6%	41.9%	20.0%	10.0%	1
0.0	13.9	95.5	5.2	59.7	64.8	20.0	10.0	1
−5.0	14.8	97.6	2.7	75.2	79.3	20.0	10.0	1
5.0	12.7	92.4	8.7	39.3	45.4	18.0	10.0	1
0.0	14.1	96.4	4.1	63.2	68.7	18.0	10.0	1
−5.0	15.0	98.2	2.0	78.7	82.8	18.0	10.0	1
5.0	13.3	92.1	9.0	41.8	46.3	20.0	11.0	1
0.0	14.4	96.0	4.6	62.9	67.1	20.0	11.0	1
−5.0	15.0	97.9	2.4	77.3	80.6	20.0	11.0	1
5.0	13.9	96.9	3.6	54.6	64.6	20.0	10.0	3
0.0	15.2	99.0	1.1	80.7	86.7	20.0	10.0	3
−5.0	15.7	99.7	0.3	93.0	95.7	20.0	10.0	3

Given these assumptions, a static asset allocation portfolio would have to be 90.9 per cent invested in the Treasury bill to assure no loss and would have an expected return of only 10.5 per cent. The expected return from a DAA program also assuring no loss over the year would be about 13.9 per cent. And if the S&P 500 rose 35 per cent over the year, the DAA program would provide a return of about 28.9 per cent.

Put another way, when the S&P 500 does well, the investor will end the year with about 95.5 per cent (1.289/1.350 = 0.955) of the wealth he would have had if he had invested all his money in the S&P 500 at the beginning of the year. Furthermore, he would not likely have done so, if he wanted to sleep at night. But with the DAA program he is assured of not losing money, no matter how far the S&P 500 declines.

This DAA program calls for an initial portfolio allocation to the S&P 500 of about 59.7 per cent. But as the S&P 500 rises, the allocation increases. Thus the portfolio's expected average allocation to the S&P 500 for the year is about 64.8 per cent—far higher than a conservative investor would normally feel comfortable with.

A less conservative investor may be satisfied with a lower minimum return over one year or the same minimum return over a longer period. Table II summarizes the characteristics of several DAA programs for a variety of assumptions about minimum returns, the riskiness of the S&P 500, the interest rate and the time horizon.

The next-to-last line of Table II shows how a more aggressive investor might fare under DAA. This investor seeks to avoid a loss over a time horizon of three years. The corresponding DAA program's expected return is about 15.2 per cent annually—only 80 basis points below the S&P 500 itself. Yet if the S&P 500 were to drop 40 per cent over the period, the DAA portfolio would not lose money. The upside capture for this program is about 99 per cent, annualized. That is, if the S&P 500 achieves a return of 20 per cent annually over the three-year period, the DAA program will provide about 18.8 per cent annually. The initial and expected average S&P 500 portfolio allocations are 80.7 and 86.7 per cent, respectively.

These examples make it clear that DAA is an attractive alternative to traditional investment techniques.

Levering Up Return. An aggressive investor might be willing to accept more downside exposure in order to achieve an expected return in excess of the S&P 500. Table II shows that a DAA program can yield expected returns quite close to those of the S&P 500 when the S&P 500 is used as the equity component of the DAA portfolio. The lower the investor's specified minimum return, other things equal, the closer a DAA program's expected return is to the expected return of its equity component.

TABLE III. CHARACTERISTICS OF DAA PROGRAMS USING THE LEVERED S&P 500

Min. Ret.	Exp. Ret.	Upside Capture	Likely Cost	Init. Lvrd. SP500 Alloc.	Exp. Avg. Lvrd. SP500 Alloc.
– 20.00%	18.20%	98.73%	1.46%	88.75%	91.06%
– 19.00	18.11	98.58	1.64	87.64	90.12
– 18.00	18.02	98.41	1.83	86.46	89.11
– 17.00	17.92	98.23	2.04	85.19	88.03
– 16.00	17.82	98.04	2.26	83.85	86.86
– 15.00	17.70	97.82	2.51	82.41	85.61
– 14.00	17.58	97.58	2.79	80.89	84.28
– 13.00	17.46	97.32	3.08	79.28	82.85
– 12.00	17.32	97.04	3.41	77.57	81.32
– 11.00	17.17	96.74	3.76	75.76	79.70
– 10.00	17.02	96.40	4.15	73.85	77.96
– 9.00	16.85	96.04	4.57	71.82	76.12
– 8.00	16.67	95.64	5.03	69.68	74.15
– 7.00	16.49	95.20	5.53	67.43	72.06
– 6.00	16.29	94.73	6.08	65.05	69.84
– 5.00	16.07	94.20	6.68	62.54	67.47
– 4.00	15.85	93.63	7.34	59.89	64.95
– 3.00	15.60	93.00	8.07	57.10	62.27
– 2.00	15.35	92.30	8.88	54.16	59.42
– 1.00	15.07	91.53	9.77	51.05	56.38
0.00	14.78	90.66	10.77	47.77	53.13

This suggests a relatively safe way of beating the S&P 500. First, choose an equity component that has an expected return above that of the S&P 500. Second, choose a minimum return low enough that the DAA program's expected return approaches that of the equity component and exceeds that of the S&P 500.

Table III summarizes the characteristics of several DAA programs that use a levered investment in the S&P 500 as their equity component. The leverage factor is 1.5. This is equivalent to an equity portfolio with a volatility of 30 per cent and an expected return of 19 per cent.[3]

According to Table III, an investor who chooses a minimum return of – 5 per cent over one year will have an expected return of 16.1 per cent. He can expect to match the performance of the S&P 500 without losing more than 5 per cent in any one year.

The investor can expect to beat the S&P 500 handily if he is willing to accept a maximum loss of 10 per cent in any one year. This DAA program has an expected return of 17 per cent annually—100 basis points above the S&P 500. Its anticipated upside capture is 96.4 per cent, measured against the performance of the levered S&P 500. To put this in perspective, suppose the S&P 500 rises 25 per cent over a year; the levered S&P 500 should then rise about 32.5 per cent [$10 + (25 - 10) \times 1.5 = 32.5$]. The DAA program will provide a return of about 27.7 per cent ($0.964 \times 1.325 = 1.277$)—some 270 basis points more than the S&P 500.

If the investor can accept a maximum one-year loss of 15 per cent, he can achieve an expected return of 17.7 per cent, or about 170 basis points above the S&P 500. This DAA program's upside capture is about 97.8 per cent. The DAA portfolio will earn about 29.6 per cent if the S&P 500 rises 25 per cent.

THE RISK-RETURN TRADEOFF

DAA is not a free lunch. But it is not clear what the tradeoffs are when an investor's expected return is increased by using DAA or a combination of DAA and leverage. In some sense, expected return can be increased only if risk is increased too. But the usual definition of risk—standard deviation of return—is inadequate when there are asymmetric payoff patterns. What is helpful is to compare the probability distributions of return for two or more investment strategies.

Table IV presents possible returns and their cumulative probabilities for the following six investment strategies:

1. a static 100 per cent allocation to the S&P 500;
2. a static allocation of 60 per cent to the S&P 500 and 40 per cent to a one-year Treasury bill;
3. a DAA program with a maximum one-year loss of 5 per cent and with the S&P 500 as its equity component;
4. a static 100 per cent allocation to the levered S&P 500;
5. a DAA program with a maximum one-year loss of 10 per cent and with the levered S&P 500 as its equity component; and
6. a DAA program with a maximum one-year loss of 15 per cent and with the levered S&P 500 as its equity component.

The top row of the table indicates a 1 per cent chance that an investment in the S&P 500 will lose 23.2 per cent or more over a year.[4] If the S&P 500 does lose 23.2 per cent over a year, then a static 60-40 portfolio mix will lose 9.9 per cent, and the levered S&P 500 will lose 39.9 per cent. The DAA portfolios shown all have minimum returns of − 15 per cent or higher, hence will earn their minimum returns under these circumstances.

Row 21 of the table shows that an investment in the S&P 500 has about a 21 per cent chance of losing money over a year. The 60-40 portfolio mix will make about 3.8 per cent if the S&P 500 breaks even. The levered S&P 500 will lose about 5.6 per cent. A DAA program with a minimum return of −5 per cent and with the S&P 500 as its equity component will lose about 2.8 per cent. The DAA portfolios (5) and (6) will lose about 10.0 and 9.0 per cent, respectively.

Row 85 of Table IV shows that there is a 15 per cent change that the S&P 500 will close a year up by more than 36.5 per cent. If the S&P 500 realizes this return, then the 60-40 portfolio mix will earn 25.9 per cent, and the levered S&P 500 will earn 49.8 per cent. DAA portfolio (3) will earn about 33.3 per cent—a much higher return than a reasonable static mix can provide. DAA portfolios (5) and (6) are even more dramatic in this case. Their returns will be about 44.4 and 46.5 per cent, respectively—far more than the S&P 500.

Another important consideration is the probability that a DAA program will earn its minimum return. Portfolio (3) is designed to provide a minimum return of −5 per cent using the S&P 500 as its equity component. Table IV shows that this portfolio will lose about 5 per cent whenever the S&P 500's return is below about −2.9 per cent. Put another way, this DAA portfolio does much better than the S&P 500 when the S&P 500 does very poorly, but does slightly worse when the S&P 500 has only a small loss. The probability that Portfolio (3) will realize its minimum return of −5 per cent (about 17 per cent) is higher than the probability that the S&P 500 will realize a return of −5 per cent or worse (about 14 per cent).

The DAA programs based upon the levered S&P 500 share this feature. Portfolio (5) has about a 19 per cent probability of achieving its minimum return of −10 per cent. The probabilities that the S&P 500 and the levered S&P 500 will lose 10 per cent or more are about 8 and 16 per cent, respectively. There is about a 13 per cent chance that Portfolio (6) will realize its minimum return of −15 per cent. The probabilities of a worse result for the S&P 500 and the levered S&P 500 are about 4 and 12 per cent, respectively.

The probability that a DAA program will realize its minimum return is higher than the probability that its equity component will realize that same return or a lower one.

DAA Versus Static Portfolios. Strictly speaking, there is no equivalence between DAA and static portfolios. It may be useful, however, to pair them in order to ascertain the regions where a DAA program will outperform its approximate static asset allocation (SAA) equivalent.

Portfolios (2) and (3) were designed to be paired this way. Portfolio (2) represents a static asset mix common in the pension world. It has about a

TABLE IV. THE PROBABILITIES OF OUTCOMES FOR VARIOUS INVESTMENT STRATEGIES

	(1) SP500 Ret.	(2) 60–40 Mix Return	(3) DAA Return (Min. = −5, SP500)	(4) Lvrd. SP500 Return	(5) DAA Return (Min. = −10, Lvrd. SP500)	(6) DAA Return (Min. = −15, Lvrd. SP500)	Cum. Prob.
1.	−23.24%	−9.94%	−5.00%	−39.86%	−10.00%	−15.00%	1.00%
2.	−19.57	−7.74	−5.00	−34.36	−10.00	−15.00	2.00
3.	−17.16	−6.29	−5.00	−30.73	−10.00	−15.00	3.00
4.	−15.29	−5.17	−5.00	−27.93	−10.00	−15.00	4.00
5.	−13.74	−4.24	−5.00	−25.61	−10.00	−15.00	5.00
6.	−12.40	−3.44	−5.00	−23.60	−10.00	−15.00	6.00
7.	−11.21	−2.72	−5.00	−21.81	−10.00	−15.00	7.00
8.	−10.13	−2.08	−5.00	−20.19	−10.00	−15.00	8.00
9.	−9.13	−1.48	−5.00	−18.69	−10.00	−15.00	9.00
10.	−8.20	−0.92	−5.00	−17.31	−10.00	−15.00	10.00
11.	−7.33	−0.40	−5.00	−16.00	−10.00	−15.00	11.00
12.	−6.51	0.09	−5.00	−14.77	−10.00	−15.00	12.00
13.	−5.73	0.56	−5.00	−13.60	−10.00	−15.00	13.00
14.	−4.98	1.01	−5.00	−12.48	−10.00	−14.38	14.00
15.	−4.27	1.44	−5.00	−11.40	−10.00	−13.33	15.00
16.	−3.58	1.85	−5.00	−10.37	−10.00	−12.32	16.00
17.	−2.91	2.25	−5.00	−9.36	−10.00	−11.34	17.00
18.	−2.26	2.64	−4.56	−8.39	−10.00	−10.39	18.00
19.	−1.63	3.02	−3.94	−7.45	−10.00	−9.47	19.00
20.	−1.02	3.39	−3.35	−6.53	−9.89	−8.57	20.00
21.	−0.42	3.75	−2.76	−5.63	−9.03	−7.69	21.00
22.	0.16	4.10	−2.19	−4.75	−8.18	−6.83	22.00
23.	0.74	4.44	−1.63	−3.89	−7.35	−5.99	23.00
24.	1.30	4.78	−1.08	−3.05	−6.54	−5.16	24.00

25.	1.86	5.11	−0.54	−2.22	−5.74	−4.35	25.00
26.	2.40	5.44	−0.01	−1.40	−4.95	−3.55	26.00
27.	2.94	5.76	0.52	−0.59	−4.17	−2.76	27.00
28.	3.47	6.08	1.04	0.20	−3.41	−1.98	28.00
29.	3.99	6.39	1.55	0.99	−2.65	−1.22	29.00
30.	4.51	6.70	2.05	1.76	−1.90	−0.46	30.00
31.	5.02	7.01	2.55	2.53	−1.16	0.29	31.00
32.	5.53	7.32	3.05	3.29	−0.43	1.04	32.00
33.	6.03	7.62	3.54	4.05	0.30	1.78	33.00
34.	6.53	7.92	4.03	4.79	1.02	2.51	34.00
35.	7.03	8.22	4.51	5.54	1.74	3.24	35.00
36.	7.52	8.51	4.99	6.28	2.45	3.96	36.00
37.	8.01	8.81	5.47	7.01	3.16	4.68	37.00
38.	8.50	9.10	5.95	7.75	3.87	5.40	38.00
39.	8.99	9.39	6.42	8.48	4.57	6.11	39.00
40.	9.47	9.68	6.90	9.21	5.27	6.82	40.00
41.	9.95	9.97	7.37	9.93	5.97	7.54	41.00
42.	10.44	10.26	7.84	10.66	6.67	8.24	42.00
43.	10.92	10.55	8.31	11.38	7.37	8.95	43.00
44.	11.40	10.84	8.79	12.11	8.07	9.66	44.00
45.	11.89	11.13	9.26	12.83	8.77	10.37	45.00
46.	12.37	11.42	9.73	13.55	9.47	11.08	46.00
47.	12.85	11.71	10.20	14.28	10.17	11.79	47.00
48.	13.34	12.00	10.68	15.01	10.87	12.50	48.00
49.	13.83	12.30	11.15	15.74	11.57	13.21	49.00
50.	14.31	12.59	11.63	16.47	12.28	13.93	50.00
51.	14.80	12.88	12.11	17.21	12.99	14.65	51.00
52.	15.30	13.18	12.59	17.94	13.70	15.37	52.00
53.	15.79	13.48	13.07	18.69	14.41	16.10	53.00
54.	16.29	13.77	13.56	19.44	15.14	16.83	54.00

TABLE IV. CONTINUED

	(1) SP500 Ret.	(2) 60–40 Mix Return	(3) DAA Return (Min. = −5, SP500)	(4) Lvrd. SP500 Return	(5) DAA Return (Min. = −10, Lvrd. SP500)	(6) DAA Return (Min. = −15, Lvrd. SP500)	Cum. Prob.
55.	16.79	14.08	14.05	20.19	15.86	17.57	55.00
56.	17.30	14.38	14.54	20.95	16.59	18.31	56.00
57.	17.81	14.69	15.04	21.71	17.33	19.06	57.00
58.	18.32	14.99	15.54	22.49	18.08	19.82	58.00
59.	18.85	15.31	16.05	23.27	18.83	20.58	59.00
60.	19.37	15.62	16.57	24.06	19.59	21.35	60.00
61.	19.90	15.94	17.08	24.85	20.36	22.13	61.00
62.	20.44	16.26	17.61	25.66	21.14	22.92	62.00
63.	20.98	16.59	18.14	26.48	21.92	23.72	63.00
64.	21.54	16.92	18.68	27.31	22.72	24.53	64.00
65.	22.10	17.26	19.23	28.15	23.53	25.35	65.00
66.	22.67	17.60	19.78	29.00	24.35	26.19	66.00
67.	23.24	17.95	20.35	29.87	25.19	27.03	67.00
68.	23.83	18.30	20.92	30.75	26.04	27.90	68.00
69.	24.43	18.66	21.51	31.64	26.91	28.77	69.00
70.	25.04	19.02	22.10	32.56	27.79	29.67	70.00
71.	25.66	19.40	22.71	33.49	28.69	30.58	71.00
72.	26.30	19.78	23.33	34.45	29.61	31.51	72.00
73.	26.95	20.17	23.96	35.42	30.55	32.47	73.00
74.	27.61	20.57	24.61	36.42	31.51	33.44	74.00
75.	28.30	20.98	25.28	37.44	32.49	34.45	75.00
76.	29.00	21.40	25.96	38.49	33.51	35.47	76.00
77.	29.72	21.83	26.67	39.58	34.55	36.53	77.00
78.	30.46	22.28	27.39	40.69	35.63	37.62	78.00

79.	31.23	22.74	28.14	41.84	36.73	38.75	79.00
80.	32.02	23.21	28.92	43.03	37.88	39.91	80.00
81.	32.84	23.71	29.72	44.27	39.07	41.12	81.00
82.	33.70	24.22	30.56	45.55	40.31	42.38	82.00
83.	34.59	24.75	31.43	46.89	41.60	43.68	83.00
84.	35.52	25.31	32.34	48.28	42.95	45.05	84.00
85.	36.50	25.90	33.29	49.75	44.36	46.49	85.00
86.	37.53	26.52	34.30	51.30	45.85	48.00	86.00
87.	38.62	27.17	35.36	52.93	47.43	49.60	87.00
88.	39.78	27.87	36.49	54.67	49.10	51.30	88.00
89.	41.02	28.61	37.70	56.53	50.89	53.12	89.00
90.	42.35	29.41	39.01	58.53	52.82	55.07	90.00
91.	43.80	30.28	40.42	60.71	54.92	57.20	91.00
92.	45.40	31.24	41.98	63.10	57.22	59.54	92.00
93.	47.17	32.30	43.71	65.75	59.79	62.14	93.00
94.	49.17	33.50	45.67	68.76	62.68	65.08	94.00
95.	51.49	34.89	47.93	72.24	66.04	68.48	95.00
96.	54.26	36.56	50.64	76.39	70.04	72.55	96.00
97.	57.74	38.64	54.03	81.60	75.07	77.64	97.00
98.	62.47	41.48	58.66	88.71	81.92	84.60	98.00
99.	70.23	46.14	66.23	100.35	93.14	95.98	99.00

TABLE V. YEARLY RETURNS FROM STATIC AND DYNAMIC ASSET ALLOCATION STRATEGIES, 1928–1983

Year	SP500 Ret.	Lvrd. SP500 Ret.	DAA Return (Min. = – 15, Lvrd. SP500)	DAA Return (Min. = – 10, Lvrd. SP500)
1983	22.60%	29.30%	25.70%	23.60%
1982	21.70	24.20	19.80	17.30
1981	– 4.90	– 13.70	– 12.20	– 8.80
1980	32.40	41.90	39.00	37.20
1979	17.90	21.00	19.40	18.50
1978	8.00	7.90	5.80	4.10
1977	– 7.20	– 13.00	– 9.50	– 6.90
1976	23.90	33.30	29.00	26.70
1975	37.30	53.80	47.60	44.00
1974	– 26.50	– 40.30	– 14.80	– 10.00
1973	– 15.50	– 25.10	– 14.60	– 9.90
1972	19.00	26.80	23.50	21.70
1971	14.30	19.20	15.30	12.60
1970	4.00	1.90	5.00	5.60
1969	– 8.50	– 15.50	– 11.70	– 8.40
1968	11.50	14.40	12.20	10.80
1967	23.90	34.80	29.40	26.60
1966	– 10.10	– 17.10	– 14.00	– 9.50
1965	12.40	16.80	15.40	13.20
1964	16.40	23.30	19.90	17.90
1963	22.80	33.70	29.20	26.60
1962	– 8.00	– 13.80	– 14.70	– 10.00
1961	28.10	43.10	36.30	32.70
1960	0.50	– 1.00	– 1.80	– 3.50
1959	11.90	16.40	13.60	11.90
1958	43.40	69.80	61.90	57.30
1957	– 10.80	– 17.60	– 13.90	– 9.60
1956	7.30	9.30	5.50	3.50
1955	31.60	48.50	42.10	37.90
1954	52.60	87.20	77.30	71.40
1953	– 1.00	– 2.70	– 2.30	– 2.30
1952	18.30	27.30	23.80	21.60
1951	21.90	33.00	27.20	23.80
1950	31.70	49.00	40.80	35.40
1949	18.80	28.20	23.10	19.70
1948	5.50	7.00	2.30	– 0.10
1947	5.70	7.70	3.80	1.70
1946	– 8.10	– 13.60	– 14.60	– 10.00
1945	36.00	57.40	49.60	44.80
1944	19.70	30.30	24.70	21.10

TABLE V. CONTINUED

Year	SP500 Ret.	Lvrd. SP500 Ret.	DAA Return (Min. = – 15, Lvrd. SP500)	DAA Return (Min. = – 10, Lvrd. SP500)
1943	26.00	40.30	30.90	25.50
1942	20.30	30.90	25.80	22.10
1941	– 11.60	– 17.50	– 14.00	– 9.70
1940	– 10.90	– 17.40	– 14.80	– 9.90
1939	– 0.40	– 2.90	– 13.10	– 9.30
1938	31.10	44.20	0.40	– 6.50
1937	– 35.00	– 49.60	– 14.70	– 10.00
1936	33.80	52.90	41.50	35.00
1935	47.80	77.20	60.70	52.00
1934	– 1.60	– 4.40	– 13.30	– 9.30
1933	53.80	75.90	3.20	– 9.40
1932	– 8.20	– 21.20	– 14.70	– 10.10
1931	– 43.30	– 59.80	– 14.60	– 10.10
1930	– 24.80	– 37.70	– 14.60	– 10.10
1929	– 8.50	– 18.80	– 15.90	– 11.30
1928	42.70	66.40	58.90	54.10
Compound Annual Return, 1928–83:	9.05%	10.54%	10.39%	10.06%

5 per cent chance of losing more than 5 per cent over a year. Portfolio (3) is designed to avoid a loss exceeding 5 per cent. In this sense, it has less downside exposure in Portfolio (2). Portfolio (2)'s expected return is 13.6 per cent; Portfolio (3)'s is 14.8 per cent—120 basis points higher. The probability that Portfolio (3) will suffer a 5 per cent loss is 17 per cent; the probability that Portfolio (2) will suffer a loss of 5 per cent or more is about 5 per cent.

Portfolio (3) will outperform Portfolio (2) whenever the S&P 500 either declines by more than about 15 per cent or rises by more than about 17 per cent. There is about a 49 per cent chance that this will occur in any particular year. When it does, Portfolio (3) is likely to *out*perform Portfolio (2) by more than it *under*performs Portfolio (2) when the S&P 500 doesn't move as much. The first three columns of Table IV illustrate this.

Portfolio (6) was designed to be roughly equivalent to the S&P 500 in terms of downside risk. It will outperform the S&P 500 whenever the S&P 500 either declines by more than 15 per cent or rises by more than 15.3 per cent. There is about a 52 per cent chance that this will occur.

Table IV makes it clear that it is much more difficult to evaluate the relative attractiveness of investment strategies when they include DAA alternatives. Comparisons based on expected return and standard deviation of return aren't adequate. But the difficulty is theoretical, not practical. By characterizing the alternatives in the manner of Table IV, and using the kind of information found in Table III, the investor can pick the strategy he finds most appealing. It is easy to avoid the difficult theoretical issues usually addressed in the finance literature.

By now it should be clear that DAA provides an attractive alternative to investors, perhaps the only alternative for beating the S&P 500 that even an aggressive investor can feel comfortable with. But would it have worked in the past?[5]

THE PROOF OF THE PUDDING[6]

DAA strategies are based upon the mathematics of option pricing theories. A particular formulation must be chosen to test if an actual DAA strategy would have enabled an investor to beat the S&P 500 in the past. The model used here was obtained by slightly modifying the Black-Scholes formula for the fair price of a European put. These modifications made the model less sensitive to errors that would ordinarily arise from fluctuating interest rates, uncertain volatility and other factors. No special attempt was made to develop a model that would have worked well over the period examined. The data consisted of daily returns for the S&P 500 and one-year Treasury bills for the period from January 1, 1928 to December 30, 1983.

Two DAA strategies were tested. Both used the levered S&P 500 as their equity component. The leverage was chosen to be 1.5. The first strategy corresponded to a minimum return of −15 per cent over each year. The second's minimum return was −10 per cent for each year. These were a series of one-year programs.

At the beginning of each year, the two DAA programs were initiated and run through the end of the year. This produced a series of 56 annual returns for both DAA programs, the S&P 500 and the levered S&P 500. Table V shows these returns.

The results indicate that the DAA programs performed as expected. The market was abnormal enough to result in disappointing upside capture in only two years—1933 and 1938.

Over the entire period, both DAA programs beat the S&P 500 handily. The DAA program with the minimum return of −15 per cent beat the S&P 500 in 58.9 per cent of the years and achieved a compound annual return of 10.4 per cent. The DAA program with the minimum return of −10 per cent beat the S&P 500 in 67.9 per cent of the years and achieved a compound annual return of 10.1 per cent. The compound annual returns achieved by the S&P 500 and the levered S&P 500 were 9.1 and 10.5 per cent, respectively.

The DAA programs beat the S&P 500 by 100 and 140 basis points, respectively.[7] This is remarkably close to the hypothetical results given in Table III, especially considering the idealized assumptions used in constructing that table. Not only does DAA work, but it is robust.

CONCLUSIONS

Both theoretical and empirical evidence indicates that DAA programs work. A substantial amount of money is now being managed this way. In principle, DAA effectively provides pleasing blends of characteristics. The particular kind of protective DAA program illustrated in this article offers a hitherto unattainable combination of long-term return, upside capture and downside protection.

Yes, Virginia, it is possible to beat the market without losing sleep. And without paying for expensive judgments, either.

FOOTNOTES

1. Outperform is meant in the sense of a positive risk-adjusted return.
2. Beat is meant in the sense of achieving a higher return.
3. This is consistent with the previous assumptions for the S&P 500 and the one-year Treasury bill and an efficient market. No talent or abnormal return is assumed.
4. Given the stated assumptions and assuming a log normal probability distribution for the price of the S&P 500.
5. Just as pension administrators know that investment managers not already hired always have attractive performance figures to show, you know that the answer is yes. But this time there is a difference. DAA programs do not need or use forecasts about the attractiveness of asset classes or the market. They cannot fail to work because someone guessed wrong about interest rates, or whatever. They are nonjudgmental in this sense. All they depend upon is a reasonable market in which equivalent securities (that can be arbitraged) sell at about the same price.
6. Is not in the eating, but the compounding.
7. A regression of the excess returns of each DAA portfolio on the excess returns of the S&P 500 was done. The estimated beta and alpha of the DAA portfolio with the minimum return of −15 per cent were 1.00 and 1.65 per cent, respectively. The corresponding figures for the DAA portfolio with the minimum return of −10 per cent were 0.83 and 2.08 per cent, respectively. The alphas are annualized. Both DAA programs appear to have an attractive alpha. I leave it to the reader to ponder whether or not these are "real" alphas. They look good in a client report in either case.

6. INSURING THE ASSET/LIABILITY RATIO

Mark P. Kritzman

Portfolio insurance has attracted a great deal of interest as a strategy for determining a pension fund's asset mix. Estimates as of year-end 1986 indicate that between $20 and $50 billion have been allocated to these strategies. Typically, the objective of portfolio insurance within the pension investment context is to protect the pension fund from generating a return below some prespecified minimum return without significantly sacrificing upside potential.

Recent changes in pension fund accounting have formalized the notion that pension investment decisions should reflect consideration of both pension assets and pension liabilities. It follows, therefore, that portfolio insurance is not an appropriate investment strategy for pension funds if it is applied only to the pension *assets*. Not only does portfolio insurance lack economic meaning within this context, but it will actually have an adverse impact on a company's financial well-being:

it introduces volatility to a pension fund's surplus value which flows through to a company's financial performance; and

it imposes an unnecessary cost on a company because it is significantly overpriced relative to protection that is economically meaningful.

These criticisms are not an indictment of portfolio insurance, in particular. Rather these problems exist with any broad pension investment strategy that ignores pension *liabilities*. Moreover, these problems do not arise as a consequence of changes in accounting practices. They are a fact of economic reality made more apparent by the provisions of Federal Accounting Standards Board Statement 87, the new pension accounting rules.

The next section of this chapter describes briefly the typical approach to portfolio insurance and the effect of risk on its cost. This section is followed by a cursory review of the elements of FASB 87 which are relevant for portfolio insurance; a discussion of the impact portfolio insurance has on the volatility of the surplus value of a pension fund; an explanation why portfolio insurance is unnecessarily expensive; and a strategy for protecting the surplus value of a pension fund is introduced; its cost is contrasted to the cost of traditional portfolio insurance. Next, these arguments are extended to an alternative insurance strategy called constant proportion portfolio insurance. The chapter is then concluded with a brief summary.

PORTFOLIO INSURANCE

Portfolio insurance is an asset allocation strategy that continually rebalances a portfolio between a risky component and a riskless component so that the total portfolio's return does not fall below some prespecified minimum return.

The cost of portfolio insurance can be thought of as lost opportunity should the risk component produce superior results, since the portfolio will not always be fully invested. Essentially, as the portfolio's value rises above the value associated with the minimum required return, its asset mix is shifted toward the risky component. As its value falls, funds are shifted to the risk-free component to protect it from penetrating the minimum-required return. The extent to which it does not capture the risky component's return when it is favorable can be thought of as the cost of the protection. This cost will increase as the standard deviation of the risky component increases, since a greater percentage of the portfolio will be allocated, on balance, to the risk-free component in order to satisfy the minimum required return. This cost is analogous to the cost of a protective put option which is positively correlated with the risk of the underlying asset.

FASB 87

FASB 87 gives accounting recognition to the economic fact that a pension fund's health is determined by the market value of both pension assets and pension liabilities. It recognizes the value of the pension fund surplus as the relevant measure of health where surplus is defined as the difference between pension assets and liabilities.

FASB 87 includes two provisions that are particularly relevant for portfolio insurance and pension investment policy in general:

Companies are required to value their liabilities using a market related discount rate, and

The pension fund surplus is reflected on both the balance sheet and the income statement.

The use of market discount rates to value pension liabilities instills economic meaning into the FASB's definition of surplus. Moreover, by refecting this value in a company's financial statements, the FASB is implicitly recognizing the pension fund surplus as an asset of the corporation.

These accounting changes have important implications for portfolio insurance. Since portfolio insurance only protects a pension fund's *asset* value, it is an economically meaningless exercise. Although portfolio insurance is without economic meaning, however, it will have a perverse economic consequence: It will actually increase the volatility of the pension fund surplus and, therefore, the net worth and earnings of the sponsoring corporation. This result is explained in the next section.

PORTFOLIO INSURANCE AND SURPLUS VOLATILITY

Two assumptions are required to demonstrate how portfolio insurance increases the volatility of the pension fund surplus. First we must assume that the duration of pension liabilities exceeds the duration of pension assets. Secondly, we must assume that the most important source of changes in the present value of pension assets and pension liabilities is a change in the rate at which these streams are discounted. The first assumption is certainly true for the preponderance of pension funds. The second assumption might be challenged in certain scenarios, but for the most part is consistent with the behavior of the capital markets.

Given these assumptions, what happens to pension liabilities, pension assets, and insured pension assets if discount rates fall? Certainly, all three values will rise, but liabilities will rise the most since they have the longest duration. Pension assets will rise by a smaller amount because they have a shorter duration than the liabilities, and insured pension assets will rise by an even smaller amount because the increase will be diluted by the cost of the protection. These relationships are illustrated in Figure 1.

In Figure 2 these effects are extended to the pension fund surplus. In the case where the assets are not insured, the surplus value will decline because the liabilities increase by more than the assets. If the assets are insured, however, the surplus will decline even further to account for the cost of the protection.

Consider the case now where discount rates rise. In this scenario liabilities decline in value by a greater amount than assets due to their longer duration.

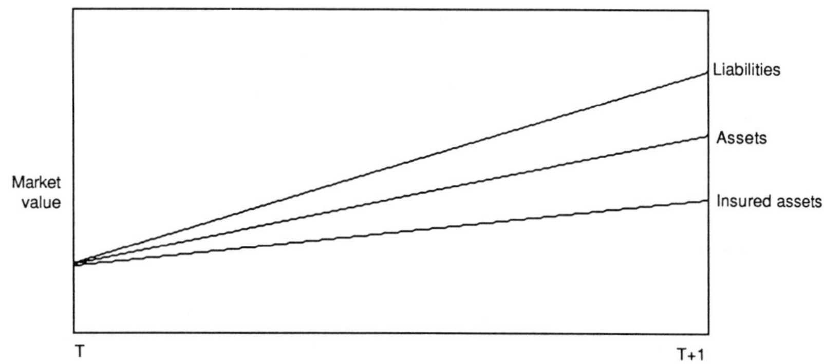

FIGURE 1. Discount rates fall

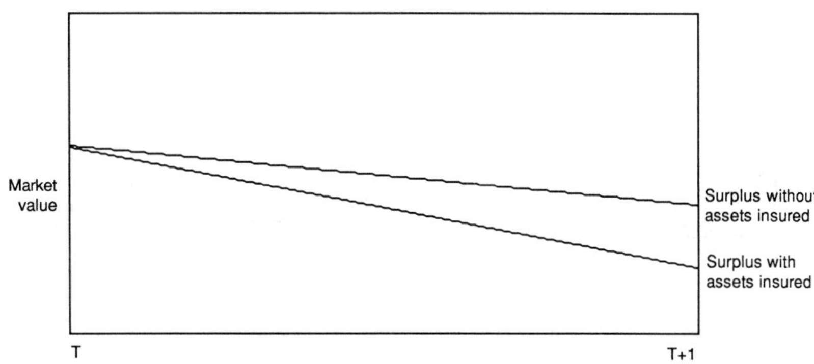

FIGURE 2. Discount rates fall

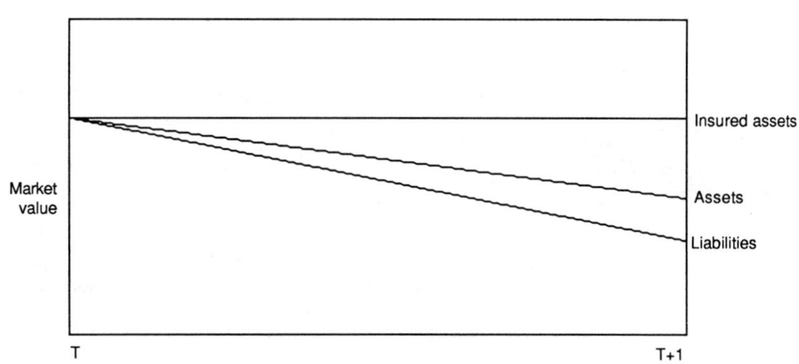

FIGURE 3. Discount rates rise

Insured assets, however, will decline even less if at all because they are protected. Despite the drop in asset values, the pension fund surplus will actually increase because the present value of the liabilities has dropped more than the present value of the assets, and it follows that if the assets are insured the surplus will increase by an event greater amount. These results are illustrated in Figures 3 and 4.

If we combine the two scenarios of both falling and rising discount rates to examine the impact on the pension fund surplus, we see that portfolio insurance has the perverse consequence of increasing the volatility of the pension fund surplus, and by extension the volatility of the net worth and earnings of the sponsoring corporation. This is illustrated in Figure 5.

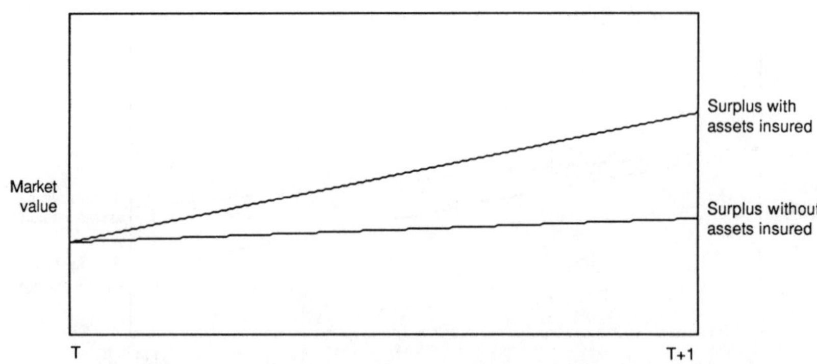

FIGURE 4. Discount rates rise

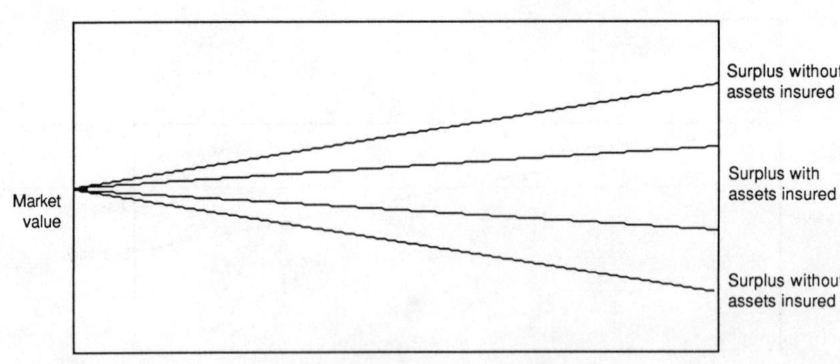

FIGURE 5. Surplus volatility

PORTFOLIO INSURANCE IS UNNECESSARILY EXPENSIVE

Not only does portfolio insurance increase volatility, it is also unnecessarily expensive given the alternative of insuring the pension fund surplus. (This strategy is described in the next section.) Pension liabilities, when measured correctly, are partly correlated with pension assets. Conceptually, we can express the present value of pension assets as:

$$\text{PVA} = \frac{C}{k - g}$$

where

PVA = present value of pension assets
C = cash flows including dividends and interest payments
k = discount rate
g = growth rate of cash flows

Similarly, we can express the present value of pension liabilities as:

$$\text{PVL} = \frac{B}{k - g}$$

where

PVL = present value of pension liabilities
B = benefit payments
k = discount rate
g = growth rate of benefit payments

Based on this conceptual model, it is apparent that when discount rates increase causing the present value of dividend and interest payments to decline to the extent that benefit payments are of equal duration and risk, their present value also declines. Therefore, the surplus value of the pension fund is *naturally hedged*, and the extent of this hedge is a function of the correlation between the pension assets and the pension liabilities. This natural hedge means that the *net* risk of pension assets and liabilities is less then the total risk of the pension assets. Since portfolio insurance is based on the total risk of the pension assets, it fails to exploit this natural hedge and, therefore, is unnecessarily expensive.

SURPLUS INSURANCE

An alternative to portfolio insurance is surplus insurance. This strategy adapts the technology of portfolio insurance to incorporate pension liabilities. Whereas portfolio insurance is designed to protect pension assets, surplus insurance is designed to protect the *ratio* of pension assets to pension liabilities. Specifically, its objective is to ensure that a minimum asset/liability ratio is met or exceeded while capturing returns in excess of changes in the value of pension liabilities.

This objective can be accomplished by substituting a *liability mimicking portfolio* for the risk-free component in the portfolio insurance strategy. Such a portfolio would track precisely any changes in the present value of the pension liabilities. Although it would be a risky portfolio in an absolute sense, it would be riskless relative to the liabilities. Within this context, any portfolio that is not perfectly correlated with the liabilities could serve as the risky component—even a portfolio that in an absolute sense was risk-free. This strategy would be executed by continually rebalancing the portfolio between the risky component and the liability mimicking component. (The mathematics of this strategy is explained in the appendix.)

Surplus insurance addresses the relevant measure of pension fund risk; that is, the net risk of the pension assets and pension liabilities. As such, it is significantly less expensive than portfolio insurance because the net risk of the pension assets and liabilities is lower than the absolute risk of the pension assets. The comparative cost of the two strategies is shown in Table 1.

The columns labled PI show the cost of portfolio insurance assuming a return of 8.0 percent for the risk-free component and a standard deviation of 15 percent for the risky component.

The columns labled SI show the cost of surplus insurance assuming a 15 per cent deviation for the risky component, a 10 percent standard deviation for the liability mimicking component, and a 75 percent correlation between the two. The minimum required return is measured relative to the return of the risk-free component, and multiple year results are annualized.

For example, consider alternative strategies with a one-year horizon and a −3 percent minimum required return. A $100 investment in a portfolio insurance strategy would ensure a terminal value one year hence of no less than $104.76 (108 times .97). If the risky component generated a 20 percent return,

TABLE 1. COMPARATIVE COST

Minimum Required Return	One Year		Two Years		Three Years	
	PI	SI	PI	SI	PI	SI
−1%	14.2%	9.2%	7.9%	5.6%	5.0%	4.0%
−2%	10.9%	6.5%	5.6%	3.6%	3.2%	2.4%
−3%	8.8%	4.8%	4.2%	2.4%	2.1%	1.6%
−4%	7.2%	3.7%	3.2%	1.7%	1.4%	1.0%
−5%	6.0%	2.9%	2.5%	1.2%	0.9%	0.7%

however, the expected terminal value of the total portfolio is \$120 times (1 − .088) or \$109.44. A surplus insurance strategy that has an initial asset/liability ratio of 100 percent would be assured of a terminal asset/liability ratio of no less than 97 percent. If the risky component generated a net return of 20 percent relative to the liability mimicking portfolio, however, the expected terminal asset/liability ratio is 120 percent times (1 − .048) or 114.24 percent.

Of course, the cost savings would increase if the liability mimicking component behaved more like the risky component. For example, if both components had a standard deviation of 15 percent and were 90 percent correlated, the cost of a one-year surplus insurance strategy with a −3 percent minimum required return would equal 2.3 percent rather than 4.8 percent. Also, the cost differential is greater the lower the risk-free rate, since the cost of portfolio insurance increases as the risk-free rate falls while the risk-free return for the surplus insurance strategy is invariant to the risk-free rate.

CONSTANT PROPORTION PORTFOLIO INSURANCE

Thus far, within the context of this chapter, the term *portfolio insurance* has been used to refer to a dynamic hedging strategy designed to replicate a protective put option. An alternative insurance strategy introduced by Robert Merton[1] and recently popularized by Andrè Perold[2], Fischer Black, and Robert Jones[3] is called *Constant Proportion Portfolio Insurance.* This strategy simply requires one to maintain an equity exposure equal to some constant multiple of a prespecified spread between the portfolio value and a minimum required value. For example, if the minimum required value (in present value terms) is \$80 and the portfolio value is \$100, then the spread equals \$20. If the chosen multiple is 4, then \$80 can be allocated to the risky component. If the portfolio value falls to \$90, then the exposure to the risky component is reduced to \$40 since the spread is only \$10 now.

This strategy is recommended by its simplicity, its insensitivity to time, and on more theoretical grounds, its compatibility with utility maximizing behavior. Nonetheless, within the context of pension fund economics, it too is susceptible to the criticisms raised in this chapter. Fortunately, this strategy can also be modified easily to overcome these problems. The minimum required value simply needs to be defined as a percentage of the market value of the pension liabilities.

[1] Footnotes appear at the end of chapter.

CONCLUSION

This chapter addresses the implications of pension fund economics on asset oriented investment strategies such as portfolio insurance. It demonstrates that portfolio insurance, as it is typically applied, has the perverse consequence of increasing risk rather than reducing risk as intended. Moreover, it is shown that portfolio insurance is unnecessarily expensive because it fails to exploit the positive correlation between pension assets and pension liabilities.

Nonetheless, portfolio insurance can be modified to incorporate pension liabilities. The key modification is to substitute a portfolio that mimics the behavior of the pension liabilities for the risk-free component and to redefine risk and return as net values. With these modifications, portfolio insurance can be adapted to protect a pension fund's surplus value and at a sharply reduced cost.

APPENDIX

The technical framework of surplus insurance is an adaptation of Margrabe's option model to exchange one asset for another.[4] After all, surplus insurance is tantamount to an option to exchange a risky portfolio for a liability mimicking portfolio or, in other words, investment in a risky portfolio with a protective put option that has an excercise price indexed to the value of the liabilities.

Based on the Margrabe model, the value of such an option equals:

$$C = N(d1)R - N(d2)L$$

$$d1 = \frac{\ln(R/L) + 1/2(SR\hat{\ }2 + SL\hat{\ }2 - 2 \times \varrho \times SR \times SL)T}{(SR\hat{\ }2 + SL\hat{\ }2 - 2 \times \varrho \times SR \times SL)\hat{\ }.5 \times T\hat{\ }.5}$$

$$d2 = d1 - (SR\hat{\ }2 + SL\hat{\ }2 - 2 \times \varrho \times SR \times SL)\hat{\ }.5 \times T\hat{\ }.5$$

where

C = price of an option to exchange R for L
R = price of risky portfolio
L = price of liability mimicking portfolio
SR = standard deviation of risky portfolio
SL = standard deviation of liability mimicking portfolio
ϱ = correlation between risky portfolio and liability mimicking portfolio
T = investment horizon
N( ) = cumulative normal density function

From put-call parity we can determine the value of a put as:

$$P = C + L - R$$

Since we are interested in replicating a strategy whereby we purchase as much of the risky portfolio as possible along with a protective put, we solve for the value of the put iteratively by changing the value of the risky portfolio such that its value, together with the value of the put, exactly matches the initial market value of the portfolio we are seeking to protect.

The initial allocation to the risky component equals N(d1)R divided by the market value of the total portfolio, and the cost of the protection equals one minus the market value of the risky portfolio as a percent of the total market value. Subsequent allocations will depend on the relative return of the two components as well as the passage of time.

The framework just described differs from the Black-Scholes framework,[5] which is used for standard portfolio insurance, in that the risk-free return equals zero since it represents the return of the liability mimicking portfolio net of changes in the present value of liabilities, and risk is defined as the standard deviation of the risky portfolio net of the standard deviation of the liability mimicking portfolio, recognizing, of course, their covariance.

FOOTNOTES

1. Robert C. Merton, "Optimum Consumption and Portfolio Rules in a Continuous Time Model," *Journal of Economic Theory*, Vol. 3, 1971.
2. Andrè F. Perold, "Constant Proportion Portfolio Insurance," Harvard Business School Working Paper, August 1986.
3. Fischer Black and Robert Jones, "Simplifying Portfolio Insurance," Goldman Sachs Research Report, August 1986.
4. William Margrabe, "The Value of an Option to Exchange One Asset for Another," *The Journal of Finance*, Vol. 33, No. 1, March 1978.
5. F. Black and M. Scholes, "The Pricing of Options and Corporate Liabilities," Chapter 19.

7. INSURING INTERNATIONAL PORTFOLIOS

Bruce J. Pullman

INTRODUCTION: INTERNATIONAL INVESTMENT

When asked to contribute an article on insuring international portfolios for what will be a predominantly American-authored book, I was struck yet again by the very real risk of insularity into which fund managers are liable to fall. To a U. K. pension fund, "international" includes the U. S. markets. To a U. S. sponsor, it is the world outside the United States which is regarded as being international. In time we may look at these labels as naive. We all live in a global marketplace. We may choose, through lack of experience or understanding, to regard the world outside our domestic capital markets as being dangerous, and thus appropriate for only a tiny portion of our assets. "Why", it may be argued, "should we invest overseas when our liabilities are domestic?"

One answer is the old argument of risk reduction. Overseas markets are imperfectly correlated with the domestic market, and hence by purchasing overseas equities we are likely to reduce our overall risk without sacrificing the high expected returns associated with equities. Opponents of overseas diversification may argue that it is difficult to obtain adequate research on foreign stocks, or that transaction costs and administrative problems make overseas investment too expensive and complicated. The answers to these criticisms must be, at least initially, to take a passive view on overseas stock selection, and invest in a basket of stocks designed to track an appropriate representative index, or to purchase a stock index futures portfolio. The development of techniques such as program trading keeps cost to a minimum and simplifies administration. It is now possible to purchase international equity exposure in the form of a series of market portfolios made up of stocks (or futures where they are available). Each portfolio will track the returns on its appropriate market index, and the allocation between these portfolios may be altered extremely rapidly, efficiently, and cost effectively.

This leaves the sponsor with an intriguing question as to what his international market allocation should be. Should he be passive, and allocate according to some passive index or benchmark? If so what should that benchmark be? Or should he adopt some dynamic allocation process?

The purpose of this article is not to discuss passive allocation benchmarks, although that is a subject in need of further research and clarification. Whether capitalization weighted, equal weighted, or maximally risk diversifying, the proper design of the benchmark portfolio is essential, particularly in an environment of performance related fees. Instead, I will focus on dynamic allocation in global markets, from a variety of perspectives and with differing objectives.

LOCAL MARKET INSURANCE

Local market insurance is the strategy on which the majority of this book is focused. It is the simplest case, but as it is dealt with extensively elsewhere, I shall assume in this section a certain level of familiarity with the strategy. Local market insurance is portfolio insurance where both the risky and the riskless assets are in the same country, typically equities and bills (or an immunized portfolio). As such, it has already been described very thoroughly for the U. S. markets. I shall discuss here the application of the strategy to the markets of other countries, from the perspective of a domestic investor.

Portfolio insurance was pioneered in the United States, and it was not until 1984 that serious consideration was given to portfolio insurance in other markets. Initially we assumed that the U. S. models would work overseas with little alteration. The first market we tested was Australia.

Basically, it failed to work. There were two tests which ex ante we required the model to fulfill:

1. Type I. A small number of returns below the insured minimum, and none far below the minimum;
2. Close tracking of the theoretical option performance on the upside, and reasonable average upside capture.

We had been seduced, in common with others in the industry, into believing these theoretical graphs which showed no returns below the minimum, tight clustering on the upside, and high upside capture. The first detailed simulations we carried out amply demonstrated that the real world was somewhat different! Our simulations were over 52 weeks of weekly equity return data, insured at 0 percent (capital preservation), with a contract commencing every week since 1 January 1969. This gave some 850 simulated one-year contracts. We accept that two contracts of the same length, one starting one week later than the other, could hardly be regarded as totally independent. Nonetheless the impact of an event (e.g., a sudden market fall) 15 weeks into a contract can have a very different effect from the same event 16 weeks into the contract. It depends on the path the market took prior to that event as to which contract is affected most. We decided that our 850 one-year contracts provided an adequate sample on which to test the model.

The first runs, using the model which had been optimized for the U. S. market, were disastrous. We missed the minimum on a number of occasions (Type I errors), and had poor and somewhat variable upside capture (Type II errors).

Back to the drawing board! We had established that modified Black-Scholes would not work for Australia nearly as well as for the U. S. market. The question was why, and what sort of modeling would work better?

The "why" related to the "fine structure" of the Australian market, and ultimately the psychological behavior of Australian investors. Black-Scholes assumes many things, but a core assumption is that security prices behave themselves. More technically, they are assumed to be lognormally distributed and to have negligible serial correlation. In English, this means that small movements in the market are much more likely than large ones, huge moves are rare, and a huge move does not indicate any increased likelihood of a compensating huge move in the opposite direction. Moreover, series of moves largely in the same direction (a "run" or "trend") occur only as frequently as they would by chance; price momentum has no value as an indicator of future performance.

Any fund manager in any market would almost certainly disagree with the assumptions in the previous paragraph. However, to keep the mathematics solvable, most academics assume this behavior. The early portfolio insurance models were no exception. You see, if you want to test your brand new portfolio insurance model, what better way than to create some normally distributed uncorrelated market returns, and run these through the model? The only problem is that in designing *both* the model and the test data, you assume this specific behavioral property for the market. Ipso facto, the model works well, and you can market with lovely theoretical graphs showing tight upside capture and no failures on the downside.

On the other hand, run the model exhaustively through not 20 but 850 simulations based on real data, and the problems start to become apparent. The reason is the existence of more large moves (and some huge moves) than a simple statistic like variance would imply, the existence of short- and long-term trends, and the existence of reversals (i.e., a trend in one direction followed immediately by a trend in the opposite direction). While these characteristics are apparent in the US market, they are nowhere near as prevalent as in a market such as Australia.

So, did we have to ditch Black-Scholes and start again? Not exactly, although the distance we have come from pure Black-Scholes means we could well have used another model of security prices which might have been a better starting point.

After many months of work, we have eventually developed portfolio insurance which works in a number of overseas markets. It has turned out not to be merely a case of exporting the domestic U. S. model and making a few minor alterations to cope with the vagaries of other markets. The two test criteria were fulfilled; not perhaps as well as our naive expectations based on other people's marketing literature, but with more than sufficient accuracy of tracking the option to be able to market the product confidently in the various markets to domestic investors.

In addition to these theoretical problems, there are significant practical issues to be addressed. First, let us consider trading. It is common practice in the United States to use very efficient, highly liquid futures markets to undertake portfolio insurance. In other markets transaction costs are likely to be significantly higher. While there has been some recent speculation that the mispricing of the futures when the market turns downward sharply will result in higher than predicted transaction costs over a full portfolio insurance contract, it is unlikely ever to be as expensive to transact portfolio insurance in the United States as it is in some overseas markets. This is because either the futures market is not terribly liquid, or there is no equity futures contract available. Australia is, to date, the only market outside North America which has a truly institutionally deep stock index futures contract. While the United Kingdom, Japan (Nikkei on SIMEX), and Hong Kong contracts are slowly developing volume, large orders ($30 million or more) would quite possibly result in significant market impact.

It is perhaps worth relating our experience in putting on a £20 million short in the United Kingdom FTSE 100 contract in September 1986. Effectively we were the market in the two days we transacted. This called for special execution skills and clever trading devices. We managed to trade at close to fair value. We could not entirely escape an element of market timing or subjective decision making, despite the fact that portfolio insurance is supposedly a passive (i.e., objective) strategy.

In practice, we believe we benefited from the need of the specialists to maintain an orderly market in the FTSE prior to the Big Bang. Whatever, trading skills are essential for successful implementation of these strategies.

More typically, overseas portfolio insurance is likely to involve physical stock transactions, and consequently higher transactions costs. One of the prerequisites for good upside capture in portfolio insurance is low and determinate transactions costs. Administrative systems must be able to handle high volume transactions, and to price portfolios accurately. Thus there are two areas which need to be addressed:

1. Provision of committed ex ante total transaction costs (including market impact);
2. A dealing structure which keeps the administrative burdens to a minimum.

A third area which must be watched is the way the portfolio insurance model handles transaction costs. This is a complex problem where a fair amount of proprietary research has been undertaken. If sensible trading rules are used in the model (e.g., what level of market movement should trigger a trade), then relatively high transaction costs will not decrease upside capture by as much as might be expected. Nonetheless, transaction costs are inevitably a drag on performance (as defined by upside capture) and so effort needs to be devoted to keeping them to a minimum.

The answer to these issues lies in a sophisticated extension of program trading. While commonplace now in the domestic markets, the idea of trading a basket of stocks at one point in time is still relatively new in overseas markets. As a pioneer in the techniques of international program trading, we have built up experience and skill in designing appropriate structures for which brokers can bid. One such structure is so-called "inventory" program trading, and it is a structure well suited to portfolio insurance where physical stock transactions are to be implemented. By way of illustration, let us consider an inventory trade for insurance based on the Tokyo Stock Exchange First Section Index. Clearly, it is infeasible, undesirable, and very expensive to transact over a thousand different names whenever the model triggers a trade (there are over 1000 stocks in the TSE First Section Index, which is the main domestic institutional benchmark).

Before setting up the portfolio insurance contract, the manager would enter into a trading agreement with an experienced broker. This is likely to be a global United States, Japanese, or United Kingdom house, given the complexity of the deal. The broker would quote a net spread on an agreed inventory of stocks. The inventory would include all the adequately liquid stocks in the TSE1, and only these stocks would be eligible for program trading in this fashion. The spread would be good for an extended period, ideally to the end of the insurance contract. Usually the spread is in practice renegotiated on a somewhat shorter term basis (typically three months). The broker would commit to trading at the predefined spread from an objective pricing source. Thus, at any time, the manager could call the broker and say that the broker has been deemed to have conducted a basket of transactions within the inventory. The conditions are that only inventory stocks are included, and that the beta and R^2 of the buy (or sell) lists lie within a certain range. Thus only index passive transactions are taking place. The manager uses the inventory as a basis for the design of a limited stock sampled index fund, and it is this basket which is traded. The complexity of the basket (the number of stocks involved) depends on how closely the client wants to track an index option.

The process transfers liquidity risk (at a fair price, the predetermined spread tendered by the broker) from the manager to the broker. The manager has a known ex ante total transaction cost, good for an extended period, which can be fed into the portfolio insurance model. The trades will usually be pro-rata transactions in the basket, and therefore administration systems can be simplified and streamlined.

The second practical issue relates to settlement problems. While futures are marked to market (same day settlement), in the United Kingdom for example, settlement may not occur for four weeks. Thus stocks may be sold, but the cash realized will not earn interest for a month. Then there are complexities over receipts of dividends, and reclaiming taxes.

A third issue relates to the pricing of the index. Is the index on which the option is based actually investable? Are the prices real; could stocks be transacted in size at the prices used in its calculation?

I could continue in a negative vein, citing problems or potential problems. It is perhaps sufficient to stress again that merely exporting a U. S. portfolio insurance model will not be sufficient to produce satisfactory local market portfolio insurance.

FOREIGN PERSPECTIVE LOCAL MARKET INSURANCE

We now move from experience to theory. International portfolio insurance is currently in its infancy. The simplest case has been implemented in institutional size (e.g., around $100 million). At this time, more complex cases of international insurance exist only on paper to our knowledge. The first extension of local market insurance is to consider a foreign investor seeking insurance in a given market. More explicitly, by way of illustration, let us consider a U. K. pension fund (£ based) appointing a manager to run portfolio insurance in the U. S. equity market.

It is unlikely that a U. K. pension fund will really be concerned to protect the asset value of its U. S. equity portfolio in U. S. dollar terms. It is irrelevant to protect the value in dollars; what is needed is protection in sterling terms. Thus, we have the noncurrency hedged U. S. equity market in sterling terms as the risky asset, and U. K. T-bills in sterling terms as the riskless asset. Put another way, the worst experience the U. K. fund wishes to encounter, is receipt of its initial sterling capital investment at the end of the insurance contract. If the return on the U. S. equity market converted into sterling terms is higher than zero, then the fund would receive that return less the option premium.

From Table 1 we see that the conventional domestic perspective local market insurance fails to meet this objective. Consider Case 5 in Table 1. If the S&P produces a zero total return, conventional portfolio insurance generates a zero return in U. S. dollar terms. If, however, the dollar depreciates by 20 percent against sterling, the "insured" return is −20 percent; hardly satisfactory insurance!

How then do you convert domestic perspective insurance into foreign perspective insurance? The answer lies in dynamic currency hedging simultaneously with the dynamic equity hedging. Let us assume the U. K. pension fund has a $100 million U. S. equity portfolio which is to be insured from a sterling perspective.

If the U. S. market rises, and the U. S. currency appreciates, the fund wants to participate in the unhedged U. S. equity market, unhedged both in equity and currency terms. If the U. S. market falls, and the currency falls, then the fund wants exposure to U. K. sterling cash.

Figure 1 schematically illustrates the hedge. For a given hedge ratio, we need to put on an equal dollar value of short S&P 500, and long British Pound contracts. As the hedge ratio varies dynamically according to the insurance model, we keep the dual hedge in parallel; equal dollar value of the two contracts.

Another variant on this exercise is a fully currency-hedged fund, where currency is removed from the risky as well as the riskless asset. This means we impose a static currency hedge on the whole fund, rather than varying it dynamically with the short S&P 500 position. The result is a return in sterling which is identical to local market insurance from a U. S. sponsor's perspective (see Table 2 for comparison with Foreign Perspective insurance).

A rather clean way of running fully currency-hedged insurance is to deposit the bulk of the portfolio in sterling Treasury-bills (the risk-free asset for the foreign investor), holding only the initial and variation margin for the dynamically varying S&P 500 contracts in U. S. dollars. The results of such a strategy would closely match the physical S&P, short S&P futures, and fully hedged long British pound futures strategy.

CURRENCY INSURANCE

The preceeding treatment of foreign perspective local market insurance caused us to consider the issue of currency risk. The advent of currency futures enables us to see clearly that a currency position can be thought of as merely another asset class. Exposure to Japanese yen in a U. S. sponsor's

TABLE 1

Case	Currency Return (£/US$)	Return on S&P 500 (US$)	Return on S&P 500 (£)	Theoretical Local Market Insurance Return* (£)	
				Domestic Perspective	Foreign Perspective
1	−20%	−20%	−36%	−20%	0%
2	+20%	−20%	−4%	+20%	0%
3	−20%	+20%	−4%	−8.8%	0%
4	0%	−20%	−20%	0%	0%
5	−20%	0%	−20%	−20%	0%
6	+20%	0%	+20%	+20%	+14%
7	0%	+20%	+20%	+14%	+14%
8	+20%	+20%	+44%	+36.8%	+30.8%

*Assume upside capture in both cases is 70%.

TABLE 2

Case	Currency Return (£/$)	Return on S&P 500 (US$)	Hedged Return on S&P 500 (£)	Theoretical Local Market Insurance Return* (£)	
				Foreign Perspective**	Fully Currency Hedged
1	− 20%	− 20%	− 20%	0%	0%
2	+ 20%	− 20%	− 20%	0%	0%
3	− 20%	+ 20%	+ 20%	0%	14%
4	0%	− 20%	− 20%	0%	0%
5	− 20%	0%	0%	0%	0%
6	20%	0%	0%	+ 14%	0%
7	0%	20%	+ 20%	+ 14%	14%
8	20%	20%	+ 20%	+ 30.8%	14%

*Assume upside capture in both cases is 70%.

**See Table 1.

(1) US equity portfolio − US stock index futures = US$ cash

(2) US$ cash + B.P. futures = £ cash

Thus, (1) + (2):

US equity portfolio + B.P. futures − US stock index futures = £ cash

FIGURE 1

portfolio (as a result of, say, long-term exposure to the Japanese equity market) can be effectively removed by a corresponding rolling short position in the yen futures contract.

However, should a sponsor make the decision to remove currency risk? In the previous section, complete removal of currency risk could have cost the sponsor 16.8 percent (see Case 8 in Table 2). More generally, the removal of currency risk removes potential for currency return. The other serious problem is that hedging currency positions may reduce diversification at the overall portfolio level. In that case, hedging will increase total portfolio volatility. If a U. S. sponsor invests abroad, his objective is to reduce risk, and to export U. S. domestic inflation. Over the long term, research indicates that complete currency hedging may increase risk, and may fail to reduce inflation exposure. Clearly then, complete hedging is unlikely to be appropriate for the prudent sponsor.

Nonetheless, poor currency returns can destroy performance. For a U. S. investor, performance will be hurt by currency exposure if the dollar strengthens against an appropriate basket of currencies, irrespective of the market or stock selections made. What is needed is an asymmetric exposure to currency risk.

Currency insurance is a more complex problem than equity or equity plus currency insurance. The currency markets are notoriously volatile, and trends followed by jumps characterize exchange rate behavior. Where equity is combined with currency, as in Foreign Perspective Local Market Insurance, then this pathological behavior is somewhat modified. However, naked currency insurance requires sophisticated modelling to cope with the vagaries of currency movements.

What, in this case, are the risky and riskless assets? As an example, consider a one-year insurance on the deutschemark for a U. S. dollar fund. If the deutschemark depreciates in value relative to the dollar, the investor would ideally like to receive the return on U. S. dollar Treasury bills. Thus, the riskless asset is, as for conventional equity insurance, the domestic Treasury-bill. Conversely, if the deutschemark appreciates, the investor would have been better off in deutschemark money market instruments. Thus, the risky asset is deutschemark Treasury-bill equivalents. The currency insurance works by dynamically altering the allocation between U. S. and German Treasury-bill equivalents. More specifically, as the deutschemark appreciates in value, U. S. Treasury-bills are sold, the proceeds are converted by a spot currency transaction into deutschemarks, and then deutschemark Treasury-bills are purchased.

This somewhat clumsy process may be simplified by putting the entire portfolio into U. S. Treasury-bills, and then using either the forward or future currency markets. The forward market would involve initially making a commitment to purchase DM to the value of say 70 percent of the portfolio one year forward. The rate agreed with the counterparty would reflect the interest rate differential between U. S. dollars and DM. As the model recommended purchases of DM (DM rises relative to U. S. $), additional forward currency contracts to buy DM on the horizon date would be taken out. As the model recommended sales of DM (DM falls relative to U. S. $), forward currency contracts committing to sell the DM on the horizon date would be entered into. At the horizon date (i.e., when the currency insurance contract matures), all the forward currency contracts would mature simultaneously, and a net profit would be received (reflecting participation in the DM's rise) or a net loss would have to be met (the option premium).

The drawbacks of the forward market are that contract size of less than $500,000 would typically result in high costs (poor forward rates) and that forward contracts cannot be undone (without significant penalty) prior to maturity. Thus it might prove expensive to terminate a forward contract currency insurance program prematurely.

Futures suffer from no such drawbacks. The contract size is sufficiently small (approximately $70,000) to be ideal for institutional clients. Futures can be sold or purchased (reversing a previous position) very quickly and with no penalty. While there may be some basis risk (i.e., moving away from the fair price as dictated by differential interest rates), this is likely to be more than offset by the cost savings and flexibility over time.

There is one variant on currency insurance which deserves brief mention. If, as a U. S. sponsor, you wish to remove the currency risk associated with an investment in the German equity market by the purchase of an option on the deutschemark, you cannot be sure of the capital value on which you need to buy the option. This capital value is clearly dependent on the performance of the German equity market over the life of the option. It is possible, using dynamic currency hedging, to replicate a currency option whose capital value is related to the performance of the related equity market.

Another version of this idea is a currency option whose quantity is *inversely* proportional to the return on the related equity market. Thus, if the equity market goes up, you are under currency hedged, and if it goes down, you are over currency hedged. It is left as an exercise for the reader to work out the entirely rational set of beliefs which would need to be held by a sponsor requiring such an option!

BOND INSURANCE

While bond insurance has not seen the interest generated by equity insurance, it is quite possible to conduct Local Market Bond Insurance from a domestic or foreign perspective in an analogous fashion to the equivalent equity strategies. The liquid international bond markets where a short futures overlay (nonintrusive hedge) strategy is possible are:

United Kingdom – Long Gilt Contract
Japan – Yen Bond
Australia – 10-year T-bond
France – 7–10-year Government Note

Other liquid bond markets where intrusive insurance (involving the purchase and sale of actual bonds) would be feasible include:

Germany
Netherlands

Bond markets tend to be less volatile than equity markets and, while portfolio insurance would tend to be less interesting or valuable, it will usually be correspondingly cheaper.

From a foreign perspective, that is, for example, bond insurance in the U. S. bond market for a U. K. pension plan that requires a minimum of the sterling investment returned at the end of the insurance period, it is not necessarily the case that bond insurance will be cheaper than equity insurance. This is because of the relatively high correlation between exchange rates and bond markets than between exchange rates and equity markets, reflecting the fact that both bond markets and exchange rates are heavily influenced by interest rate changes. The result may be a higher relative foreign perspective volatility (compared to domestic volatility) for bonds than for equities, thus increasing the relative cost of insurance.

Bond market returns tend to behave more normally than currency returns, and so overseas bond insurance programs should be easier to model than pure currency portfolio insurance.

MULTIPLE ASSET INSURANCE

My final topic, before returning to the issues I raised in my introduction, is insurance on a number of international assets. Multiple asset insurance has the objective of giving a return equal to the best performing of the assets less an option premium. For an example, see Table 3.

The numbers in Table 3 are fictional. However, if there are two assets which are negatively correlated (as one goes up, most of the time the other goes down), then the option to be in the better performing one is very valuable and hence expensive.

There are various types of multiple asset insurance:

I. Single equity/ single currency – A variant on Foreign Perspective Local Market Insurance where the currency hedge and equity hedge are not kept in parallel. The possible asset returns are:

1. Zero in domestic currency terms
2. Foreign currency return (i.e., fully equity hedged)
3. Equity return in foreign currency
4. Equity return in domestic currency (i.e., fully currency hedged)

TABLE 3. ANNUAL RETURNS

Case	UK Equities (%)	Japan Equities (%)	Germany Equities (%)	Insured Level (US$) (%)	Portfolio Return US$ (%)
1	+25	−6	+12	0	+13
2	+15	+65	−19	0	+45
3	+21	+19	+23	0	+11
4	−8	−21	−7	0	0

		The strategy would automatically (no subjective judgement) vary the currency hedge as appropriate to generate the best of the four possible returns (the last three being less the option premium).
II. Single equity/ single bond/ single currency	–	An extension of strategy (I), giving two additional asset classes: 5. Bond return in foreign currency 6. Bond return in domestic currency
III. Multiple stocks, currencies (+ bonds)	–	This is the no-holds barred product. As the number of assets increase, the usefulness of the product decreases and costs will rise. But for, say, five overseas equity markets, the S&P 500 and the Shearson Lehman bond index, this would be a hard product to beat.

I will focus briefly on strategy III. Let us assume we are appointed as manager of a global equity-only portfolio (for the purposes of illustration). The mandate precludes stock selection; that is, we have to invest in index funds or stock index futures in the local markets. Our target is the Financial Times-Actuaries World Market Index. Now it turns out that the target index can be tracked quite well by using only the five major markets (United States, Japan, United Kingdom, Germany, and Australia). The sponsor is giving us an equity mandate, and, believing the world's equity markets (in U. S. $ terms) to be not very highly correlated, and that there is a *long-term* upward trend in all the markets, he reckons at least one market will give a positive return each year. Thus, he tells us not to concern ourselves about a minimum return in dollars; rather, on a year-by-year basis, seek to be invested in the better performing markets. This is very much the sort of mandate (not perhaps as clearly defined) given to global managers at this time.

We know we can track the target benchmark by holding some 25 German equities, and long futures/cash positions in the other four markets. The question is, can we beat that index without imposing subjective market timing judgements? With a properly constructed multiple asset option model, the answer is almost certainly, yes.

It should be stressed that this option involves no subjective judgements. Nonetheless, because the markets underlying these options are not highly correlated over time, the dynamic allocation replicating this option is likely to outperform the passive FT-A World Market Index. Thus, providing the option replicating model works well and can be implemented accurately and in a timely fashion, this is an objective dynamic strategy which will beat the static composite index.

CONCLUSION: BRAVE NEW BENCHMARKS

I raised in my introduction the question of what a U. S. sponsor should use as his neutral "no view" international market allocation.

First, I would argue that it should not be a passive allocation. The passive benchmark, the FT World Index, can, as we have seen, almost certainly be beaten in the long term by an option replicating strategy of some kind. Secondly, a U. S. sponsor would probably like some downside protection, on either his market or currency exposure, and possibly on both.

Novel dynamic allocation techniques will permit the sponsor to tailor precisely his expected payoff diagram to meet his desired investment objectives. It is clearly unlikely to be appropriate to insure the U. S. equity portfolio, and not to carry out some form of insurance for the overseas portion of his fund. Such a mismatch can result in very peculiar and illogical expected return profiles. Given a sponsor's particular requirements (technically, his utility function and risk aversion), an objective option can be designed which will meet his needs, and which can be replicated by the manager. This objective strategy may well beat a passive benchmark which is less appropriate for the sponsor.

The design and pricing of these complex options, and the reverse engineering of a sponsor's requirements, will inevitably involve the development of new skills and modelling for both fund managers and pensions consultants.

Last, let us remember that however well designed the complex option, it will only spell out a no-view neutral portfolio at any point in time. If the manager has market alpha, that is, he can identify relative value across markets, the imposition of his subjective judgements will inevitably add value, and produce a higher return than the complex option.

Complex options may well eventually spell the demise of a passive benchmark for international managers. Nonetheless, there will always be a place for competent subjective judgements as to the relative attraction of one overseas market over another.

8. THE BEST-RETURN STRATEGY

Oldrich Vasicek

INTRODUCTION

Portfolio insurance is a technique that allows the investor to participate in the upside potentential of a risky portfolio (called the target asset), while reducing or eliminating the downside risk. Typically, this means guaranteeing a specified minimum return over a given investment horizon. The cost of the insurance is paid in terms of a return differential by which the investment return lags behind the performance of the target asset.

The target asset itself can be a portfolio containing a number of investment assets. For instance, the target portfolio can be a balanced fund consisting of equities, bonds, and mortgages. The allocation of funds within this portfolio can be fixed, or can vary according to a passive or active strategy. The insurance then applies to the total fund, and depends only on its total performance rather than on the performance of the individual components. Although the insured portfolio consists of multiple assets, from the viewpoint of the insurance strategy it is a single target asset.

In this chapter, we address a different type of multiple asset strategy, called *the best return strategy*. Instead of insuring the performance of a combination of assets, this strategy assures that the return on the total investment will be that of the best performance of the individual assets, less the known cost of the strategy. Thus, if the individual assets are stocks, bonds, and mortgages, and if stocks happen to perform the best of the three, the return on the strategy will be that of the stock portion, less the known cost. If bonds perform better over the investment horizon than stocks and mortgages, the investment return will equal the return on bonds, less cost. If mortgages do better than stocks or bonds, the investor will realize the return, after costs, of the mortgage portfolio on his total investment.

Moreover, if one of the assets has a fixed return over the investment horizon, this strategy guarantees a specified minimum return in addition to assuring the best of the remaining asset returns. This minimum guaranteed return is the return on such safety asset less the known costs. Thus, if the assets include a pure discount bond maturing at the end of the investment horizon in addition to stocks, bonds, and mortgages, the strategy will yield a specified minimum return even if stocks, bonds, and mortgages all perform poorly.

There is no restriction on the number of assets used in the best return strategy. It can be applied to individual securities (such as getting the best of several individual stock returns), to portfolios (for example, assuring that the return achieved by the best—or luckiest—of several portfolio managers is realized on the total plan), or to whole markets (for instance, obtaining the best performing of several international equity markets). The cost of the strategy, of course, increases with the number of assets involved. In addition to the number of assets, the costs depend on the riskiness of the assets (the riskier the assets the higher the costs), on the correlations among the assets (the higher correlated they are, the lower the costs), and on the length of the investment horizon (the costs per year decrease with increasing horizon length).

The strategy is implemented by a dynamic allocation of the investment funds among the several assets. The proportions of the total investment allocated to the individual assets are continuously monitored and adjusted, depending on their performance to date, and on the time remaining to the horizon date.

THE OBJECTIVE

The best return strategy is a generalization of portfolio insurance to multiple assets. To understand the connection, consider the objective of portfolio insurance. The objective function can be written in the following form:

$$R_I = \max (R_T - c, R_{min})$$

where R_I is the total investment return, R_T is the target asset return, R_{min} is the assured minimum return, and c is the insurance cost. (Throughout this chapter, all returns are assumed to be expressed in terms of annual, continuously compounded rates.)

Portfolio insurance is nothing other than getting the better of two asset returns. Indeed, when the insurance plan is implemented by means of dynamic asset allocation, it is necessary to utilize a second asset that has a fixed return over the insurance horizon, such as a pure discount bond with no default risk. The difference between the second asset return and the assured minimum return can be viewed as a second insurance cost, assigned to this second asset. The objective function can then be written as

$$R_I = \max(R_1 - c_1, R_2 - c_2)$$

where R_1, R_2 are returns on the two assets and c_1, c_2 are the corresponding insurance costs. A minimum return guarantee is just a special case when one of the two assets has a fixed terminal value. (In a world of changing interest rates, however, that asset is also risky, since its value fluctuates during the horizon.)

The two insurance costs, c_1, c_2 (both of which must be positive) are subject to a pricing equation that determines one of them if a value for the other is selected. This equation reduces to a version of the Black-Scholes (1973) option pricing formula if one of the assets is a bond and interest rates are deterministic and constant, and to Merton's (1973) extension of that formula if one asset is a pure discount bond and the variability of interest rates is independent of their level. Margrabe (1978) has provided a formula for two risky assets. In general, the insurance costs will depend on the risk structure of the two assets throughout the horizon (i.e., their instantaneous covariance matrix as a function of time and state variables) and the length of the horizon.

It is a natural generalization of the two-asset case to postulate an objective function of the form

$$R_I = \max(R_1 - c_1, R_2 - c_2, \ldots, R_n - c_n)$$

where $n \geqslant 2$ is the number of assets, $R_1, R_2, \ldots, R_n$ are their returns, and $c_1, c_2, \ldots, c_n$ are the corresponding insurance costs. This objective is to get the best of multiple risky asset returns, less the cost of insurance. This constitutes the goal of the best return strategy.

THE COSTS

The valuation formula from which the costs of the best return strategy are calculated is a single equation for the n costs, so that $n - 1$ of the costs can be independently chosen (subject to feasibility constraints) and the remaining one is then determined. Alternatively, $n - 1$ relationships can be imposed on the costs (such as that they be all equal) to determine their values.

The formula depends on the number of assets, the risk structure of the n-dimensional stochastic process that describes their behavior over the horizon, and the horizon length. For diffusion processes, the valuation formula involves $(n - 1)$-dimensional cumulative normal distribution functions with covariance matrices that are transformations of the n-dimensional instantaneous covariance matrix of the assets, integrated over the horizon. In addition to the two-asset formulas of Black and Scholes, Merton, and Margrabe mentioned earlier, the other result previously available in Stulz's (1982) formula for two risky and one riskless asset.

The values of the costs are determined by the investor's preferences, much like in the case of portfolio insurance. In that special case of two assets, the investor chooses a trade-off between the minimum guaranteed return (which is the fixed return of the safety asset less the cost attributed to the safety asset), and the return differential between the target asset return and the total investment return (which is the cost attributed to the target asset). Thus, portfolio insurance strategies can guarantee a relatively high minimum return at a high cost of the insurance, or a lower minimum return at a more modest insurance cost.

In the best return strategy, one alternative is to choose the costs to be all equal,

$$c_1 = c_2 = \ldots = c_n.$$

In that case, the objective function of the strategy has a particularly simple form

$$R_I = \max(R_1, R_2, \ldots, R_n) - c,$$

where the common value c of the n costs is determined from the valuation formula. This case, which will be called uniform cost allocation, assigns the costs equally to all of the assets included in the objective.

As an example, consider n assets whose stochastic behavior is described by a logarithmic Wiener process. Let the instantaneous covariance matrix be specified by standard deviations all equal to 15 percent annual, with correlations among the assets all equal to .4, and assume a five-year horizon. Table 1 lists the value c of the uniform costs, in annual percent, as a function of the number of assets:

TABLE 1. UNIFORM COSTS IN ANNUAL PERCENT

n =	2	3	4	5	6	8	10
c =	2.7	4.1	5.0	5.7	6.2	7.0	7.6

TABLE 2. BEST RETURN STRATEGY

Uniform Costs (in Annual %)

Horizon Length (yrs): 5.0
Standard Deviation (%): 15.0

	Number of Assets										
Corr.	2	3	4	5	6	7	8	9	10	11	12
.0	3.4	5.2	6.3	7.2	7.9	8.4	8.9	9.2	9.6	9.9	10.2
.1	3.3	4.9	6.0	6.9	7.5	8.0	8.4	8.8	9.1	9.4	9.7
.2	3.1	4.7	5.7	6.5	7.1	7.6	8.0	8.3	8.7	8.9	9.2
.3	2.9	4.4	5.4	6.1	6.7	7.1	7.5	7.8	8.1	8.4	8.6
.4	2.7	4.1	5.0	5.7	6.2	6.6	7.0	7.3	7.6	7.8	8.0
.5	2.5	3.8	4.6	5.2	5.7	6.1	6.4	6.7	6.9	7.2	7.4
.6	2.3	3.4	4.1	4.7	5.1	5.5	5.8	6.0	6.2	6.4	6.6
.7	2.0	3.0	3.6	4.1	4.5	4.8	5.0	5.2	5.4	5.6	5.8
.8	1.6	2.4	3.0	3.4	3.7	3.9	4.1	4.3	4.5	4.6	4.7
.9	1.2	1.7	2.1	2.4	2.6	2.8	2.9	3.1	3.2	3.3	3.4

These costs are the price to pay for getting the best out of a number of asset returns. Suppose that the values of the parameters chosen for the example are descriptive of the international equity markets. It is possible to implement a strategy whose realized return is equal to the highest of six separate national stock markets, over a five-year period, less 6.2 percent annual. It goes without saying that no prediction is needed as to which of these markets will have the highest return, or, for that matter, what are the expected returns of each.

Table 1 is an extract from Table 2, which lists the values of the uniform costs as a function of the number of assets and of the correlation among them, assumed to be the same between any pair. The investment horizon is taken to be five years and the standard deviations of the individual asset returns are assumed to be all equal to 15 percent per year. It can be seen that the costs decrease drastically with an increase in the correlation among the assets. The uniform costs under the same assumptions but for a one-year horizon are given in Table 3.

NONUNIFORM COSTS

The costs of the strategy do not have to be made equal. It is possible to choose them in such a way that a disproportionate part of the burden is borne by those assets in which the investor has a secondary interest. For instance, consider

TABLE 3. BEST RETURN STRATEGY

Uniform Costs (in Annual %)

Horizon Length (yrs): 1.0
Standard Deviation (%): 15.0

	Number of Assets										
Corr.	2	3	4	5	6	7	8	9	10	11	12
.0	8.1	12.2	14.9	16.8	18.4	19.6	20.7	21.6	22.3	23.1	23.7
.1	7.7	11.6	14.1	16.0	17.4	18.6	19.6	20.5	21.2	21.9	22.5
.2	7.3	11.0	13.4	15.1	16.5	17.6	18.5	19.3	20.1	20.7	21.3
.3	6.8	10.3	12.5	14.2	15.4	16.5	17.4	18.1	18.8	19.4	19.9
.4	6.3	9.5	11.6	13.1	14.3	15.3	16.1	16.8	17.4	18.0	18.5
.5	5.8	8.7	10.6	12.0	13.1	14.0	14.7	15.4	16.0	16.5	16.9
.6	5.2	7.8	9.5	10.8	11.8	12.6	13.2	13.8	14.3	14.8	15.2
.7	4.5	6.8	8.3	9.4	10.2	10.9	11.5	12.0	12.4	12.8	13.2
.8	3.7	5.6	6.8	7.7	8.4	8.9	9.4	9.8	10.2	10.5	10.8
.9	2.6	4.0	4.8	5.5	5.9	6.3	6.7	7.0	7.2	7.5	7.7

TABLE 4. BEST RETURN STRATEGY COSTS

Number of assets:	4			
Horizon length (years):	5.0			
Standard deviations (%):	15.7	11.7	15.2	1.3
Correlation matrix:	1.00	.25	.24	−.08
		1.00	.97	.74
			1.00	.75
				1.00

Costs (in annual %):

Case	Stocks	Bonds	Mortgage	Bills
Uniform	3.8	3.8	3.8	3.8
1	4.1	4.1	4.1	3.0
2	3.0	5.8	5.8	3.0
3	2.2	9.0	9.0	3.0
4	4.9	4.9	4.9	2.0
5	4.2	4.2	7.3	2.0
6	3.4	7.0	8.0	2.0
7	6.4	6.4	6.4	1.0
8	2.0	5.0	5.0	6.0

the case of four assets with standard deviations of 15.7 percent, 11.7 percent, 15.2 percent, and 1.3 percent, and a correlation matrix as shown in Table 4. These values correspond to historical estimates of volatilities and correlations (over the period 1/79 to 12/80) for S&P 500 stock index, Lehman government/corporate bond index, GNMA index, and Treasury bill index. For a five-year horizon, the uniform costs are 3.8 percent annually. This means that the best return strategy applied to these four assets assures the investor a return equal to the highest of the realized annual returns over the five-year period of stocks, bonds, mortgages, and cash, less 3.8 percent. For instance, if stocks turned out to do the best of these four assets with an annual return of 20 percent, the investor would realize 16.2 percent annually over the horizon. If stocks, bonds, and the GNMA portfolio all lost money, the strategy would still provide a return equal to that realized on Treasury bills, less 3.8 percent.

Now suppose that it is essential to the investor to maintain a five-year return of no less than that of Treasury bills less 2 percent, while retaining as much of the upside potential of stocks, bonds, and GNMAs as possible. The costs of a best return strategy can be chosen as

$$c_1 = 4.9\%, c_2 = 4.9\%, c_3 = 4.9\%, c_4 = 2.0\%$$

(Case #4 in Table 4). This choice of costs would assure a minimum performance of Treasury bill return less 2 percent, while keeping the possibility open to participate in the performance of the three riskier assets if any one of them turns out to do well.

If mortgages were less important to the investor than stocks and bonds, perhaps the following cost assignment may be a preferred choice:

$$c_1 = 4.2\%, c_2 = 4.2\%, c_3 = 7.3\%, c_4 = 2.0\%$$

(Case #5 in Table 4). This cost allocation would attribute lower costs to stocks and bonds than the previous case, and higher costs to the less important mortgage portfolio.

Table 4 lists a number of possible alternatives for the cost allocation. Note that these are just a few possibilities out of an infinite range of feasible cost allocations, with no particular meaning to the order in which the cases are listed.

STRATEGY IMPLEMENTATION

The strategy is executed by a dynamic allocation of investment funds among the several assets. The amounts allocated to the individual assets are maintained to be proportional to the partial derivatives, with respect to the asset

TABLE 5. BEST RETURN STRATEGY SIMULATION

Plan #5: Best of Four Assets

Best	Name	Costs (%)	Description	
1	Stocks	8.76	Standard & Poor's 500 Stock Index	Inception date 1-01-81
2	Bonds	8.76	Shearson Lehman Government Corporate Bond Index	Horizon date 12-31-81
3	Morg	8.76	Shearson Lehman GNMA Pass Through Index	Horizon length 1.00yrs
4	Bills	8.76	U. S. Treasury Bill Index	
				Init'l. investment $10,000,000
				Rnd. trip trans. costs .25%

Date	Yrs to Horiz	Stocks	Bonds	Mortg	Bills	Plan Sched.	Plan Actual Before T/costs	Plan Actual After T/costs		
1-01-81	1.00									
Required allocation		36.07%	8.71%	28.79%	26.42%				Investment value	$10,000,000
2-01-81	.91									
Return in last period		−4.20%	−0.03%	0.68%	1.21%	−1.03%	−1.00%	−1.00%	Investment value	$9,899,676
Return since inception		−4.20%	−0.03%	0.68%	1.21%	−1.03%	−1.00%	−1.00%	Turnover	13.65%
Current allocation		34.90%	8.80%	29.28%	27.01%				Transaction costs	$3,391
Required allocation		23.28%	6.78%	34.46%	35.49%					
3-01-81	.84									
Return in last period		1.71%	−1.63%	−3.68%	1.18%	−.55%	−.56%	−.60%	Investment value	$9,840,655
Return since inception		−2.57%	−1.66%	−3.03%	2.41%	−1.57%	−1.56%	−1.59%	Turnover	14.23%
Current allocation		23.81%	6.70%	33.38%	36.11%				Transaction costs	$3,517
Required allocation		28.06%	8.00%	19.13%	44.81%					
4-01-81	.75									
Return in last period		4.03%	2.39%	2.05%	1.62%	2.09%	2.44%	2.40%	Investment value	$10,077,098

Return since inception	1.36%	0.68%	−1.04%	4.06%	.49%	.84%	.77%	Turnover	6.55%
Current allocation	28.50%	7.99%	19.06%	44.45%				Transaction costs	$1,662
Required allocation	33.79%	9.25%	17.03%	39.93%					
5-01-81 .67									
Return in last period	−1.97%	−3.22%	−6.28%	0.64%	−1.62%	−1.77%	−1.79%	Investment value	$9,896,627
Return since inception	−0.63%	−2.56%	−7.26%	4.73%	−1.14%	−.95%	−1.03%	Turnover	16.41%
Current allocation	33.72%	9.12%	16.25%	40.91%				Transaction costs	$4,074
Required allocation	29.60%	9.01%	4.06%	57.33%					
6-01-81 .59									
Return in last period	0.21%	3.19%	6.97%	1.25%	1.24%	1.35%	1.31%	Investment value	$10,026,188
Return since inception	−0.42%	0.55%	−0.79%	6.05%	.09%	.39%	.26%	Turnover	11.79%
Current allocation	29.27%	9.18%	4.28%	57.28%				Transaction costs	$2,965
Required allocation	23.49%	5.60%	16.06%	54.85%					
7-01-81 .50									
Return in last period	−0.63%	0.15%	−3.04%	1.46%	.12%	.18%	.15%	Investment value	$10,040,793
Return since inception	−1.05%	0.70%	−3.81%	7.60%	.21%	.57%	.41%	Turnover	16.97%
Current allocation	23.30%	5.60%	15.54%	55.56%				Transaction costs	$4,275
Required allocation	18.08%	10.15%	3.78%	67.98%					
8-01-81 .42									
Return in last period	0.23%	−1.79%	−3.28%	1.07%	.31%	.46%	.42%	Investment value	$10,082,992
Return since inception	−0.82%	−1.10%	−6.96%	8.75%	.52%	1.03%	.83%	Turnover	11.24%
Current allocation	18.04%	9.93%	3.64%	68.39%				Transaction costs	$2,848
Required allocation	15.04%	4.63%	0.69%	79.64%					
9-01-81 .33									
Return in last period	−5.81%	−1.68%	−4.58%	1.16%	.36%	−.06%	−.09%	Investment value	$10,074,200
Return since inception	−6.58%	−2.77%	−11.22%	10.01%	.88%	.97%	.74%	Turnover	15.80%
Current allocation	14.17%	4.56%	0.66%	80.61%				Transaction costs	$3,997
Required allocation	2.25%	1.30%	0.01%	96.43%					

TABLE 5. CONTINUED

Plan #5: Best of Four Assets

Date	Yrs to Horiz	Stocks	Bonds	Mortg	Bills	Plan Sched.	Plan Actual Before T/costs	Plan Actual After T/costs		
10-01-81	.25									
Return in last period		−4.94%	0.02%	−0.67%	1.57%	1.47%	1.40%	1.36%	Investment value	$10,211,184
Return since inception		−11.19%	−2.75%	−11.82%	11.73%	2.36%	2.39%	2.11%	Turnover	3.12%
Current allocation		2.11%	1.29%	0.01%	96.59%				Transaction costs	$810
Required allocation		0.06%	0.22%	0.00%	99.72%					
11-01-81	.17									
Return in last period		5.43%	5.45%	9.27%	1.56%	1.57%	1.57%	1.57%	Investment value	$10,371,085
Return since inception		−6.37%	2.55%	−3.65%	13.48%	3.96%	4.00%	3.71%	Turnover	.31%
Current allocation		0.07%	0.23%	0.00%	99.71%				Transaction costs	$94
Required allocation		0.05%	0.53%	0.01%	99.41%					
12-01-81	.08									
Return in last period		4.11%	8.04%	12.22%	1.51%	1.62%	1.55%	1.54%	Investment value	$10,531,296
Return since inception		−2.52%	10.79%	8.13%	15.19%	5.65%	5.60%	5.31%	Turnover	8.07%
Current allocation		0.05%	0.56%	0.01%	99.38%				Transaction costs	$2,135
Required allocation		0.00%	7.10%	1.54%	91.37%					
12-31-81	.00									
Return in last period		−2.55%	−3.19%	−7.37%	0.79%	.69%	.38%	.36%		
Return since inception		−5.01%	7.25%	0.16%	16.10%	6.37%	6.01%	5.69%	Investment value	$10,569,185

values, of the valuation function (the same function which is also used initially to determine the costs of the strategy). The required allocation changes continuously as a function of the asset performance to date, and the remaining time to the horizon.

An example of the strategy is provided in Table 5. The strategy is simulated over a one-year investment horizon from 1/1/81 to 12/31/81, using the four assets described. The risk parameters are those listed in Table 4, as measured over a prior period from 1/79 to 12/80. The costs, allocated uniformly, are 8.8 percent for each asset. The simulations assume monthly rebalancing, with transaction costs of .25 percent round-trip (since the rebalancing can be executed by trading futures).

The initial allocation was 36.1 percent, 8.7 percent, 28.8 percent, and 26.4 percent among stocks, bonds, mortgages, and cash, respectively. One month later, based on the market moves over the month, the allocation was changed to 23.3 percent, 6.8 percent, 34.5 percent, and 35.5 percent, respectively, for a turnover of 13.6 percent. The rebalancing is continued each month until the horizon date.

Table 5 lists, for each rebalancing period, the last month performance and the performance since inception of the four assets, as well as the scheduled performance of the plan (the performance, calculated from the valuation formula, that is expected from the strategy given the performance of the

TABLE 6. SIMULATION SUMMARY

Plan #5: Best of Four Assets

Plan Inception Date	1-01-81	Horizon Length	1.00 Yrs
Plan Horizon Date	12-31-81	Initial Investment	$10,000,000

	Stocks	Bonds	Mortg	Bills
Return Since Inception:				
Total	−5.01%	7.25%	0.16%	16.10%
Per/yr (Annl. Comp)	−5.01%	7.25%	0.16%	16.10%
Per/yr (Cont. Comp)	−5.14%	7.00%	0.16%	14.93%

	Plan Scheduled	Plan Actual Before T/Costs	Plan Actual After T/Costs
Return Since Inception:			
Total	6.37%	6.01%	5.69%
Per/yr (Annl. Comp)	6.37%	6.01%	5.69%
Per/yr (Cont. Comp)	6.18%	5.83%	5.54%

Investment Value	$10,569,185
Total Turnover	118.14%
Total Trans. Costs	$29,768

individual assets), and the actual performance of the plan before and after transaction costs.

The summary of the strategy performance is provided in Table 6. Over the one-year horizon, the annual continuously compounded returns for the four assets were −5.1 percent for stocks, 7.0 percent for bonds, .2 percent for mortgages, and 14.9 percent for cash. The scheduled return was 6.2 percent, equal to the best of the four asset returns (Treasury bills in this case) less 8.8 percent. The actual performance of the plan was 5.8 percent before, and 5.5 percent after transaction costs, very close to the schedule. The difference between the actual and promised performance is due to monthly (rather than continuous) rebalancing and to the actual risk parameters over the investment horizon differing from the assumed values (which were estimated over a previous period).

METHODS

9. STRUCTURING A PORTFOLIO INSURANCE PROGRAM

Steven Paul Somes

Portfolio insurance, formally introduced to investors in the early 1980s, remains an essentially new strategy for managing investment portfolios. As a result, practitioners have focused their energies in four separate directions: improvement upon the basic option algorithm; expansion of the availability of the strategy; improvement upon current implementation techniques; and development of procedures to ensure that the strategy is most effectively applied.

Other contributors deal with the issues associated with these first three areas and furnish the reader with the tools necessary to structure a portfolio insurance program.

The purpose of this chapter is to develop a procedure to utilize them effectively in order to structure the desired program. One such procedure, described as "investment engineering," seeks to methodologically evaluate the overall plan, and then structure a program best-suited to the sponsor's objectives.

This chapter introduces the investment engineering approach and describes five steps necessary to structuring the program:

1. Identifying the sponsor's objectives and constraints.
2. Structuring a program to meet the objective.
3. Projecting expected results.
4. Identifying the sources and impact of underperformance.
5. Identifying the program's "next step."

IDENTIFYING THE OBJECTIVE AND CONSTRAINTS

The design of a successful structured program is critically dependent upon careful consideration of the sponsor's objectives and constraints. As such, the first step to structuring the program is to recognize these characteristics.[1]

Identifying the Objective. Perhaps the most difficult aspect to structuring the program is identifying the sponsor's investment objective. It is not uncommon to encounter multiple, and potentially contradictory, objectives. For example, consider a plan in which the value of the assets precisely equals the liabilities, yet in which the stated objective is to simultaneously preserve the value of the assets one year hence and to ensure that the present value of the liabilities will not exceed the assets. Such dual objectives cannot always be achieved with certainty.

The first step in identifying the objective is to review the plan's stated objectives. The firm's stated objective can generally be found in the plan's investment policy statement. This statement presents the strategic objective of the plan and may include rate-of-return, funding, or distributional targets. Once the stated objective has been reviewed, the next step is to determine whether any tactical objectives exist. For example, the sponsor may have as a tactical objective increasing the plan's exposure to equities or preserving the level of the surplus.

Whatever the actual portfolio objective may be, however, it should be clearly articulated. Though portfolio insurance is a powerful technique, it requires a precise identification of the investment objective in order to set the minimum return requirements or absolute levels of risk used in the portfolio insurance algorithm.

Required return. For institutional investors, return requirements are generally long term in nature and only loosely based on the assumptions of the plan's actuary. FASB 87, however, will undoubtedly focus more attention on the plan's overall performance and the return on plan assets versus liabilities. Under FASB 87, defined benefit pension plans must repeat a pension deficit on the firm's balance sheet.[2]

Return requirements are generally of more importance at eleemosynary institutions which confront short-term distribution requirements. For these institutions, the program must be carefully constructed to account for overall return and distribution requirements.

Tolerance for Risk. A plan's tolerance for risk is a function of such factors as its expected liabilities or obligations, the current value of its assets, and the

[1] Footnotes appear at end of chapter.

anticipated level of future contributions. For example, a plan which is substantially overfunded may be willing to accept more risk than one which is only marginally overfunded. However, despite these factors, many plans base the level of risk that they are willing to tolerate on factors such as market expectations or "normal" levels of risk. This tendency is evident in the cluster of plans toward a 60/40 stock and bond asset allocation.[3]

In portfolio insurance programs we define risk, and consequently a sponsor's tolerance for risk, differently. Risk, in portfolio insurance programs, is defined in terms of a minimum return requirement, asset value, funded ratio, or plan surplus value rather than in terms of traditional measures of volatility. Defined in this way, the plan's return requirement and risk tolerance become essentially identical.

For example, consider a university endowment fund unwilling to absorb plan losses in excess of 10 percent in any calendar year. We would consider this figure both in their absolute risk tolerance and their minimum return requirement. To address this risk, we would structure a program which would prevent losses in excess of 10 percent, the fund's minimum rate of return requirement.

In light of the exceptional degree to which portfolio insurance can address risk, it is essential that investors carefully articulate their tolerance for risk at the time the portfolio insurance program is structured. If the sponsor's risk tolerance cannot be specified in this fashion, or if it is exceedingly large, then portfolio insurance may not be an appropriate investment strategy.

Identifying the Constraints. Having articulated an objective, investors must also pay attention to the constraints upon which the program must adhere. Such constraints include tax considerations, liquidity requirements, and time horizons. Among these factors, the sponsor's time horizon will exert the greatest influence over the expected results of the program.

Tax Considerations. Though taxes are of little concern to pension plans, they may create acute constraints for banks, insurance companies, and eleemosynary institutions. While taxes must be carefully evaluated in evaluating any investment strategy, they are especially important in portfolio insurance strategies because, as earlier chapters explain, portfolio insurance programs typically generate capital gains or losses which cannot be fully anticipated. Although it is beyond the scope of this chapter to identify the tax consequences of portfolio insurance strategies, such consequences are critically important to the structuring of programs with taxable plans.

Liquidity Constraints. Liquidity constraints only rarely influence the structuring of insurance programs, but for plans with explicit requirements regarding liquidity levels or when liquid assets are required at short notice, this constraint may prove binding. However, even in these instances, such requirements can be largely offset through the implementation techniques employed. For example, in the case of a plan termination where instant liquidity is required, the program could be managed entirely through the futures market with cash assets invested in liquid, short-term securities. This would enable the sponsor to retain substantial liquidity while enjoying the benefits of portfolio insurance.

Time Horizon. The plan's time horizon enters the portfolio algorithm directly through the option pricing formula and, as such, it exerts a significant influence over the cost, or upside capture, of the program. As a result, the horizon is a critical parameter which should be carefully defined by the plan's sponsor at the outset.

Interestingly enough, despite the higher cost of shorter-term programs, when portfolio insurance was first introduced, most programs were initiated with one- or two-year durations. However, because this period was characterized by such high interest rates, the cost imposed by adopting such severe time constraints was largely concealed.

Because the cost of portfolio insurance declined with longer time horizons, plan sponsors should seek to adopt the longest program consistent with their time horizon. We have found that for many plans, this suggests that their program's time horizon should equal the length of their liabilities.

The objectives and constraints described above define the environment in which the portfolio insurance program must be structured. The proposed program must meet the stated investment objective yet satisfy each of the sponsor's constraints.

STRUCTURING A PROGRAM TO MEET THE OBJECTIVE

Once we identify a plan's objectives and constraints, we can proceed to the second stop in the "engineered" approach: structuring the program. To structure the program, we must first prepare an inventory of the plan's assets and liabilities, then analyze the current investment environment, and finally select the parameters of the program.

Before conducting such a procedure, however, we should ask ourselves whether portfolio insurance is the most efficient way to satisfy the sponsor's objective. Portfolio insurance cannot meet all investment objectives and may not operate in a manner consistent with the sponsor's investment philosophy. For example, portfolio insurance is not appropriate whenever the sponsor, or his managers, possess market timing capabilities. In this instance, insurance of any type is unnecessary. Also, portfolio insurance cannot be easily applied to illiquid assets. Finally, because portfolio insurance buys appreciating assets and sells depreciating assets, it may operate in a manner inconsistent with the sponsor's philosophy.

Asset and Liability Selection. If portfolio insurance can satisfy the sponsor's objectives and is selected for evaluation, then the practitioner should first prepare an inventory of the plan's assets and liabilities, then estimate certain capital market assumptions for each of the various security classes and the liabilities. Such capital market assumptions include estimates of expected return, volatility, and covariance. In addition, because most insurance programs consider transactions costs, the practitioner should include estimates of transaction costs for each of the asset classes. Depending upon the requirements of the model selected, additional assumptions such as expected dividends may be required.

Although the program may not include all of the assets or liabilities inventoried, they should still be considered to evaluate how the structured program will fit within the context of the overall plan. This topic is discussed in more detail in the section on projecting expected results.

Having taken stock of the plan's current assets and liabilities, we must identify which assets and, if appropriate, which liabilities to include in the program. As a rule, the ideal assets to include are those which are very liquid and can be hedged by using the futures market. As a result, equities and fixed income securities have proven the most popular assets. It is less clear which liabilities should be included, but those which are most certain are best the best candidates. These would include retired lives.

One other asset should also be included in this step of the analysis. In any insurance program, there is a risk-free asset. The risk-free asset is defined by the program. It is always a fixed income asset with a duration equal to the duration of the insurance program. For example, in one-year programs, a one-year Treasury bill is the risk-free asset. As the desired program is structured, estimates of the return, volatility, covariance, and transactions costs for the risk-free asset should be calculated and included with the other estimates.

Estimating the Program Parameters. Once our inventory of plan assets and liabilities and their capital market estimates are complete, we have all the inputs required to structure the program. Now we must translate the objectives and constraints into program parameters. The program parameters include the type of program, whether it is asset- or liability-based; the term of the program; the minimum rate of return, the level of the surplus, or funded ratio; and which assets are to be included.

Asset-based Strategies. For simplicity, we divide portfolio insurance programs into asset- or liability-based programs. As the name suggests, asset-based strategies are designed to provide a minimum rate of return for one or more asset classes over a defined time horizon. Such programs account for the vast majority of the insurance programs currently in force.

In practice, asset-based strategies have been returned to provide minimum rates of return as low as −10 percent and as high as 5 percent per annum. The time horizon has ranged from as short as several months to as long as five years. The choice of assets has included equities, bonds, and balanced funds, and has accounted for everything from a small percentage of total assets to the entire plan. Probably the most frequent program, however, is one with two- to three-year term, 0 percent minimum return, and which includes only equities.

An asset-based portfolio insurance program is the most straightforward strategy to structure. The program's minimum rate of return can be taken directly from the sponsor's minimum return requirement or risk tolerance. The sponsor's time horizon, if unstated, can be inferred by comparing the relative cost and level of protection inherent in programs with varying time horizons. This process, which may need to be repeated, provides a good illustration of the tradeoffs between both the cost of insurance and level of protection.

The selection of assets in asset-based programs also tends to be quite simple. By and large, sponsors usually choose to include equities in these programs, which is logical given the high expected return from this asset class. More recently, however, some sponsors have also placed their fixed income assets in these programs. This is at least partly attributed to the increase in the level of interest rate volatility.

Liability-based Strategies. Liability-based insurance programs are the most recent portfolio insurance innovation proposed by practitioners. In this strategy the minimum return requirement and program horizon are based on the plan's expected liability schedule. One application of this strategy sets the program's minimum return modestly less than the yield-to-maturity on a fixed income portfolio constructed to fund the liability schedule and sets the program horizon equal to the length of the liabilities.

Equities are the active asset of this application, but a plan may choose any other liquid asset which has an expected return in excess of the risk-free asset. The risk-free asset is typically an immunized bond portfolio constructed to reduce the interest rate risk of funding the liabilities.

Liability-based strategies can be structured in a variety of ways and practitioners have recently proposed several alternatives. Among the alternatives proposed include strategies to protect the dollar value of a plan's surplus and strategies to protect some level of the plan's funded ratio. (The funded ratio is equal to the market value of the plan assets divided by the present value of the plan's liabilities.) Additional innovations permit sponsors to select program time horizons shorter than the life of the liabilities. Such

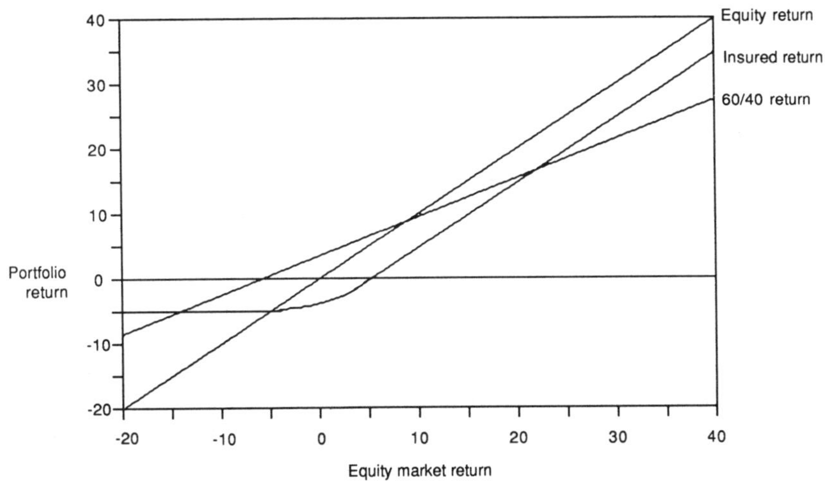

FIGURE 1. Projected return analysis

enhancements enable sponsor's to address long-term objectives with shorter, more flexible programs.

Because of the flexibility of this strategy and its ability to protect a plan's funded position from a precise amount of market risk, the liability-based strategy is an excellent strategy for dealing with the investment implications of FASB 87.

PROJECTING EXPECTED RETURNS

One of the advantages to using a structured approach is that we can project the expected results from the program with some degree of accuracy. This section describes the three-step process that we can use to evaluate structured investment programs and presents a simple example for portfolio insurance. It is important to note that in each step of the analysis, we compare the expected results of the structured program with a comparison benchmark, such as a portfolio with a "normal" asset allocation, or an alternative strategy designed to meet the specified objective.

In the first step of the evaluation process, we project the expected results of the structured program and the comparison benchmark only. Typically these results are presented graphically (see Figure 1). Figure 1 shows how such a graph can be constructed. This graph shows the return on an asset-based strategy where the active asset is equities, the minimum return is −5 percent, and the time horizon is one year. The comparison portfolio in this case is a 60/40 equity and fixed income portfolio. For purposes of comparison, a 45-degree line is included to show the performance of an unprotected equity portfolio.

The graph shows the projected results after one year from three alternative investment strategies and gives a range in equity return of −20 percent to 40 percent. The projected return from portfolio insurance, which is shown by the dashed line, is compared with the expected results from investing all the program assets in equities (the solid line) and the results from the 60/40 strategy (the dotted line).

The relative benefit and cost of pursuing a portfolio insurance program has typically been measured by comparing the results from the insured portfolio with the results from the uninsured portfolio. The expected benefit and cost is then equivalent to the vertical distance between the solid line and the dashed line. If the return on the equity market is less than −4 percent, the program benefits the sponsor; if the return on the equity market exceeds approximately −4 percent, the program is a cost. In addition to determining the approximate "breakeven" point at which the benefit from insurance becomes a cost, the graph also illustrates the relative magnitude of the cost and benefit. The cost is fairly constant for market returns in excess of 4 percent, but the benefit increases in a linear fashion for market declines.

Although the foregoing analysis of the cost and benefit from portfolio insurance is important, it may not accurately describe the costs and benefits to the sponsor. For example, what if the sponsor would never contemplate a 100 percent position in equities? If this is the case, then the foregoing analysis will not provide an accurate comparison of the benefits and costs from pursuing the strategy. Consequently, we must compare the portfolio insurance strategy with a comparison benchmark, in this case we determined that a 60/40 static asset allocation benchmark is appropriate.

The use of a comparison benchmark reveals a substantially different picture of the relative benefits and costs from pursuing the insurance strategy. In this case, portfolio insurance proves to be beneficial if the market return exceeds approximately 22 percent, or if the market return is less than about −14 percent. In addition, the magnitude of the potential benefits and costs is both large and variable. For example, if the market's return is near zero, we would expect that the cost could reach approximately 6 percent. Clearly, this graph provides a more revealing indication of expected results. In fact, after reviewing such an analysis, a sponsor may come to a very different conclusion about the attractiveness of this particular insurance program. If the sponsor concludes that results from this program are unattractive, then we would return to the previous step and restructure the program.

However, let us assume that the program originally proposed is suitable. Now we can proceed to the second step of the evaluation process and project results for the entire plan. (If the portfolio insurance program includes all plan assets then we would proceed directly to the third step of the analysis.)

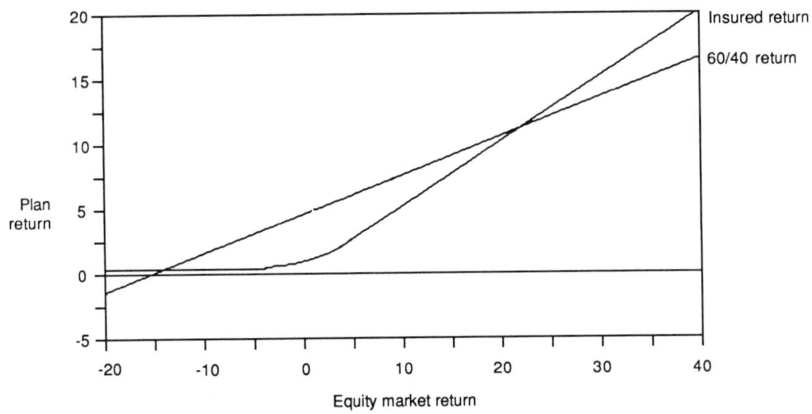

FIGURE 2. Projected return analysis

For simplicity, I have assumed that 50 percent of plan assets will be invested in either the portfolio insurance program or the 60/40 strategy, and that the balance will be invested in a Guaranteed Investment Contract (GIC) maturing one year hence and yielding 5 percent. Because the return on the contract is guaranteed, and because it matures in one year, its results will be insensitive to the performance of the investment markets.

Figure 2 shows the plan's expected performance, given our range of equity returns. The graph shows how the structured program and comparison benchmark fit with the balance of our assets at each of a variety of equity market returns. Again we can compare relative benefit and cost by comparing the vertical distance between the insured return (the solid line) and the 60/40 strategy return (the dotted line) for each given equity return. As in our previous case, we benefit from this portfolio insurance strategy if the equity market return exceeds 22 percent or is less than −14 percent; and we incur a relative cost if the equity return is between −14 percent and 22 percent. In addition, the magnitude of the benefit and cost is variable and large. At this point these projected results should be carefully analyzed. If the results are unattractive, an alternative program must be designed.

The third step in evaluating projected results adds the plan's liabilities or funding targets. To evaluate projected results in this step, we convert our graph from expected returns to the expected value of the plan's surplus one year hence. In this example I have assumed that the plan has \$120 in assets, that the present value of the liabilities is \$100, and that the surplus is \$20.

Figure 3 compares the ending value of the plan's surplus from investing its assets in the portfolio insurance program and GIC (the solid line) with investment of the plan's assets in the 60/40 portfolio and the GIC (the dotted line). Note that in this graph the portfolio insurance strategy does not provide

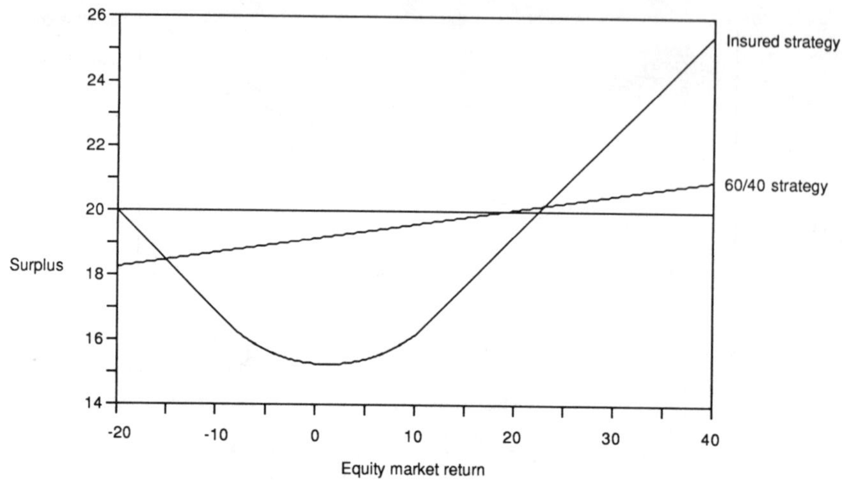

FIGURE 3. Projected return analysis

a minimum floor value for the surplus. This is attributable to the structure of the program, which is asset-based, rather than liability-based. A liability-based program would put a minimum floor value on the surplus.

Despite the absence of a floor, the relative benefit and cost pattern from the proposed insurance strategy remains intact. We benefit from the insurance strategy for equity returns greater than 24 percent and less than −14 percent and we incur a relative cost when the equity return falls within the −14 percent to 24 percent range. Similarly, the magnitude of the relative benefit and cost remains large and variable. The graph shows that we need an equity return in excess of 18 percent under either strategy to maintain our current surplus, or an equity return of less than −20 percent in the insured strategy.

In our three-step evaluation process, we projected results for the insurance strategy and a comparison benchmark over a range of equity returns. These steps can be repeated, using various capital market assumptions, to provide an even richer description of expected results. In addition, given the capability of some models to evaluate interim results, we can provide additional information about what an investor may expect during the program.

IDENTIFYING THE SOURCES AND IMPACT OF UNDERPERFORMANCE

The projected results described in the previous section were based on the expected results from our portfolio insurance model using hypothetical capital market assumptions. Because these results are dependent on a number of assumptions, the actual performance of our structured program may deviate rather substantially from our expectations. Consequently, we must identify the sources of underperformance and the impact of these sources on our expected results.

The three most common sources of underperformance are deficiencies in the option model selected, implementation factors, and the impact of the markets themselves. By definition, an option model is incomplete since all option models must, in one way or another, simplify the enormous complexities of the marketplace. For example, the Black-Scholes model assumes that interest rates are constant and trading is continuous. Obviously, such assumptions reduce the accuracy of our projections and inevitably introduce a potential for underperformance.

The complex models with which we are familiar, incorporate many of the dynamics of the marketplace, but even they cannot provide perfect estimates of expected results. Therefore, we should understand the extent to which the model selected can incorrectly estimate expected results.

Implementation factors weigh heavily in the actual performance of insurance strategies. By implementation factors, we mean trading acumen, selection of alternative investment vehicles, and implementation philosophy. Trading acumen, the ability to add value through the trading process, can be measured as it would be in conventional asset management programs. Essentially we should determine whether the trading process adds value relative to a theoretical benchmark.

The use of alternative instruments, such as options, to implement insured programs is currently receiving increasing attention. The use of these instruments can, under certain circumstances, reduce the cost of the structured program. Unfortunately, these instruments may also increase the expected cost of insurance. If the structured program will include alternative instruments, their potential impact should be identified.

The third factor is the manager's implementation philosophy, defined as how actively the structured program is managed. Will the manager use the model as a loose guide for asset allocation, will he mechanistically implement the program, or will he use a modest degree of active judgement? If all else is held constant, we would expect only mechanistically implemented programs to produce results in line with the projections. However, mechanistically implemented programs may also experience considerable difficulties in choppy markets.

Of the three sources of underperformance, the behavior of the investment markets has the greatest potential impact on actual results. All portfolio insurance programs depend on estimates to calculate expected results and to run the model selected. As a consequence, the accuracy of our estimates will have a significant impact on both the accuracy of our projections and the performance of our program.

Because it is unlikely that we will precisely quantify the actual behavior of the investment markets, we should attempt to estimate the potential impact of any deviations. At a minimum, we can estimate the impact of greater transactions costs and/or market volatility. These estimates can then be included in the projection of expected results to illustrate the impact of different estimates.

PREPARING FOR THE "NEXT STEP"

Rarely are portfolio insurance programs left undisturbed to run to maturity. More typically, these programs are reinitialized in order to capture current market gains, rolled into new programs, or prematurely terminated. The explanations for such changes are varied, but can generally be traced to a fundamental change in the sponsor's objectives or constraints. For example, a sponsor who reinitializes to capture market gains may do so because it enables him to ensure a higher minimum return on his assets.

Because portfolio insurance is such a flexible investment strategy, it can easily accommodate unanticipated changes in a sponsor's investment objectives. In fact, greater flexibility can be built into the program through the use of the futures markets. These markets enable practitioners to effect fairly substantial changes quickly and at minimum cost. Despite the flexibility of such programs, however, it is generally worthwhile to prepare for possible future changes in advance.

The most visible instances for program revision come when portfolio insurance has been used to achieve a tactical objective. For example, if portfolio insurance is used to increase equity exposure temporarily, then the sponsor may be able to define those circumstances where the program is no longer necessary. Such conditions might include a market rally of some magnitude or duration. In these applications, the sponsor should try to identify those events which would trigger reevaluation of the program and outline potential courses of action prior to initiation.

For liability-based programs, the reevaluation of the liability schedule may create a need to revise the program. Portfolio insurance can quite effectively ameliorate the investment risk in funding liabilities, but cannot address the actuarial factors which determine the liability schedule. As a result, liability-based programs should be reevaluated whenever the liability schedule is analyzed.

In the light of the rapidity with which market conditions can change, portfolio insurance programs should be managed in close cooperation between the manager and the sponsor. Given his proximity to the markets, the manager can continuously monitor the investment environment and, given the plan sponsor's timely input, change the structure of the program when it becomes appropriate.

SUMMARY

Structuring the portfolio insurance program may be the single most important determinant of the success of the insurance program. As a result, it is imperative that the sponsor, practitioner, and consultant develop a consistent approach to structuring these programs.

In this chapter we have introduced the five sequential steps of the investment engineering approach, and showed how to structure and evaluate portfolio insurance investment strategies. We argued that it is crucial that these programs be based principally upon the sponsor's objectives and constraints. Thus our first step was to identify the sponsor's investment and constraints, and then the second step was to translate these attributes into program parameters.

In the third step of the approach, we projected the expected results from the structured program and compared these with the results from an alternative strategy. This step served as a critical check to ensure that the structured program satisfied the sponsor's objectives and constraints.

The final steps of the approach were essentially educational. They served to increase our understanding of how our actual results could differ from our expectations, and when revisions occur, what changes we might expect.

Portfolio insurance is a new investment strategy. As such, we expect continual refinements will be made in the models and implementation techniques used and the applications proposed. However, regardless of its progress, we believe that a sound approach to structuring these programs will remain an essential element to their success.

FOOTNOTES

1. For a complete discussion of investment constraints for institutional investors see Jay Vawter, "Determination of Portfolio Policies: Institutional Investors," in *Managing Investment Portfolios: A Dynamic Process*, Maginn, John and Tuttle, Donald L., Eds., Boston, Mass: Warren, Gorham & Lamont, 1983.
2. For a review of FASB 87 and discussion of how portfolio insurance can be used to mitigate the risks embodied in this rule, see Steven P. Somes and Mark A. Zurack, "Pension Plans, Portfolio Insurance and FASB 87: An Old Risk in a New Light," forthcoming in *Financial Analysts Journal*, 1987.
3. This tendency to accept a "normal" asset allocation is documented in Zvi Bodie, Jay O. Light, Randall Morck, and Robert A. Taggart, Jr., "Corporate Pension Policy: An Empirical Investigation," *Financial Analysts Journal*, September/October 1985, pp. 10–16.

10. THE MANY DIMENSIONS OF RISK

Wayne H. Wagner

Portfolio insurance is an investment management technology that, in its most general form, reduces risk through systematic reallocation of the portfolio holdings between a "risk" asset and a "reserve" asset. *How* it works has been adequately covered elsewhere. *That* it works is not at issue; within its own premises it cannot fail to work, although the costs encountered may exceed expectations.

Portfolio insurance, like similar policies that create option-style payoffs, place new and powerful tools in the hands of the pension officer and his investment managers. These tools provide pension funds with an opportunity to *prespecify* the conditions under which it chooses to win (overperform) relative to market outcomes. No free lunch; since the cost of applying this strategy cannot be avoided, there must be some market outcomes under which the fund will lose (underperform). No one can use this technique to be a relative winner under all future outcomes.

The hands-on reshaping of the payoffs greatly extends the power of investment management. *With this power to choose payoffs comes an ability to choose wrong*; an ability to shape outcomes implies the ability to misshape. It follows that a clear understanding of how risk affects each specific pension fund is crucial to the successful use of these techniques.

Portfolio insurance is very clear about what it defines as risk: The possibility of achieving a return less than some threshold amount over the period of insurance. This operational definition of risk is presumed to be reasonably coincident with the pension plan's real susceptibility to risk. If it is not, the future may unfold some consequences that were unanticipated in the original decision to insure. What was believed to be a riskless reserve asset may actually *create* risks of a different nature than those the portfolio insurance decision was designed to *alleviate*. The panacea may become more like a creation of Pandora.

RISK AND RETURN

The purpose of pension investment is to fund the liability stream. That sounds straightforward, but note that it is quite a different objective from maximizing the value of the pension assets. The difference is akin to the difference between investment and speculation.

The assumption of anyone who acts to reduce risk is that risk is bad, and the less of it one is subject to, the more comfortable one feels. Yet *risk policy* is the control lever on any investment portfolio; one cannot control returns except by eliminating risk and accepting a lower expectation of return.

We know that certain risks, specifically market risks, are positively related to returns, both historically and expectationally. The assignment of the pension officer is not to simply minimize all risks, but to *eliminate uncompensated risks* and then to strike a balance between compensated risks/expected returns and the requirement to fund the liabilities at minimum cost and maximum stability.

This balance requires a clear understanding of the goals of the pension fund, which are, in decreasing order of importance:

The Fiduciary Objective. Maximizing the probability that the fund meets its funding obligations;

The Funding Objective. Minimizing the cost of the funding source; and

The Stability Objective. Enhancing predictability in the sequence of obligations of the funding source.

What makes life interesting for the pension executive is that these three goals are not compatible. In general, the higher return strategies that best achieve the Fiduciary and Funding objectives are achieved only at the cost of Stability.

Overly concentrating on risk reduction emphasizes stability, perhaps at the sacrifice of the more important objectives.

It is not difficult to deduce the source of this interest in stability and risk reduction.

Corporate management expends great energy promoting stability and growth of company income. Volatile pension funding demands disrupt this corporate planning; thus most pension plans try to create predictable annual pension expenses. As FASB 87 causes pension experience to more strongly impact balance sheets and income statements, sponsors will be even more attracted to strategies that stabilize pension assets.

The long-term danger of ignoring stability is that the tolerance and patience of the funding source may be exhausted, placing the continuance of the plan (and the job of the pension executive) in jeopardy. A pension officer who fails to respond to management's desire for stable pension expense holds a bomb timed to explode with the next major bear market.

Yet the pension executive retains responsibility for the three objectives stated above, and is duty-bound to present management with intelligent choices. To do this, the manager needs to prepare a pension risk analysis: an informed, explicit analysis of the risks facing the pension plan, how they relate to the goals, and the tradeoffs that need to be made.

A complete risk analysis of a pension plan:

1. Seeks to identify the dimensions of risk and to assess their importance to this particular plan, and
2. Minimizes or controls these risks by the least expensive means available.

A SUMMARY OF PENSION RISK

In the following sections we will explore the nature of pension investment risk, and identify some of the factors that amplify or dampen these risks for a given pension plan. Before setting forth, however, it is useful to provide a roadmap.

Pension risks can be summarized as follows:

1. *Specific Risks.* Over-emphasizing sensitivity to specific economic scenarios, by design or inadvertently; failing to take advantage of diversification; ignoring risks generated within the funding source.
2. *Mismatching Risks.* Creating asset portfolios whose time horizons differ from those of the liability stream; investing in securities whose economic sensitivities differ from those of the pension obligations.
3. *Business Risks.* Creating excessive demands or instabilities on the funding source that exhaust the patience of managers and the shareholders/taxpayers/contributors who bear the pension obligation.

THE PENSION PROMISE

Each of these risks derive from the unique agreement struck between a corporation and its employees to provide funds for retirement.

To truly understand risk we must know something of the purposes of the investment. The place to start is with *purpose* of the pension fund, the nature of the fiduciary goal. We call this the *Pension Promise.*

Pension plans exist for two reasons: The employer creates them to promote workforce stability, and society sanctions them through favored tax status as a means of providing for future living expenses when retirees will have no contemporaneous earning ability.

The Pension Promise is an implicit employment agreement that assures the employee of a "decent standard of living during his retirement." It is the expectation of the Pension Promise that leads an employee to trade off current income in favor of income years later.

It is the pension benefit review process, rather than the actuarial process, that provides the best view of the Pension Promise: Both employer and employee consider the long-term economic effects of pension contracts. As they evolve over time, pension contract changes reflect:

An assessment of anticipted retirement living standards, and

The desire to share company success with the employees.

As a practical matter, companies have contributed and will continue to contribute additional funds needed to maintain retiree living standards. In the late 1970s/early 1980s, raging inflation eroded buying power, and many companies were called upon to "chip in" additional benefits that were neither anticipated nor agreed to.

Employee expectations must also reflect the *micro* economic, company gains in productivity, which affect the company's ability to meet the Pension Promise. As many American workers have sadly learned in recent years, a company that does not keep pace with productivity gains cannot continue to support the same standard of pension (or compensation) promises.

Both of these issues reflect changes in productivity. Changes in living standards reflect the economy's gain in productivity; the company's pension (or compensation) policy ultimately must reflect company gains in productivity. *An adequate view of pension economics includes an appreciation of how productivity changes affect the evolution of pension obligations.*

It follows that pension policy must account for expected gains in productivity, not only until the employee retires, but as long as he collects retirement benefits.

To summarize, the real risk to pension beneficiaries plan is that the company will not be able to fulfill the Pension Promise. The Pension Promise of an adequate standard of living is inexorably linked to changes in productivity.

REDUCING PRODUCTIVITY RISK

Productivity risk arises when pension portfolios do not fully participate in productivity gains, thus opening a difference between Pension Promise obligations and accumulated assets. Fortunately, it is a risk that is easily offset, and most funds do offset this risk. Equity securities, as the residual claim on the earning power of productive assets, automatically participate in productivity gains.

Many observers have noted that the higher theoretical and experienced equity returns virtually ensure that equities dominate other investment vehicles over the long term. Down this path one is led to the conclusion that stocks are not risky to a pension plan: A patient pension executive with an all-equity strategy would find that the compounding effects of higher returns ultimately overwhelm the "risks" due to return variability.

The problem with this logic is that the horizon has stretched out to infinity, unrelated to the liability stream. The stability objective is completely forgotten. Pension payments are not made at the end of some mystical, never-reached horizon, they must be made to current retirees on a month-by-month basis. Thus the horizon of a pension plan has finite components, and an all-equity policy does not protect the pension plan's need for stability and on-going pension payments.

THE SHADOW ASSET—A MAJOR SOURCE OF PENSION RISK

The ability of a pension fund sponsor to fulfill the Pension Promise depends on two major factors:

Investment performance on previous contributions in excess of the assumed actuarial return, in combination with

Continuing contributions with the company,[1]

a. to fund past service credits,
b. to fund new service benefits as accrued,
c. to fund new benefits that are granted,
d. to fund any shortfalls in investment returns, and
e. to provide additional funding in case retirement expenses rise.

The present value of expected contributions can be thought of as a Shadow Asset of the pension plan. It is very real, but it doesn't show in the accounting reports. It is probably the largest asset of most pension plans.

[1] Footnotes appear at end of chapter.

To the pension beneficiary, it is a uniquely hazardous asset: It is undiversified, and in all the worst ways. It is subject to the same economic pitfalls as the employee's other major asset, his current and future earnings stream. In a very real sense, the shadow asset puts the General Motors Pension Plan substantially into the automotive business. Simultaneously, it puts General Motors in the pension finance business in a major way.

Typically, the shadow asset is not considered by investment managers as they pursue individualistic "styles." As a result, pension portfolios are far less diversified than commonly thought. Economic events or scenarios that strain corporate cash flow could compound and confound pension risks, thus simultaneously weakening both the pension plan and the company itself.

Pension sponsors need to explicitly consider how the risk characteristics of the funding source relate to pension promise risks. Different companies react differently to such factors as energy costs, capital costs, labor costs, and so on. These risks are easily diversified by orienting holdings away from the specific dimensions of funding source risk.[2] The pension portfolio needs to incorporate portfolio strategies that reduce this vulnerability.

FUNDING STATUS AND RISK

The sensitivity of the pension plan to shadow asset risk depends on the level of funding relative to the level of obligations.

More fully funded pension plans have less vulnerability to shadow asset risk, simply because they are less dependent on the funding source for the funds required to meet the Pension Promise. Their high susceptibility to company fortunes lies in the past, and is no longer relevant to risk management decisions, unless poor investment performance or large liability increases results in the disappearance of the surplus.

The major risk for fully funded plans is the possibility of differing growth experience patterns for the assets and the liabilities, that is, the productivity risk. As long as both the assets and the liabilities respond alike to economic events, the funding status is maintained.

Here is a situation wherein portfolio insurance may result in an *increase* in long-term risk. As portfolio insurance reduces the portfolio's exposure to equity-related productivity gains, pension assets are less likely to keep pace with productivity-related rises in the liabilities.

HORIZON AND RISK

Horizon plays a key role in the determination of what is risky and what is not. A risk reduction strategy appropriate for a longer horizon may be quite dangerous if applied to an investment problem with a short horizon, and vice versa.

When the horizon covers a short period of time such as a year, the strategy is typically to match these current liabilities with current assets; for example, cash.

For a funding stream of intermediate horizon, such as the previously promised pension benefits for current retirees, risk minimization involves ensuring against interest rate changes through the use of fixed income investments. But bonds alone cannot cover all the risks of a pension plan, since bonds do not participate in productivity gains.[3]

The principal long-term risks have been previously identified as productivity risks: That investment returns may be left behind by economic productivity gains. Only equities, with their automatic participation in productivity gains, can adequately ensure against long-term risks. A second long-term risk is that the company may not complete its promised payments, a risk that can be reduced by specific diversification against company risk.

THE DIVERSIFYING EFFECTS OF PENSION LIABILITIES

One of the most powerful recent developments in financial applications is the realization that liabilities, as well as the assets, can be a source of diversification.

An insurance company hedges its annuity obligations with investments that produce income step-for-step with the required outgo. The same concept can be applied to a pension fund by constructing a fixed income portfolio whose cash production matches the pension payments. This *dedication* approach is most commonly applied to payments to current retirees (retired lives).

When interest rates are high and actuarial rates low, a corporation can reduce its pension payments by annuitizing the retired lives obligations through dedication. This is an artificial situation which cannot last; either bond rates must come down or actuarial rates rise to accurately reflect inflation. Simple dedication seems little more than an accounting gimmick that abuses the actuary for his limited frame of reference, while doing nothing for the long-term health of the pension plan.

A valuable extension of this concept creates the portfolio insurance arrangement called "surplus insurance" where the reserve asset is a dedicated bond portfolio. Risks are taken when a surplus of pension assets exists, and risks are reduced if the surplus deteriorates. Without a link to the productive equity assets, however, this policy is likely to lead to longer term underfunding unless favorable—but uncertain—market conditions keep enlarging the surplus.

* * *

In the preceding sections we have explored pension risk management. In the next section, these insights are drawn together into a broad brush procedure that can be undertaken by a pension executive.

REDUCING AND CONTROLLING PENSION PORTFOLIO RISK

Earlier we defined the assignment of the pension officer as the elimination of uncompensated risks and the balancing of compensated risks/expected returns with the requirement to fund the liabilities at minimum cost.

A comprehensive risk analysis begins with a firm understanding of the nature of the specific provisions of the pension plan, the timing of its obligations, and an awareness of how future developments are likely to change those assumptions, that is, the implications of the Pension Promise.[4]

Start with the Projected Benefit Obligation (PBO) as defined by FASB 87. This figure includes an estimate of the obligations that will accrue to participants in a percent-of-final-pay plan as a result of future salary increases. (It is assumed that salary increases reflect productivity gains until time of retirement.) Add to that figure an estimate of the Pension Promise increases in benefits prior to retirement. Then add an expectation for benefit increases *after* retirement, on the assumption that the Pension Promise continues after retirement.

This determines the best estimate of the future stream of benefits to be paid.

Now, take a look at the nature of the company and its vulnerabilities. It is dependent on cheap energy? Foreign earnings? What scenarios could cause real strains on the cash flows? What kind of assets could be held in the portfolio to alleviate these vulnerabilities? Use *diversification* to reduce these risks. For example, an airline could load up on energy stocks to offset its vulnerability to business trains stemming from rising fuel costs.

Next, assess how much of the year-by-year obligations are likely to be tied to productivity increases. The present value of this determines the amount that should be placed in equities to *match* the productivity risk.

Now, *match* the intermediate term obligations with bonds of similar duration, and lay aside sufficient cash assets to pay the current liabilities.

This combination of protective (fixed income) and productive (equity) investments is the best match to the duration/nature of the liability stream. This is a reserve asset that minimizes the risk of the pension plan. It is not, however, constructed with the goal of (short-term) stability in mind.

If it is desirable to increase short-term stability, this portfolio could be hedged with *surplus insurance* to either a specific floor or to a dedicated portfolio that reflected only the actuarial liabilities. This opens up the possibility of productivity risk, but this is a risk the company may wish to take to increase stability of pension contributions.

Alternatively, if the corporation was financially strong and confident of its future, it could become more aggressive by writing *surplus insurance* in the other direction, using this protective portfolio as the reserve asset and building a risk portfolio containing more equities. In so doing, it could hope to increase its competitive position by gaining pension assets and minimizing future costs. The attractiveness of this approach depends to a large extent on how much financial statement instability the company is willing to tolerate. Companies with underfunded pension plans may not be able to afford this luxury.

Finally, the corporation could try for a little extra kick from the short-term assets by putting up some option premium and moving into equities with *floor insurance* in force.

The following table summarizes the techniques that can be used to reduce or manage risk, and suggests where each of these might be applied:

1. *Diversification.* Eliminates uncompensated risk taking; zero expectational cost; particularly effective in reducing shadow asset risk.
2. *Matching.* Eliminates mismatching risks by tying duration and nature of security investments to the duration/nature of the liability requirements.
3. *Low risk, reserve assets.* Reduces volatility and increases stability. Cannot reduce risk without concomitant decreases in expected returns. Most suitable for eliminating risk for very short term obligations.
4. *Surplus insurance.* Reduces actuarial risk at low "insurance" cost. Increases year-to-year stability. Ineffective at reducing Pension Promise risk, unless equities form part of the reserve asset.
5. *Floor insurance.* Guarantees minimum floor value for specified period. Expensive insurance. In effect, makes stability the primary goal. Useful for building a little low risk action into otherwise locked in returns.

Pension liabilities, while fixed-dollar obligations to the actuary and the accountant, are *real* liabilities, and imply a commitment by the funding source to preserve real purchasing power; the Pension Promise.

The best defense against pension funding risk is a policy that uses diversification and matching to reduce most risks. Portfolio insurance fits on top of the diversification/matching policy to promote stability or increase aggressiveness without losing control of the risk.

FOOTNOTES

1. "Company" here is used generically. The residual responsibility for funding the pension obligation falls on the shareholders of a corporation, the taxpayers of a public fund, or the contributors of an endowment or foundation.

2. Curiously, much of corporate strategy, particularly mergers and acquisition activity, is concerned with increasing company diversification and decreasing susceptibility to specific economic scenarios. Yet here in the pension plan holdings is an asset:

   that under FASB 87 and 88 has a direct effect on the financial statements;

   that has a major claim on corporate cash flow, probably larger than the effect of most acquisitions;

   whose diversification contribution can be adjusted virtually instantaneously and at minimal cost, and

   whose management requires little intensity and nuts-and-bolts specialized skills from corporate staff.

   Despite these advantageous features, the pension plan is virtually ignored as an asset whose risk profile can be easily adjusted to compensate for other corporate risks.
3. This is the classic error made in the past by many public funds. Restrictions on the levels of equity holdings result in a mismatch that tries to fund benefits, which correlate to productivity gains, with assets such as bonds that do *not* participate in productivity gains.

11. STOCK INDEX AND FINANCIAL FUTURES

Larry Martin

In the minds of many investors, futures contracts connote high-pressure sales tactics and speculation on agricultural commodities. But since the introduction of futures contracts on financial instruments in the early 1970s, futures markets have come to be dominated by institutional investors who employ them in pursuit of legitimate investment, hedging, arbitrage, and asset allocation strategies.

Portfolio insurance and dynamic hedging make a prime example of the best institutional use of futures markets. Dynamic hedging is basically an ongoing process of constantly revising a portfolio's asset allocation between classes. The transaction costs and operational inconveniences associated with implementing these revisions can be minimized by the intelligent use of futures contracts on stock price indexes and other financial assets.

A futures contract is an exchange-traded contract obligating buyer and seller to respectively take and make delivery of an underlying financial instrument, at a predetermined time in the future. At maturity some contracts call for physical transfer of the underlying financial instrument; others call for a settlement in cash based on the market price of the underlying instrument. The prices of futures contracts are set in a free auction market on the floors of various regulated exchanges, principally in Chicago and New York. Contracts can be bought or sold with only a small "initial margin" deposit; the integrity of the marketplace is assured by the requirement of the exchanges' clearinghouses that holders of futures contracts settle their unrealized profit or loss in cash each day.

The futures contracts most often employed in portfolio insurance programs are those on stock index futures—the most popular is the S&P 500 Index contract traded on the Chicago Mercantile Exchange. Introduced in 1982, trading in this contract now regularly accounts for a greater value than that of total New York Stock Exchange volume. Other less popular contracts are traded on the Major Market Index, the New York Stock Exchange Composite, the Value Line Composite, and the Frank Russell Indexes.

To understand how these contracts work, let's work through a simple example. Let's assume that, with the S&P 500 Index at 285.00, a futures contract with three months maturity can be traded at 286.40. If we were to buy a single contract, we would be required to post an initial margin of $10,000 with the exchange's clearinghouse—we could satisfy this requirement by posting a Treasury bill, so we would not lose the power to earn interest on our money.

As long as we hold the contract, we will have to settle our unrealized profits and losses each day in cash. For example, suppose that on the first day we hold the contract its price rises $1\frac{1}{2}$ points, from the 286.40 we paid to 287.90. To determine our total unrealized profit, we multiply the $1\frac{1}{2}$ points profit by the "contract multiplier" of $500—our total profit is thus $750. We are free to withdraw this amount from our futures account and reinvest it any way we wish. If, on the other hand, the contract's price had *declined* $1\frac{1}{2}$ points, to 284.90, we would be required to *deposit* $750 in cash. This process repeats each day until the maturity of the contract. Finally, on the last day of the contract's life, we would settle our ultimate profit and loss against that day's opening price of the *underlying index itself* (rather than against the daily closing price of the futures contract, as we had done every day prior).

Our position of one S&P 500 futures contract could be said to have an initial underlying value of $142,500—the initial index price of 285.00 times the contract multiplier of $500. We could think of the risk exposure of the position as similar to owning 500 "shares" of the index. But it is important to note that at no time were we required to pay the full value of the contract. We are able to achieve the risk exposure of a position in the index itself without having to ever actually pay the price of the index—just our $10,000 margin deposit, which we get back when the contract is closed out. This explains why we might be willing to pay 286.40 for the futures contract when the underlying index is priced lower, at 285.00.

There is a simple and exact formula that can determine the *fair price* or *theoretical value* of a stock index futures contract, given the price of the underlying index.

$$\begin{aligned}\text{Futures Value} \;=\; & \text{Index price} + \text{Interest on index price} \\ & - \text{Index dividends}\end{aligned}$$

Buying the futures contract allows us to reinvest the price of the index, which would have been tied up had we purchased the index itself. In an efficient market the interest that can be earned this way must *raise* the futures price. On the other hand, owning the index itself allows us to earn the dividends paid by the component stocks, while owning the futures contract does not. In an efficient market the value of the dividends must *lower* the futures price.

When the interest that can be earned on the price of the index is *greater* than the dividends paid by the component stocks, the theoretical value of the futures contract will be *higher* than the price of the index. On the other hand, when the interest that can be earned is *less* than the dividends, the theoretical value of the futures contract will be *lower* than the price of the index.

The theoretical value of 286.40 for the three-month contract used in the example assumed that the annual interest rate was 5 percent, and the annual dividend yield was 3 percent.

Futures Value	=	Index price	+	Interest on index price	−	Index dividends
286.40	=	285.00	+	$3.56	−	2.16

The theoretical value formula calculates a futures price at which a position in the futures is economically equivalent to an alternate investment in the index itself. Herein lies the key to how futures can be employed to implement the frequent asset allocation shifts required by dynamic hedging programs. If, as the formula suggests, a futures contract is economically equivalent to a position in the index, and if an equity portfolio to be insured is strongly correlated to the index, then trading futures can be freely substituted for trading the insured portfolio.

For example, let us assume that an investor holds a $10 million position distributed equally between stocks (indexed to the S&P 500) and cash. Let us further assume that he is initiating a portfolio insurance program, and that the dynamic hedging model he employs suggests that his equity exposure should be $85\frac{5}{8}$%, an increase of $35\frac{5}{8}$% over the current exposure of 50 percent. On the one hand, he could buy $3,562,500 in stocks, depleting his cash account by the same amount. On the other hand, he could leave his cash position intact and buy 25 S&P 500 Index futures contracts with a total underlying value of $3,562,500.

Index price	×	Contract multiplier	×	Contracts	=	Total underlying value
285.00	×	$500	×	25	=	$3,562,500

Whether he buys stocks or futures, he achieves his higher desired level of equity exposure. By buying the futures he pays a premium over the index price and foregoes receipt of dividends, but earns a perfectly offsetting amount of interest on the $3,562,500 in cash that he otherwise would have had to spend.

If trading futures is the economic equivalent of trading stocks, what factors might lead an investor to prefer one over the other? One significant consideration is convenience—it is often far easier to achieve a given level of equity exposure by trading a single futures contract than by trading a lengthy list of stocks. This can be especially important for portfolio insurance programs designed to hedge the overall activities of multiple investment managers; futures provide the ability to adjust equity exposure of all the managers at once, without disrupting any of their actual positions.

While futures offer convenience of trading, they also impose their own special administrative inconvenience: the need to settle unrealized profits and losses in cash on a daily basis. Of course, this is not a problem if one's position is in profit—one can happily reinvest the cash received and earn interest on it as an unexpected boost to performance. But if one's position is at a loss, the opposite will occur—the need to deliver cash diverts funds that would otherwise be earning interest, contributing to an unexpected drag on performance.

This phenomenon makes futures positions effectively larger than they seem to be. Profits are amplified by earned interest, and losses are amplified by foregone interest. Therefore, the effect of the daily settlement process can be hedged by making one's futures position somewhat smaller than one would have in the absence of the daily settlement requirement. In the following example, we would reduce the position to 98.7 percent of 25 contracts, or 24.69 contracts. The formula for determining the precise reduction factor is based on the periodic interest rate corresponding to the maturity of the contract (with annual rates at 5 percent, the periodic rate for a three-month contract would be $1\frac{1}{4}$ percent). As the contract matures, the reduction factor is continuously recalculated.

$$\text{Reduction factor} = \text{Inverse of 1 plus periodic interest rate}$$

$$98.7\% = \frac{1}{1.0125}$$

In this example the reduction factor is not sufficient to cause us to change our position by a whole contract; since fractional contracts cannot be traded, we would probably make no adjustment at all. But in practice positions can easily become large enough to make some adjustments well worth implementing.

An important consideration arguing in favor of futures is their relatively low transactions costs. Assuming an average price per share of $50, and an average commission of 5¢ per share, it would cost $7125 to buy and then resell shares of stock equivalent to the 25-contract position in S&P 500 futures cited in the example. At $25 round-trip (covering both the initial buy and subsequent sell) per contract, total commissions for the 25 contracts would be only $625.

Futures enjoy a similar advantage in terms of market impact as represented by the spread between bid and offer prices. If we assume that we would have to pay $\frac{1}{8}$ of a point per share of stock, we would pay a market-impact cost of \$8906.25 to buy shares of stock equivalent to 25 S&P 500 contracts. Assuming we would pay 0.05 per contract to buy the futures, our total market-impact cost would be the same as our total commissions—only \$625.

An element which sometimes argues in favor of futures, and at other times argues in favor of stocks, is the occasional inefficiency of pricing in the futures markets. When futures contracts are priced *above* their theoretical values, they are relatively unattractive to *buy* (but correspondingly attractive to *sell*). On the other hand, when they are priced *below* their theoretical value, they are relatively unattractive to *sell* (but correspondingly attractive to *buy*).

There are a host of other less tangible considerations that may make a given investor prefer stocks to futures, or vice versa. Because buyers of futures do not own actual shares of stock, they cannot vote to elect corporate directors, or participate in corporate policy decisions. While this may be a disadvantage to many investors, it may be a benefit to moral investors who wish to participate in the broad market without explicitly participating in the management of companies with policies deemed immoral.

The wide variety of actively traded futures contracts makes it possible to easily implement complex dynamic hedging programs across many asset classes, all using the futures markets. For example, the asset/liability ratio insurance program discussed in earlier chapters could be implemented by trading in stock index futures and a combination of Treasury bond, note, and bill futures. Similarly, international portfolio insurance could be implemented by trading in futures contracts in the Financial Times Stock Exchange Index (United Kingdom), the All-Ordinaries Share Price Index (Australia), the Nikkei Average (Japan), the Hang Seng Index (Hong Kong) and the Toronto Stock Exchange 300 (Canada).

12. LISTED STOCK INDEX OPTIONS

Sumner Abramson, Ren Y. Cheng, and Don Elan

Many forms of dynamic hedging seek to create patterns of risk and return that might be called "synthetic options." For example, the process of portfolio insurance closely resembles protection of a portfolio by a hypothetical put option. In certain cases it may be appropriate, as an alternative to the complex management processes of dynamic hedging, *to utilize actual exchange-traded options contracts.*

Listed options on common stocks began trading on the Chicago Board Options Exchange (CBOE) in 1973. Prior to that time, private options contracts traded over-the-counter. In the new listed options market, contract terms were standardized and a central clearinghouse acted as issuer and guarantor of the contracts. These innovations made possible the development of deep and liquid secondary markets in these previously illiquid instruments.

Ten years later, the CBOE introduced trading in options on a stock price index—the Standard & Poor's 100. Following enthusiastic public and institutional acceptance, other options exchanges quickly moved to introduce index options contracts of their own. Today contracts are actively traded on the S&P 100, the S&P 500, the Major Market Index, the Value Line Composite, the New York Stock Exchange Composite, and the Institutional Index.

WHAT ARE INDEX OPTIONS?

An index option is a standardized exchange-traded contract between a buyer and a seller. There are two kinds of contracts: calls and puts. A *call* stipulates that in exchange for a negotiated dollar consideration (the *price* or *premium* of the option), the buyer gets the right (but not the obligation), for a fixed period of time, to *exercise* the call and thereby *buy* the index from the call seller at a fixed *strike-price*. A *put*, on the other hand, gives the buyer the right (but not the obligation), for a fixed period of time, to exercise the put and thereby *sell* the index to the put seller at a fixed *strike-price*.

Most index options can be exercised at any time up to and including the day they expire. Options on the S&P 500 and the Institutional Index, however, cannot be exercised prior to expiration.

Exercising an index option does not result in the actual buying or selling of physical shares of stock. Instead, exercises of index options are *cash-settled*. On the day of exercise, the owner of a call receives in cash from the call seller any amount by which the index's closing price is *above* the call's strike-price. The owner of the put, on the other hand, receives in cash from the put seller any amount by which the index's closing price is *below* the put's strike-price. For both calls and puts, the difference between the index price and the strike-price is multiplied by the *contract multiplier* (generally $100) to determine the actual amount of the cash settlement.

If the contract terms of index options seem a little complex, it can be useful to consider actual examples of exactly how a call and a put would perform in practice. Let's begin by reviewing the *Wall Street Journal*'s quotations for S&P 100 options as of February 24, 1987, when the index closed at 232.72 (Figure 1).

Note that three expiration terms and a wide selection of strike-prices are available. First, let's consider what would happen if we were to buy an April

Monday, February 23, 1987

Chicago Board

S&P 100 INDEX

Strike	Calls—Last			Puts—Last		
Price	Mar	Apr	May	Mar	Apr	May
220	53	....	....	1/16	....	....
225	48	49	....	1/16	3/16	....
230	44	45	....	1/16	¼	....
235	39¼	37½	....	1/16	⅜	11/16
240	35	35	....	⅛	9/16	1
245	28½	31½	31½	3/16	⅞	1⅝
250	24	27	24½	7/16	1 7/16	2⅜
255	19	20⅜	23	¾	2⅛	3⅜
260	14¾	17	18½	1⅝	3⅜	4¾
265	10⅞	14⅛	15½	2⅞	4⅞	6⅝
270	7⅜	10½	12⅞	4⅞	7¼	8¾
275	5	7⅞	10¼	7⅜	9⅜	10⅝
280	3⅛	5¾	7¾	10½	12⅛	12⅞
285	1 13/16	4¼	6¼	14	17½	....
290	15/16	2¾	4½	18	19½	....

Total call volume 224,986 Total call open int. 474,173
Total put volume 212,461 Total put open int. 1,320,314
The index: High 275.11; Low 268.97; Close 272.21, −2.85

FIGURE 1. Index options quotations

270.00 call, quoted in the *Journal* at $10\frac{1}{2}$. The actual dollar cost of the contract, exclusive of brokerage commissions, would be \$1050—the premium of $10\frac{1}{2}$ times the contract multiplier of \$100.

Because the call gives us the right to receive, in cash, \$100 times any amount by which the index price is *above* the 270.00 strike-price, we can easily determine the potential profit and loss in this investment as a simple function of the price of the underlying index as of expiration in April. Clearly, if the index is below the 270.00 strike-price, the call will be worthless. In this case we would lose our entire initial investment of \$1050, but it is important to note that this is the most we could possibly lose, even if the index price were to fall all the way to zero. On the other hand, our profit potential is unlimited on the upside. If, for example, the index were to close at 290.00 on expiration, we would receive \$2000 in cash, a \$950 profit on an investment of \$1050.

Index price		Strike price		Contract multiplier		Cash settlement
(290.00	−	270.00)	×	\$100	=	\$2000

If the index were to close at 310.00, we would receive \$4000 for a profit of \$2950.

Index price		Strike price		Contract multiplier		Cash settlement
(310.00	−	270.00)	×	\$100	=	\$4000

We can easily depict the range of possible outcomes in a simple profit-and-loss graph (Figure 2). The horizontal axis represents the price of the underlying index at expiration, and the vertical axis represents profit or loss.

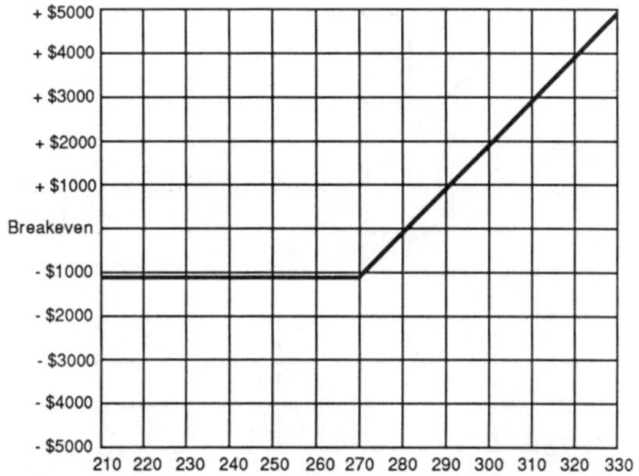

FIGURE 2. Profit-and-loss graph: index call option

Note the fundamental assymetry of this pattern. On the downside our losses are limited to the $1050 initial investment, but our upside potential is virtually unlimited. It may seem that, as the *buyer* of the call, we have a great advantage over the call's *seller*—the most he can hope to earn is our maximum loss of $1050, and his losses are potentially limitless. This is why the buyer must pay the initial premium to the seller, and not the other way around. Presumably, the premium will be negotiated at a level that makes the transaction fair for buyer and seller.

Now let's see what the results would be of buying a put, rather than a call. If we were to buy the April 270.00 put at the *Journal*'s quotation of $7\frac{1}{4}$, our initial cost, exclusive of brokerage commissions, would be $725. Again, our profit or loss at expiration will be a simple function of the price of the underlying index, because the put gives us the right to receive, in cash, $100 times any amount by which the index price is *below* the 270.00 strike-price. If the index is above the 270.00 strike-price, the put will be worthless, and we will lose our entire initial investment of $725. On the other hand, our profit potential on the downside is limited only by the fact that the index can't go below zero. If, for example, the index were to close at 250.00 on expiration, we would receive $2000 in cash, a $1275 profit on an investment of $725.

Strike price		Index price		Contract multiplier		Cash settlement
(270.00	−	250.00)	×	$100	=	$2000

Again, we can depict the range of possible outcomes in a simple profit-and-loss graph (Figure 3).

FIGURE 3. Profit-and-loss graph: index put option

FACTORS IN THE PRICING OF INDEX OPTIONS

Premiums for listed options are set by the free market in the auction environment of the various options exchanges. It is possible to suggest a set of parameters that can be understood as influencing premiums.

Exercise Value

The difference betwen the index price and an option's strike-price is it's exercise value—the amount received, in cash, upon exercise. A call whose strike-price is above the index price is said to be out of the money because it has no exercise value; conversely, a call whose strike-price is below the index price is said to be in the money because it has an exercise value. On the other hand, a put whose strike-price is below the index price is said to be out of the money because it has no exercise value, while one whose strike-price is above the index price is said to be in the money because it has an exercise value. Options that can be exercised at any time rarely trade below their exercise value—an alert owner of an option would always prefer to exercise it rather than sell it for less than its exercise value.

Expiration Term

The more time remaining until expiration, the higher the option premium. There are two reasons for this:

1. The longer the time remaining until expiration, the more opportunity there is for the option to be in the money at some point in its life.
2. Options are levered instruments. In the case of a call, the buyer "borrows" the strike-price for the life of the option. The longer he has this "loan," the more valuable the option is. The opposite is true for puts. The put buyer "lends" the strike-price to the put seller for the life of the option, so time works *against* the put buyer, negatively affecting premiums. However, in most cases the first effect dominates this one, so long-term puts are more valuable than short-term puts.

Anticipated Volatility

Because the buyer of an option cannot lose more than his initial investment, while the seller's losses are potentially limitless, high anticipated volatility in the underlying index will cause a buyer to be willing to pay more for an option, and a seller to insist that he do so. Therefore, the higher the anticipated volatility, the higher the option premium; conversely, the lower the anticipated volatility, the lower the option premium. Of course, neither party knows with certainty what the actual volatility of the index will be during the life of the option.

Interest Rates

As previously discussed, because options transactions involve implicit borrowing and lending, the level of general interest rates affects option premiums. Because buying a call involved implicit borrowing, the higher the interest rate the higher the call premium. Conversely, because buying a put involves implicit lending, the higher the interest rate the *lower* the put premium.

Dividends

Option buyers benefit only from price movements in the underlying index, not dividend payments. Dividends tend to reduce the price level of the index (other things being equal), so the *higher* the dividend yield the *lower* the call premium, and the *higher* the put premium.

LISTED INDEX OPTIONS FOR PORTFOLIO INSURANCE

The profit-and-loss graph depicted in Figure 3 makes it clear that an index put option is very much like an insurance policy. On the upside, when protection is not needed, the premium representing the cost of insurance is lost. On the downside, the value of the put expands to compensate for losses in the underlying index.

Buying listed index puts enjoys two significant advantages over creating "synthetic puts" through dynamic hedging. First, buying a single exchange-traded instrument is more convenient, and may invoke lower transaction costs, than constantly monitoring and adjusting a dynamic hedging program. Second, buying a listed put option precisely locks in the cost of insurance —it cannot be more than the put's premium. Uncertainties in the process of dynamic hedging, on the other hand, can lead to significant unpredictability in the cost of insurance.

There are several reasons, unfortunately, that prevent us from naively treating index put options as "listed portfolio insurance policies." First, exchange-imposed position limits set a maximum number of contracts that can be held by a single investor, restricting the value of portfolios that can be insured with listed puts to under $1 billion. Second, liquidity in the longest-term contracts is insufficient to allow economical execution of even relatively small transactions. Third, the standardized strike-prices, spaced at even five-point intervals, often do not offer the precise levels of protection desired.

Fourth, and most significant, index options are not presently listed with sufficiently long expiration terms to meet the needs of most portfolio insurance programs. Although the exchanges have listed long-term contracts, the longest currently available term is two years—most portfolio insurance programs require terms considerably longer. At first glance one might expect that a series of short-term listed options could be strung together into a single long-term program, but a close inspection of the quotations in the *Wall Street Journal* reveals why this would not be economical. Note that the March, April, and May 270.00 puts were quoted at $4\frac{7}{8}$, $7\frac{1}{4}$, and $8\frac{3}{4}$ respectively. While each successive option is more expensive than the previous one, the difference between them becomes successively smaller. The difference between the first two contracts is $2\frac{3}{8}$, but the difference between the second two is only $1\frac{1}{2}$. If puts with further expirations were listed, this pattern would continue—each additional unit of time is less expensive than the previous unit. Therefore, it would be unnecessarily costly to string together a series of expensive short-term options into what should be a single, economical long-term option.

By no means should this be taken to mean that listed options have no role in dynamic hedging programs. While their naive use could be highly uneconomical, their judicious applications can lead to substantial benefits. For example, when an insurance program has run into its final months, the dynamic hedging process can be terminated and replaced with short-term options contracts. There would be no economic penalty for using short-term contracts because their term would perfectly match the remaining term of the program. And the employment of a single convenient instrument, purchased at a known cost, would replace the dynamic hedging process at the point in the program when it is least stable and most cost-intensive.

The following chapter discusses how listed puts can be successfully integrated into longer-term programs.

13. INTEGRATING LISTED STOCK INDEX OPTIONS

Andrew Harmstone-Rakowski and Roger Saylor

The portfolio insurance technique was developed using the Black-Scholes option pricing model. Therefore, strictly speaking, it is valid only if the assumptions used to develop the Black-Scholes model are correct. An important implementation issue is how to run an insurance program given that the Black Scholes assumptions are not all realistic.

One significant source of performance uncertainty of an insurance program is the risk that the volatility of the insured asset will fluctuate randomly. The integration of listed put options in a portfolio insurance program can significantly reduce this risk. Furthermore, if the Black-Scholes assumption of constant perceived and realized volatility proves to be correct then the put options, if used correctly, will not affect the cost of the portfolio insurance program.

Chapter 12 discusses why the naive use of listed put options raises the cost of a portfolio insurance program. This is based on the observation that the cost of consecutively buying four three-month put options at the same strike price is considerably more expensive than buying a one-year put option at the strike price, if the market and the other key variables are stable over the year. But it must be understood that consecutive purchases of three-month equity index put options offer significantly more protection to an equity portfolio than buying a one-year put option at the same strike price. This is because, assuming the equity portfolio tracks the index underlying the options, the consecutive purchase strategy causes the protection level for the equity portfolio to equal the strike price four times during the year. In contrast, the one-year strategy protects the equity portfolio at the strike price level only once during the year: on the last day of the year. Furthermore, the one-year put option strategy has a protection level which is lower than the consecutive purchase strategy for most of the year. Only during the last three months of the year is level of protection for the one-year strategy equal to the level of protection for the consecutive purchase strategy. Therfore, comparing the consecutive purchase of short-term puts at a given strike price with the purchase of one long-term put at the same strike price is comparing two dissimilar protection strategies. If short-term put options are purchased in a way which offers the same level of protection as the long-term put at all points in time, then assuming the Black Scholes assumptions are valid, the cost of using the short-term options will equal the cost of using the long-term option. The reason for this will be discussed below.

The notion of a constant volatility of the insured asset—the standard deviation of the natural log of the asset's rate of return—is a central premise of the Black-Scholes model, and yet it is violated in reality. For example, a reasonable long run estimate of the volatility of the S&P 500 Index is 15 percent, and yet this value can be seen to vary randomly by as much as five percentage points, depending on the period chosen for empirical estimation.

A complete discussion of the impact of random volatility changes on portfolio insurance programs quickly becomes very technical. A particular kind of volatility change, however, can illustrate some of its most important general effects. Suppose that the volatility of an insured asset, say the S&P 500, changes just once right after a portfolio insurance program is put in place. Let us assume that the index's actual and perceived volatility are 15 percent when the program begins, but the day after the program starts some unexpected economic event raises actual and perceived volatility to 20 percent, where it remains through the life of the program. The dynamic hedging process underlying the insurance program is designed to replicate the protection afforded by a hypothetical put on the index. But this dramatic rise in volatility will cause the results of the process to diverge sharply—and disappointingly—from the results of owning the hypothetical put. Theoretically, a put option increases in value in response to rises in volatility—and yet there is nothing in the dynamic hedging process that would cause a corresponding increase in value. For this reason typical dynamic hedging processes based on the assumption of constant volatility will tend to perform more poorly than expected when volatility rises. On the other hand, when volatility falls dynamic hedging processes tend to perform better than expected.

Dynamic hedging programs tend to underperform when volatility rises because none of the assets used to typically implement them—stocks, stock index futures, and cash—are responsive to volatility changes. Listed puts *are* explicitly sensitive to volatility changes. If listed puts are used to implement portfolio insurance programs, underperformance attributable to rises in volatility will tend to be offset by a corresponding increase in the value of the listed puts. This is because the price of a listed put can be interpreted as discounting the effect of future volatility in the underlying index. In a sense, when listed puts are purchased, volatility is being paid for "up front." If actual volatility turns out to be greater than that implied in the put price, the buyer is protected because he has "locked in" the lower rate implied at the time of purchase. If, on the other hand, actual volatility turns out to be less than that implied in the put price, then there is an opportunity cost to the put buyer—in principle, the buyer would have done better replicating the put through dynamic hedging.

But when listed puts are included in the dynamic hedging process, various adjustments in the program must be made to accommodate them. Their presence must not raise the expected cost of the program assuming the Black-Scholes assumptions are valid. If the Black-Scholes assumptions are valid then it is easy to show that this objective can be satisfied. This result is an immediate implication of the fact that in a Black-Scholes world both the hypothetical put of the protection program and the listed puts can be replicated by a trading strategy moving between stocks and cash. If, at any moment in time, x stocks must be sold to replicate the hypothetical put and y stocks must be sold to replicate the listed puts, then if listed puts are included in an insurance program, $x - y$ stocks need to be sold. In other words, if $x - y$ stocks are sold, and the listed put is held then the result is the same as if x stocks were sold. But since the effect is the same as if x stocks were sold then the hypothetical put is being replicated perfectly. If the hypothetical put is replicated perfectly at every point in time, then the characteristics of the put, such as its delta and the protection level it can give to an equity portfolio, are also perfectly replicated. Of course, even in a Black-Scholes world, if listed puts do not trade at their fair value then using listed puts could affect the cost of a protection program. If puts are overpriced then the cost would probably be raised. Similarly if puts are underpriced then the cost would probably be lowered.

This analysis also shows why a series of short-term puts, when used in a particular way, can have the same cost as using one long-term put, assuming the Black-Scholes assumptions are valid. The long-term put can be replicated by a trading strategy. Suppose at any given time that x shares of stock need to be sold to replicate the long-term put on that stock. Therefore, all that is necessary for short-term puts on the stock to replicate a long-term put is that at every point in time the short-term puts be held in the appropriate quantities such that if each put option were replicated with a trading strategy then the cumulative required trades would be a sale of x shares of stock.

The more interesting question is whether using puts adds to the cost of the protection program when the Black-Scholes assumptions are *not* valid. This answer depends on whether the aggregate utility function of investors is neutral with respect to possible fluctuations in volatility. This question is distinct from the question of whether investors are risk averse. Another way of looking at volatility risk is to ask whether, given a particular expected return, and given a particular expected value of the standard deviation of the return, the typical investor would require payment to bear the risk of fluctuations of the standard deviation of returns around the expected value of the standard deviation. If the typical investor requires a payment to bear volatility risk defined in this way then listed put options will be cheaper than if the typical investor is indifferent or partial to volatility risk. This is true because listed put options are explicitly sensitive to volatility risk and therefore the buyer of puts would require a discount in price in return for being exposed to the volatility risk of the put.

If listed put option prices include a discount because they are exposed to volatility risk, then using listed put options may lower the expected cost of an insurance program. But, it is also possible that listed put options include a premium because investors like volatility risk. In this case there may be an added cost from using the puts. Determining which of these cases holds is a complex empirical question which depends critically on how the fair value of the put option is calculated once its volatility is not assumed to be constant.

In sum, listed put options can be very important for practical applications of portfolio insurance. By including put options in an insurance program the tendency of the puts to rise in value when volatility rises will offset the tendency of a portfolio insurance program to underperform its objectives when volatility rises unexpectedly. In this way, listed put options act as a hedge against volatility risk in a portfolio insurance program. If the Black-Scholes assumptions are valid, then volatility is constant; in this case there is no volatility risk, and using listed puts has no effect on the cost of a protection program. If the Black-Scholes assumptions are not valid, and volatility is not constant, then one critical factor is whether the typical investor dislikes volatility risk. The more the investor dislikes volatility risk the lower the equilibrium price of put options will be. This is because buyers of puts are exposed to the volatility risk of the put and will require a discount in the put price. Lower put prices because of investor dislike for volatility risk will, of course, reduce the cost of a protection program which uses put options. Without a complex empirical investigation investor attitudes towards volatility risk are unknown and therefore the full incremental cost or benefit of using listed put options cannot be determined. It is equally likely that using put options raises or lowers the cost of a portfolio insurance program when volatility is uncertain, but the size of this effect is likely to be small.

14. ESTIMATING VOLATILITY

Jeremy Evnine

Chapter 13 discussed how integrating listed index puts into a portfolio insurance (PI) or dynamic hedging program can hedge against the risk of changes in the insured asset's volatility. This risk arises from assumptions implicit in the options pricing models which typically drive the dynamic hedging process.

To be sure, it is possible to guarantee a floor without resorting to option pricing models. For example, a stop-loss order may be employed. A preferred method may be the so-called Constant Proportion Portfolio Insurance (CPPI), originally proposed by Brennan and Solanki,[1] and more recently by Perold,[2] and Black and Jones.[3] This method involves a dynamic adjustment of an asset mix, as does the more traditional replication of a Black and Scholes[4] type protective put. But, in the CPPI scheme, no assumption need be made about the stochastic process followed by the assets, and so no volatility estimation is required.

The most popular forms of PI, however, do rely on assumptions concerning the stochastic process followed by the assets involved. The earliest, and perhaps still the most popular form of PI is the replication of a protective put over a relatively short time horizon, typically one year. Following the methodology of Black and Scholes,[4] the riskless rate is assumed to be known and constant over the life of the policy, and the risky asset, usually a common stock portfolio, is assumed to follow a lognormal diffusion process (which we define later). It is well known that in order to replicate a put option on the risky

[1] Bibliography appears at the end of chapter.

asset, we need to know the volatility of the lognormal process, but not the drift (expected return).

A more general approach relies on the model of Margrabe,[5] which is an extension of the Black and Scholes model. In Margrabe's model, instead of one risky and one riskless asset, there are two risky assets, the relative returns of which are assumed to follow a lognormal diffusion process. It is then possible to price an option to exchange one of the risky assets for the other. This is the appropriate type of model to use if we wish to insure, for example, a stock portfolio against a "safe" asset which is a bond portfolio of relatively long duration, say 10 or 15 years. This type of strategy is being increasingly considered by sponsors of pension plans in response to the FASB 87 regulations, since such a safe asset corresponds more closely to the liabilities of the pension plan.

The volatility that enters into Margrabe's pricing formula is the relative volatility of the two assets, which is the volatility of the difference of their logarithmic returns. If the volatilities of the two assets are denoted by s_1 and s_2 respectively, and the correlation coefficient of the two processes by ϱ, then the relative volatility s is defined by:

$$s^2 = s_1^2 - 2 \cdot s_1 \cdot s_2 \cdot \varrho + s_2^2$$

Estimation of s can be attempted either by direct estimation from observations drawn from the relative price process, or by estimating s_1, s_2 and ϱ separately, and computing s from the above formula.

When implementing a protective put strategy via dynamic replication, misestimation of the volatility will cause the payoff of the strategy, contingent on the returns on the assets, to be different than predicted. For example, if volatility turns out to be less than we predicted, we may achieve a greater return than anticipated (i.e., our upside participation will be greater) if the put expires out of the money, since we will have wasted (in an *ex post* sense) less money on the put. If volatility turns out to be greater than predicted, we may achieve less upside participation. In either case, if the put expires in the money, we will achieve exactly our protected minimum. It is also possible to construct a strategy where uncertainty about the volatility is reflected in uncertainty in the protected minimum, but upside capture is independent of volatility.

It is also possible to implement portfolio insurance without resorting to a Black and Scholes type of replication. For example, a protective put can be purchased, either in the listed options market, or, what is more likely, over-the-counter. In this case, we would like to predict volatility, so that we can compare it with the volatility implied by the price of the option. We can then predict whether it would be cheaper to buy the option or to replicate it dynamically.

An alternative route using options is to construct a portfolio of short-term options that looks like a longer-term option. This portfolio would have to be readjusted periodically as options expired, or if the portfolio of short-term options began to look insufficiently similar to the long-term option. In this case, we need to predict the volatility that will be implied by the options' future prices. Unless we have reason to believe that option implied volatilities consistently over- or under-estimate true volatility, this problem simply reduces to that of predicting future volatility.

ESTIMATION AND PREDICTION

Before proceeding further, we now define the two terms *estimation* and *prediction*, which are often used rather loosely, and interchangeably. When we talk about estimation, we shall mean the attempt to identify, ex post, the parameters of a stochastic process (which are not, unfortunately, directly observable), from a limited set of information about the process. By prediction, we shall mean the formulation of a rule to determine, to the best of our ability, the values that these parameters will assume in the future.

Estimation is usually a forerunner of prediction. To construct a prediction model, we may estimate historically some values of the parameters that we seek to predict, and then construct some predictors, the values of which could have been known prior to the period over which the estimated values were computed. The predictors may, of course, be lagged values of the same parameters, as well as other quantities which may be thought to have predictive content. Next, on a historical basis, we estimate a relationship by which the predictors best explained the subsequent estimated values of the parameters. If we wish, we may withhold part of the available data set from the estimation of this relationship, so that we can perform an out-of-sample test of the relationship to see how robust it is. Finally, we have no choice but to assume that the relationship that held historically between estimated outcomes and predictors will hold between future realized outcomes and the current set of predictors.

Thus, we may regard estimation as a necessary first step in prediction. Most of the classical literature dealing with volatility deals with estimation, rather than prediction.

THE LOGNORMAL PROCESS

The classical assumption in option pricing theory is the lognormal diffusion process. The lognormal hypothesis may be stated as follows: Over any period of time of length t_i, the natural logarithm of one plus the rate of return is normally distributed with mean $u \cdot t_i$ and variance $v \cdot t_i$. In addition, the returns over disjoint periods are independent of each other.

The rate at which variance evolves is v, and its square root is referred to as the volatility. We will concentrate our attention on variance, rather than volatility, since variance will be found to have more tractable properties than volatility.

This is not the only possible specification of a stochastic process, to be sure. We have already alluded to Margrabe's model, in which two assets may follow a joint lognormal process. In this case, the difference of the logarithmic returns (which is equal to the logarithm of the ratio of one plus the returns) satisfies the lognormal hypothesis, in addition to each asset separately satisfying the lognormal hypothesis. Other stochastic processes which have been used to model stock price behavior in the option pricing literature include the constant elasticity of variance model, the jump process, and the jump diffusion process (see Cox and Ross[6]).

When modeling the behavior of fixed income assets, the lognormal diffusion process is conceptually inconsistent. If a 10-year note is being employed in a policy of length 5 to 10 years, we cannot allow the price to follow an unconstrained random walk, since the price must converge to par at the end of 10 years. For a one-year policy, a lognormal diffusion process may be a reasonable approximation. For fixed income modelling, it is more appropriate either to specify an alternate process for the price dynamics, such as a "bridge" diffusion process in which the price is tied down to the current price now, and to the par value at maturity (see, for example, Ball and Torous[7]). An alternative is to assume a stochastic process for interest rates, from which the price dynamics follow (see, for example, Brennan and Schwartz[8]).

We will limit ourselves to the case of the lognormal diffusion process, however, since this is the most widely used assumption in portfolio insurance. Many of the techniques described here can also be used to estimate and predict other classes of stochastic processes, but the analysis would become quite complex and lengthy.

PROPERTIES OF ESTIMATORS

What are the properties that make one estimate better than another? There are essentially two properties that we seek in an estimator: that it be unbiased and efficient.

To explain what these terms mean, suppose that the true, but unobservable, variance is v, and that we have an estimator for v, which we denote by $\hat{v}$. $\hat{v}$ is constructed from observations of the process whose variance is v, and these observations are random variables whose distribution depends on v. Thus $\hat{v}$ is a random variable whose distribution depends on v. Different sets of observations would yield different values of $\hat{v}$. Let us denote the difference between $\hat{v}$ and v by the random variable e.

We say that $\hat{v}$ is an unbiased estimator of v if the expected value of e, E(e), is zero. In this case, while our estimated value $\hat{v}$ may not hit v on the button, we know that, on average, $\hat{v}$ will be neither too high nor too low.

The efficiency of $\hat{v}$ is determined by the variance of e, V(e). The smaller this quantity is, the tighter is the distribution of $\hat{v}$ around its expected value, which will be v, if the estimator is unbiased. If V(e) is small, $\hat{v}$ is less likely to be far from v, than if V(e) is large. The efficiency of one estimator relative to another is measured by the ratio of their respective values of V(e), the estimation error variance. If $\hat{v}_1$ has an error variance which is 3 times that of $\hat{v}_2$, we would say that $\hat{v}_2$ is 3 times as efficient as $\hat{v}_1$.

An inefficient estimator produces an interesting side effect in option pricing that can potentially affect PI. Suppose that $\hat{v}$ is an unbiased estimate of v, and we evaluate an option using a pricing formula, such as Black and Scholes,[4] which depends on v, using $\hat{v}$ as a substitute for the unknown v. Then the resulting option value is not an unbiased estimate of the *true* option value, which corresponds to the pricing formula evaluated at v. This is because the pricing formula is not a linear function of v. To see how efficiency is important, let f(v) denote the option pricing formula as a function of the variance. Since

$$\hat{v} = v + e$$

and e is small relative to v, we can approximate $f(\hat{v})$ by a Taylor series expansion around v. This gives

$$f(\hat{v}) = f(v) + f'(v) \cdot e + 1/2 \cdot f''(v) \cdot e^2 + \ldots$$

If $\hat{v}$ is an unbiased estimate of v, then $E(e) = 0$, and $E(e^2) = V(e)$, so taking expectations of both sides, we obtain

$$E(f(\hat{v})) = f(v) + 1/2 \cdot f''(v) \cdot V(e) + \ldots$$

Hence, the bias in $f(\hat{v})$ as an estimate of the true option value f(v) is directly proportional to V(e). The more efficient is $\hat{v}$, the less biased will be $f(\hat{v})$. This demonstrates that efficiency is a highly desirable property of a variance estimator, or predictor. For a complete discussion of this bias, see Boyle and Ananthanarayanan.[9]

ESTIMATION

Before proceeding with our estimation, we must specify precisely the process to be estimated, and also the information available about the process. The

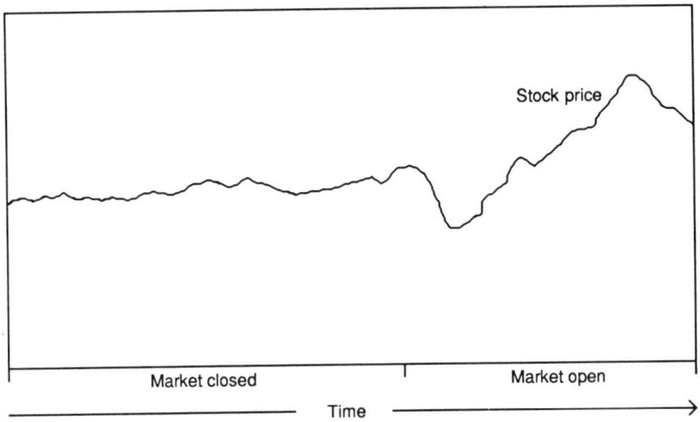

FIGURE 1. 24-hour trading day

lognormal diffusion hypothesis precisely stated is an ideal one which allows for elegant mathematical manipulations of the type found in the pricing literature. At the macroscopic level it appears to be a fairly good description of the world. For example, if we look at a graph of weekly price levels for a stock index, the lognormal hypothesis appears to be a good one. However, if we use only weekly observations of the price process, then over any reasonably short period, say one year, we will have relatively few observations with which to construct an estimator, and our estimator will turn out to be relatively inefficient.

We can increase the efficiency of our estimator by increasing the frequency of our observations. When viewed microscopically, however, the lognormal hypothesis may not appear quite so good. Most importantly, we note that during nontrading hours (nights and weekends) we have very little information about the process. The one piece of information which we can obtain, namely the return from the market close to the next day's open, leads us to believe that if stocks do follow a lognormal diffusion process overnight, then they certainly have much lower variance than during trading hours. This view of a 24-hour day is depicted in Figure 1.

Another problem, which can become significant if variance is being estimated from tick-by-tick data, is that prices do not take values on a continuum. Stocks trade in eighths, and stock indices are quoted to the nearest 0.05. As Marsh and Rosenfeld[10] show, this rounding problem can cause problems with both the bias and efficiency of certain variance estimators.

How we construct estimators and deal with these problems is strongly tied to the data that are available. Generally, for stocks or stock indices, the maximal data set that may be readily available would consist of daily values of closing price, high and low values, and possibly opening prices as well. If the asset whose variance we wish to estimate is, say, a stock portfolio other than a quoted index, we may have nothing more than closing values available.

We will describe estimates based on two types of information: sample returns, and extreme values; and two methods of constructing estimates: sample statistics, and maximum likelihood. These are the most well known, and have received the most attention in literature.

SAMPLE RETURN STATISTICS

The simplest variance estimate is constructed from sample returns. We assume that we have available a set of returns from the process whose variance is to be estimated. For instance, if we are estimating the variance of the price process for a stock index, we assume that we have a set of logarithmic returns over N disjoint time intervals (not necessarily of equal length).

If u and v denote the drift and variance rates, respectively, of the process per year, then the lognormal hypothesis states that over each interval i:

$$R_i \sim N(u \cdot t_i, v \cdot t_i)$$

That is, each of the (logarithmic) returns R_i has normal distribution, with the stated means and variances. In addition, all of the R_i are independent of one another.

Referring to Figure 1, we must now decide how to deal with nontrading hours. If we have daily returns, this means dealing with weekends and holidays. If we also have opening prices, so that we have some returns measured over trading hours and some returns measured over nontrading hours, then this means dealing with differential processes for daytime and nighttime returns as well.

One solution is to assume that the relative price process continues during nontrading hours just as it does during trading hours. Both casual and meticulous empiricism tell us that this is not a good idea. Another solution is to assume that during nontrading hours, the process follows a lognormal random walk, but with different drift and variance rates. Unfortunately, this means that we now have twice as many parameters to estimate. What we would really like to estimate is the average rate at which drift and variance occur. Even if at the micro level this contradicts the pure lognormal hypothesis, at the macro level of PI and option pricing, both of which are based on dynamic rebalancing on a reasonably infrequent basis, this average variance rate should do very well.

This suggests the third, and probably the best, solution. That is to assume a fixed relationship between the rate at which drift and variance occur during trading and nontrading hours, such as a nontrading period rate of 1/4 or

1/2 the rate during trading hours. This relationship is probably much more stable across stocks and time periods than drift and variance themselves, and so we can estimate it from historical data. Recall that under the lognormal hypothesis, the drift and variance of return over a time interval of length t_i are both directly proportional to t_i. If u and v for nontrading hours are the same fraction of the respective rates for trading hours, then another way of viewing this solution is to think of time as running slower. In other words, since the only way in which time manifests itself in a lognormal diffusion process is by the unfolding of drift and variance, we cannot distinguish between a rescaling of the drift and variance on the one hand, and a slower clock on the other.

It also appears from the lognormal hypothesis that in order to estimate v, we will also have to estimate u. This is unfortunate, since we do not need to estimate or predict u for the purposes of option pricing or PI. We will present an estimator for the drift; however, as we shall see, under normal circumstances variance can be estimated quite accurately without any estimate of the drift whatsoever.

Estimation of Drift. To estimate u, from our statement of the lognormal hypothesis above, it follows that

$$R_i/t_i \sim N(u, v/t_i)$$

Thus for ech i, i = 1, . . . , N, the estimator

$$\hat{u}_i = R_i/t_i$$

is an unbiased estimator of u, since its expected value is u. The estimation error variance of $\hat{u}_i$ is v/t_i. We now have N independent estimators for u, and we can combine them to produce an unbiased estimator of u which has a much lower estimation error variance, simply by averaging them. Thus we define

$$\hat{u} = (\hat{u}_1 + \cdots + \hat{u}_N)/N$$

Since expected values are linear, it follows that $E(\hat{u}) = u$. To find the variance of $\hat{u}$, we use the fact that the variance of a sum of independent random variables is the sum of the variances. Hence

$$\begin{aligned} Var(\hat{u}) &= (v/t_1 + \cdots + v/t_N)/N^2 \\ &= (1/t_1 + \cdots + 1/t_N) \cdot v/N^2 \end{aligned}$$

To see how much more efficient $\hat{u}$ is than any of the individual u_i, suppose that the N observations are equally spread over T years. Then

$$t_i = T/N$$

for each i. Substituting for each t_i in the expression for Var($\hat{u}$), we obtain

$$\mathrm{Var}(\hat{u}) = v/T$$

whereas

$$\mathrm{Var}(\hat{u}_i) = v/t_i$$

The ratio of these two quantities is the ratio of T to t_i, which is just N, so $\hat{u}$ is N times as efficient as $\hat{u}_i$.

Estimation of Variance. To estimate v, we return again to our lognormal hypothesis and observe that

$$(R_i - u \cdot t_i)/\sqrt{t_i} \sim N(0, v)$$

Now recall that the variance of a random variable is just the expected value of the squared variable minus the square of the expected value. For a random variable with an expected value of 0, as we have here, it follows that the expected value of the square is exactly the variance. Thus we are led to define an estimator as the square of the above random variable. That is,

$$\hat{v}_i = (R_i - u \cdot t_i)^2/t_i$$

Then $\hat{v}_i$ is an unbiased estimator of v. Note, however, that the definition of $\hat{v}_i$ involves the unobservable quantity u. We could substitute for u an unbiased estimate of u, such as $\hat{u}$ above, but unfortunately this will not make $\hat{v}_i$ unbiased.

Instead, we define a new estimator, v_i', by

$$v_i' = R_i^2/t_i$$

In other words, v' is obtained from $\hat{v}$ by ignoring u, or assuming that u = 0. Certainly it is true that if $\hat{v}$ is unbiased, then v' cannot be unbiased. But just how big is the bias? Dropping the subscript i for brevity, let us define the difference between the two estimators

$$\begin{aligned} D &= v' - \hat{v} \\ &= R^2/t - (R - u \cdot t)^2/t \\ &= (2 \cdot R \cdot u \cdot t - u^2 \cdot t^2)/t \end{aligned}$$

The proportional difference, D/v' is thus

$$D/v' = 2 \cdot (u \cdot t/R) - (u \cdot t/R)^2$$

What happens to the magnitude of $u \cdot t/R$ when the time interval t becomes small (e.g., 1/365 of a year)? From the distribution of R, we can write

$$R = u \cdot t + \sqrt{v \cdot t} \cdot Z$$

where Z is a standard normal random variable (with mean 0 and variance 1). But as t shrinks towards zero, $\sqrt{t}$ becomes enormous compared to t, and so R becomes enormous relative to $u \cdot t$ (in a probabilistic sense which we do not define formally here). Thus $u \cdot t/R$ tends to zero, and of course the square of this quantity tends to zero twice as fast. Intuitively, the idea is that for small values of t, the drift, being of order t, becomes negligible relative to the standard deviation, which is of order $\sqrt{t}$.

This means that we can use v_i' in place of $\hat{v}_i$, even though v_i' is slightly biased, since the magnitude of this bias will be very small if our observations are sufficiently frequent. Certainly with daily data the bias should be negligible. As before, we can obtain an estimator of v of much higher efficiency by defining v' as

$$v' = (v_1' + \cdots + v_N')/N$$

Let us proceed on the assumption that we can ignore u, that is, we assume that $u = 0$, and therefore that v' is unbiased. The estimator v' is just an equal weighted average of the estimators v_i'. Since each individual v_i' is an unbiased estimator of v, any weighted average of the v_i' will also be unbiased, provided the weights sum to one. So we may ask, for what set of weights w_i, which sum to one, does the estimator

$$(w_1 \cdot v_1' + \cdots + w_N \cdot v_N')$$

have minimal variance? This would be the best estimator that we can get from a linear combination of the v_i'. It is not hard to show (e.g., see Thorp[11]) that choosing $w_i = 1/N$ for all i is the minimum variance estimator, so that v' is the theoretically best way of combining the v_i'.

An alternative weighting scheme worthy of consideration is the following. First, define T by

$$T = t_1 + \cdots + t_N$$

Now choose

$$w_i = t_i/T, \qquad i = 1, \ldots, N$$

Using these weights, the quantities t_i cancel, and the weighted average value of the v_i' provides us with the estimator

$$v'' = (R_1^2 + \cdots + R_N^2)/T$$

Even though in theory v'' has a greater estimation error variance than v', it may under certain conditions be a better estimator. For example, if the values of the individual t_i are unavailable, or subject to measurement error, but T is known with certainty, then v'' is preferred.

A situation such as this can arise when trying to measure the variance experienced over some period by a dynamically rebalanced PI scheme. The experienced variance is that realized from trade to trade. Intratrade variance does not count, since it does not cause a whipsaw, and so will not contribute to the cost of the insurance. If trades are infrequent (say, several days apart), then v' may be easily calculated. However, if there is more than one trade per day, then the time between trades, t_i, may be unobservable. If the trades are not time stamped, but only date stamped, then the time between two trades on the same day is lost. Even if the trades are time stamped, to measure t_i properly, we must address the issue of differential variance rates during daytime and nighttime. In any event, the estimated t_i will be subject to considerable error. Since the time elapsed between intraday trades is small (less than 1/275 years), a slight error in its measurement can cause a huge error in the contribution of R_i^2 to v'. On the other hand, v'' will not suffer from this problem, since T is simply the total time over which the consecutive returns were realized.

To test for the possible severity of this effect, we calculated v' and v'' for a two-year PI program that had been in effect from mid-1986 until the end of 1986. This period included September 11 and 12, when the stock market declined about 5 percent in two days. During the half-year period, there were several days when the hedge ratio was adjusted twice in one day, and one day (September 11) when it was adjusted three times. To estimate the t_i for these trades, we assumed that all trades took place at equally spaced intervals during the day. The resulting value of v' was about $30^2\,\%^2$, compared to about $16^2\,\%^2$ for v''!

Conceptually, we can think of t_i as a random variable instead of a known constant. In this case, the summand R_i^2/t_i in v' is the quotient of two random variables. We have already made assumptions about R_i^2, by virtue of the log-normal hypothesis. Depending on what assumptions we make about the distribution of the estimated value of t_i, the ith summand would have some probability distribution, for which some other value of the weights w_i, rather than $1/N$, may minimize the variance of v'. Using v'' obviates the necessity to make assumptions about the t_i. If the t_i have fairly similar values, then there will be very little difference between v' and v'', so in many cases v'' may be preferred to v'.

Before turning to the question of the estimation error variance of v' and the construction of confidence intervals for v, we return to the question of how the process evolves during nontrading hours. By using v' instead of $\hat{v}$, we are assuming that $u = 0$, and so do not have to address the question of whether the scale factor from trading days to nontrading days is the same for u as for v, since any scale factor will work for zero!

To estimate the scale factor for v, we computed the average value of R_i^2 over weekends (of which there were 208 in our example below) and over single days, and found that the ratio of the two was 1.275. In other words, the total amount of variance that evolves from Friday's close to Monday's close is on average only 1.275 times the amount of variance that evolves between the close on contiguous days, and not three times the amount as we would expect for a perfect lognormal process in real time. French and Roll[12] estimated a ratio around 1.1 for individual stocks. Using our value of 1.275, we would suggest using one day as the elapsed time between contiguous days (and over single day holidays), and 1.275 days as the elapsed time between returns over three (or more) days. In this case, there are $4 + 1.275 = 5.275$ days in a week, and $52 \cdot 5.275 + 1 = 275$ days per year. Thus t_i is 1/275 years for weekdays, and 1.275/275 years for weekends.

The error induced by assuming that the variance from Friday's close to Monday's close is the same as that over contiguous days, however, will be small. If we do not divide the squared weekend return by, say, 1.275, then its contribution to the sum of squares will be too large, so the sum of squares will be too large. However, to be consistent, we must calculate the number of "days" per year as $52 \cdot 5 + 1 = 261$ (ignoring holidays). This will tend to offset the excess in the sum of squared returns, so that the resulting error can probably be ignored.

Similarly, if we assume that the variance evolves at the same rate on the weekend as on weekdays, then the squared return from Friday to Monday will be divided by 3, and will make too small a contribution to v′. But now we must annualize by multiplying v′ by 365, and so the error will be approximately offset. In short, as long as we take care to annualize our estimate appropriately, the result should not be sensitive to assumptions about the weekend variance rate.

Error variance and confidence intervals. The lognormal hypothesis with zero drift states that

$$R_i \sim N(0, v \cdot t_i)$$

If we define Z_i by

$$Z_i = R_i/\sqrt{(v \cdot t_i)}$$

then Z_i has the standard normal distribution, and the Z_i are all independent. Substituting Z_i for R_i in the definition of v′, we obtain

$$v' = v \cdot (Z_i^2 + \cdots + Z_N^2)/N$$

Now the square of a standard normal random variable has chi-squared distribution with one degree of freedom, and the sum of N independent chi-squared variables has chi-squared distribution with N degrees of freedom. This distribution has variance $2 \cdot N$. Hence the standard deviation of v′ is

$$\begin{aligned} \text{Std}(v') &= (v/N) \cdot \sqrt{(2 \cdot N)} \\ &= v \cdot \sqrt{(2/N)} \end{aligned}$$

The variance of v′ is thus inversely proportional to N, the number of observations. Of course, the true variance of v′ depends on v, the true variance of the process, so without knowing v we cannot know the true value of the estimation error variance of v′. We can estimate it by using v′ in place of v. Thus we are led to define

$$s = v' \cdot \sqrt{(2/N)}$$

Then s is an unbiased estimate of the standard deviation of v′. We can now construct confidence intervals for v by examining the percentiles of the chi-squared distribution.

When the number of degrees of freedom, N, is large, the chi-squared distribution looks very much like the normal distribution. Thus, a 95 percent confidence interval can be found as for the normal distribution, by computing the interval $(v' - 1.96 \cdot s, v' + 1.96 \cdot s)$. Other confidence intervals can be constructed from the percentiles of the normal distribution, which can be found from tables.

Example. To illustrate the computations, we construct the relative daily returns of the S&P 500 to six-month Treasury bills for the years 1982 through 1985 as follows. From a time series of daily closing price levels of the S&P 500, we computed the natural logarithms of the price relatives (which are one plus the daily returns). From a time series of daily yields on Treasury bills, we computed the daily return on the bills (arising from price change and accrued interest), and computed the logarithms of one plus these returns. The relative returns were then computed as the difference between the logarithmic returns on the S&P 500 and Treasury bills. There were 990 such returns, which we denote by R_i, $i = 1, \ldots, 990$. We denote by d_i the number of days over which each return was realized, and by t_i the number of years corresponding to d_i, which is just d_i divided by the number of days per year.

First, we assumed that d_i is 1 for weekdays, and 1.275 for weekends. To estimate u, the drift, we computed

$$\begin{aligned} \hat{u} &= (R_1/t_1 + \cdots + R_N/t_N)/N \\ &= (R_i/d_i + \cdots + R_N/d_N) \cdot 275/N \end{aligned}$$

and obtained $\hat{u} = 5.27\%$. u is the average risk premium of stocks over bills during the four-year period.

To estimate the variance, we computed $\hat{v}$, which subtracts the drift term before squaring. This gave $\hat{v} = 0.018903$, which has a square root of 13.749 percent for the volatility. Ignoring the drift, we computed v' as the average (time adjusted) squared return, and obtained $v' = 0.018910$, which corresponds to a volatility of 13.751 percent. As expected, the difference between $\hat{v}$ and v' is trivial. We also computed v'', which is the sum of squared returns divided by the total time period, and obtained $v'' = 0.018907$, which corresponds to a volatility of 13.751 percent. We expect v'' to be extremely close to v' when the time intervals are approximately equal.

To construct confidence intervals for v', we computed s as

$$s = 0.018910 \cdot \sqrt{(2/990)} = 0.000849$$

This produces a 95 percent confidence interval for v' of

$$\begin{aligned}(v' - 2 \cdot s, v' + 2 \cdot s) \\ &= (0.018910 - 2 \cdot 0.000849, 0.018901 + 2 \cdot 0.000849) \\ &= (0.018833, 0.020610)\end{aligned}$$

We obtain a 95 percent confidence interval for volatility by taking the square root of the end points of the interval for v', and obtain the interval

$$(13.12\%, 14.36\%)$$

Finally, we reestimated v' assuming that all returns corresponded to a time interval of one day (in other words, ignoring weekend effects). In this case, there are $52 \cdot 5 + 1 = 261$ days per year (ignoring holidays). The value of v' so obtained was 0.018842, which corresponds to a volatility of 13.727 percent. This is trivially different from the value of v' computed using our weekend adjustment, and shows that the sensitivity of the estimated variance to assumptions about weekend variance rates is quite small, when computed from large data sets.

THE EXTREME VALUE METHOD

The extreme value method is generally attributed to Parkinson.[13] The idea stems from the observation that given a diffusion process with zero drift, if time is divided into discrete intervals, then the high and low values of the process in the interval contain a lot of information about the volatility of the process. We might expect that the high and low values will contain much more information about volatility than the return over the period, for the following reason. If we take the value of the process at the beginning of the interval as given, then the return over the interval is nothing more than the value of the process at the end of the interval, whereas the high and low values contain information about every single value of the process in the interval, since we know that they are all lower than the high value, and higher than the low value.

In fact, the volatility estimate obtained from the high and low values is about five times more efficient than the estimate obtained from the interval return, under ideal conditions. Garman and Klass[14] constructed an estimator by combining the high, low and ending value of the process over each interval, which is about seven times more efficient than the standard benchmark.

Some words of caution also apply to the high–low estimator. First, the estimator only applies to processes with zero drift. As in the case of the sample return variance discussed above, if we have decided *a priori* that the drift is zero, then this is a moot point. Also as before, as the measurement interval grows smaller, the error introduced by erroneously assuming a zero drift rapidly diminishes.

Second, if the volatility clock runs at a different rate when the market is closed, then the high–low estimator is only of value in estimating variance while the market is open. If we wish to think in terms of an average daily variance which governs the process as if each day were an "atomic" unit (i.e., this variance is responsible for generating close to close returns), then the observed high–low range during the period of high volatility (trading hours), may be a biased estimate of variance over a 24-hour period. The same problem holds for weekends.

The third point is that even for that part of the day while the market is open, we do not know the true high and low values of the process, since we are not able to monitor the process continuously, but only at discrete points in time. This will tend to bias the high–low range downwards. This bias diminishes as the frequency of observations increases. Garman and Klass provide tables to estimate the bias as a function of the daily trading volume, which is essentially a measure of the average frequency of observation. For an index such as the S&P 500 or the S&P 100, the frequency of observations is so great that this should not be a problem. However, Marsh and Rosenfeld[10] have shown that for stocks, the mere bid–ask spread is enough to reduce enormously the efficiency of the high–low variance estimator. Even though stock indices are computed in real time to the nearest 0.05, this value will not move in such a way as to bounce back and forth between the bid and the ask, since the result of such liquidity trading in individual stocks will be diversified away in a stock index.

A final comment is that the high–low estimator is sensitive to reporting errors. If there is one quote in the day for which, for example, a decimal point is entered incorrectly, the reported high or low value may be grossly distorted. For an index such as the S&P 500, if the price of one stock is grossly incorrect, this error will be diversified away in the computation of the index level, so an index may be less sensitive to reporting errors than individual stocks.

As a result, it is not clear exactly what is the bias and efficiency of the high–low estimator, although it should be better for a stock index than for individual stocks. This may make it less useful as an estimate of ex post realized variance. However, as long as any bias is consistent, it may be extremely useful as a predictor of future variance! This emphasizes the point that in a prediction model, the predictors do not themselves necessarily have to be good estimates of the quantity to be predicted. We will see other examples of this later.

If we wish to construct the high–low estimate of relative return between two assets, then we need to know the high and low values of the relative process, which is not the same as the difference between the high values and low values of the two processes independently, since the extremes of each process will almost certainly not be attained simultaneously. This being the case, we should probably construct the high–low estimate of each process independently, and combine them according to the formula for computing the relative variance from the variance of each of two processes.

Let us denote by A_i the opening price on day i, or else the closing price on day i $-$ 1, depending on whether we are trying to estimate variance over the trading day or over the 24-hour day. Let B_i denote the closing price on day i. Let H_i and L_i denote the high and low prices on day i. We convert B_i, H_i, and L_i to (relative) logarithmic values by defining

$$C_i = \ln(B_i) - \ln(A_i)$$
$$U_i = \ln(H_i) - \ln(A_i)$$
$$D_i = \ln(L_i) - \ln(A_i)$$

Parkinson's variance estimate is given by

$$\hat{v}_i = (U_i - D_i)^2/(4 \cdot \ln(2))$$

In theory, this estimator has an efficiency of about 5.2 relative to the close-to-close estimator. Garman and Klass[14] improve this estimator by considering the joint effect of C_i, U_i, and D_i. Their estimate is given by

$$\hat{v}_i = 0.5 \cdot (U_i - D_i)^2 - (2 \cdot \ln(2) - 1) \cdot C_i^2$$

and has a theoretical efficiency of about 7.4 relative to C_i^2. If A_i denotes Friday's closing price, we might consider dividing C_i^2 by 1.275, as discussed above. Of course, $(U_i - D_i)^2$ should also be adjusted to reflect the three-day interval, but the nature of the adjustment is not clear.

Having computed $\hat{v}_i$ for many days i, we then average the estimates by adding them over N days, and dividing by N. Then we annualize the variance estimate by multiplying by 275 (or 261, or 365 as appropriate). This is analogous to the procedure for combining the individual daily variance estimators for the traditional close to close estimator.

For a more complete description of the high–low estimator, the reader is referred to Garman and Klass.[14]

THE MAXIMUM LIKELIHOOD METHOD

This is a classical statistical method, which seeks the values for the parameters of the stochastic process which make the observed realization the most likely. If we can formulate the probability density of the observed outcomes as a function of the parameters of the stochastic process, then we can differentiate this function to find the parameter values for which it is maximized.

To illustrate this, suppose the observed outcome is a set of logarithmic relative close-to-close returns, such as we have already analyzed above. Once again, we can write the lognormal hypothesis as

$$(R_i - u \cdot t_i)/\sqrt{(v \cdot t_i)} \sim N(0, 1)$$

That is, the standardized returns are normally distributed with zero mean and unit variance, and in addition are independent of each other. The probability density function of the normal distribution is given by

$$f(Z_i) = (1/\sqrt{(2 \cdot \pi \cdot v)}) \cdot \exp(-Z_i^2/2)$$

where Z_i is the standardized return. Since the standardized returns are independent of each other, the probability density function of the joint set of outcomes $\{Z_1, \ldots, Z_N\}$ is given by

$$\begin{aligned} L &= f(Z_1) \cdot \cdots \cdot f(Z_N) \\ &= (2 \cdot \pi \cdot v)^{-N/2} \cdot \exp(-(Z_1^2 + \cdots + Z_N^2)/2) \end{aligned}$$

We wish to find the values of u and v which maximize the function L. However, rather than do this, we instead maximize the function ln(L), the natural logarithm of L. Since the ln function is an increasing function, ln(L) attains its maximum at the same point as L, but ln(L) is easier to manipulate algebraically than L. Referring to this function as g(u, v), we seek to maximize g, where

$$g(u, v) = -N \cdot \ln(v) - (Z_1^2 + \cdots + Z_N^2)$$

where we have omitted an additive constant, and multiplied throughout by 2, since these operations also do not affect the value of u and v for which g attains its maximum. Equating to zero the partial derivative of g with respect to u yields

$$\begin{aligned} 0 &= \partial g/\partial u \\ &= -(2/v) \cdot ((R_1 - u \cdot t_1) + \cdots + (R_N - u \cdot t_N)) \end{aligned}$$

Hence our estimate of u is given by

$$\hat{u} = (R_1 + \cdots + R_N)/(t_1 + \cdots + t_N)$$

Equating to zero the partial derivative of g with respect to v yields

$$0 = \partial g/\partial v = -N/v + (1/v^2) \cdot ((R_1 - u \cdot t_1)^2/t_1 + \cdots + (R_N - u \cdot t_N)^2/t_N)$$

To achieve a maximum, both partial derivatives must vanish simultaneously, and so we can substitute û for u to obtain

$$v = (1/N) \cdot ((R_1 - \hat{u} \cdot t_1)^2/t_1 + \cdots + (R_N - \hat{u} \cdot t_N)^2/t_N)$$

How do these estimates compare to the sample estimates obtained previously? If the time intervals, t_i, are all of the same length, then

$$t_i = (t_1 + \cdots + t_N)/N$$

In this case, the maximum likelihood and sample estimates of u are identical to each other. If the intervals are of different lengths, as they are in Friday to Monday closes are identified with more than one day's worth of variance, then they will in general be different, but we recognize in the maximum likelihood estimator the alternative weighting scheme for the individual $\hat{u}_i$ that we considered to construct the estimator v″ in (a).

For the data set used to illustrate the preceding sample estimates, we associated each return with either 1 or 1.275 days worth of variance. The sum of these intervals over the period 1982 through 1985 is 1039.5 days. The sum of the logarithmic relative returns over the period is 16.2325 percent, so the maximum likelihood estimate of the drift is 0.0156%/day, which is 4.2943%/year, based on a 275 day year. This compares to 5.27%/year obtained from the sample mean.

Once the drift parameter has been established, the maximum likelihood estimator of the variance is seen to be identical to the sample variance estimator. As for the sample variance estimator, the choice of mean becomes insignificant when the interval sizes are small.

The maximum likelihood estimator has also been derived for the case when high and low values are available. This extends the maximum likelihood estimators in the same way that Parkinson's method extends the sample estimators. However, the solution is no longer of closed form, and numerical search techniques must be employed to find the solution. The interested reader is referred to Ball and Torous.[15]

PREDICTION

Having established procedures for estimating variance, ex post, we now turn out attention to the considerably harder problem of predicting variance. First, we must decide what quantities may be useful in predicting variance. Next, we must decide on a functional form for the relationship between predictors and subsequent realized variance. Finally, we must consider any difficulties in estimating the model.

Predictors. In a Black-Scholes world, in which the variance rate is constant, any historical estimate of variance will be as good a predictor as it is an estimator. In reality, however, we suspect that the variance rate does change through time. It should be pointed out, however, that this is not obvious. It is not enough simply to observe that over two adjacent periods the estimated variance is different. For any process with stationary variance, there is some probability that the realized outcome, which produced different variance estimates over different periods, will, in fact, occur.

However, for a given constant variance, it is possible to compute the probability that the realized outcome will occur. The method is essentially that outlined above to compute the maximum likelihood estimate. If this probability is small enough, we would reject the hypothesis that the true variance rate was constant over the periods that produced the different estimates. For most asset price series it is not hard to reject the hypothesis of constant variance over periods of a few years, given sufficiently frequent observations.

If the variance rate is not constant over the life of a PI program, then a key assumption of the Black-Scholes or Margrabe models is violated. However, assuming that variance is constant and equal to the average variance rate over the whole period will probably render these option pricing models sufficiently valid for the purpose of constructing insurance policies.

Thus our problem is to predict the average variance rate over the life of the PI program, which may be typically one to three years, but may become increasing longer as pension sponsors respond to the FASB 87 regulations. We know of at least one PI program which has a horizon of 12 years! Predicting variance rates over such long periods is indeed a difficult task. We now consider potential predictors of variance.

Lagged Estimates. Lagged estimates of the variance rate may be good predictors of future variance. If variance rates wander around in a random walk, then the most recent estimated variance will be the best predictor of future average variance. If variance rates revert to some long-run mean, then a recent estimate will still contain information about future variance. We may use the lagged values of any or all of the estimates considered in this chapter, although using more than one may cause collinearity problems if not handled carefully.

Factor Model Predictors. To predict the variance of any stock or portfolio, we may use an equity factor model, many of which are now commonly available. A factor model is a model of the form:

$$R = x_1 \cdot f_1 + \cdots + x_K \cdot f_K + e$$

where the f_i represent the returns to random factors which account for virtually all of that part of a stock's return which is correlated with the return of other stocks. The x_i denote the exposure, or sensitivity, of the stock's return to the return on factor i. These might be such attributes as company capitalization, stock yield, P/E ratio, B/P ratio, and so on. The residual e denotes that portion of the stock's return which is uncorrelated with other stocks; that is, the e of one stock is uncorrelated with that of another stock, and uncorrelated with the factor returns, f_i.

One reason for using such a return-generating model for stocks is the assumption that while the distribution of stock return (i.e., variance) changes through time, the cause is that the attributes, x_i, change through time. Hopefully, the joint distribution of the factor returns, f_i, is substantially more stationary than the distribution of stock returns. If this is the case, then we can estimate the joint distribution of the factors over a recent period (say, the most recent 60 months), and use that as a predictor of the future joint distribution of the factors. This joint distribution may then be combined with the current attributes of a stock or portfolio, and a good predictor of stock variance will result. In particular, if a good prediction of the covariance matrix of the factors is available, then the variance of a portfolio may be computed by simple matrix algebra. For a well diversified portfolio or index, the effect of the residuals, e, will be negligible.

Many commercial factor models of this type are available. For a good description of factor models, see Sharpe.[16] A model of this type may give a good prediction of long-term variance. If the factor model is expressed in terms of proportional return, as opposed to logarithmic return, then the variance rate may be converted to a logarithmic rate according to the formula:

$$v = \ln(1 + s^2/(1 + m)^2)$$

where s^2 denotes the variance of proportional return, and m denotes the expected proportional return. If no estimate of m is available, the term rate (to the expiration of the policy) on a riskless instrument may be used as a proxy.

Unfortunately, most factor models have relatively short histories. The oldest ones go back to the early or mid 1970s. This does not allow for extensive testing to see how well such models predict future variance over horizons of one or more years. Also, care must be taken not to estimate a variance prediction rule in the same period over which the factor model was estimated. This will result in an in-sample use of the factor model, and the factor model predictor will probably show extraordinarily high predictive content.

Implied Variance. The implied variance of an option is that value of the variance which, when used as input to an option pricing model, produces a model value equal to the market price of the option. If we assume that market participants are in the aggregate using this pricing model, then the implied variance is the market's aggregate prediction of variance over the life of the option. Latané and Rendleman[17] have shown that this implied variance contains useful information for predicting future variance. Presumably, the more liquid the option contract, the more informationally efficient will be the implied variance. Two salient questions are, therefore, which option should we use, and which pricing model should we use to compute the implied variance?

The answers to these two questions depend on what variance we are trying to predict. If we wish to predict the variance of a stock portfolio, then we should use an option on an index which is similar to the portfolio in question. Several of these are available:

1. The S&P 500 (SPX), a capitalization weighted portfolio of 500 stocks. European style options on the SPX trade on the Chicago Board Options Exchange (CBOE).
2. The S&P 100 (OEX), a capitalization weighted portfolio of 100 stocks, each of which has options trading on the CBOE. The OEX correlates highly with the SPX. American style options on the OEX trade on the CBOE.

3. The Amex Major Market Index (XMI), a price weighted index of 20 stocks. The XMI correlates highly with the Dow Jones average of 30 industrials. American style options on the XMI trade on the American Stock Exchange (AMEX).
4. The Amex Institutional Index (XII), a capitalization weighted index of 75 stocks that have the largest holdings in institutional portfolios. The XII correlates highly with the SPX. European style options on the XII trade on the AMEX.

If the stock portfolio in question is not one of these indices, and does not correlate highly with one of them, then the implied variance of the index may not be a good predictor of the variance of the stock portfolio. If the stock portfolio is similar or identical to the S&P 500, then three of the above indices are useful proxies. The SPX and XII have the advantage of perfect or extremely high correlation with the S&P 500, and in addition the options traded on them are European, meaning that they cannot be exercised prior to expiration. This makes the Black-Scholes formula a more theoretically appropriate model from which to infer a variance.

The OEX correlates slightly less well with the S&P 500 than the other two indices, but is a vastly more liquid contract. OEX options are American, which means that they can be exercised prior to expiration. In theory, this means that the Black-Scholes formula is inappropriate for pricing these options. However, because the dividend yield on the OEX is fairly smooth and significantly lower than interest rates, it can be shown that for call options there is no value to early exercise unless the call is extremely deep in-the-money. Thus, the Black-Scholes model may be used for OEX calls also.

Having decided on the appropriate index, which option series should be used? In general, different option series will imply different variances, since the market prices of options will not all equal their Black-Scholes values for any one choice of variance. It can be shown that the Black-Scholes price is most sensitive to the variance when the option is approximately at-the-money. It follows from this that the implied variance from the at-the-money option is least sensitive to the market price of the option (which may differ from its equilibrium price). Also, as time to expiration increases, the sensitivity of the implied variance to option price also decreases, since more of the option's price is derived from time premium. We would like to use a long maturity option, since its implied variance will be a predictor of variance over a longer-term period. Unfortunately, while longer maturities may correspond more closely to the horizon of the PI program, the liquidity of index option contracts drops off sharply as maturity increases past about three months, and this is likely to reduce the efficiency of the implied variance as a predictor.

One choice, therefore, is to use the at-the-money call option with a maturity of about three months. This is by far the simplest choice. Another choice is to compute the implied variance for all options on the same underlying instrument, and to compute their weighted average, where the weights are the inverses of the sensitivities of the implied variance to the option price (i.e., the partial derivative of the Black-Scholes option value to variance). A third possibility, suggested by Latané and Rendleman,[17] is to find the variance which minimizes, in some sense, the aggregate pricing error across all option series.

Both the second and third choices require extensive computation, and are only justifiable if there is reason to believe that they would provide better predictors of variance than the variance implied by a single option. In fact, Beckers[18] found that the at-the-money call options contain the most accurate predictive information. In addition, better predictive ability can be obtained by computing the implied variance at several points in time, and averaging them.

While we indicated above that the Black-Scholes model is the appropriate model for comparing model values to market prices, some points should be noted. First, the index level should be dividend adjusted before being used in the formula. The theory indicates that if a dividend yield to expiration, d, is known with certainty, then the index level, S, may be replaced by $S \cdot (1 - d)$, and the Black-Scholes formula will hold. If the dividend amount, D, rather than the yield is assumed to be known with certainty, we can approximate d by D/S, so that S is replaced in the formula by $S - D$. See Jarrow and Rudd[19] for a complete explanation of the effect of dividends on the Black-Scholes formula.

The second point concerns the impact of futures trading on index option prices. Given the existence of options and futures on the same underlying instrument, such as the S&P 500, under the assumptions of the Black-Scholes model there are formulae which relate any pair of instruments. A call options should price off the underlying spot instrument according to the Black-Scholes formula. Ignoring the difference between a future and a forward contract, the futures contract should price off the underlying spot instrument according to the well known cost of carry formula (e.g., see Sharpe[20]). Marrying these two models together produces Black's[21] formula which relates the price of the call to the futures price. All of these relationships are derived from no-arbitrage conditions in perfect markets.

In practice, however, it is relatively easy to arbitrage the relationship between the option and the futures contracts, since both instruments are easily traded. By comparison, it is relatively difficult to arbitrage the relationship between the underlying index and its derivative instruments. This is because the underlying instrument is an index, and it is hard to trade a large portfolio of stocks efficiently enough to engage in arbitrage. As a result, the options and the futures tend to trade in lock step with each other, even though they may both be mispriced relative to the underlying index.

In practice, options on the SPX, XII, and OEX all tend to trade off the S&P 500 futures price, rather than off the price of the spot S&P 500 index. For example, if the S&P 500 futures are underpriced relative to their model value, this will tend to drag the OEX calls down, and the puts up. Under these circumstances, if the implied variance of an OEX call is computed from the Black-Scholes formula using the OEX index value, it will be biased downwards. The opposite holds if the futures are trading at a premium.

To avoid this problem, two solutions are available. The first is to use the Black formula to compute the option's implied variance from the futures price. The second is to use the Black-Scholes formula only when the S&P 500 futures seem to be fairly priced.

Whichever model is used, the implied variance cannot be solved analytically from the formula. Thus, numerical search procedures must be employed. The most popular technique is the Newton-Raphson search method. This can be easily implemented in a spreadsheet. We will outline the method for computing the implied standard deviation (the square root of variance) from the Black-Scholes formula.

Let s denote the volatility, and let f(s) denote the difference between the Black-Scholes option value, considered as a function of s, and the market price of the option. Our objective is to find a root of f; that is, a value of s for which $f(s) = 0$. In addition to f(s), we need its derivative with respect to s, which we denote $f'(s)$. This is just the partial derivative of the option value with respect to volatility. The Black-Scholes formula and its partial derivatives can be found in books by Cox and Rubinstein[22] and by Jarrow and Rudd.[19] To compute these formulae requires values of the distribution and density functions for the standard normal distribution. Formulae for these can also be found in both books. Start with a guess for s, say .15 in annual units, and compute f(s) and $f'(s)$. Then replace s by a new guess:

$$s \leftarrow s - f(s)/f'(s)$$

Keep repeating this procedure until f(s) is sufficiently close to zero. Usually no more than three or four iterations are necessary.

The value of the implied volatility will be affected by other parameters of the model. One of these, the riskless rate, is ambiguous; a suitable choice for this is the broker call loan rate. Another is the dividend yield through expiration of the option. The dividend adjusted pricing formula should be used to account for dividends.

Another point which can have an effect on the implied volatility is the problem of nonsimultaneity. The stock exchanges stop trading at 4 P.M., e.s.t., while options trading continues until 4:15. If a significant event occurs during the 15 minutes in between, then the closing option price may not correspond to the closing stock price, and the implied volatility will contain noise. Using an average value over several days will help alleviate this problem.

Finally, the same problem holds for implied variances as holds for stock factor model variance predictions, namely a short history. Options on the OEX (the first index options) began trading in 1982. The XII options only began trading in 1986. Thus, while it is possible to test whether index options can predict short-term variance, it is too early to tell whether they can usefully predict long-term variance.

Macro-Economic Variables. It seems likely that the long-term volatility of both the stock market and the fixed income market are influenced by the environment of the economy in which they are imbedded. An inherent danger in using historical market data without referencing economic variables is that conclusions might be drawn that may have been valid in economic environments of the past, but are irrelevant in the current and prospective environment. To avoid this problem, it would be desirable to use economic variables as predictors of volatility.

Little work has been done in this area by financial economists, although the recent Arbitrage Pricing Theory (APT) has provided some impetus for work in this direction. The APT assumes that asset returns are generated by a factor model, and statistical evidence suggests that the number of factors is small, perhaps four or five (see Chen, Roll and Ross[22]). APT researchers have therefore focused on factor models in which the factors are macro-economic, rather than the micro-economic factors used in traditional factor models. While the power of these macro-based models to explain and predict short-term variance is low compared to the micro-based factor models, they do provide a basis for using macro-economic variables to predict long term volatility.

The type of factors included in Chen, Roll and Ross[23] are: Growth rates in industrial production returns on market indices, changes in the risk premium (between high- and low-grade corporate bonds), growth rates in real consumption and growth rates in oil prices.

Estep, Hanson and Johnson[24] describe a model whose five factors are: Growth in defense spending, growth in oil prices, growth in GNP, decline in interest rates, and growth in inflation.

These are the type of factors one would expect to be of use in describing the impact of the economic environment on future stock market volatility. Models incorporating macro-economic factors like these are now beginning to become commercially available. As with traditional factor models, they may suffer the deficiency of not having sufficiently long histories to be able to test whether they can really do a good job of predicting volatility.

Prediction Models. Whatever predictors we have decided to include, we must define a structural form that our prediction model will take. The simplest one is the linear form, in which we put the observed outcome on the left-hand side, and specify the right-hand side of the equation as the sum of our predictors, multiplied by coefficients, which may be estimated by linear regression.

For example, if we are trying to predict one-year variances, we could estimate annual variance by the previously suggested methods, and use these values as our dependent variable values, one per year, as far back as we can go. The independent variables could be any values that were known prior to the beginning of the year for which estimated variance appears as the dependent variable. These might be the estimated variance from the previous year, perhaps the average estimated variance from the preceding five years, the implied variance from index options (if available) from the end of the preceding year, a factor model prediction of variance, the high–low variance estimator, and so on. The coefficients on these predictors might then be estimated by a simple ordinary least squares regression.

One problem that is likely to arise if we specify the model in such a way is that of collinearity between the independent variables. Some of the predictors may be highly correlated with others, and this will cause the regression to be unstable. There are various ways to get around this. One possibility is to regress one independent variable on others that tend to correlate with it. Then, instead of using that variable in its raw form, we could substitute the residual from the latter regression. This represents the information in the predictor that is not already contained in the other predictors with which it correlates.

Another possible specification might be to use as a new predictor the average of the individual raw predictors, and then substitute in place of the raw predictors their deviations from their common mean.

There is no right way to specify a prediction model. The use of too complex a model requires a subtle understanding of the statistical and economic issues involved. At the other extreme, an extremely simple model is one which requires no estimation at all. For example, we could simply use last period's estimated variance as our prediction of next period's variance. Or we could use a fixed average of a lagged sample variance estimate, a lagged high–low estimate of a lagged sample variance estimate, a lagged high–low estimate and a recent average of implied variances from a particular index option. However, without testing out such a prediction rule, we cannot have any idea how good it is. But it may be that estimating a more complex rule will add very little to the predictive ability of the model.

One advantage of not having to estimate a prediction rule is that all of the available data can be used to test the predictive ability of the rule. If limited data are available, and we must use some of it to estimate the prediction rule, then little or no data may be left to use in an out-of-sample test of the rule.

For an interesting attempt to predict the short-term variance of individual stocks using many of the estimates described in this chapter, see Beckers.[25]

BIBLIOGRAPHY

1. Brennan, M., and Solanki, R. 1981. "Optimal Portfolio Insurance." *Journal of Financial and Quantitative Analysis*, Vol. 16 (September) pp. 279–300.
2. Perold, A. 1986. "Constant Proportional Portfolio Insurance." Draft paper, Harvard Business School (1986).
3. Black, F., and Jones, R. 1986. "Simplifying Portfolio Insurance." Goldman, Sachs Research Report (August).
4. Black, F., and Scholes, M. 1973. "The Pricing of Options and Corporate Liabilities." *Journal of Political Economy*, Vol. 81 (May/June) pp. 637–59.
5. Margrabe, W. 1978. "The Value of an Option to Exchange One Asset for Another." *Journal of Finance*, Vol. 33, pp. 177–186.
6. Cox, J., and Ross, S. 1976. "The Valuation of Options for Alternative Stochastic Processes." *Journal of Financial Economics* (January) pp. 145–166.
7. Ball, C., and Torous, W. 1983. "Bond Price Dynamics and Options." *Journal of Financial and Quantative Analysis*, Vol. 18, pp. 517–531.
8. Brennan, M., and Schwartz, E. 1982. "An Equilibrium Model of Bond Pricing and a Test of Market Efficiency." *Journal of Financial and Quantative Analysis*, Vol. 17, pp. 301–329.
9. Boyle, P., and Ananthanarayanan, A. 1977. "The Impact of Variance Estimation in Option Valuation Models." *Journal of Financial Economics*, Vol. 5, pp. 375–387.
10. Marsh, T., and Rosenfeld, E. 1986. "Non Trading, Market Making, and Estimates of Stock Price Volatility." *Journal of Financial Economics*, Vol. 15 (March) pp. 359–372.
11. Thorp, E. 1976. "Common Stock Volatilities in Optin Formulas." Proceedings, Seminar on the Analysis of Security Prices, Vol. 21, No. 1, May 13–14.
12. French, K., and Roll, R. 1985. "Stock Return Variances: The Arrival of Information and the Reaction of Traders." UCLA working paper.
13. Parkinson, M. 1980. "The Extreme Value Method for Estimating the Variance of the Rate of Return." *Journal of Business*, Vol. 53 (January) pp. 61–65.
14. Garman, M., and Klass, M. 1980. "On the Estimation of Security Price Volatility from Historical Data." *Journal of Business*, Vol. 53 (January) pp. 67–78.
15. Ball, C., and Torous, W. 1984. "The Maximum Likelihood Estimation of Security Price Volatility: Theory, Evidence, and Application to Option Pricing." *Journal of Business*, Vol. 57 (January) pp. 97–112.
16. Sharp, W. 1982. "Factors in New York Stock Exchange Security Returns, 1931–1979." *Journal of Portfolio Management* (Summer) pp. 5–19.
17. Latane, H., and Rendleman, R. 1976. "Standard Deviations of Stock Price Ratios Implied in Option Prices." *Journal of Finance*, Vol. 31 (May) pp. 369–382.
18. Beckers, S. 1981. "Standard Deviations Implied in Option Prices as Predictors of Future Stock Price Variability." *Journal of Banking and Finance* (September) pp. 363–382.
19. Jarrow, R., and Rudd, A. 1983. "Option Pricing." Dow-Jones Irwin.
20. Sharpe, W. 1985. "Investments." Third edition, Prentice Hall.

21. Black, F. 1976. "The Pricing of Commodity Contracts." *Journal of Financial Economics* (May) pp. 167–179.

22. Cox, J., and Rubinstein, M. 1985. "Options Markets." Prentice-Hall.

23. Chen, N., Roll, R., and Ross, S. 1984. "Economic Forces and the Stock Market: Testing the APT and Alternative Asset Pricing Theories." Seminar on the Analysis of Security Prices (May).

24. Estep, P., Hanson, N., and Johnson, C. 1983. "Sources of Value and Risk in Common Stocks." *Journal of Portfolio Management* (Summer).

25. Beckers, S. 1983. "An Empirical Test of Security Price Volatility Estimators Incorporating High, Low and Closing Price Observations." *Journal of Business* (January).

15. THE INSURANCE COMPANY GUARANTEE

Ralph S. Tate

The various kinds of portfolio "insurance" discussed up to now in this volume share many common characteristics. One of the most interesting is that none represent *true* insurance. The important characteristics of insurance—most notably the existence of a legally binding obligation to perform—do not exist. Instead buyers of this "insurance" find a best-efforts form of asset management. It is true that the more sophisticated applications of portfolio protection techniques (especially those grouped under the rubric of dynamic hedging) provide economic outcomes that mimic the existence of a portfolio insured against a worse-than-expected outcome. It remains true that the confidence in the attainment of the desired outcome cannot be made absolute in the absence of real insurance.

Portfolio assurance programs can fail to provide the expected downside protection for several reasons. One of these is some failure in the hedging technology. While it is clear that the basic theoretical underpinnings for the dynamic hedging process are well understood, it is, of course, possible that the hedging manager would apply a faulty theoretical construct and thus fail to meet the specified minimum. In the absence of the guarantee, the client would simply be left to find a new manager for his hedging program. A similar outcome would arise from the intrusion of operator error into the hedging process. Failure to follow the dictates of the hedging algorithm either through inattention or a desire to outguess the market is the most obvious potential source of trouble here. Whatever the source of error, the portfolio insurance buyer is left holding the shortfall.

Finally, and perhaps most importantly, the potential for a discontinuous change in market values represents a case where the hedging process—even the most carefully constructed and monitored—cannot guarantee a prespecified outcome. Although the sort of discontinuity that would seriously damage the ability of the dynamic hedging program to produce the prespecified outcome is extraordinarily rare, it is not unthinkable. A catastrophic market decline —400 points on the Dow in a single day, for example—has the potential for making a portfolio insurance program miss its target.

GUARANTEEING THE HEDGING PROCESS

To solve some of these problems Aetna Life has developed a true insurance product it calls Guaranteed Equity Management (GEM). This product begins with the basic dynamic hedging process as developed by Leland, O'Brien and Rubinstein, and wraps around it a literal guarantee of the minimum outcome specified. The precise nature of this guarantee is modeled after the well understood Guaranteed Investment Contract (GIC) sold by most of the major U. S. life insurers. This GEM contract specifies that the depositor has the right to receive at the end of the agreed upon guarantee period either a minimum amount specified in the contract, or, alternatively, the market value of the Life Company Separate Account. In normal circumstances (i.e., in the absence of error or discontinuous market declines) this market value will always equal or exceed the guaranteed amount.

There are several noteworthy items about this guaranteed application of the dynamic hedging process. It does, of course, eliminate the criticism that portfolio insurance is not really insurance at all—in this format, it is in fact *true* portfolio insurance. The guarantee is subject to the same sort of insurance regulation (and hence confidence) that GIC's are subject to and thus can go a long way toward reassuring users of the hedging technology. Realized results cannot be below the prespecified minimum. It is important to note that the guarantee does not specify the precise extent of upside capture. Said another way, the insurance extends to the minimum value—the strike-price of the synthetic put that is created—but not the opportunity cost—the premium associated with the put—that exists on the upside.

Users of this guaranteed hedging alternative have generally not used it as a methodology for hedging the market risk of their entire portfolio, but instead have treated it as a specialty equity product that allows them to attain higher equity exposure without increasing downside risk. For some users it is an equity substitute. In this application, it is employed as either a short-term catastrophe insurance (e.g., a one-year, maximum 10% program) or an intermediate term no-loss guarantee (e.g., a three-year, 0% per annum minimum).

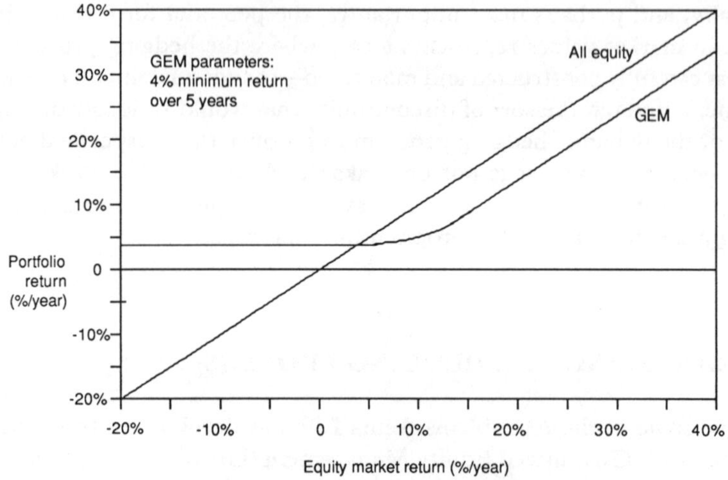

FIGURE 1. GEM payoff pattern

TABLE 1

	1 Year, −10%	3 Year, 0%
Initial Equity	.83	.716
Upside Capture	.987	.986

Upside Capture defined as $\frac{1 + \text{rate of return of protected portfolio}}{1 + \text{rate of return of Equity Portfolio}}$

As noted in Table 1, these programs give excellent equity exposure while eliminating the possibility of negative surprise.

Other users have viewed this as a way to create a "convertible GIC." Like a highly simplified convertible bond, this instrument has a bullet maturity with an insured return slightly below the existing market rate and the potential for upside participation in price appreciation above a certain level. A representative example in the current interest rate environment might be a five-year, 4 percent minimum return guarantee. The characteristics of this instrument are sketched on Figure 1.

NEW USES FOR THE GUARANTEED EQUITY MANAGEMENT CONCEPT

The existence of a literal guarantee offers the potential for uses beyond the pension arena where GEM has enjoyed its initial successes. As with all the dynamic hedging based products, GEM's key strength is that it allows asset pools to attain exposure to the higher expected returns of equities but protects the assets from the short-term negative volatility that heretofore have been the inevitable result of equity ownership. One such use that holds significant promise is in savings (defined contribution) and profit sharing plans. As plans of this sort grow in importance as sources of retirement income, it is increasingly important that short-term considerations do not unduly limit the investments undertaken for these assets. Historically, individuals have been very conservative in their savings plan asset allocation decisions—typically allocating under 20 percent of assets to the higher returning equity investments. While this clearly reflects the conservative bias of these decision-makers, it will tend to reduce longer-term returns. GEM serves to offset this negative outcome longer term by controlling short term uncertainty.

There are other uses for GEM that involve very long liability streams. One classic example would be a nuclear decommissioning fund. Theoretically, very long duration liabilities might justifiably use a 100 percent equity allocation. Regulatory authorities have been reluctant to allow an entirely unguaranteed use of equities in such a fund despite the fact that the very long-term nature of the future liabilities makes equities the investment medium of choice. A GEM structure could be targeted to solve both the regulatory concern and the desire for exposure to the higher equity returns. Other similar structured settlement programs could similarly benefit from GEM's unique risk control features.

Finally, we are hopeful that the existence of the guarantee will allow the successful development of a retail oriented product that will satisfy the consumer's desire for liquidity, for a known worse case outcome for his savings and for significant participation in the market's upside gains over time. Development of an appropriate retail vehicle will allow us to combine the power of the guaranteed outcome and the flexibility of the dynamic hedging process to produce a highly liquid, guaranteed equity vehicle.

16. CONSTANT HORIZON PORTFOLIO INSURANCE

Robert Clancy, Douglas Holmes, Larry Martin, and Scott Stewart

Portfolio insurance products have enjoyed growing popularity among institutional investors in recent months. The financial press has estimated that over 50 billion dollars in portfolios are currently insured in one form or another.

This chapter briefly describes two basic insurance strategies, discusses their advantages and disadvantages, and proposes a new method which is simpler to implement and suitable for commingling. The last two sections of the chapter present the results of a historical simulation and provide a summary.

CURRENT METHODS

Portfolio insurance is an investment strategy which ensures that the market value of a fund does not fall below a specified level while providing upside potential. The products currently offered by insurance vendors include option replication systems and constant proportion strategies. Option replication insurance offers performance similar to a put option on the insured portfolio. Through time, a hedge position is managed to provide the same sensitivity to the underlying portfolio as an option. Constant proportion portfolio insurance provides downside protection by monitoring the difference between the program's floor of protection and current value, and investing a portion of this difference in a risky asset.

Both forms of portfolio insurance are custom strategies tailored to individual funds. Each requires custom management, separate custodial services, and individual trading accounts. This is due to the parameter-dependent nature of portfolio insurance programs. When a hedging strategy is initiated, an investor must decide upon his floor, the size of his protected fund, and in some cases, his time horizon. During operation, the hedging strategy is monitored daily and is adjusted as time and market values change. As a result, an insurance program's current strategy will differ across systems if only one parameter differs. For example, suppose two accounts exhibit the same risky and riskless assets, identical floors and initial length of protection, and the same underlying model. The hedge position (and value of the insurance) will differ between the two accounts if the programs were not initiated at the same point in time.

In addition to being unsuitable for commingling, option replication strategies exhibit several idiosyncrasies. For example, as the system approaches its time horizon, the hedge position reaches a boundary solution or becomes very volatile. Nearby out-of-the-money replication programs are close to 100 percent in the market, in-the-money systems are close to 100 percent hedged and at-the-moneys vacillate significantly around a 50 percent hedge position. The insured party must also define a specific time horizon for the insurance program.

Constant proportion portfolio insurance (CPPI) does not require defining a time horizon and avoids boundary and volatile hedge positions. Unfortunately, it is difficult to estimate the "cost" of such a program in advance. For reasons discussed next, this makes it difficult to operate a separately managed insurance program using CPPI technology.

Portfolio insurance strategies which are managed independently of the protected fund involve setting up a short position in futures as a hedge against market declines. If the market rises, this short position will create a loss. If the market is higher at expiration than the initial value, the loss equals the cost of the insurance. The cost of option replication insurance can be estimated at any time using an option valuation formula.

Perold (1986)[1] has provided a method for estimating the value of an investment following a CPPI strategy given the price of the underlying risky asset, a volatility figure and a risk-free rate of return. However, we cannot estimate the cost of a CPPI insurance program independent of the underlying asset value. Depending on the hedging factor, there is a high boundary on the losses that the hedge position could generate. As a result, a large reserve or periodic contributions would be required to fund the hedging strategy. This makes it impractical to manage the constant proportion insurance independently of the protected fund.

[1] Footnotes appear at end of chapter.

CONSTANT HORIZON PORTFOLIO INSURANCE

Constant horizon portfolio insurance (CHPI)[2] is a strategy which provides clear boundaries, offers a defined cost and doesn't require specifying a time horizon. The strategy lends itself to commingling and therefore lower fees. When futures contracts are used to manage the hedging strategy, the system can both be run independently of the protected fund and provide daily liquidity. The product provides participants with the ability to take active bets, protect accumulated gains, or reduce volatility of pension fund returns.

The method is based on a modified Black-Scholes option valuation model which assumes a *constant* one year time to horizon. As a result, the strategy is path independent in frictionless markets, its hedge position depends only on market movements and its cost may be defined explicitly. Investors may contribute the cost of the put into one of a set of commingled funds, each differing only in its offered strike-price. Participants can realize any custom strategy by investing in several funds and modifying their participation through time. The required contribution to the fund equals the cost of the insurance and the fund's unit value increases when the stock market declines, offsetting the protected portfolio's decline in value.

We calculated some numerical examples to illustrate the behavior of the constant horizon method of portfolio insurance relative to the option replication and constant proportion strategies (Table 1). Suppose that annualized short-term rates are 5 percent, annual market volatility is 15 percent and no trading frictions exist. Table 1 lists hypothetical performance for the three strategies when the market either rises, remains the same, or decreases over a one-year period. The figures in Panel A were estimated using Black/Scholes (1973)[3] valuation formulas, the values in Panel B were computed from Perold's (1986)[1] constant proportion valuation formulas and the figures in Panel C were estimated from Monte Carlo simulations.

Panel A illustrates that it would cost $3.76 to insure a $100 portfolio against loss for one year while providing upside potential. If the market drops below its initial value, option replication insurance will protect the fund's value from falling below $100. When the market increases, the fund will participate fully in the rise. If the market remains flat, the $103.76 investment falls to $100.

Panel B illustrates the performance of a constant proportion strategy using a 2.5 investment factor under the same market scenarios. The reserve was set equal to the present value of $100 at a 5 percent discount rate, or $95.24. A $103.76 investment would yield a higher return than the option replication strategy when the market declined or was flat, but a lower return when the market rose substantially. It is important to note that the values listed will change when the proportion figure is adjusted.

The performance of the constant horizon strategy is illustrated in Panel C. In up markets, the strategy outperforms the constant proportion strategy and

TABLE 1. SAMPLE PERFORMANCE OF PORTFOLIO INSURANCE STRATEGIES (15% annual volatility, 5% short-term rates, protecting 100% of $100)

Panel A: Option Replication

	Initial	One Year Later Market Position		
		No Change	Up 20%	Down 20%
Portfolio	$100.00	$100.00	$120.00	$ 80.00
Insurance	3.76	0.00	0.00	20.00
Total	$103.76	$100.00	$120.00	$100.00

*Panel B: Constant Proportion**

	Initial	One Year Later Market Position		
		No Change	Up 20%	Down 20%
Reserve	$ 95.24	$100.00	$100.00	$100.00
Cushion	8.52	7.59	11.98	4.35
Total	$103.76	$107.59	$111.98	$104.35

Panel C: Constant Horizon

	Initial	One Year Later Market Position		
		No Change	Up 20%	Down 20%
Portfolio	$100.00	$100.00	$120.00	$ 80.00
Insurance	3.76	3.13	−0.53	17.33
Total	$103.76	$103.13	$119.47	$ 97.33

*Proportion factor = 2.5, initial reserve = 100 × (1/1.05).

in flat markets, outperforms the option replication strategy. CHPI provides a lower level of protection in down markets than the other strategies. This is because the modified option model's floor at every point in time equals the present value of the model's strike price. The option replication strategy's floor is also the present value of the strike, but this value increases as the time to horizon shrinks. The constant horizon's time to expiration never shrinks, however.

The value of the strategy at any point in time can be estimated roughly as a one year put option using the Black-Scholes formula. This estimate is biased however, because it ignores the interest earned through time on the cash balance. As an example, Table 1, Panel C lists a value of 17.33 for the constant horizon strategy when the market drops by 20%. A one-year Black-Scholes option under the same conditions would be worth 16.03.

Both Monte Carlo and real data simulations suggest that CHPI is path dependent. This means that the current value of a fund following the constant horizon strategy depends on the path the underlying assets followed before reaching their current level, not just the current level. Under real world conditions however, both CPPI and option replication strategies are clearly path dependent.

The constant horizon feature has a very clear advantage over the option replication strategy. Once an option replication program reaches its time horizon, its protection stops. Reinstituting the protection requires paying another cost. Under most conditions, constant horizon insurance does not require restarting. This compensates, in part, for the strategy's softer downside protection and is an added benefit under flat and up market conditions.

Constant horizon portfolio insurance also offers less extreme hedge positions than the option replication strategy. Table 2 presents hedge positions for the two strategies one month prior to expiration. When the market value of the underlying fund switches from 1 percent above the floor to 1 percent below, constant horizon portfolio insurance requires changing the effective hedge from 32 percent to 37 percent of the protected fund's market value. This represents a 5 percent change in the hedge with a 2 percent change in the value of the risky asset. With the same market changes, the hedge of an option replication strategy switches between 36 percent and 55 percent. This involves changing the hedge by 19 percent of the fund's value when the market changes by only 2 percent. If the market has risen 20 percent above the insurance floor, a constant horizon strategy would require hedging 5 percent while a replication system would recommend no hedging at all.

TABLE 2. SAMPLE HEDGING POSITIONS OF CONSTANT HORIZON AND OPTION REPLICATION INSURANCE STRATEGIES (15% annual volatility, 5% short-term rates, one month prior to expiration of the replicated option*)

Market Position Relative to Floor	Constant Horizon	Option Replication
Up 1%	32%	36%
Down 1%	37%	55%
Up 20%	5%	0%
Down 20%	86%	100%

*Hedging values were calculated from Black-Scholes valuation formulas.

It is important to note that the results in Tables 1 and 2 depend on the assumed parameter values. Varying the short-term rates and volatility figures will not change the Tables' implications, but will change the actual values.

In practice, volatility has a large impact on portfolio insurance programs. The volatility estimate affects the hedge strategy of both option replication and constant horizon insurance systems directly through the option valuation model. Realized volatility affects the hedge strategy of CPPI indirectly, through the size of the investment cushion. Ex post performance for all three methods of insurance are affected by volatility. The cost of portfolio insurance actually realized depends on the level of volatility experienced, not estimated.

SIMULATION RESULTS

We conducted a historical simulation of the constant horizon strategy between 1966 and 1985 to illustrate the performance of the insurance under realistic conditions. At the beginning of each year, we calculated a cost figure using a Black-Scholes valuation formula based upon the average 90-day Treasury bill yield, 15 percent market volatility and a fully insured $100 market weighted portfolio of all AMEX and NYSE common stocks. Each day we calculated the optimal hedge ratio and compared it with the current position. If the two levels differed by more than 3 percent, we adjusted the current hedge at a transaction cost of .35 percent.

The results are presented in Table 3. The table lists constant horizon insurance costs, year-end insured and uninsured portfolio values, and annualized Treasury bill yields for each of 20 years. The average cost in up markets was 3.03 percent when the insured fund averaged 125.04 compared to 125.49 for the underlying portfolio. The results show that the cost of the insurance was underestimated in several years. This is due to imperfect prediction of market volatility. In down markets, the cost averaged 2.93 and the total insured fund returned 97.41 compared to the underlying portfolio's 87.84.

The bottom panel in Table 3 lists compounded returns on both insured and uninsured investment strategies. The constant horizon system exhibited a return 8.20 percent higher than the uninsured investment over the 20 years, even though only 6 of the 20 years experienced down markets.

AN ADDED FEATURE

The previous sections have illustrated the performance of the constant horizon strategy when followed over one year periods. This section briefly

TABLE 3. HISTORICAL PERFORMANCE OF THE CONSTANT HORIZON STRATEGY (20 years of year-end performance, protection set at 100%*)

Year	Average T-bill Rate %	Beginning Protected Portfolio	Beginning Insurance	Ending Protected Portfolio	Ending Insurance	Ending Total Position
1966	4.76	100.00	3.81	91.24	7.35	98.59
1967	4.21	100.00	4.02	128.62	−1.42	127.20
1968	5.21	100.00	3.64	114.37	−0.29	114.08
1969	6.58	100.00	3.15	89.20	8.66	97.86
1970	6.53	100.00	3.17	100.19	3.10	103.29
1971	4.39	100.00	3.95	116.01	−1.14	114.87
1972	3.84	100.00	4.17	117.33	−0.70	116.63
1973	6.93	100.00	3.04	82.02	12.76	94.78
1974	8.00	100.00	2.70	72.84	20.38	93.22
1975	5.80	100.00	3.42	137.70	−2.33	135.37
1976	5.08	100.00	3.68	126.43	−1.57	124.86
1977	5.12	100.00	3.67	95.96	5.90	101.86
1978	7.18	100.00	2.95	108.01	0.16	108.17
1979	10.38	100.00	2.06	123.26	0.10	123.36
1980	11.24	100.00	1.86	132.62	−1.62	131.00
1981	14.71	100.00	1.20	95.79	2.36	98.15
1982	10.54	100.00	2.02	120.06	−0.84	119.22
1983	8.80	100.00	2.47	123.70	−0.57	123.13
1984	9.85	100.00	2.19	104.56	1.67	106.23
1985	7.72	100.00	2.79	130.94	−0.83	130.11

Averages

Market Type	Beginning Portfolio	Beginning Insurance	Ending Portfolio	Ending Insurance	Ending Total
Up Market (14)	100.00	3.03	125.49	−0.45	125.04
Down Market (6)	100.00	2.93	87.84	9.57	97.41

Compounded Return on Total Investment, 1966–1985

	Portfolio Alone	Protected Investment
% Compounded Return	460.38	468.58

*Trading conducted at a .35% cost when optimal and actual hedge position differs by more than 3%; portfolio return based on value weighted average of all AMEX and NYSE common stock returns; annual volatility set at 15%.

describes how custom portfolio insurance strategies may be implemented within a constant horizon commingled framework.

Suppose that a manager offers several commingled constant horizon funds, differing in strike prices, each with its own unit value. The hedging position for each fund is known by the manager at any point in time because he directs the allocation between the risky and riskless assets. By offering daily liquidity, investors can move assets between the different funds frequently.

The manager can offer custom hedging strategies by directing the allocation of clients' assets between the available funds. If an investor wishes to follow a hedging strategy which changes as a function of time in addition to market movements, the advisor can monitor the exposure and adjust the level of assets between funds through time. Any (non-negative) hedge may be replicated using the commingled funds by adjusting both the exposure between and the total contribution in the funds.

SUMMARY

Constant horizon portfolio insurance provides investors with an inexpensive method for limiting declines in the value of a fund while preserving upside market exposure. The strategy offers a cost which may be estimated with high confidence, doesn't require periodic contributions to renew protection and exhibits homogeneity across accounts invested in the same risky asset. These features are ideal for creating a family of commingled insurance products differing in strike-price and offering investors protection, daily liquidity, simplicity, and low fees. In addition, custom hedging strategies may be created by investing in more than one fund and adjusting the contributions through time.

FOOTNOTES

1. André Perold, "Constant Proportion Portfolio Insurance," Harvard Business School working paper, August 1986.
2. State Street Bank & Trust, "Portfolio Insurance: Technical Details," October, 1986.
3. Chapter 19: Fischer Black and Myron Scholes, "The Pricing of Options and Corporate Liabilities."

ROOTS

17. THE INTELLECTUAL ORIGINS OF PORTFOLIO INSURANCE

Michael R. Granito

Insuring a portfolio entails managing it in a way that alters the probabilities of particular return outcomes, compared with the risk profile of the unprotected or *reference* portfolio. The most common example is where the reference portfolio consists of a diversified portfolio of stocks, but the managed or *protected* portfolio is to have a zero probability of a return, as of some fixed horizon, below a defined level, say, −5 percent. We often call the difference between a zero return and the minimum acceptable return the *deductible*. Otherwise the protected portfolio should have a return distribution similar to that of the reference portfolio.

In the example we have chosen, the analogy between portfolio insurance and an option is immediate. The desired protection would be obtained by purchasing a put option on the portfolio with exercise price equal to 95 percent of the current portfolio value. The cost of the protection is the cost of the put. In more general settings, we might wish to have a more complex *payoff pattern*. For instance, we might want to keep the −5 percent deductible, a *floor return* of −5 percent, but we might also stipulate that between −5 percent and 20 percent we want a return comparable to the reference portfolio, and above 20 percent we will accept a return lower than the reference portfolio return. We might be willing to forego the upside in this example to help reduce the cost of the insurance. The ranges might also be selected so as to complement our subjective view of market return possibilities. In fact, we could specify a completely general payoff function that would state the portfolio value we sought, on the selected horizon, as a function of the value of the reference portfolio. The particular function we might want should reflect our view on the market, compared with concensus views, as well as our attitude toward risk in a very comprehensive sense.

It is evident that this expanded example of what we might mean by portfolio insurance goes well beyond the simple concept of owning a put. Instead we are talking about a generalized option. This suggests three questions. How do we know the precise option that an individual *should* want? How do we price such an option? Once we have identified the desired option, how do we obtain it in a market where only the simplest put and call options are actually traded? These questions have occupied much attention in financial theory since the late 1960s beginning with Merton's[1,2] pioneering work on dynamic portfolio optimization in a continuous time model. His analysis introduced into mainstream financial theory the model for security prices and the associated optimization principles that would lead to important theoretical advances in asset pricing and investor behavior. Two topics have received particular attention: option pricing and the individual's investment/consumption decision—topics which hold the answers to our questions. The papers in this section are an important contribution to this literature that have particular relevance to portfolio insurance. Our objective in this introduction is to provide an overview of how financial theory answers these questions, with particular reference to the cited works.

WHAT OPTION SHOULD AN INDIVIDUAL WANT?

In trying to determine the type of option an individual might want, financial theory does not start with option analysis per se. Instead it begins with the more general question of how an investor decides to allocate investment and consumption over time, when faced with uncertain prices, asset returns, income, and so on. In fact, Merton's[2] original analysis, which used a continuous time model to build on the discrete time multi-period models of Hakansson,[3] Long[4] and others, provided the general theory of this problem. That theory allowed us to specify an economy in which critical parameters are functions of new variables, called *state variables*, which themselves evolve randomly in a prescribed way. By appropriate choice of the state variables, and the economic system's dependence on them, we could make our model as realistic as we wished. One of the important features of this overall method is that we can normally obtain certain broad conclusions regarding optimal investor behavior, regardless of the complexity of the model. In particular, it will be optimal generally for the individual to manage his assets using a method that we now call *dynamic hedging*. That is, the optimal percentages in different asset categories should be systematically and continuously varied as a function of portfolio value and other factors, including the values of the state variables.

[1] Footnotes appear at end of chapter.

The problem with general models that capture many of the uncertainties of the real world is that the specific rules for an individual's behavior cannot be determined. All we can do is identify a differential equation whose solution gives the answer, but for which there is no known analytic solution. Consequently, much research has focused on a simpler problem that is soluable, but which contains important implications for behavior in more general settings. Specifically, researchers assumed that the individual had to continuously allocate funds between consumption and investment. There was a single consumption good and two investment vehicles—cash earning a constant rate of return, and a single risky asset whose expected rate of return and standard deviation were fixed parameters. The individual's problem was to maximize his lifetime expected utility, subject to the constraint that his resources were limited to an initial wealth endowment. We call this paradigm the *standard model.*

Merton[2] was the first to solve this problem in a continuous time model under a particular assumption for the individual's utility function. Specifically, he assumed a general form called the hyperbolic absolute risk aversion (HARA) utility which is viewed as an important class because of its ability to represent the behavior of many individuals.[5] Although Merton did not focus on this specific application, this form is particularly important for portfolio insurance. The reason is that it allows us to assign a sensible measure of utility to wealth levels above some critical value, but infinite negative utility to wealth levels equal or lower than the critical value—a value which itself could be moving over time. The resulting investor behavior would then represent the following objective: Maximize the appropriate measure of economic well-being in a way that assures wealth will not fall below some target level.

In terms of our original question—what option should an individual want? —the importance of Merton's work is that relatively simple adaptations of his model lead to investment allocation rules that provide portfolio insurance. Moreover, the rules have normative significance since they result from a utility optimization problem. That is, they get at the question of what the investor *should want*. Of course, we have not yet drawn the conclusion that the resulting investment resembles an option. This finding would await the results of Black[6] and Cox and Leland.[7]

Before publishing his celebrated option paper coauthored with Myron Scholes,[8] Black examined certain dynamic properties of the simple consumption/investment problem considered by Merton, but assuming a completely general utility function. By examining the process of obtaining the optimal solution, he found a general equation that the optimal investment rule would always obey. In this case, the investment rule would be expressed as the amount of money the individual would choose to invest in the risky asset as a function of wealth and time (along with a subsidiary equation representing an initial condition). In fact, Black found that any specific investment rule that obeyed this equation, along with a consistent rule expressing consumption as a function of wealth and time, would represent an optimal program for some utility maximizing individual.

For our purpose, the importance of this finding is that it gives us a new framework for evaluating investment strategies. The traditional method is to start with a utility function and derive the optimal investment rule—a difficult process that often fails to produce an analytic expression for the desired rule due to the complexity of the associated solution process. In contrast, we frequently have an investment rule in mind based upon intuition regarding a practical solution for the investment problem at hand. Black's equation now lets us evaluate whether the rule is optimal. Specifically, if the investment rule —along with any associated rule for withdrawals from the fund that would represent consumption—obeys Black's equation, then the rule is optimal for some plausible attitude toward risk and return.

Black's work foresaw the importance of engineered solutions to investment problems. As an example, the paper offers a simple solution for a practical task of protecting the value of a portfolio that corresponds to the HARA utility formulation of Merton. This method is referred to as *constant proportion portfolio insurance* in a recent paper by Perold.[9] An implication of Black's approach is that it may be easier to invent a solution to the problem, and then justify its optimalability, than the reverse. A similar spirit characterizes the work of Cox and Leland,[7] whose work complement's Black's to enable us to reach our original goal—identify the option characteristics of optimal investment strategies.

Ten years after Black's analysis, Cox and Leland[7] considered the question of what type of investment strategies cause the investor's wealth level at a future date to be a function of only time and price of the risky asset. That is, future wealth should not depend on the path taken by the risky asset price, but only on its ending value. They call this condition *path independence*. Assuming the same economic model as Merton[2] and Black,[6] they find a general equation that the investment rule must obey in order for path independence to obtain. Remarkably, the condition for path independence is identical to Black's equation, which assures optimality. Moreover, if path independence holds at a particular point, it will at each intervening point. That is, a strategy that causes wealth to be a function of time and the risky asset price, as of a particular horizon, allows this same result for any horizon over which the path independence condition continuously holds.

What conclusions can be drawn for our original question—what option should an individual want? In the simple world with a constant risk-free rate and a single risky asset whose return mean and variance are also constant, a utility optimal investment rule satisfies Black's equation. Cox and Leland show that this same equation, which we now refer to as the Black, Cox, Leland equation, implies path independence. Consequently, an optimal policy can be represented by the payoff that it produces at a future date. This is simply a generalized option—a function that specifies the desired portfolio value as a function of the value of the risky asset price. Of course, this finding is predicated on the simple economic model the authors assumed. The results break down in more general settings such as economies with random interest rates, random expected risky asset returns, and so on. In general, a path independent solution may not be optimal, or even obtainable, in such cases. Nonetheless, the normative implications of path independent models have had profound impact on the thought process of providing portfolio insurance. Several studies now document the efficiency loss associated with suboptimal path dependent policies. See for instance Rubinstein[10] and Dybvig.[11]

Our discussion has, to now, simply justified the notion that the individual should want an investment rule that is executed through dynamic hedging and that, under the assumptions of the standard model, some form of an option is optimal. We have not yet considered what type of option is appropriate. In general, this depends on the utility function of the individual. In fact, when we know in advance that the assumptions of the model imply path independence, we can use a shortcut for determining the desired option, without using the solution method outlined by Merton.[2] Leland[12] employs this method to draw conclusions regarding the option appropriate for the representative investor. In general, the optimal payoff function depends on the investor's marginal utility function, his subjective probability distribution for market returns, and the cost of providing a payoff in particular states of nature. Buying portfolio insurance causes a portfolio payoff function to be more convex—to be flatter for low risky asset prices and then rise more steeply. Consequently, Leland associates the theoretical preconditions for wanting a more convex payoff with the motivation to insure. He finds two conditions that would lead to a more convex payoff, and hence a disposition to insure: (1) the individual is more optimistic than consensus; or (2), the individual is, in a particular sense, more aggressive than average. In either case, the individual often has a *more* risky portfolio than otherwise but insures the portfolio to reduce downside risk. Related findings have been obtained by Brennan and Solanski.[13]

In reviewing our findings for the type of option an investor would want, it is worth stressing the absence of theoretical support for a simple fixed horizon, conventional put option. First, even in the standard model where path independence is optimal, and a generalized option strategy represents the desired outcome, the *horizon* must be carefully interpreted. When we pick a horizon, we must make sure that the payoff required on that date agrees with the optimal program implied by Black's equation. Otherwise, inefficiency costs will creep in. Second, the payoff function itself is expected to be a smooth increasing function of the risky asset price—not kinked. Perhaps most surprising of all, in theory investors frequently demand portfolio insurance to not to reduce risk but to ultimately increase risk—by buying a higher risk portfolio and insuring it.

HOW DO WE PRICE SUCH AN OPTION?

After identifying the option that is appropriate for an investor, the valuation process is essential for two reasons. First, and obvious, the parameters of the option payoff must be adjusted so that the investor can afford it. Second, the valuation method is intimately linked with the problem of providing the option, a question we deal with in the next section. In this section, we review the major findings in options pricing.

Although option pricing had been studied for some time, it was not until the well known Black-Scholes paper that a fully rigorous general equilibrium solution for put and call pricing was advanced. Using methods introduced by Merton, and assuming the standard model employed in the last section, Black-Scholes made the following observations. If the option price was a function of only time and the risky asset price, then it is possible to form a position in the option and the risky asset that would be riskless, over a short period of time. This implied that the net capital tied up in the position must earn the risk-free rate of return. The differential equation expressing this relationship is then solved to yield the Black-Scholes formula. The same method could be used to price a put or a call, although given one, put-call parity—that had been advanced by Stoll[14] somewhat earlier—would price the other.

What distinguished the Black-Scholes paper from earlier attempts is their use of arbitrage to price the option. This frees them from having to make assumptions regarding investor utility functions, wealth endowments, or other features of the economy. Their method for constructing a riskless hedge would become a standard approach in the analysis of any *contingent claim*—a security whose value derives solely from the values of other securities.

In the period surrounding the Black-Scholes paper, and during the subsequent five years, there were a significant number of important papers on option pricing, which today represent the main body of theory. For example, at the same time as Black-Scholes, Merton[15] published a classic paper that examined diverse facets of the theory including relationships between European and American options and an extension of the standard model to allow certain forms of random interest rates—a topic of particular importance in applied settings for providing portfolio insurance. Cox[16] examined option pricing when the variance of return on the risky asset is not a constant, but depends on the asset price in a particular way. Cox and Ross[17] consider alternative stochastic processes for the risky asset price—including jump processes, or cases where price movements can be randomly discontinuous in a particular way. In providing exact pricing for particular types of options, these models expanded our understanding of valuation methodology. Two particularly important contributions that would have major influence on both the theory, as well as the practice of general option valuation, are risk neutral valuation and the binomial model.

The original Black-Scholes paper illustrated that the option price was a type of expected present value of the option payoff. But the present value was computed as if the expected return on the risky asset was the risk-free rate! This observation was generalized by Cox and Ross[17] who articulated the concept of risk neutral valuation. Since the option is priced by arbitrage, the solution must be consistent with any risk preference structure. Consequently, we can also compute the option's price via the expected utility method, but where the expected rates of return agree—in the sense of an economic equilibrium—with the preferences assumed. The simplest structure would be a world of risk neutral investors, in which case, the equilibrium expected return on the risky asset must equal the risk-free rate—or an arbitrage would occur. In this world, the option price is simply the expected present value of the future payoff, discounted at the risk-free rate.

The concept of risk neutral valuation has had important generalizations to allow extensions of option pricing to other economic settings—that is, beyond the standard model of a constant risk-free rate and constant mean and variance of return on the risky asset. Specifically, in more general settings we have the concept of a risk-adjusted expected present value. These methods amount to rules for identifying the probability distribution that should be used for computing the present value of the option's payoff. A related idea that emerged, in a series of papers, is the notion that we can identify today's cost of a dollar payment in particular future state of the world. For instance, we could identify the cost today of receiving $1 at the horizon, if the risky asset price turns out to equal say, $105. The total value of the option is simply the sum of the values of all the contingent payoffs. This concept was also implicit in the original Black-Scholes analysis, and has been extended to more general economic models. See Ross[18] and Breeden and Litzenberger.[19]

These developments provide us with a rich understanding of how to theoretically value a generalized option, with important extensions for how to proceed in circumstances outside the standard model. It often turns out however that, in practice, the most difficult step is to numerically value the option—that is, perform the theoretical calculations. One of the most important solution methods in applied problems, that allows extensions beyond the standard model, is the binomial method advanced by Cox, Ross and Rubinstein.[20] In developing a pricing formula for a standard call option, they illustrate how to replace the continuous time model for security prices with a binomial model, and then recursively apply a solution procedure to compute today's option value. Their method of calculation illustrates the underlying economics of option valuation, and can be adjusted to reflect additional complexities of a real world problem. As a numerical procedure for obtaining option values, their method can be compared with alternative methods within the general realm of numerical analysis. Because of its focus on successive present value calculations it is known as an *explicit* method. Alternative *implicit* methods exist that have certain computational advantages. Nonetheless, the binomial method clarifies the economics of the problem, and has enjoyed widespread use in practice for valuing many types of options both within and beyond the standard model.

HOW DO WE PROVIDE THE DESIRED OPTION?

Once we have identified and priced the desired option, providing it is a theoretically simple task that can be fraught with real world problems. We begin with recognition that no traded option is likely to satisfy our requirements. Consequently we must use a *replication* technique that was implicit in the original Black-Scholes methodology, but first stressed as a practical technique by Rubinstein and Leland.[21]

From the arbitrage mechanism by which options are priced we know that a position in the option and an offsetting position in the risky asset produces a cash return. By reversing this reasoning, a position in cash and the risky asset must reproduce the option's return. By continuously adjusting the amount in cash—as a function of time, the risky asset price and other factors—we can synthetically produce the option return. A similar procedure is, in principle, used to replicate any option, including those outside of the standard model.

While this is simple enough in theory, practical difficulties emerge. First, the risky asset is normally a diversified reference portfolio that is not easily traded. This has led to the use of futures to adjust market exposure. While futures are more liquid (although not perfectly liquid), they possess an imperfect correlation with the reference portfolio, and so, an element of tracking error is introduced. Moreover, futures can be subject to pricing error that can work to the disadvantage of the program.

A second problem has to do with random variation in parameters not accounted for in the standard model. The two primary variables are interest rates and randomness in the variance of the risky asset. It turns out that, subject to a few assumptions about the risk of interest rate movements, the interest rate problem can be accounted for using an adjustment to the standard model, leading to a revised option formula. An adjustment method outlined by Merton[15] is often employed. The more serious problem involves random volatility. Fluctuations in volatility can substantially influence the cost of the replicated insurance. There is no general method for eliminating this uncertainty unless we are allowed to trade in instruments whose prices are themselves influenced by volatility. Essentially, this means that we must use traded options in the replication program to hedge uncertain volatility.

A third problem relates to the fixed and variable transaction costs associated with trading—even aside from the problem of needing to use futures in lieu of the cash securities. There is a commission involved in most trades, as well as a potential market impact. Moreover, trading cannot be literally continuous as theory dictates, and so, we must decide how to trade at discrete intervals so as to optimize the program outcome. We should also measure the impact of the trading approach we employ in order to adjust—in advance—the estimated cost of the option. These are difficult problems.

Leland[22] has developed a transaction cost adjusted option price in the standard model, when transactions occur at regular intervals. However, in general this will not be optimal. The timing of trades, and their magnitude, is best determined using an optimized dynamic model that reflects diverse features of the program as well as its current status—time to expiration, risky asset price, assured market value, interest rate, volatility, and so on.

A fourth problem is the impact of discontinuous markets that are not contemplated by the standard model. Such occurrences can immobilize the dynamic trading process, thus causing the replication technique to fail.

The complexity of these issues, particularly as they relate to replicating a conventional kinked payoff pattern, have lead researchers and practitioners alike to look for simpler, more robust forms of insurance. One direction of research seeking to simplify insurance has led back to Merton's[2] model outlining the optimal program for an individual with a HARA class utility. It may be recalled, Black also examined this framework as a way to provide portfolio insurance. Under the assumptions of the standard model, a rather simple allocation rule is optimal—thus avoiding some of the complexities of specific valuation models. Moreover, this allocational rule still gives a fairly simple and useful outcome even when we relax assumptions of the standard model to include random interest rates and volatility—even though it may no longer be an optimal rule for the HARA utility. The method also appears rather flexible with respect to the definition of the minimum acceptable market value. Calling it Constant Proportion Portfolio Insurance, Andre Perold[9] has explored this method at length, including adjustments for the effect of transaction costs. A great deal of work is currently underway that further explores and generalizes this approach. See for instance Black and Perold.[23]

Other avenues of research seek ways to mitigate the impact of market discontinuities. One approach employs the concept of a generalized option that is implicit in Merton's[2] analysis, where the risky asset is itself a managed portfolio containing valuation judgments. Discussed by Granito,[24] this method merges asset allocation and insurance to reduce the transaction intensiveness of the process, while providing a portfolio outcome that is theoretically preferred under certain conditions. Other approaches employ option valuation models allowing jumps in market prices, such as Cox and Ross[17] and Merton.[25] New insights are likely to emerge, and progress made, as insurance techniques continue to be reshaped and improved by practice.

FOOTNOTES

1. Robert C. Merton, "Lifetime Portfolio Selection Under Uncertainty: The Continuous-Time Case," *Review of Economic Statistics*, August, 1969.
2. Robert C. Merton, "Optimum Consumption and Portfolio Rules in a Continuous-Time Model," *Journal of Economic Theory*, December, 1971.
3. Nils Hakansson, "Optimal Investment and Consumption Strategies For a Class of Utility Functions," Western Management Science Institute, UCLA Working Paper, June 1966.
4. John B. Long, "Consumption-Investment Decisions and Equilibrium in the Securities Market," In Studies in the Theory of Capital Markets, M. C. Jensen editor, Preager, 1972.
5. See for instance, Irwin Friend and Marshall Blume, "The Demand for Risky Assets," *American Economic Economic Review*, 1975.
6. Chapter 18: Fischer Black, "Individual Investment and Consumption Strategies Under Uncertainty."
7. John C. Cox and Hayne E. Leland, "On Dynamic Investment Strategies," Proceedings of the Seminar on the Analysis of Security Prices, Volume 27, No. 2, November 1982.
8. Chapter 19: Fischer Black and Myron Scholes, "The Pricing of Options and Corporate Liabilities."
9. Andre F. Perold, "Constant Proportion Portfolio Insurance," Harvard Business School, working paper, August, 1986.
10. Chapter 2: Mark Rubinstein, "Alternative Paths to Portfolio Insurance."
11. Philip Dybvig, "Inefficient Dynamic Portfolio Strategies," Yale University School of Organization and Management, working paper, 1986.
12. Chapter 21: Hayne E. Leland, "Who Should Buy Portfolio Insurance."
13. Michael Brennan and R. Solanski, "Optomal Portfolio Insurance," *Journal of Financial and Quantitative Analysis*, September, 1981.
14. Hans Stoll, "The Relationship Between Put and Call Prices," *Journal of Finance*, December, 1969.
15. Robert C. Merton, "The Rational Theory of Option Pricing," *Bell Journal of Economics and Management Science*, Spring, 1973.
16. John C. Cox, "Constant Elasticity of Variance Option Pricing," unpublished manuscript.
17. John C. Cox and Stephen A. Ross, "The Valuation of Options for Alternative Stochaster Processes," *Journal of Financial Economics*, January–March, 1976.
18. Stephen A. Ross, "Options and Efficiency," Quarterly Journal of Economics, 1976.
19. Douglas Breeden and Robert Litzenberger, "Determining State Prices Implicit in Option Prices," *Journal of Business*, 1978.
20. Chapter 20: John C. Cox, Stephen A. Ross and Mark Rubinstein, "Option Pricing: A Simplified Approach."
21. Chapter 22: Mark Rubinstein and Hayne Leland, "Replicating Options with Positions in Stock and Cash."
22. Hayne E. Leland, "Option Replication with Transaction Costs," *Journal of Finance*, 1985.
23. Fischer Black and Andre Perold, "The Theory of Constant Proportional Portfolio Insurance," Harvard Business School Working Paper, October 1987.
24. Michael R. Granito, "Redefining Portfolio Insurance: The Safety Net," The Money Management Forum, Institutional Investor, November 1987.
25. Robert C. Merton, "Option Pricing for Jump Processes," Journal of Financial Economics, 1976.

18. INDIVIDUAL INVESTMENT AND CONSUMPTION UNDER UNCERTAINTY

Fischer Black

OVERVIEW

This paper is an analysis of how the individual, attempting to maximize the total utility over his lifetime of his consumption and his final wealth, should decide on his level of investment and his rate of consumption at each point in time.

The analysis shows that instead of specifying his utility function on consumption and final wealth, the individual may specify his rate of comsumption as a function of wealth and time, and his initial level of investment as a function of wealth. These functions determine his utility function, but may be used to derive his investment function without finding his utility function at all.

Writing x(w, t) for the individual's investment function, c(w, t) for his consumption function, and y(w) for his initial investment function, the equations that determine the individual's investment function given his consumption and initial investment functions are as follows:

$$x_2 = (r - c_1)x - (wr - c)x_1 - \tfrac{1}{2}s^2x^2x_{11}$$

$$x(w, 0) = y(w)$$

When the consumption function is linear in wealth at each point in time, and the initial investment function is linear in wealth, these equations may be solved analytically. The resulting investment function is linear in wealth at each point in time, and its derivative with respect to wealth is constant in time.

When the consumption function is strictly proportional to wealth at each point in time, and the initial investment function is strictly proportional to wealth, the solution has the following form:

$$x = bw$$

This investment function is independent of the consumption function, and is constant in time.

The assumptions underlying this analysis include the following: (1) That the individual can borrow or lend as much as he wants, either for investment or for consumption, at a reasonable interest rate; (2) That he invests only in a "market portfolio"; and (3) that his rate of consumption at one point in time does not influence the utility of his rate of consumption at any other time.

INTRODUCTION

One of the earliest papers to treat the problem of the individual's portfolio allocation and consumption decisions through time, taking into account the uncertainty in the returns on the individual's portfolio, was that of Phelps.[1] He looked at the case where there is a single investment opportunity with an uncertain return, and where an individual, in any period, may consume a unit of income or wealth, or may invest it in the single investment opportunity. He assumed that the individual's utility of lifetime consumption had a very special form, equal to the sum over all periods of a single utility function applied to consumption in that period, discounted at a constant rate to the present.

His restrictive assumption about the individual utility function was not too serious, but his assumption that the individual has only two choices—consumption or investment in the risky opportunity—was serious. Because he did not include borrowing or lending as one of the individual's choices, he was not able to obtain realistic analytic solutions.

He did, however, introduce the technique of dynamic programming that most later researchers have used in working on this problem. The individual maximizes his expected utility over the possible values of next period consumption, using a derived utility function on his wealth at the end of the next period. By applying this equation to each consumption period in the individual's life, he gets a closed form solution to the individual's investment and consumption decision problem.

[1] Footnotes appear at end of chapter.

Tobin[2] deviated from this technique, and therefore solved a different problem. He assumed a utility function on final wealth only, with no intermediate consumption. And he assumed that the individual must decide ahead of time how much he is going to have invested in each period, rather than deciding in each period how much he will have invested, on the basis of the outcomes of his investments in previous periods. As a result of this assumption, he found that the optimal strategy involves the individual keeping the same amount invested in each period (if the interest rate is zero), and thus providing diversification over time as well as diversification across securities.

Mossin[3] presented a model that offered the investor a choice of two assets, one risky and one riskless, so he was able to obtain realistic and closed-form solutions that Phelps was not able to obtain. He allowed the investor to base his decision on how much to invest in each asset in each period on the outcomes of previous investments, so he avoided the restrictive assumptions of Tobin's model. His solutions were not as simple as they might have been, however, because he used discrete periods rather than continuous time. And he did not include the consumption decision at all.

The most general form of the methodology introduced by Phelps is developed by Fama.[4] Fama uses a completely general utility function on lifetime consumption,[4] and shows that the individual can make his decision on allocation of his wealth between consumption and investment in one or more assets as if he had a utility function that depended only on his next-period consumption and his end-of-period wealth. He does not, however, derive any specific investment and consumption strategies for specific utility functions.

Levhari and Srinivasan[5] extend Phelps' analysis by giving the individual the choice of two risky assets, but they do not change the form of Phelps' utility function on the individual's lifetime consumption stream.

Samuelson[6] and Merton[7] carry Mossin's analysis one step further by introducing consumption into his model, and by going to a continuous time model from a discrete time model. They maintain the special type of utility function used by Phelps, and by Levhari and Srinivasan.

Meyer[16] uses a continuous time model with consumption, and analyzes both the Phelps utility function and an analogous multiplicative utility function. He considers the case where an individual has an infinite lifetime rather than a finite lifetime.

Merton[9] extends the analysis to a completely general additive utility function of the type that will be described below. Many of his results parallel those derived in this paper.

The papers previously discussed are all set in a world of uncertainty. They were based in part on previous analyses of the individual's lifetime investment and consumption strategy under certainty, by such authors as Fisher,[10] Friedman,[11] and Modigliani and Brumberg.[12] The principal contribution of this work to the development of individual strategy under uncertainty was the idea that the individual makes his consumption and investment decisions in the light of his expected income throughout his lifetime, rather than paying attention only to this current level of income.

There is a radically different approach to individual investment strategy that was originated by Markowitz,[13] by Latané,[14] and by Latané and Tuttle.[15] This approach takes the view that the individual wants to maximize the "expected long-run rate of return" of his portfolio, rather than the expected utility of his terminal wealth. Since it does not use the principle of maximizing expected utility, it is inconsistent with most of economic theory. In addition, the results that Latané and Tuttle obtain do not seem reasonable: The optimum portfolio strategy for an individual, using their approach, turns out to be completely independent of his risk preferences.

INVESTMENT AND CONSUMPTION STRATEGY

We will assume that the individual decides, at each point in time, on a level of investment in the market portfolio, and on a rate of consumption, in order to maximize the expected utility of his lifetime consumption and his final wealth. His decision process is dynamic, in that the level of investment in the market portfolio and his rate of consumption may depend on the outcome of past investments, and on changes in his anticipated future income.

We will assume that the amount that the individual can have invested in the market portfolio is not limited either by his current wealth or by his rate of consumption. We will assume that he is able to lend any part of his wealth that he does not want to invest in the market portfolio, and that he can borrow as much as he wants if he wants to have more than his current wealth invested in the market portfolio. Thus the individual has just two decision variables at any point in time: The level of his investment in the market portfolio, and his rate of consumption.

The most general utility function on lifetime consumption and terminal wealth that the individual can have would have the following form:

$$U(C_1, C_2, \ldots, C_n, W_n, W_{n+1}; S_n)$$

This form, which was introduced by Fama,[4] gives the individual's utility as a function of his consumption C_k in each of n periods, his terminal wealth W_n, and a variable S_n describing the state of the world.

We will assume a more restrictive utility function, in which the variable S_n is omitted, and in which total utility is the sum of separate utility functions for each period:

$$U_1(C_1) + U_2(C_2) + \cdots + U_n(C_n) + U_{n+1}(W_{n+1})$$

This type of utility function is sometimes called an "additive" utility function. It implies, in particular, that the level of past consumption does not affect the utility of current consumption.

We assume also that the utility functions U_k change continuously, so that $U_{k+1}(C)$ is not very different from $U_k(C)$.

Finally, we assume that individuals prefer more wealth to less wealth, and that each individual is risk-averse:

$$\begin{aligned} \frac{\partial}{\partial C_k} U_k(C_k) &> 0 \\ \frac{\partial^2}{\partial C_k^2} U_k(C_k) &< 0 \end{aligned} \tag{1}$$

We define the individual's total wealth as his current wealth, plus the present market value of his anticipated future income from all sources. Writing W_k for his total wealth in period k, W_k^0 for his current wealth in period k, $\tilde{I}_j$ for his uncertain income in future period j, and $PV(\tilde{I})$ for the present market value of income $\tilde{I}$, we have:

$$W_k = W_k^0 + PV(\tilde{I}_{k+1}) + PV(\tilde{I}_{k+2}) + \cdots + PV(\tilde{I}_n) \tag{2}$$

The concept of the market value of an individual's future income is a little odd, since individuals do not usually sell shares in their future income. Indeed, some economists claim that if an individual were able to sell shares in even a small fraction of his future income, the value of his future income would decline, because his incentive to increase his future income would be reduced. But we can define the concept of the market value of an individual's future income without allowing the individual himself to sell shares in his future income. The market value can be the value that would be placed on the individual's income by other individuals, making side bets. In other words, there could be a market for shares in an individual's income, with some investors holding long positions and other investors holding short positions, without the individual himself being able to participate in the market. Equivalently, we may assume that the individual has no future income, or that all his future income is certain.

Using either set of assumptions, the individual's investment and consumption decisions in each period will depend only on his total wealth at the start of the period, and on his utility function.

We assume that the distribution of possible returns on the market portfolio is the same in each period, and that the short-term interest rate at which an individual may borrow or lend is the same in each period. We will write $\Delta\tilde{M}_k$ for the excess return on the market portfolio in period k (the return minus the short term interest rate), and R for the short-term interest rate.

Writing C_k for the amount the individual consumes in period k, and X_k for the amount he has invested in the market portfolio, his wealth in period $k + 1$ will be related to his wealth in period k by:

$$\tilde{W}_{k+1} = W_k + W_k R - C_k + X_k \Delta \tilde{M}_k \quad (3)$$

Now we can define a series of derived utility functions $EU_k(W_k)$ that give the expected utility in period k of the individual's optimal investment and consumption strategy, starting with wealth W_k. The derived utility function for period k can be written in terms of the derived utility function for period $k+1$ as follows:

$$EU_k[W_k] = \max_{C_k, X_k} E[U_k(C_k) + EU_{k+1}[W_k + W_k R - C_k + X_k \Delta \tilde{M}_k]] \quad (4)$$

Taking the indicated maximum over all possible values of C_k and X_k defines the individual's consumption strategy and investment strategy as a function of his wealth, and all of the derived utility functions.

$C_k(W_k)$	Consumption strategy.
$X_k(W_k)$	Investment strategy.
$EU_k(W_k)$	Derived utility functions.

Thus the individual's consumption strategy gives his consumption as a function of his wealth and time; and his investment strategy gives the level of his investment in the market portfolio as a function of his wealth and time.

This framework is consistent with the general consumption function introduced by Modigliani and Brumberg[12] for the case of certainty. In their notation, the consumption function is:

$$\bar{c}_\tau = f(v_t, t, \tau) \quad \tau = t, t + 1, \ldots, L$$

$$v_t = \sum_{\tau=t}^{N} \frac{y_\tau}{(1 + r)^{\tau+1-t}} + a_t$$

In these equations, t is the age of the individual, τ is a time variable, y_τ is the individual's income at time τ, r is the rate of interest, and a_t is his wealth at age t.

The framework developed above is also consistent with the "permanent income hypothesis" developed by Friedman.[11] Temporary increases in income affect total wealth, and thus the individual's rate of consumption, much less than increases that are expected to be permanent.

THE CONTINUOUS TIME CASE

The preceding equations were written for the case in which the investor makes his consumption and investment decisions at discrete intervals. We will now turn to the case where he makes his consumption and investment decisions continuously. His consumption strategy gives his rate of consumption as a function of his wealth and time, and his investment strategy gives his level of investment in the market as a function of his wealth and time. Time is now a continuous variable.

Instead of C_k for the individual's consumption in period k, we will write c for the individual's rate of consumption. Instead of X_k for the individual's level of investment in the market portfolio in period k, we will write x for the individual's level of investment in the market portfolio. Instead of $U_k(C_k)$ for the increment to the individual's utility from his consumption in period k, we will write v(c, t) for the rate of increase in his utility with rate of consumption c at time t. Instead of $U_{n+1}(W_{n+1})$ for the individual's utility of final wealth, we will write z(w) for his utility of final wealth. Instead of R for the interest earned in a single period, we will write r for the rate of interest. Thus the correspondence is:

Discrete Time	Continuous Time
W_k	w
C_k	c
X_k	x
$U_k(C_k)$	v(c, t)
$U_{n+1}(W_{n+1})$	z(w)
R	r

We will assume that the return on the market portfolio over any period follows a lognormal distribution. Since the returns on the market portfolio in successive periods are independent, the variance of the log of one plus the return on the market must be proportional to the length of the period. The constant of proportionality we will write as s^2. For small intervals, the distribution of the return on the market is approximately normal, and the variance of the distribution is approximately $s^2\Delta t$. In the limit, as Δt goes to zero, this approximation becomes exact. So we can speak of s^2 as the rate of variance of the return on the market portfolio.

Similarly, we can write a for the rate of expected excess return on the market. (The excess return on a portfolio in any period is the return on the portfolio minus the interest earned in that period.) The expected excess return on the market in a short interval is approximately $a\Delta t$. In the limit as

Δt goes to zero, this approximation becomes exact. So we can speak of a as the rate of expected excess return on the market.

We will use $\Delta\tilde{m}$ for the actual excess return on the market over a small interval Δt. Writing E[ ] for expected value, we have the following relations, which become exact in the limit as Δt goes to zero.

$$E[\Delta\tilde{m}] = a\Delta t$$
$$E[(\Delta\tilde{m} - a\Delta t)^2] = s^2\Delta t$$

We will write the individual's investment and consumption functions as x(w, t) and c(w, t). Thus x(w, t) is the amount that the individual holds of the market portfolio if he has wealth w at time t, and c(w, t) is his rate of consumption if he has wealth w at time t.

Instead of $EU_k(W_k)$, we will use u(w, t) for the expected utility of the individual's lifetime consumption and final wealth, starting with wealth w at time t, and following optimal investment and consumption strategies. Following Mossin[3] and Fama,[4] we may also call u(w, t) the individual's "derived utility function over wealth" for time t.

Finally, we will write y(w) for the individual's "initial investment function."

$$y(w) = x(w, 0)$$

The function y(w) gives the amount that the individual would currently hold of the market portfolio as a function of his wealth w.

Les us assume, in this section, that we are given the utility functions v(c, t) and z(w), and that we want to find the optimal investment strategy x(w, t) and consumption strategy c(w, t) for these utility functions.

Rewriting equation (4) for continuous time, we have:

$$u(w, t) \doteq \max_{c,x} (E[u(w + wr\Delta t - c\Delta t + x\Delta\tilde{m}, t + \Delta t)] + v(c, t)\Delta t) \quad (5)$$

This equation corresponds exactly to an equation of Fama's [2, p. 5, equation (6)].

Writing t* for the time at which the investor evaluates his final wealth, the boundary condition for this equation is:

$$u(w, t^\star) = z(w) \quad (6)$$

Using equation (5) we can work backward from $u(w, t + \Delta t)$ to u(w, t), starting from $u(w, t^\star)$, and getting the optimal investment strategy x(w, t) along the way.

To put equation (5) into the form of a differential equation, we begin by expanding the right hand side, using the first two terms of a Taylor's series.

In the equations that follow, a subscript on a function refers to the partial derivative of the function with respect to the variable indicated by the subscript.

$$\begin{aligned} & u(w + wr\Delta t - c\Delta t + x\Delta\tilde{m}, t + t\Delta t) \\ = \; & u(w, t) + u_1(w, t)[wr\Delta t - c\Delta t + x\Delta\tilde{m}] + u_2(w, t)\Delta t \\ & + \tfrac{1}{2}u_{11}(w, t)[wr\Delta t - c\Delta t + x\Delta\tilde{m}]^2 \\ & + u_{12}(w, t)[wr\Delta t - c\Delta t + x\Delta\tilde{m}]\Delta t + \tfrac{1}{2}u_{22}(w, t)\Delta t^2 \qquad (7) \end{aligned}$$

Taking the expected value of both sides of equation (7), and eliminating terms in Δt^2, we have:

$$\begin{aligned} & E[u(w + wr\Delta t - c\Delta t + x\Delta\tilde{m}, t + \Delta t)] = u(w, t) \\ & + u_1(w, t)[wr + xa - c]\Delta t + u_2(w, t)\Delta t + \tfrac{1}{2}u_{11}(w, t)x^2 s^2 \Delta t \qquad (8) \end{aligned}$$

In deriving this expression, we make use of the fact that:

$$E[\Delta\tilde{m} - E[\Delta\tilde{m}])^2] = E[\Delta\tilde{m}^2] - E[\Delta\tilde{m}]^2$$

so that:

$$E[\Delta\tilde{m}^2] = s^2\Delta t + a^2\Delta t^2$$

The second term in this expression is a term in Δt^2, so it does not appear in equation (8).

Thus equation (5) becomes:

$$\begin{aligned} u(w, t) = \max_{c,x} \; & [u(w, t) + u_1(w, t)[wr + xa - c]\Delta t + u_2(w, t)\Delta t \\ & + \tfrac{1}{2}u_{11}(w, t)s^2x^2\Delta t + v(c, t)\Delta t] \qquad (9) \end{aligned}$$

Equation (9) simplifies to:

$$\begin{aligned} u_2(w, t) = -u_1(w, t)wr - \max_{c,x} \; & [\tfrac{1}{2}u_{11}(w, t)s^2x^2 \\ & + u_1(w, t)[xa - c] + v(c, t)] \qquad (10) \end{aligned}$$

Taking the partial derivative with respect to c of the expression to be maximized, we have:

$$-u_1(w, t) + v_1(c, t) = 0 \qquad (11)$$

This equation is an implicit definition of the consumption function c(w, t) in terms of the functions v(c, t) and u(w, t):

$$v_1(c, t) = u_1(w, t) \tag{12}$$

Taking the partial derivative with respect to x of the expression in equation (10) to be maximized, and setting it equal to zero, we have:

$$u_{11}(w, t)s^2x + u_1(w, t)a = 0 \tag{13}$$

This equation defines the investment function x(w, t) in terms of the derived utility function u(w, t):

$$x(w, t) = -\frac{au_1(w, t)}{s^2u_{11}(w, t)} \tag{14}$$

Equation (14) has a particularly interesting form, because Pratt[8] has shown that the appropriate measure of "absolute local risk aversion" is, in our notation, $-u_{11}(w, t)/u_1(w, t)$. Thus equation (14) states that the amount that the investor keeps in the market portfolio is inversely proportional to his absolute local risk aversion.

This is intuitively appealing. It says that the more risk-averse an individual is, the less he keeps in the market portfolio. Very risk-averse individuals keep almost nothing in the market portfolio. And the amount he keeps in the market portfolio is strictly proportional to the inverse of his risk aversion.

We can use equation (14) to simplify equation (10), keeping in mind that the maximum values of x and c in equation (10) are given by the functions x(w, t) and c(w, t).

$$u_2(w, t) = -u_1(w, t)[\tfrac{1}{2}ax(w, t) + wr - c(w, t)] - v(c(w, t), t) \tag{15}$$

The economic interpretation of equation (15) is not entirely clear. Except for the factor $\frac{1}{2}$, the expression multiplying $u_1(w, t)$ is the expected rate of increase in the individual's wealth. So the first term on the right-hand side of equation (15) seems to be the rate of change in the individual's derived utility due to changes in his wealth, while the second term seems to be the rate of change in his derived utility due to his rate of consumption.

Collecting equations (12), (14), (15), and (6), we have a system of differential equations defining the functions u(w, t), c(w, t), and x(w, t) in terms of the functions v(c, t) and z(w).

$$v_1(c(w, t), t) = u_1(w, t) \tag{12}$$

$$x(w, t) = -\frac{au_1(w, t)}{s^2 u_{11}(w, t)} \tag{14}$$

$$u_2(w, t) = -u_1(w, t)[\tfrac{1}{2}ax(w, t) + wr - c(w, t)] - v(c(w, t), t) \tag{15}$$

$$u(w, t^\star) = z(w) \tag{6}$$

Since the functions v(c, t) and z(w) make up the individual's utility function, we can say that these four equations define the individual's optimal investment and consumption strategies through time in terms of his utility function on lifetime consumption and final wealth.

Meyer[16] has derived equations (12), (14), and (15) independently, starting from a utility function of the type used by Phelps. His equations (12a), (13), and (14a) correspond to my equations (12), (14), and (15).

The analysis done by Mossin[3] corresponds to the case where we set consumption equal to zero, and eliminate the function v(c, t). The individual's utility function is described entirely by the function z(w) that gives his utility of final wealth. A utility function with constant "relative local risk aversion" (see Pratt[8]) may be written in one of the following ways:

$$\begin{aligned} z(w) &= (w - k)^{1-\frac{1}{b}} && b > 1 \\ &= \log(w - k) && b = 1 \\ &= -(w - k)^{-\left(\frac{1}{b}-1\right)} && b < 1 \end{aligned} \tag{16}$$

For a utility function of this form, we get an analytic solution to equations (12), (14), (15), and (6) as follows:

$$x(w, t) = b(w - ke^{r(t-t^\star)}) \tag{17}$$

Defining p as $ke^{-rt^\star}$, this investment function may also be written:

$$x(w, t) = b(w - pe^{rt}) \tag{18}$$

For a utility function of this form, the individual's optimal investment strategy is a linear function of his wealth. The slope of the function is constant, but the intercept changes through time. The utility function defined by (16) is a member of the HARA (hyperbolic absolute risk-aversion) class. Merton[9] has shown that the investment function is linear in wealth if and only if the utility function is a member of the family of HARA functions.

One effect of this investment strategy is to guarantee that the individual will have final wealth greater than k. As his current wealth drops toward an amount that would grow to k if invested at the short-term interest rate, he reduces his level of investment in the market.

Mossin's solution for this case is similar, except that he omits the factor k, so that he is working with a more restrictive form of utility function than (16). Thus his solution, in our notation, is:

$$x(w, t) = bw$$

ELIMINATING THE UTILITY FUNCTION

It is possible to eliminate the individual's utility function entirely from equations (12), (14), (15), and (6), giving a set of equations involving only his investment function and his consumption function. For these equations to have a unique solution, however, we must add an additional equation specifying the individual's initial investment function.

The resulting set of equations can be viewed as defining the individual's investment function through time in terms of his consumption function and his initial investment function.

This derivation is not completely a mathematical exercise. It can be argued that it is easier for the individual to specify the functions c(w, t) and y(w) than the functions v(c, t) and z(w). "Utility" is a foreign concept for most individuals, and the traditional way of mapping an individual's utility function is to ask him about his preferences among a number of gambles.

Instead of stating his preferences among various gambles, the individual can specify his consumption function and his initial investment function. He can give the rate at which he would consume his wealth at various times in the future as a function of the amount of his wealth at those times. And he can tell how much he would invest currently in the market portfolio as a function of his current wealth.

For the special kind of utility function that we have been assuming, in which total utility is the integral over time of a function v(c, t) of the rate of consumption and time, plus a function of final wealth, specifying the consumption function c(w, t) and the initial investment function y(w) is equivalent to specifying the utility function. Either can be derived from the other using equations (12), (14), (15), and (6).

Let us begin by rewriting equation (14) as follows:

$$u_{11}(w, t) = -\frac{au_1(w, t)}{s^2x(w, t)} \tag{19}$$

Taking the derivative with respect to w of both sides of equation (15), we have:

$$u_{21}(w, t) = -u_{11}(w, t)[\tfrac{1}{2}ax(w, t) + wr - c(w, t)] - u_1(w, t)[\tfrac{1}{2}ax_1(w, t) + r - c_1(w, t)] - v_1(c(w, t), t)c_1(w, t) \quad (20)$$

Using equations (19) and (12), we may rewrite this as follows:

$$u_{21}(w, t) = +\frac{au_1(w, t)}{s^2x(w, t)}[\tfrac{1}{2}ax(w, t) + wr - c(w, t)] - u_1(w, t)[\tfrac{1}{2}ax_1(w, t) + r - c_1(w, t)] - u_1(w, t)c_1(w, t) \quad (21)$$

Collecting terms, and using equation (15), we obtain:

$$u_{21}(w, t) = -\frac{a}{s^2x(w, t)}[u_2(w, t) + v(c(w, t), t)] - u_1(w, t)[\tfrac{1}{2}ax_1(w, t) + r] \quad (22)$$

Taking the derivative with respect to w of both sides of this equation, we have:

$$u_{211}(w, t) = -\frac{a}{s^2x(w, t)}[u_{21}(w, t) + v_1(c(w, t), t)c_1(w, t)] + \frac{ax_1(w, t)}{s^2x(w, t)^2}[u_2(w, t) + v(c(w, t), t)] - u_{11}(w, t)[\tfrac{1}{2}ax_1(w, t) + r] - \tfrac{1}{2}au_1(w, t)x_{11}(w, t) \quad (23)$$

Using equations (15), (19), and (12), we have:

$$u_{211}(w, t) = -\frac{a}{s^2x(w, t)}[u_{21}(w, t) + u_1(w, t)c_1(w, t)] + \frac{au_1(w, t)}{s^2x(w, t)^2}[-\tfrac{1}{2}ax(w, t)x_1(w, t) - wrx_1(w, t) + c(w, t)x_1(w, t) + \tfrac{1}{2}ax(w, t)x_1(w, t) + rx(w, t)] - \tfrac{1}{2}au_1(w, t)x_{11}(w, t) \quad (24)$$

Collecting terms, this becomes:

$$u_{211}(w, t) = -\frac{au_{21}(w, t)}{s^2x(w, t)} - \frac{au_1(w, t)c_1(w, t)}{s^2x(w, t)} + \frac{au_1(w, t)}{s^2x(w, t)^2} \times [rx(w, t) - wrx_1(w, t) + c(w, t)x_1(w, t)] - \tfrac{1}{2}au_1(w, t)x_{11}(w, t) \quad (25)$$

Taking the derivative with respect to time of equation (19), we have:

$$u_{112}(w, t) = -\frac{au_{12}(w, t)}{s^2x(w, t)} + \frac{au_1(w, t)x_2(w, t)}{s^2x(w, t)^2} \tag{26}$$

But assuming that u(w, t) is a well behaved function, with continuous derivatives, we know that $u_{211}(w, t)$ must be equal to $u_{112}(w, t)$, so we have:

$$\frac{au_1(w, t)x_2(w, t)}{s^2x(w, t)^2} = \frac{au_1(w, t)}{s^2x(w, t)^2}[rx(w, t) - wrx_1(w, t)$$
$$+ c(w, t)x_1(w, t) - c_1(w, t)x(w, t)] - \tfrac{1}{2}au_1(w, t)x_{11}(w, t) \tag{27}$$

This simplifies to:

$$x_2(w, t) = [r - c_1(w, t)]x(w, t) - [wr - c(w, t)]x_1(w, t)$$
$$- \tfrac{1}{2}s^2x^2(w, t)x_{11}(w, t) \tag{28}$$

Equation (28) involves only the investment and consumption functions. The utility function v(c, t) and the derived utility function u(w, t) have been eliminated.

Equation (28) may be interpreted as defining a relationship that must hold between the functions c(w, t) and x(w, t) if they are to be consistent with maximization of a lifetime utility function of the form given by functions v(c, t) and z(w). It defines a feasible class of pairs [x(w, t), c(w, t)] consistent with maximization of an additive utility function. Thus it defines a feasible class of consumption and investment strategies for an individual.

Neither the individual's consumption strategy alone nor his investment strategy alone is limited by equation (28). Given any consumption function c(w, t) that is reasonably well behaved, equation (28) defines a family of investment functions consistent with it. And given any investment function x(w, t) that is reasonably well behaved, equation (28) defines a family of consumption functions that is consistent with it. Only combinations of choices of c(w, t) and x(w, t) are limited by equation (28).

Let us now add to equation (28), as a boundary condition, the individual's initial risk function.

$$x(w, 0) = y(w) \tag{29}$$

This boundary condition defines a unique investment strategy that is consistent with a given consumption strategy and equation (28).

ANALYTIC SOLUTIONS

Equations (28) and (29) may be solved analytically if the consumption and initial investment functions are both linear in wealth.

It does not seem to be much of a restriction to require an individual to specify a consumption function that is linear in wealth if we allow the constants of the function to depend on time. Let us write such a consumption function as follows:

$$c(w, t) = wf(t) + g(t) \tag{30}$$

The function f(t) gives the rate at which the individual's consumption increases as his wealth increases. For example, a typical value of f(t) might be 2 percent per year. This would mean that if you added \$10,000 to the individual's wealth, he would increase his rate of consumption by \$200 per year.

We would expect f(t) to increase through time, as the individual gets older. When he is very old, he might spend each dollar of additional wealth at the rate of 10 percent a year, simply because he hasn't got much time left in which to spend it. This doesn't mean, of course, that his absolute level of consumption will increase over time. If he is spending at a high rate, his wealth will probably be decreasing through time, so the product of his rate of consumption as a percentage of wealth and his wealth may well be decreasing through time.

Similarly, it does not seem to be much of a restriction to require an individual to specify an initial investment function that is linear in wealth, if we allow an additive constant as well as a multiplicative constant. Let us write such an initial investment function as follows:

$$y(w) = b(w - p) \tag{31}$$

The constant b allows the individual to specify his aggressiveness. It tells how much his level of investment in the market portfolio will increase for each dollar increase in his wealth. A timid investor might specify a b of 0.5: for each added \$10,000 in wealth, he increases his investment in the market portfolio by \$5000. On the other hand, an aggressive investor might specify a b of 2.0: for each added \$10,000 in wealth, he increases his investment in the market portfolio by \$20,000, borrowing, if necessary, to do so.

The constant p allows the investor's overall aggressiveness to vary with his wealth. For example, if he sets p equal to \$100,000, and b is equal to 2.0, then if he has wealth of only \$150,000, he will be relatively timid: He will have only \$100,000 invested in the market portfolio. But if he has wealth of \$500,000, he will be relatively aggressive: He will have \$800,000 invested in the market portfolio.

Thus the solutions that we will show below for equations (28) and (29) are not meant simply as solutions that we happened to be able to obtain; they are meant as reasonable consumption and investment strategies for a wide variety of individuals.

The solution to equations (28) and (29) given a consumption function of the form (30) and an initial investment function of the form (31), is as follows:

$$x(w, t) = b\left[w + e^{\int(r - f(t))dt}\left[-p + \int g(t)e^{-\int(r - f(t))dt}dt\right]\right] \tag{32}$$

This solution can be verified by substituting it in equations (28) and (29). The process by which I derived it is too long to record here.

In equation (32), any expression of the form

$$\int h(t)dt$$

is to be taken as an abbreviation for

$$\int_0^t h(s)ds.$$

We can simplify equation (32) considerably by looking at the case where $g(t) = 0$:

$$x(w, t) = b[w - pe^{\int(r - f(t))dt}] \tag{33}$$

This is the solution when the consumption function is strictly proportional to wealth. This class of solutions is still a fairly large class, and most individuals would probably be happy with investment and consumption strategies from this class.

The individual can still specify the constant of proportionality $f(t)$ in his consumption function as a function of time, and he can still specify a level of aggressiveness b and a minimum level of wealth p in his initial investment function.

The investment function given by (33) has a constant slope, so the added investment in the market portfolio that results from an increment to the individual's wealth is independent of time. The intercept, however, changes through time. When $f(t)$ is greater than r, which seems like a reasonable assumption for most individuals, the intercept with the x-axis shifts constantly to the left.

When the consumption function and the initial investment function are both strictly proportional to wealth, so that $g(t) = 0$ and $p = 0$, the investment

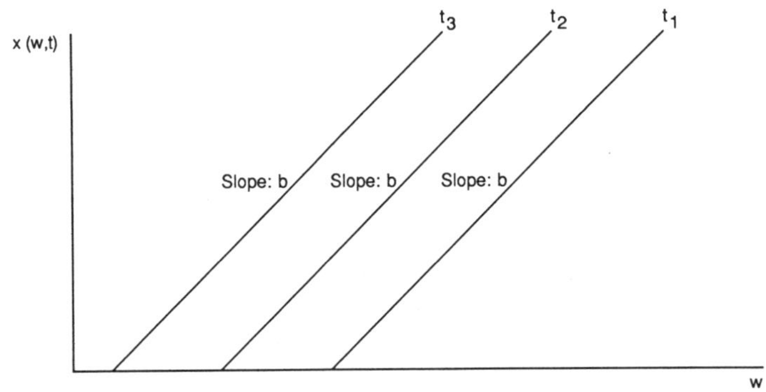

FIGURE 1. A graphical display of the investment strategy given in equation (33)

strategy given by (33) becomes:

$$x(w, t) = bw \tag{34}$$

The individual's investment strategy in this case is completely independent of time.

Even this case gives enough degrees of freedom for a large number of individuals. The individual can still specify d(t), which we can call his "lifetime consumption pattern," and b, which we can call his "willingness to accept risk." It turns out, as shown by equation (34), that his investment strategy is completely independent of his consumption strategy, as well as independent of time. The investment strategy (34) depends on b but not on d(t).

This case is the generalization to a world with consumption as well as investment of Mossin's analysis[3] of a case in which a "stationary strategy" with "complete myopia" is optional.

PRACTICAL IMPLICATIONS

There is a commonly recommended investment strategy called "dollar averaging." To follow this strategy, by an individual adds a constant number of dollars to his holdings of the market portfolio at regular intervals. The theory is that he will get more shares when the market is down, and fewer shares when the market is up, so that his average cost per share will be low. The implication is that he will be better off using this strategy than investing all of his money in the market as soon as he has the opportunity.

The preceding analysis shows that dollar averaging will almost never be an optimal strategy. The trouble with it is that it causes the individual to have larger and larger amounts invested as he grows older, so that his lifetime investment results are too dependent on what happens to the market near the end of his lifetime.

For most individuals, a realistic consumption strategy will give a rate of consumption high enough that the individual's total wealth tends to decline through time. (Recall that his total wealth includes both his current wealth and the market value of his uncertain future income. His current wealth may increase through time, but the market value of his future income is likely to decline faster than his current wealth increases.)

If the individual's total wealth declines through time, and if his optimal investment strategy has the form $x(w, t) = bw$, then the level of his investment in the market portfolio should decline through time. But the level of investment of most individuals rises through time.

In evaluating his level of investment, an individual should keep in mind that his future income is uncertain. This means that his investment in himself is partially equivalent to investment in the market portfolio. So an individual in an occupation whose returns are particularly uncertain should have less invested in the market portfolio, other things (including his risk preferences) being equal, than an individual in an occupation whose returns are fairly certain.

In general, however, an individual should have more invested when he is young than he typically does. He should adopt an investment strategy that will tend to keep his level of investment in the market portfolio from growing rapidly over time.

The most direct way for an individual to invest more when he is young would be for him to borrow for investment against his future income. For various reasons, however, it is difficult for an individual to borrow on his future income.

If he cannot borrow on his future income, the individual can at least consider shifting funds from other assets to the market. He can borrow on his house, or liquidate his savings account. He can buy securities on margin.

If these measures do not increase his investments enough, he should consider buying securities with built-in leverage, such as the common stocks of companies with large amounts of debt outstanding, or warrants and call options. He should be careful in choosing this course of action, however. Since there are many investors looking for securities with built-in leverage, such securities tend to be somewhat overpriced.

These recommendations do not follow in a completely rigorous way from the theory presented above. But they illustrate the kinds of implications that the theory has, and the ways in which these implications differ from commonly used investment strategies.

Some of the basic ideas used in formulating this problem in continuous time came from Jack L. Treynor. Comments by Jan Mossin and Michael Jensen on earlier drafts of the paper were very helpful.

FOOTNOTES

1. Phelps, Edmund S., "The Accumulation of Risky Capital: A Sequential Utility Analysis," *Econometrica* (October, 1962) pp. 729–743.
2. Tobin, James, "The Theory of Portfolio Selection," in F. H. Hahn and F. P. R. Brechling, eds., *The Theory of Interest Rates*. London: Macmillan, 1965, pp. 3–51.
3. Mossin, Jan, "Optimal Multiperiod Portfolio Policies," *Journal of Business* (April, 1968) pp. 215–229.
4. Fama, Eugene F., "Multiperiod Consumption-Investment Decisions," *American Economic Review* (March, 1970) pp. 163–174.
5. Levhari, D., and T. N. Srinivasan, "Optimal Savings Under Uncertainty," *Review of Economic Studies* (April, 1969) pp. 153–163.
6. Samuelson, Paul A. "Lifetime Portfolio Selection by Dynamic Stochastic Programming," *Review of Economics and Statistics* (August, 1969) pp. 239–246.
7. Merton, Robert C., "Lifetime Portfolio Selection Under Uncertainty: The Continuous-time Case," *Review of Economics and Statistics* (August, 1969) pp. 247–257.
8. Pratt, John W., "*Risk Aversion in the Small and in the Large*," *Econometrica* (January-April, 1964) pp. 122–136.
9. Merton, Robert C., "Optimum Consumption and Portfolio Rules in a Continuous-time Model," *Journal of Economic Theory*, Vol. 3, No. 4 (December, 1971).
10. Fisher, Irving, *The Theory of Interest Rates*. New York: Macmillan, 1930.
11. Friedman, Milton, *A Theory of the Consumption Function*, Princeton: Princeton University Press, 1957.
12. Modigliani, Franco, and Richard Brumberg, "Utility Analysis and the Consumption Function: An Interpretation of Cross-Section Data," in K. K. Kurihara, ed., *Post-Keynesian Economics*, London: George Allen and Unwin, 1955, pp. 388–436.
13. Markowitz, Harry M., *Portfolio Selection*. New York: Wiley, 1967.
14. Latané, Henry A., "Criteria for Choice Among Risky Ventures," *Journal of Political Economy* (April, 1959) pp. 144–155.
15. Latané, Henry A., and Donald L. Tuttle, "Criteria for Portfolio Building," *Journal of Finance* (September, 1967) pp. 359–373.
16. Meyer, Richard F., "On the Relationship Among the Utility of Assets, the Utility of Consumption, and Investment Strategy in an Uncertain, but Time-Invariant World," *Proceedings of the 5th International Conference on Operational Research*. London: Tavistock Publications, 1970, pp. 627–648.

19. THE PRICING OF OPTIONS AND CORPORATE LIABILITIES

Fischer Black and Myron Scholes

INTRODUCTION

An option is a security giving the right to buy or sell an asset, subject to certain conditions, within a specified period of time. An "American option" is one that can be exercised at any time up to the date the option expires. A "European option" is one that can be exercised only on a specified future date. The price that is paid for the asset when the option is exercised is called the "exercise price" or "striking price." The last day on which the option may be exercised is called the "expiration date" or "maturity date."

The simplest kind of option is one that gives the right to buy a single share of common stock. Throughout most of the paper, we will be discussing this kind of option, which is often referred to as a "call option."

In general, it seems clear that the higher the price of the stock, the greater the value of the option. When the stock price is much greater than the exercise price, the option is almost sure to be exercised. The current value of the option will thus be approximately equal to the price of the stock minus the price of a pure discount bond that matures on the same date as the option, with a face value equal to the striking price of the option.

Reprinted from *Journal of Political Economy*, May–June 1973

Received for publication November 11, 1970. Final version received May 9, 1972.

The inspiration for this work was provided by Jack L. Treynor (1961a, 1961b). We are grateful for extensive comments on earlier drafts by Eugene F. Fama, Robert C. Merton, and Merton H. Miller. This work was supported in part by the Ford Foundation.

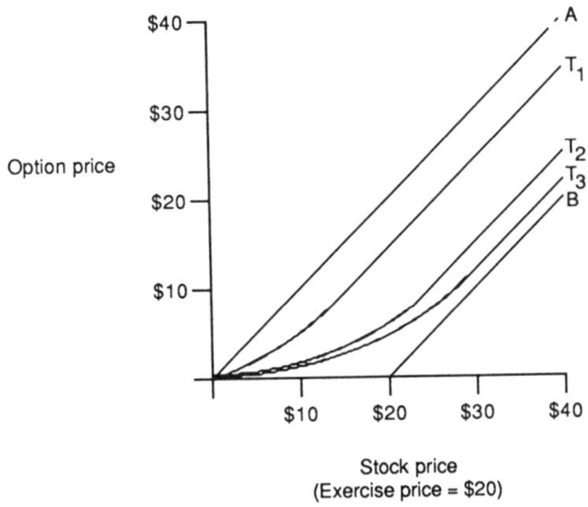

FIGURE 1. The relation between option value and stock price

On the other hand, if the price of the stock is much less than the exercise price, the option is almost sure to expire without being exercised, so its value will be near zero.

If the expiration date of the option is very far in the future, then the price of a bond that pays the exercise price on the maturity date will be very low, and the value of the option will be approximately equal to the price of the stock.

On the other hand, if the expiration date is very near, the value of the option will be approximately equal to the stock price minus the exercise price, or zero, if the stock price is less than the exercise price. Normally, the value of an option declines as its maturity date approaches, if the value of the stock does not change.

These general properties of the relation between the option value and the stock price are often illustrated in a diagram like Figure 1. Line A represents the maximum value of the option, since it cannot be worth more than the stock. Line B represents the minimum value of the option, since its value cannot be negative and cannot be less than the stock price minus the exercise price. Lines T_1, T_2, and T_3 represent the value of the option for successively shorter maturities.

Normally, the curve representing the value of an option will be concave upward. Since it also lies below the 45° line, A, we can see that the option will be more volatile than the stock. A given percentage change in the stock price, holding maturity constant, will result in a larger percentage change in the option value. The relative volatility of the option is not constant, however. It depends on both the stock price and maturity.

Most of the previous work on the valuation of options has been expressed in terms of warrants. For example, Sprenkle (1961), Ayres (1963), Boness

(1964), Samuelson (1965), Baumol, Malkiel, and Quandt (1966), and Chen (1970) all produced valuation formulas of the same general form. Their formulas, however, were not complete, since they all involved one or more arbitrary parameters.

For example, Sprenkle's formula for the value of an option can be written as follows:

$$kxN(b_1) - k^\star cN(b_2)$$

$$b_1 = \frac{\ln kx/c + \frac{1}{2}v^2(t^\star - t)}{v\sqrt{(t^\star - t)}}$$

$$b_2 = \frac{\ln kx/c - \frac{1}{2}v^2(t^\star - t)}{v\sqrt{(t^\star - t)}}$$

In this expression, x is the stock price, c is the exercise price, $t^\star$ is the maturity date, t is the current date, v^2 is the variance rate of the return on the stock,[1] ln is the natural logarithm, and $N(b)$ is the cumulative normal density function. But k and $k^\star$ are unknown parameters. Sprenkle (1961) defines k as the ratio of the expected value of the stock price at the time the warrant matures to the current stock price, and $k^\star$ as a discount factor that depends on the risk of the stock. He tries to estimate the values of k and $k^\star$ empirically, but finds that he is unable to do so.

More typically, Samuelson (1965) has unknown parameters α and β, where α is the rate of expected return on the stock, and β is the rate of expected return on the warrant or the discount rate to be applied to the warrant.[2] He assumes that the distribution of possible values of the stock when the warrant matures is log-normal and takes the expected value of this distribution, cutting it off at the exercise price. He then discounts this expected value to the present at the rate β. Unfortunately, there seems to be no model of the pricing of securities under conditions of capital market equilibrium that would make this an appropriate procedure for determining the value of a warrant.

In a subsequent paper, Samuelson and Merton (1969) recognize the fact that discounting the expected value of the distribution of possible values of the warrant when it is exercised is not an appropriate procedure. They advance the theory by treating the option price as a function of the stock price. They also recognize that the discount rates are determined in part by the requirement that investors be willing to hold all of the outstanding amounts of both the stock and the option. But they do not make use of the fact that investors

[1] The variance rate of the return on a security is the limit, as the size of the interval of measurement goes to zero, of the variance of the return over that interval divided by the length of the interval.

[2] The rate of expected return on a security is the limit, as the size of the interval of measurement goes to zero, of the expected return over that interval divided by the length of the interval.

must hold other assets as well, so that the risk of an option or stock that affects its discount rate is only that part of the risk that cannot be diversified away. Their final formula depends on the shape of the utility function that they assume for the typical investor.

One of the concepts that we use in developing our model is expressed by Thorp and Kassouf (1967). They obtain an empirical valuation formula for warrants by fitting a curve to actual warrant prices. Then they use this formula to calculate the ratio of shares of stock to options needed to create a hedged position by going long in one security and short in the other. What they fail to pursue is the fact that in equilibrium, the expected return on such a hedged position must be equal to the return on a riskless asset. What we show below is that this equilibrium condition can be used to derive a theoretical valuation formula.

THE VALUATION FORMULA

In deriving our formula for the value of an option in terms of the price of the stock, we will assume "ideal conditions" in the market for the stock and for the option:

a) The short-term interest rate is known and is constant through time.

b) The stock price follows a random walk in continuous time with a variance rate proportional to the square of the stock price. Thus the distribution of possible stock prices at the end of any finite interval is lognormal. The variance rate of the return on the stock is constant.

c) The stock pays no dividends or other distributions.

d) The option is "European," that is, it can only be exercised at maturity.

e) There are no transaction costs in buying or selling the stock or the option.

f) It is possible to borrow any fraction of the price of a security to buy it or to hold it, at the short-term interest rate.

g) There are no penalties to short selling. A seller who does not own a security will simply accept the price of the security from a buyer, and will agree to settle with the buyer on some future date by paying him an amount equal to the price of the security on that date.

Under these assumptions, the value of the option will depend only on the price of the stock and time and on variables that are taken to be known constants. Thus, it is possible to create a hedged position, consisting of a long position in the stock and a short position in the option, whose value will not depend on the price of the stock, but will depend only on time and the values of known constants. Writing $w(x, t)$ for the value of the option as a function of the stock price x and time t, the number of options that must be sold short against one share of stock long is:

$$1/w_1(x, t). \tag{1}$$

In expression (1), the subscript refers to the partial derivative of $w(x, t)$ with respect to its first argument.

To see that the value of such a hedged position does not depend on the price of the stock, note that the ratio of the change in the option value to the change in the stock price, when the change in the stock price is small, is $w_1(x, t)$. To a first approximation, if the stock price changes by an amount Δx, the option price will change by an amount $w_1(x, t)\,\Delta x$, and the number of options given by expression (1) will change by an amount Δx. Thus, the change in the value of a long position in the stock will be approximately offset by the change in value of a short position in $1/w_1$ options.

As the variables x and t change, the number of options to be sold short to create a hedged position with one share of stock changes. If the hedge is maintained continuously, then the approximation mentioned above become exact, and the return on the hedged position is completely independent of the change in the value of the stock. In fact, the return on the hedged position becomes certain.[3]

To illustrate the formation of the hedged position, let us refer to the solid line (T_2) in Figure 1 and assume that the price of the stock starts at \$15.00, so that the value of the option starts at \$5.00. Assume also that the slope of the line at that point is 1/2. This means that the hedged position is created by buying one share of stock and selling two options short. One share of stock costs \$15.00, and the sale of two options brings in \$10.00, so the equity in this position is \$5.00.

If the hedged position is not changed as the price of the stock changes, then there is some uncertainty in the value of the equity at the end of a finite interval. Suppose that two options go from \$10.00 to \$15.75 when the stock goes from \$15.00 to \$20.00, and that they go from \$10.00 to \$5.75 when the stock goes from \$15.00 to \$10.00. Thus, the equity goes from \$5.00 to \$4.25 when the stock changes by \$5.00 in either direction. This is a \$.75 decline in the equity for a \$5.00 change in the stock in either direction.[4]

In addition, the curve shifts (say from T_2 to T_3 in Figure 1) as the maturity of the options changes. The resulting decline in value of the options means an increase in the equity in the hedged position and tends to offset the possible losses due to a large change in the stock price.

Note that the decline in the equity value due to a large change in the stock price is small. The ratio of the decline in the equity value to the magnitude

[3] This was pointed out to us by Robert Merton.

[4] These figures are purely for illustrative purposes. They correspond roughly to the way Figure 1 was drawn, but not to an option on any actual security.

of the change in the stock price becomes smaller as the magnitude of the change in the stock price becomes smaller.

Note also that the direction of the change in the equity value is independent of the direction of the change in the stock price. This means that under our assumption that the stock price follows a continuous random walk and that the return has a constant variance rate, the covariance between the return on the equity and the return on the stock will be zero. If the stock price and the value of the "market portfolio" follow a joint continuous random walk with constant covariance rate, it means that the covariance between the return on the equity and the return on the market will be zero.

Thus the risk in the hedged position is zero if the short position in the option is adjusted continuously. If the position is not adjusted continuously, the risk is small, and consists entirely of risk that can be diversified away by forming a portfolio of a large number of such hedged positions.

In general, since the hedged position contains one share of stock long and $1/w_1$ options short, the value of the equity in the position is:

$$x - w/w_1. \tag{2}$$

The change in the value of the equity in a short interval Δt is:

$$\Delta x - \Delta w/w_1. \tag{3}$$

Assuming that the short position is changed continuously, we can use stochastic calculus[5] to expand Δw, which is $w(x + \Delta x, t + \Delta t) - w(x, t)$, as follows:

$$\Delta w = w_1 \Delta x + \tfrac{1}{2} w_{11} v^2 x^2 \Delta t + w_2 \Delta t. \tag{4}$$

In equation (4), the subscripts on w refer to partial derivatives, and v^2 is the variance rate of the return on the stock.[6] Substituting from equation (4) into expression (3), we find that the change in the value of the equity in the hedged position is:

$$-\left(\tfrac{1}{2} w_{11} v^2 x^2 + w_2\right)\Delta t/w_1. \tag{5}$$

Since the return on the equity in the hedged position is certain, the return must be equal to $r\Delta t$. Even if the hedged position is not changed continuously, its risk is small and is entirely risk that can be diversified away, so the expected

[5] For an exposition of stochastic calculus, see McKean (1969).

[6] See footnote 1.

return on the hedged position must be at the short term interest rate.[7] If this were not true, speculators would try to profit by borrowing large amounts of money to create such hedged positions, and would be in the process force the returns down to the short term interest rate.

Thus the change in the equity (5) must equal the value of the equity (2) times $r\Delta t$.

$$-\left(\tfrac{1}{2}w_{11}v^2x^2 + w_2\right)\Delta t/w_1 = (x - w/w_1)r\Delta t. \tag{6}$$

Dropping the Δt from both sides, and rearranging, we have a differential equation for the value of the option.

$$w_2 = rw - rxw_1 - \tfrac{1}{2}v^2x^2w_{11}. \tag{7}$$

Writing $t^\star$ for the maturity date of the option, and c for the exercise price, we know that:

$$\begin{aligned} w(x, t^\star) &= x - c, \qquad x \geqslant c \\ &= 0, \qquad x < c. \end{aligned} \tag{8}$$

There is only one formula $w(x, t)$ that satisfies the differential equation (7) subject to the boundary condition (8). This formula must be the option valuation formula.

To solve this differential equation, we make the following substitution:

$$\begin{aligned} w(x, t) = {} & e^{r(t-t^\star)}y\,[(2/v^2)(r - \tfrac{1}{2}v^2)[\ln x/c - (r - \tfrac{1}{2}v^2)(t - t^\star)], \\ & - (2/v^2)(r - \tfrac{1}{2}v^2)^2(t - t^\star)]. \end{aligned} \tag{9}$$

With this substitution, the differential equation becomes:

$$y_2 = y_{11}, \tag{10}$$

[7] For a thorough discussion of the relation between risk and expected return, see Fama and Miller (1972) or Sharpe (1970). To see that the risk in the hedged position can be diversified away, note that if we don't adjust the hedge continuously, expression (5) becomes:

$$-\left(\tfrac{1}{2}w_{11}\Delta x^2 + w_2\Delta t\right)/w_1. \tag{5$'$}$$

Writing Δm for the change in the value of the market portfolio between t and $t + \Delta t$, the "market risk" in the hedged position is proportional to the covariance between the change in the value of the hedged portfolio, as given by expression (5′), and Δm: $-\frac{1}{2}w_{11}$ cov $(\Delta x^2, \Delta m)$. But if Δx and Δm follow a joint normal distribution for small intervals Δt, this covariance will be zero. Since there is no market risk in the hedged position, all of the risk due to the fact that the hedge is not continuously adjusted must be risk that can be diversified away.

and the boundary condition becomes:

$$\begin{aligned} y(u, 0) &= 0, & u &< 0 \\ &= c[e^{u(\frac{1}{2}v^2)/(r-\frac{1}{2}v^2)} - 1], & u &\geqslant 0. \end{aligned} \tag{11}$$

The differential equation (10) is the heat-transfer equation of physics, and its solution is given by Churchill (1963, p. 155). In our notation, the solution is:

$$y(u, s) = 1/\sqrt{2\pi} \int_{-u/\sqrt{2s}}^{\infty} c[e^{(u+q\sqrt{2s})(\frac{1}{2}v^2)/(r-\frac{1}{2}v^2)} - 1]e^{-q^2/2}dq. \tag{12}$$

Substituting from equation (12) into equation (9), and simplifying, we find:

$$\begin{aligned} w(x, t) &= xN(d_1) - ce^{r(t-t^\star)}N(d_2) \\ d_1 &= \frac{\ln x/c + (r + \frac{1}{2}v^2)(t^\star - t)}{v\sqrt{t^\star - t}} \\ d_2 &= \frac{\ln x/c + (r - \frac{1}{2}v^2)(t^\star - t)}{v\sqrt{t^\star - t}} \end{aligned} \tag{13}$$

In equation (13), $N(d)$ is the cumulative normal density function.

Note that the expected return on the stock does not appear in equation (13). The option value as a function of the stock price is independent of the expected return on the stock. The expected return on the option, however, will depend on the expected return on the stock. The faster the stock price rises, the faster the option price will rise through the functional relationship (13).

Note that the maturity $(t^\star - t)$ appears in the formula only multiplied by the interest rate r or the variance rate v^2. Thus, an increase in maturity has the same effect on the value of the option as an equal percentage increase in both r and v^2.

Merton (1973) has shown that the option value as given by equation (13) increases continuously as any one of $t^\star$, r, or v^2 increases. In each case, it approaches a maximum value equal to the stock price.

The partial derivative w_1 of the valuation formula is of interest, because it determines the ratio of shares of stock to options in the hedged position as in expression (1). Taking the partial derivative of equation (13), and simplifying, we find that:

$$w_1(x, t) = N(d_1). \tag{14}$$

In equation (14), d_1 is as defined in equation (13).

From equations (13) and (14), it is clear that xw_1/w is always greater than one. This shows that the option is always more volatile than the stock.

AN ALTERNATIVE DERIVATION

It is also possible to derive the differential equation (7) using the "capital asset pricing model." This derivation is given because it gives more understanding of the way in which one can discount the value of an option to the present, using a discount rate that depends on both time and the price of the stock.

The capital asset pricing model describes the relation between risk and expected return for a capital asset under conditions of market equilibrium.[8] The expected return on an asset gives the discount that must be applied to the end-of-period value of the asset to give its present value. Thus, the capital-asset pricing model gives a general method for discounting under uncertainty.

The capital-asset pricing model says that the expected return on an asset is a linear function of its β, which is defined as the covariance of the return on the asset with the return on the market, divided by the variance of the return on the market. From equation (4) we see that the covariance of the return on the option $\Delta w/w$ with the return on the market is equal to xw_1/w times the covariance of the return on the stock $\Delta x/x$ with the return on the market. Thus, we have the following relation between the option's β and the stock's β:

$$\beta_w = (xw_1/w)\beta_x. \tag{15}$$

The expression xw_1/w may also be interpreted as the "elasticity" of the option price with respect to the stock price. It is the ratio of the percentage change in the option price to the percentage change in the stock price, for small percentage changes, holding maturity constant.

To apply the capital-asset pricing model to an option and the underlying stock, let us first define a as the rate of expected return on the market minus the interest rate.[9] Then the expected return on the option and the stock are:

$$E(\Delta x/x) = r\Delta t + a\beta_x\Delta t, \tag{16}$$

$$E(\Delta w/w) = r\Delta t + a\beta_w\Delta t. \tag{17}$$

[8]The model was developed by Treynor (1961b), Sharpe (1964), Lintner (1965), and Mossin (1966). It is summarized by Sharpe (1970), and Fama and Miller (1972). The model was originally stated as a single-period model. Extending it to a multi-period model is, in general, difficult. Fama (1970), however, has shown that if we make an assumption that implies that the short-term interest rate is constant through time, then the model must apply to each successive period in time. His proof also goes through under somewhat more general assumptions.

[9]See footnote 2.

Multiplying equation (17) by w, and substituting for β_w from equation (15), we find:

$$E(\Delta w) = rw\Delta t + axw_1\beta_x\Delta t. \tag{18}$$

Using stochastic calculus,[10] we can expand Δw, which is $w(x + \Delta x, t + \Delta t) - w(x, t)$, as follows:

$$\Delta w = w_1\Delta x + \tfrac{1}{2}w_{11}v^2x^2\Delta t + w_2\Delta t. \tag{19}$$

Taking the expected value of equation (19), and substituting for $E(\Delta x)$ from equation (16), we have:

$$E(\Delta w) = rxw_1\Delta t + axw_1\beta_x\Delta t + \tfrac{1}{2}v^2x^2w_{11}\Delta t + w_2\Delta t. \tag{20}$$

Combining equations (18) and (20), we find that the terms involving a and β_x cancel, giving:

$$w_2 = rw - rxw_1 - \tfrac{1}{2}v^2x^2w_{11}. \tag{21}$$

Equation (21) is the same as equation (7).

MORE COMPLICATED OPTIONS

The valuation formula (13) was derived under the assumption that the option can only be exercised at time $t^\star$. Merton (1973) has shown, however, that the value of the option is always greater than the value it would have if it were exercised immediately $(x - c)$. Thus, a rational investor will not exercise a call option before maturity, and the value of an American call option is the same as the value of a European call option.

There is a simple modification of the formula that will make it applicable to European put options (options to sell) as well as call options (options to buy). Writing $u(x, t)$ for the value of a put option, we see that the differential equation remains unchanged.

$$u_2 = ru - rxu_1 - \tfrac{1}{2}v^2x^2u_{11}. \tag{22}$$

The boundary condition, however, becomes:

$$\begin{aligned} u(x, t^\star) &= 0 \qquad && x \geqslant c \\ &= c - x, && x < c. \end{aligned} \tag{23}$$

[10] For an exposition of stochastic calculus, see McKean (1969).

To get the solution to this equation with the new boundary condition, we can simply note that the difference between the value of a call and the value of a put on the same stock, if both can be exercised only at maturity, must obey the same differential equation, but with the following boundary condition:

$$w(x, t^\star) - u(x, t^\star) = x - c. \tag{24}$$

The solution to the differential equation with this boundary condition is:

$$w(x, t) - u(x, t) = x - ce^{r(t-t^\star)}. \tag{25}$$

Thus the value of the European put option is:

$$u(x, t) = w(x, t) - x + ce^{r(t-t^\star)}. \tag{26}$$

Putting in the value of $w(x, t)$ from (13), and noting that $1 - N(d)$ is equal to $N(-d)$, we have:

$$u(x, t) = -xN(-d_1) + ce^{-rt^\star}N(-d_2). \tag{27}$$

In equation (27), d_1 and d_2 are defined as in equation (13).

Equation (25) also gives us a relation between the value of a European call and the value of a European put.[11] We see that if an investor were to buy a call and sell a put, his returns would be exactly the same as if he bought the stock on margin, borrowing $ce^{r(t-t^\star)}$ toward the price of the stock.

Merton (1973) has also shown that the value of an American put option will be greater than the value of a European put option. This is true because it is sometimes advantageous to exercise a put option before maturity, if it is possible to do so. For example, suppose the stock price falls almost to zero and that the probability that the price will exceed the exercise price before the option expires is negligible. Then it will pay to exercise the option immediately, so that the exercise price will be received sooner rather than later. The investor thus gains the interest on the exercise price for the period up to the time he would otherwise have exercised it. So far, no one has been able to obtain a formula for the value of an American put option.

If we relax the assumption that the stock pays no dividend, we begin to get into some complicated problems. First of all, under certain conditions it will pay to exercise an American call option before maturity. Merton (1973) has shown that this can be true only just before the stock's ex-dividend date. Also, it is not clear what adjustment might be made in the terms of the option to

[11] The relation between the value of a call option and the value of a put option was first noted by Stoll (1969). He does not realize, however, that his analysis applies only to European options.

protect the option holder against a loss due to a large dividend on the stock and to ensure that the value of the option will be the same as if the stock paid no dividend. Currently, the exercise price of a call option is generally reduced by the amount of any dividend paid on the stock. We can seen that this is not adequate protection by imagining that the stock is that of a holding company and that it pays out all of its assets in the form of a dividend to its shareholders. This will reduce the price of the stock and the value of the option to zero, no matter what adjustment is made in the exercise price of the option. In fact, this example shows that there may not be any adjustment in the terms of the option that will give adequate protection against a large dividend. In this case, the option value is going to be zero after the distribution, no matter what its terms are. Merton (1973) was the first to point out that the current adjustment for dividends is not adequate.

WARRANT VALUATION

A warrant is an option that is a liability of a corporation. The holder of a warrant has the right to buy the corporation's stock (or other assets) on specified terms. The analysis of warrants is often much more complicated than the analysis of simple options, because:

a) The life of a warrant is typically measured in years, rather than months. Over a period of years, the variance rate of the return on the stock may be expected to change substantially.

b) The exercise price of the warrant is usually not adjusted at all for dividends. The possibility that dividends will be paid requires a modification of the valuation formula.

c) The exercise price of a warrant sometimes changes on specified dates. It may pay to exercise a warrant just before its exercise price changes. This too requires a modification of the valuation formula.

d) If the company is involved in a merger, the adjustment that is made in the terms of the warrant may change its value.

e) Sometimes the exercise price can be paid using bonds of the corporation at face value, even though they may at the time be selling at a discount. This complicates the analysis and means that early exercise may sometimes be desirable.

f) The exercise of a large number of warrants may sometimes result in a significant increase in the number of common shares outstanding.

In some cases, these complications can be treated as insignificant, and equation (13) can be used as an approximation to give an estimate of the warrant value. In other cases, some simple modifications of equation (13) will improve the approximation. Suppose, for example, that there are warrants outstanding, which, if exercised, would double the number of shares of the company's common stock. Let is define the "equity" of the company as the sum of the value of all of its warrants and the value of all of its common stock. If the warrants are exercised at maturity, the equity of the company will increase by the aggregate amount of money paid in by the warrant holders when they exercise. The warrant holders will then own half of the new equity of the company, which is equal to the old equity plus the exercise money.

Thus, at maturity, the warrant holders will either receive nothing, or half of the new equity, minus the exercise money. Thus, they will receive nothing or half of the difference between the old equity and half the exercise money. We can look at the warrants as options to buy shares in the equity rather than shares of common stock, at half the stated exercise price rather than at the full exercise price. The value of a share in the equity is defined as the sum of the value of the warrants and the value of the common stock, divided by twice the number of outstanding shares of common stock. If we take this point of view, then we will take v^2 in equation (13) to be the variance rate of the return on the company's equity, rather than the variance rate of the return on the company's common stock.

A similar modification in the parameters of equation (13) can be made if the number of shares of stock outstanding after exercise of the warrants will be other than twice the number of shares outstanding before exercise of the warrants.

COMMON STOCK AND BOND VALUATION

It is not generally realized that corporate liabilities other than warrants may be viewed as options. Consider, for example, a company that has common stock and bonds outstanding and whose only asset is shares of common stock of a second company. Suppose that the bonds are "pure discount bonds" with no coupon, giving the holder the right to a fixed sum of money, if the corporation can pay it, with a maturity of 10 years. Suppose that the bonds contain no restrictions on the company except a restriction that the company cannot pay any dividends until after the bonds are paid off. Finally, suppose that the company plans to sell all the stock it holds at the end of 10 years, pay off the bond holders if possible, and pay any remaining money to the stockholders as a liquidating dividend.

Under these conditions, it is clear that the stockholders have the equivalent of an option on their company's assets. In effect, the bond holders own the company's assets, but they have given options to the stockholders to buy the assets back. The value of the common stock at the end of 10 years will be the value of the company's assets minus the face value of the bonds, or zero, whichever is greater.

Thus, the value of the common stock will be $w(x, t)$, as given by equation (13), where we take v^2 to be the variance rate of the return on the shares held by the company, c to be the total face value of the outstanding bonds, and x to be the total value of the shares held by the company. The value of the bonds will simply be $x - w(x, t)$.

By subtracting the value of the bonds given by this formula from the value they would have if there were no default risk, we can figure the discount that should be applied to the bonds due to the existence of default risk.

Suppose, more generally, that the corporation holds business assets rather than financial assets. Suppose that at the end of the 10 year period, it will recapitalize by selling an entirely new class of common stock, using the proceeds to pay off the bond holders, and paying any money that is left to the old stockholders to retire their stock. In the absence of taxes, it is clear that the value of the corporation can be taken to be the sum of the total value of the debt and the total value of the common stock.[12] The amount of debt outstanding will not affect the total value of the corporation, but will affect the division of that value between the bonds and the stock. The formula for $w(x, t)$ will again describe the total value of the common stock, where x is taken to be the sum of the value of the bonds and the value of the stock. The formula for $x - w(x, t)$ will again describe the total value of the bonds. It can be shown that, as the face value c of the bonds increases, the market value $x - w(x, t)$ increases by a smaller percentage. An increase in the corporation's debt, keeping the total value of the corporation constant, will increase the probability of default and will thus reduce the market value of one of the corporation's bonds. If the company changes its capital structure by issuing more bonds and using the proceeds to retire common stock, it will hurt the existing bond holders, and help the existing stockholders. The bond price will fall, and the stock price will rise. In this sense, changes in the capital structure of a firm may affect the price of its common stock.[13] The price changes will occur when the change in the capital structure becomes certain, not when the actual change takes place.

Because of this possibility, the bond indenture may prohibit the sale of additional debt of the same or higher priority in the event that the firm is recapitalized. If the corporation issues new bonds that are subordinated to the existing bonds and uses the proceeds to retire common stock, the price of the existing bonds and the common stock price will be unaffected. Similarly, if the company issues new common stock and uses the proceeds to retire completely

[12]The fact that the total value of a corporation is not affected by its capital structure, in the absence of taxes and other imperfections, was first shown by Modigliani and Miller (1958).

[13]For a discussion of this point, see Fama and Miller (1972, pp. 151–52).

the most junior outstanding issue of bonds, neither the common stock price nor the price of any other issue of bonds will be affected.

The corporation's dividend policy will also affect the division of its total value between the bonds and the stock.[14] To take an extreme example, suppose again that the corporation's only assets are the shares of another company, and suppose that it sells all these shares and uses the proceeds to pay a dividend to its common stockholders. Then the value of the firm will go to zero, and the value of the bond will go to zero. The common stockholders will have "stolen" the company out from under the bond holders. Even for dividends of modest size, a higher dividend always favors the stockholders at the expense of the bond holders. A liberalization of dividend policy will increase the common stock price and decrease the bond price.[15] Because of this possibility, bond indentures contain restrictions on dividend policy, and the common stockholders have an incentive to pay themselves the largest dividend allowed by the terms of the bond indenture. However, it should be noted that the size of the effect of changing dividend policy will normally be very small.

If the company has coupon bonds rather than pure discount bonds outstanding, then we can view the common stock as a "compound option." The common stock is an option on an option on . . . an option on the firm. After making the last interest payment, the stockholders have an option to buy the company from the bond holders for the face value of the bonds. Call this "option 1." After making the next-to-last interest payment, but before making the last interest payment, the stockholders have an option to buy option 1 by making the last interest payment. Call this "option 2." Before making the next-to-the-last interest payment, the stockholders have an option to buy option 2 by making that interest payment. This is "option 3." The value of

[14]Miller and Modigliani (1961) show that the total value of a firm, in the absence of taxes and other imperfections, is not affected by its dividend policy. They also note that the price of the common stock and the value of the bonds will not be affected by a change in dividend policy if the funds for a higher dividend are raised by issuing common stock or if the money released by a lower dividend is used to repurchase common stock.

[15]This is true assuming that the liberalization of dividend policy is not accompanied by a change in the company's current and planned financial structure. Since the issue of common stock or junior debt will hurt the common shareholders (holding dividend policy constant), they will normally try to liberalize dividend policy without issuing new securities. They may be able to do this by selling some of the firm's financial assets, such as ownership claims on other firms. Or they may be able to do it by adding to the company's short-term bank debt, which is normally senior to its long-term debt. Finally, the company may be able to finance a higher dividend by selling off a division. Assuming that it receives a fair price for the division, and that there were no economies of combination, this need not involve any loss to the firm as a whole. If the firm issues new common stock or junior debt in exactly the amounts needed to finance the liberalization of dividend policy, then the common stock and bond prices will not be affected. If the liberalization of dividend policy is associated with a decision to issue more common stock or junior debt than is needed to pay the higher dividends, the common stock price will fall and the bond price will rise. But these actions are unlikely, since they are not in the stockholders' best interests.

the stockholders' claim at any point in time is equal to the value of option $n + 1$, where n is the number of interest payments remaining in the life of the bond.

If payments to a sinking fund are required along with interest payments, then a similar analysis can be made. In this case, there is no "balloon payment" at the end of the life of the bond. The sinking fund will have a final value equal to the face value of the bond. Option 1 gives the stockholders the right to buy the company from the bond holders by making the last sinking fund and interest payment. Option 2 gives the stockholders the right to buy option 1 by making the next-to-the-last sinking fund and interest payment. And the value of the stockholders' claim at any point in time is equal to the value of option n, where n is the number of sinking fund and interest payments remaining in the life of the bond. It is clear that the value of a bond for which sinking fund payments are required is greater than the value of a bond for which they are not required.

If the company has callable bonds, then the stokholders have more than one option. They can buy the next option by making the next interest or sinking fund and interest payment, or they can exercise their option to retire the bonds before maturity at prices specified by the terms of the call feature. Under our assumption of a constant short-term interest rate, the bonds would never sell above face value, and the usual kind of call option would never be exercised. Under more general assumptions, however, the call feature would have value to the stockholders and would have to be taken into account in deciding how the value of the company is divided between the stockholders and the bond holders.

Similarly, if the bonds are convertible, we simply add another option to the package. It is an option that the bond holders have to buy part of the company from the stockholders.

Unfortunately, these more complicated options cannot be handled by using the valuation formula (13). The valuation formula assumes that the variance rate of the return on the optioned asset is constant. But the variance of the return on an option is certainly not constant: it depends on the price of the stock and the maturity of the option. Thus the formula cannot be used, even as an approximation, to give the value of an option on an option. It is possible, however, that an analysis in the same spirit as the one that led to equation (13) would allow at least a numerical solution to the valuation of certain more complicated options.

EMPIRICAL TESTS

We have done empirical tests of the valuation formula on a large body of call-option data (Black and Scholes 1972). These tests indicate that the actual prices at which options are bought and sold deviate in certain systematic ways from the values predicted by the formula. Option buyers pay prices that are consistently higher than those predicted by the formula. Option writers, however, receive prices that are at about the level predicted by the formula. There are large transaction costs in the option market, all of which are effectively paid by option buyers.

Also, the difference between the price paid by option buyers and the value given by the formula is greater for options on low-risk stocks than for options on high-risk stocks. The market appears to underestimate the effect of differences in variance rate on the value of an option. Given the magnitude of the transaction costs in this market, however, this systematic misestimation of value does not imply profit opportunities for a speculator in the option market.

REFERENCES

Ayres, Herbert F. "Risk Aversion in the Warrants Market." *Indus. Management Rev.* 4 (Fall 1963): 947–505. Reprinted in Cootner (1967), pp. 497–505.

Baumol, William J.; Malkiel, Burton G.; and Quandt, Richard E. "The Valuation of Convertible Securities." *Q.J.E.* 80 (February 1966): 48–59.

Black, Fischer, and Scholes, Myron. "The Valuation of Option Contracts and a Test of Market Efficiency." *J. Finance* 27 (May 1972): 399–417.

Boness, A. James. "Elements of a Theory of Stock-Option Values." *J.P.E.* 72 (April 1964): 163–75.

Chen, Andrew H. Y. "A Model of Warrant Pricing in a Dynamic Market." *J. Finance* 25 (December 1970): 1041–60.

Churchill, R. V. *Fourier Series and Boundary Value Problems*, 2d ed. New York: McGraw-Hill, 1963.

Cootner, Paul A. *The Random Character of Stock Market Prices.* Cambridge, Mass.: M.I.T. Press, 1967.

Fama, Eugene F. "Multiperiod Consumption-Investment Decisions." *A.E.R.* 60 (March 1970): 163–74.

Fama, Eugene F., and Miller, Merton H. *The Theory of Finance.* New York: Holt, Rinehart & Winston, 1972.

Lintner, John. "The Valuation of Risk Assets and the Selection of Risky Investments in Stock Portfolios and Capital Budgets." *Rev. Econ. and Statis.* 47 (February 1965): 768–83.

McKean, H. P., Jr. *Stochastic Integrals.* New York: Academic Press, 1969.

Merton, Robert C. "Theory of Rational Option Pricing." *Bell J. Econ. and Management Sci.* (1973): in press.

Miller, Merton H., and Modigliani, Franco. "Dividend Policy, Growth, and the Valuation of Shares." *J. Bus.* 34 (October 1961): 411–33.

Modigliani, Franco, and Miller, Merton H. "The Cost of Capital, Corporation Finance, and the Theory of Investment." *A.E.R.* 48 (June 1958): 261–97.

Mossin, Jan. "Equilibrium in a Capital Asset Market." *Econometrica* 34 (October 1966): 768–83.

Samuelson, Paul A. "Rational Theory of Warrant Pricing." *Indus. Management Rev.* 6 (Spring 1965): 13–31. Reprinted in Cootner (1967), pp. 506–32.

Samuelson, Paul A., and Merton, Robert C. "A Complete Model of Warrant Pricing that Maximizes Utility." *Indus. Management Rev.* 10 (Winter 1969): 17–46.

Sharpe, William F. "Capital Asset Prices: A Theory of Market Equilibrium Under Conditions of Risk." *J. Finance* 19 (September 1964): 425–42.

——. *Portfolio Theory and Capital Markets*: New York: McGraw-Hill, 1970.

Sprenkle, Case. "Warrant Prices as Indications of Expectations." *Yale Econ. Essays* 1 (1961): 179–232. Reprinted in Cootner (1967), 412–74.

Stoll, Hans R. "The Relationship Between Put and Call Option Prices." *J. Finance* 24 (December 1969): 802–24.

Thorp, Edward O., and Kassouf, Sheen T. *Beat the Market*. New York: Random House, 1967.

Treynor, Jack L. "Implications for the Theory of Finance." Unpublished memorandum, 1961. (*a*)

——. "Toward a Theory of Market Value of Risky Assets." Unpublished memorandum, 1961. (*b*)

20. OPTION PRICING: A SIMPLIFIED APPROACH

John C. Cox, Stephen A. Ross, and Mark Rubinstein

1. INTRODUCTION

An option is a security which gives its owner the right to trade in a fixed number of shares of a specified common stock at a fixed price at any time on or before a given date. The act of making this transaction is referred to as exercising the option. The fixed price is termed the striking price, and the given date, the expiration date. A call option gives the right to buy the shares; a put option gives the right to sell the shares.

Options have been traded for centuries, but they remained relatively obscure financial instruments until the introduction of a listed options exchange in 1973. Since then, options trading has enjoyed an expansion unprecedented in American securities markets.

Option pricing theory has a long and illustrious history, but it also underwent a revolutionary change in 1973. At that time, Fischer Black and Myron Scholes presented the first completely satisfactory equilibrium option pricing model. In the same year, Robert Merton extended their model in several important ways. These path-breaking articles have formed the basis for many subsequent academic studies.

As these studies have shown, option pricing theory is relevant to almost every area of finance. For example, virtually all corporate securities can be

Reprinted from *Journal of Financial Economics*, September 1979.

interpreted as portfolios of puts and calls on the assets of the firm.[1] Indeed, the theory applies to a very general class of economic problems—the valuation of contracts where the outcome to each party depends on a quantifiable uncertain future event.

Unfortunately, the mathematical tools employed in the Black–Scholes and Merton articles are quite advanced and have tended to obscure the underlying economics. However, thanks to a suggestion by William Sharpe, it is possible to derive the same results using only elementary mathematics.[2]

In this article we will present a simple discrete-time option pricing formula. The fundamental economic principles of option valuation by arbitrage methods are particularly clear in this setting. Sections 2 and 3 illustrate and develop this model for a call option on a stock which pays no dividends. Section 4 shows exactly how the model can be used to lock in pure arbitrage profits if the market price of an option differs from the value given by the model. In section 5, we will show that our approach includes the Black–Scholes model as a special limiting case. By taking the limits in a different way, we will also obtain the Cox–Ross (1975) jump process model as another special case.

Other more general option pricing problems often seem immune to reduction to a simple formula. Instead, numerical procedures must be employed to value these more complex options. Michael Brennan and Eduardo Schwartz (1977) have provided many interesting results along these lines. However, their techniques are rather complicated and are not directly related to the economic structure of the problem. Our formulation, by its very construction, leads to an alternative numerical procedure which is both simpler, and for many purposes, computationally more efficient.

Section 6 introduces these numerical procedures and extends the model to include puts and calls on stocks which pay dividends. Section 7 concludes the paper by showing how the model can be generalized in other important ways and discussing its essential role in valuation by arbitrage methods.

2. THE BASIC IDEA

Suppose the current price of a stock is $S = \$50$, and at the end of a period of time, its price must be either $S^\star = \$25$ or $S^\star = \$100$. A call on the stock is

[1] To take an elementary case, consider a firm with a single liability of a homogeneous class of pure discount bonds. The stockholders then have a 'call' on the assets of the firm which they can choose to exercise at the maturity date of the debt by paying its principal to the bondholders. In turn, the bonds can be interpreted as a portfolio containing a default-free loan with the same face value as the bonds and a short position in a put on the assets of the firm.

[2] Sharpe (1978) has partially developed this approach to option pricing in his excellent new book, *Investments*. Rendleman and Bartter (1978) have recently independently discovered a similar formulation of the option pricing problem.

TABLE 1. ARBITRAGE TABLE ILLUSTRATING THE FORMATION OF A RISKLESS HEDGE

	Present date	Expiration date	
		$S^* = \$25$	$S^* = \$100$
Write 3 calls	$3C$	–	– 150
Buy 2 shares	– 100	50	200
Borrow	40	– 50	– 50
Total		–	–

available with a striking price of $K = \$50$, expiring at the end of the period.[3] It is also possible to borrow and lend at a 25% rate of interest. The one piece of information left unfurnished is the current value of the call, C. However, if riskless profitable arbitrage is not possible, we can deduce from the given information *alone* what the value of the call *must* be!

Consider forming the following levered hedge:

(1) Write 3 calls at C each,
(2) buy 2 shares at \$50 each, and
(3) borrow \$40 at 25%, to be paid back at the end of the period.

Table 1 gives the return from this hedge for each possible level of the stock price at expiration. Regardless of the outcome, the hedge exactly breaks even on the expiration date. Therefore, to prevent profitable riskless arbitrage, its current cost must be zero; that is,

$$3C - 100 + 40 = 0.$$

The current value of the call must then be $C = \$20$.

If the call were not priced at \$20, a sure profit would be possible. In particular, if $C = \$25$, the above hedge would yield a current cash inflow of \$15 and would experience no further gain or loss in the future. On the other hand, if $C = \$15$, then the same thing could be accomplished by buying 3 calls, selling short 2 shares, and lending \$40.

Table 1 can be interpreted as demonstrating that *an appropriately levered position in stock will replicate the future returns of a call.* That is, if we buy

[3] To keep matters simple, assume for now that the stock will pay no cash dividends during the life of the call. We also ignore transaction costs, margin requirements and taxes.

shares and borrow against them in the right proportion, we can, in effect, duplicate a position in calls. In view of this, it should seem less surprising that all we needed to determine the *exact* value of the call was its *striking price, underlying stock price, range of movement in the underlying stock price, and the rate of interest*. What may seem more incredible is what we do not need to know: among other things, *we do not need to know the probability that the stock price will rise or fall*. Bulls and bears must agree on the value of the call, relative to its underlying stock price!

This example is very simple, but it shows several essential features of option pricing. And we will soon see that it is not as unrealistic as it seems.

3. THE BINOMIAL OPTION PRICING FORMULA

In this section, we will develop the framework illustrated in the example into a complete valuation method. We begin by assuming that the stock price follows a multiplicative binomial process over discrete periods. The rate of return on the stock over each period can have two possible values: $u - 1$ with probability q, or $d - 1$ with probability $1 - q$. Thus, if the current stock price is S, the stock price at the end of the period will be either uS or dS. We can represent this movement with the following diagram:

$$S \begin{cases} uS & \text{with probability } q, \\ dS & \text{with probability } 1 - q. \end{cases}$$

We also assume that the interest rate is constant. Individuals may borrow or lend as much as they wish at this rate. To focus on the basic issues, we will continue to assume that there are no taxes, transaction costs, or margin requirements. Hence, individuals are allowed to sell short any security and receive full use of the proceeds.[4]

Letting r denote one plus the riskless interest rate over one period, we require $u > r > d$. If these inequalities did not hold, there would be profitable riskless arbitrage opportunities involving only the stock and riskless borrowing and lending.[5]

To see how to value a call on this stock, we start with the simplest situation: the expiration date is just one period away. Let C be the current value of the call, C_u be its value at the end of the period if the stock price goes to uS, and C_d be its value at the end of the period if the stock price goes to dS. Since there is now only one period remaining in the life of the call, we know that the terms

[4] Of course, restitution is required for payouts made to securities held short.

[5] We will ignore the uninteresting special case where q is zero or one and $u = d = r$.

of its contract and a rational exercise policy imply that $C_u = \max[0, uS - K]$ and $C_d = \max[0, dS - K]$. Therefore,

$$C \begin{cases} C_u = \max[0, uS - K] & \text{with probability } q, \\ C_d = \max[0, dS - K] & \text{with probability } 1 - q. \end{cases}$$

Suppose we form a portfolio containing Δ shares of stock and the dollar amount B in riskless bonds.[6] This will cost $\Delta S + B$. At the end of the period, the value of this portfolio will be

$$\Delta S + B \begin{cases} \Delta uS + rB & \text{with probability } q, \\ \Delta dS + rB & \text{with probability } 1 - q. \end{cases}$$

Since we can select Δ and B in any way we wish, suppose we choose them to equate the end-of-period values of the portfolio and the call for each possible outcome. This requires that

$$\begin{aligned} \Delta uS + rB &= C_u, \\ \Delta dS + rB &= C_d. \end{aligned}$$

Solving these equations, we find

$$\Delta = \frac{C_u - C_d}{(u - d)S}, \qquad B = \frac{uC_d - dC_u}{(u - d)r}. \tag{1}$$

With Δ and B chosen in this way, we will call this the hedging portfolio.

If there are to be no riskless arbitrage opportunities, the current value of the call, C, cannot be less than the current value of the hedging portfolio, $\Delta S + B$. If it were, we could make a riskless profit with no net investment by buying the call and selling the portfolio. It is tempting to say that it also cannot be worth more, since then we would have a riskless arbitrage opportunity by reversing our procedure and selling the call and buying the portfolio. But this overlooks the fact that the person who bought the call we sold has the right to exercise it immediately.

Suppose that $\Delta S + B < S - K$. If we try to make an arbitrage profit by selling calls for more than $\Delta S + B$, but less than $S - K$, then we will soon find that we are the source of arbitrage profits rather than their recipient. Anyone could make an arbitrage profit by buying our calls and exercising them immediately.

[6] Buying bonds is the same as lending; selling them is the same as borrowing.

We might hope that we will be spared this embarrassment because everyone will somehow find it advantageous to hold the calls for one more period as an investment rather than take a quick profit by exercising them immediately. But each person will reason in the following way. If I do not exercise now, I will receive the same payoff as a portfolio with ΔS in stock and B in bonds. If I do exercise now, I can take the proceeds, $S - K$, buy this same portfolio and some extra bonds as well, and have a higher payoff in every possible circumstance. Consequently, no one would be willing to hold the calls for one more period.

Summing up all of this, we conclude that if there are to be no riskless arbitrage opportunities, it must be true that

$$\begin{aligned} C &= \Delta S + B \\ &= \frac{C_u - C_d}{u - d} + \frac{uC_d - dC_u}{(u - d)r} \\ &= \left[\left(\frac{r - d}{u - d}\right) C_u + \left(\frac{u - r}{u - d}\right) C_d\right] \Big/ r, \end{aligned} \tag{2}$$

if this value is greater than $S - K$, and if not, $C = S - K$.[7]

Eq. (2) can be simplified by defining

$$p \equiv \frac{r - d}{u - d} \quad \text{and} \quad 1 - p \equiv \frac{u - r}{u - d},$$

so that we can write

$$C = [pC_u + (1 - p)C_d]/r. \tag{3}$$

It is easy to see that in the present case, with no dividends, this will always be greater than $S - K$ as long as the interest rate is positive. To avoid spending time on the unimportant situations where the interest rate is less than or equal to zero, we will now assume that r is always greater than one. Hence, (3) is the exact formula for the value of a call one period prior to expiration in terms of S, K, u, d, and r.

[7] In some applications of the theory to other areas, it is useful to consider options which can be exercised only on the expiration date. These are usually termed European options. Those which can be exercised at any earlier time as well, such as we have been examining here, are then referred to as American options. Our discussion could be easily modified to include European calls. Since immediate exercise is then precluded, their values would always be given by (2), even if this is less than $S - K$.

To confirm this, note that if $uS \leqq K$, then $S < K$ and $C = 0$, so $C > S - K$. Also if $dS \geqq K$, then $C = S - (K/r) > S - K$. The remaining possibility is $uS > K > dS$. In this case, $C = p(uS - K)/r$. This is greater than $S - K$ if $(1 - p)dS > (p - r)K$, which is certainly true as long as $r > 1$.

This formula has a number of notable features. First, the probability q does not appear in the formula. This means, surprisingly, that even if different investors have different subjective probabilities about an upward or downward movement in the stock, they could still agree on the relationship of C to S, u, d, and r.

Second, the value of the call does not depend on investors' attitudes toward risk. In constructing the formula, the only assumption we made about an individual's behavior was that he prefers more wealth to less wealth and therefore has an incentive to take advantage of profitable riskless arbitrage opportunities. We could obtain the same formula whether investors are risk-averse or risk-preferring.

Third, the only random variable in which the call value depends is the stock price itself. In particular, it does not depend on the random prices of other securities or portfolios, such as the market portfolio containing all securities in the economy. If another pricing formula involving other variables was submitted as giving equilibrium market prices, we could immediately show that it was incorrect by using our formula to make riskless arbitrage profits while trading at those prices.

It is easier to understand these features if it is remembered that the formula is only a relative pricing relationship giving C in terms of S, u, d, and r. Investors' attitudes toward risk and the characteristics of other assets may indeed influence call values indirectly, through their effect on these variables, but they will not be separate determinants of call value.

Finally, observe that $p \equiv (r - d)/(u - d)$ is always greater than zero and less than one, so it has the properties of a probability. In fact, p is the value q would have in equilibrium if investors were risk-neutral. To see this, note that the expected rate of return on the stock would then be the riskless interest rate, so

$$q(uS) + (1 - q)(dS) = rS,$$

and

$$q = (r - d)/(u - d) = p.$$

Hence, the value of the call can be interpreted as the expectation of its discounted future value in a risk-neutral world. In light of our earlier observations, this is not surprising. Since the formula does not involve q or any measure of attitudes towards risk, then it must be the same for any set of preferences, including risk neutrality.

It is important to note that this does not imply that the equilibrium expected rate of return on the call is the riskless interest rate. Indeed, our argument has shown that, in equilibrium, holding the call over the period is exactly equivalent to holding the hedging portfolio. Consequently, the risk and expected rate of return of the call must be the same as that of the hedging portfolio. It can be shown that $\Delta \geqq 0$ and $B \leqq 0$, so the hedging portfolio is equivalent to a particular levered long position in the stock. In equilibrium, the same is true for the call. Of course, if the call is currently mispriced, its risk and expected return over the period will differ from that of the hedging portfolio.

Now we can consider the next simplest situation: a call with two periods remaining before its expiration date. In keeping with the binomial process, the stock can take on three possible valus after two periods,

$$\begin{array}{ccccc} & & & & u^2S, \\ & & uS & \diagup & \\ S & \begin{array}{c}\diagup \\ \diagdown\end{array} & & \diagdown & dUS, \\ & & dS & \diagup & \\ & & & \diagdown & d^2S; \end{array}$$

similarly, for the call,

$$\begin{array}{ccccl} & & & & C_{uu} = \max[0, u^2S - K], \\ & & C_u & \diagup & \\ C & \begin{array}{c}\diagup \\ \diagdown\end{array} & & \diagdown & C_{du} = \max[0, duS - K], \\ & & C_d & \diagup & \\ & & & \diagdown & C_{dd} = \max[0, d^2S - K]. \end{array}$$

C_{uu} stands for the value of a call two periods from the current time if the stock price moves upward each period; C_{du} and C_{dd} have analogous definitions.

At the end of the current period there will be one period left in the life of the call and we will be faced with a problem identical to the one we just solved. Thus, from our previous analysis, we know that when there are two periods left,

$$C_u = [pC_{uu} + (1 - p)C_{ud}]/r,$$

and

$$C_d = [pC_{du} + (1 - p)C_{dd}]/r. \tag{4}$$

Again we can select a portfolio with ΔS in stock and B in bonds whose end-of-period value will be C_u if the stock price goes to uS and C_d if the stock price goes to dS. Indeed, the functional form of Δ and B remains unchanged. To get the new values of Δ and B, we simply use eq. (1) with the new values of C_u and C_d.

Can we now say, as before, that an opportunity of profitable riskless arbitrage will be available if the current price of the call is not equal to the new value of this portfolio or $S - K$, whichever is greater? Yes, but there is an important difference. With one period to go, we could plan to lock in a riskless profit by selling an overpriced call and using part of the proceeds to buy the hedging portfolio. At the end of the period, we knew that the market price of the call must be equal to the value of the portfolio, so the entire position could be safely liquidated at that point. But this was true only because the end of the period was the expiration date. Now we have no such guarantee. At the end of the current period, when there is still one period left, the market price of the call could still be in disequilibrium and be greater than the value of the hedging portfolio. If we closed out the position then, selling the portfolio and repurchasing the call, we could suffer a loss which would more than offset our original profit. However, we could always avoid this loss by maintaining the portfolio for one more period. The value of the portfolio at the end of the current period will always be exactly sufficient to purchase the portfolio we would want to hold over the last period. In effect, we would have to readjust the proportions in the hedging portfolio, but we would not have to put up any more money.

Consequently, we conclude that even with two periods to go, there is a strategy we could follow which would guarantee riskless profits with no net investment if the current market price of a call differs from the maximum of $\Delta S + B$ and $S - K$. Hence, the larger of these is the current value of the call.

Since Δ and B have the same functional form in each period, the current value of the call in terms of C_u and C_d will again be $C = [pC_u + (1 - p)C_d]/r$ if this is greater than $S - K$, and $C = S - K$ otherwise. By substituting from eq. (4) into the former expression, and noting that $C_{du} = C_{ud}$, we obtain

$$\begin{aligned} C &= [p^2 C_{uu} + 2p(1 - p)C_{ud} + (1 - p)^2 C_{dd}]/r^2 \\ &= [p^2 \max[0, u^2 S - K] + 2p(1 - p)\max[0, duS - K] \\ &\quad + (1 - p)^2 \max[0, d^2 S - K]]/r^2. \end{aligned} \tag{5}$$

A little algebra shows that this is always greater than $S - K$ if, as assumed, r is always greater than one, so this expression gives the exact value of the call.[8]

[8] In the current situation, with no dividends, we can show by a simple direct argument that if there are no arbitrage opportunities, then the call value must always be greater than $S - K$ before the expiration date. Suppose that the call is selling for $S - K$. Then there would be an easy arbitrage strategy which would require no initial investment and would always have a positive return. All we would have to do is buy the call, short the stock, and invest K dollars in bonds. See Merton (1973). In the general case, with dividends, such an argument is no longer valid, and we must use the procedure of checking every period.

All of the observations made about formula (3) also apply to formula (5), except that the number of periods remaining until expiration, n, now emerges clearly as an additional determinant of the call value. For formula (5), $n = 2$. That is, the full list of variables determining C is S, K, n, u, d, and r.

We now have a recursive procedure for finding the value of a call with any number of periods to go. By starting at the expiration date and working backwards, we can write down the general valuation formula for any n:

$$C = \left[\sum_{j=0}^{n} \left(\frac{n!}{j!(n-j)!}\right) p^j (1-p)^{n-j} \max[0, u^j d^{n-j} S - K]\right] \Big/ r^n. \quad (6)$$

This gives us the complete formula, but with a little additional effort we can express it in a more convenient way.

Let a stand for the minimum number of upward moves which the stock must make over the next n periods for the call to finish in-the-money. Thus a will be the smallest non-negative integer such that $u^a d^{n-a} S > K$. By taking the natural logarithm of both sides of this inequality, we could write a as the smallest non-negative integer greater than $\log(K/Sd^n)/\log(u/d)$.

For all $j < a$,

$$\max[0, u^j d^{n-j} S - K] = 0,$$

and for all $j \geqq a$,

$$\max[0, u^j d^{n-j} S - K] = u^j d^{n-j} S - K.$$

Therefore,

$$C = \left[\sum_{j=a}^{n} \left(\frac{n!}{j!(n-j)!}\right) p^j (1-p)^{n-j} [u^j d^{n-j} S - K]\right] \Big/ r^n.$$

Of course, if $a > n$, the call will finish out-of-the-money even if the stock moves upward every period, so its current value must be zero.

By breaking up C into two terms, we can write

$$C = S\left[\sum_{j=a}^{n} \left(\frac{n!}{j!(n-j)!}\right) p^j (1-p)^{n-j} \left(\frac{u^j d^{n-j}}{r^n}\right)\right] - Kr^{-n}\left[\sum_{j=a}^{n} \left(\frac{n!}{j!(n-j)!}\right) p^j (1-p)^{n-j}\right].$$

Now, the latter bracketed expression is the complementary binomial distribution function $\Phi[a; n, p]$. The first bracketed expression can also be interpreted as a complementary binomial distribution function $\Phi[a; n, p']$, where

$$p' \equiv (u/r)p \quad \text{and} \quad 1 - p' \equiv (d/r)(1 - p).$$

p' is a probability, since $0 < p' < 1$. To see this, note that $p < (r/u)$ and

$$p^j(1 - p)^{n-j}\left(\frac{u^j d^{n-j}}{r^n}\right) = \left[\frac{u}{r}p\right]^j\left[\frac{d}{r}(1 - p)\right]^{n-j} = p'^j(1 - p')^{n-j}.$$

In summary:

Binomial Option Pricing Formula

$$C = S\Phi[a; n, p'] - Kr^{-n}\Phi[a; n, p],$$

where

$p \equiv (r - d)/(u - d)$ and $p' \equiv (u/r)p$,

$a \equiv$ the smallest non-negative integer greater than $\log(K/Sd^n)/\log(u/d)$

If $a > n$, $C = 0$.

It is now clear that all of the components we made about the one period valuation formula are valid for any number of periods. In particular, the value of a call should be the expectation, in a risk-neutral world, of the discounted value of the payoff it will receive. In fact, that is exactly what eq. (6) says. Why, then, should we waste time with the recursive procedure when we can write down the answer in one direct step? The reason is that while this one-step approach is always technically correct, it is really useful only if we know in advance the circumstances in which a rational individual would prefer to exercise the call before the expiration date. If we do not know this, we have no way to compute the required expectation. In the present example, a call on a stock paying no dividends, it happens that we can determine this information from other sources: the call should never be exercised before the expiration date. As we will see in section 6, with puts or with calls on stocks which pay dividends, we will not be so lucky. Finding the optimal exercise strategy will be an integral part of the valuation problem. The full recursive procedure will then be necessary.

For some readers, an alternative 'complete markets' interpretation of our binomial approach may be instructive. Suppose that π_u and π_d represent the state-contingent discount rates to states u and d, respectively. Therefore, π_u

would be the current price of one dollar received at the end of the period, if and only if state u occurs. Each security—a riskless bond, the stock, and the option—must all have returns discounted to the present by π_u and π_d if no riskless arbitrage opportunities are available. Therefore,

$$1 = \pi_u r + \pi_d r,$$

$$S = \pi_u(uS) + \pi_d(dS),$$

$$C = \pi_u C_u + \pi_d C_d.$$

The first two equations, for the bond and the stock, imply

$$\pi_u = \left(\frac{r - d}{u - d}\right)\frac{1}{r} \quad \text{and} \quad \pi_d = \left(\frac{u - r}{u - d}\right)\frac{1}{r}.$$

Substituting these equalities for the state-contingent prices in the last equation for the option yields eq. (3)

It is important to realize that we are not assuming that the riskless bond and the stock and the option are the only three securities in the economy, or that other securities must follow a binomial process. Rather, however, these securities are priced in relation to others in equilibrium, among themselves they must conform to the above relationships.

From either the hedging or complete markets approaches, it should be clear that three-state or trinomial stock price movements will not lead to an option pricing formula based solely on arbitrage considerations. Suppose, for example, that over each period the stock price could move to uS or dS or remain the same at S. A choice of Δ and B which would equate the returns in two states could not in the third. That is, a riskless arbitrage position could not be taken. Under the complete markets interpretation, with three equation in now three unknown state-contingent prices, we would lack the redundant equation necessary to price one security in terms of the other two.

4. RISKLESS TRADING STRATEGIES

The following numerical example illustrates how we could use the formula if the current *market price* M ever diverged from its *formula value* C. If $M > C$, we would hedge, and if $M < C$, 'reverse hedge', to try and lock in a profit.

Suppose the values of the underlying variables are

$$S = 80, \quad n = 3, \quad K = 80, \quad u = 1.5, \quad d = 0.5, \quad r = 1.1$$

In this case, $p = (r - d)/(u - d) = 0.6$. The relevant values of the discount factor are

$$r^{-1} = 0.909, \quad r^{-2} = 0.826, \quad r^{-3} = 0.751.$$

The paths the stock price may follow and their corresponding probabilities (using probability p) are, when $n = 3$, with $S = 80$,

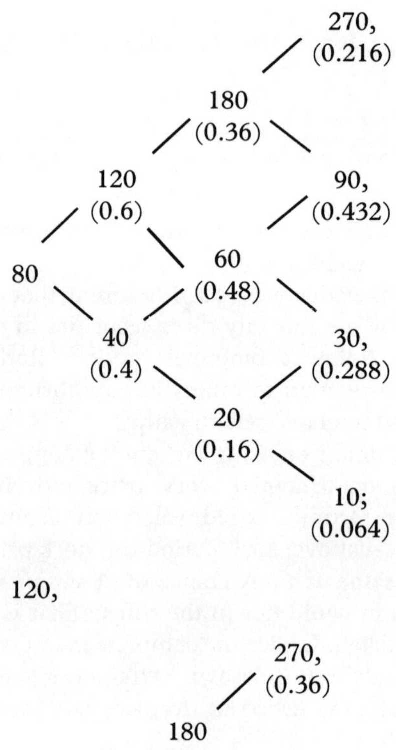

when $n = 2$, if $S = 120$,

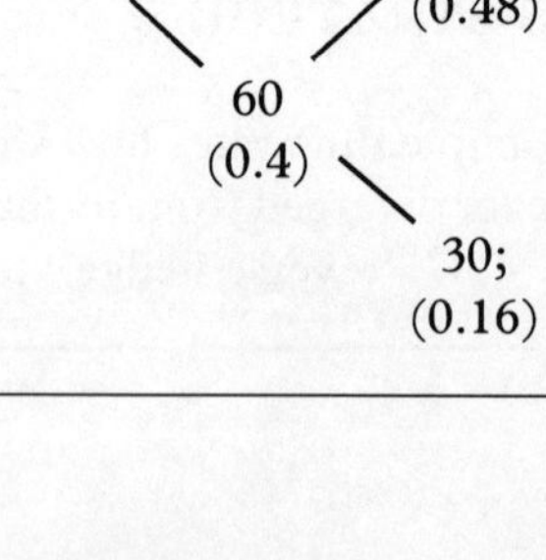

when $n = 2$, if $S = 40$,

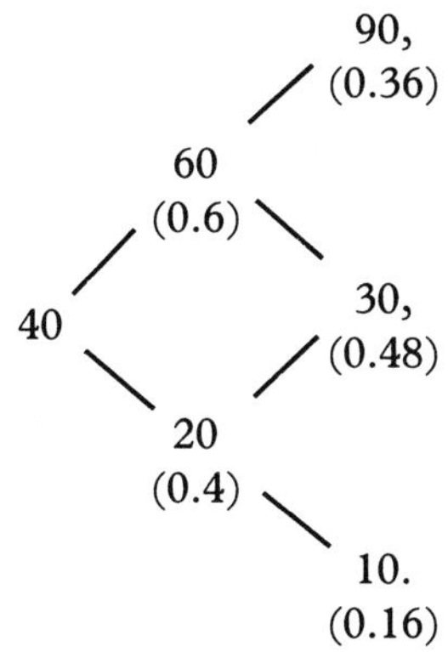

Using the formula, the current value of the call would be

$$\begin{aligned} C &= 0.751[0.064(0) + 0.288(0) + 0.432(90 - 80) + 0.216(270 - 80)] \\ &= 34.065. \end{aligned}$$

Recall that to form a riskless hedge, for each call we sell, we buy and subsequently keep adjusted a portfolio with ΔS in stock and B in bonds, where $\Delta = (C_u - C_d)/(u - d)S$. The following tree diagram gives the paths the call value may follow and the corresponding values of Δ:

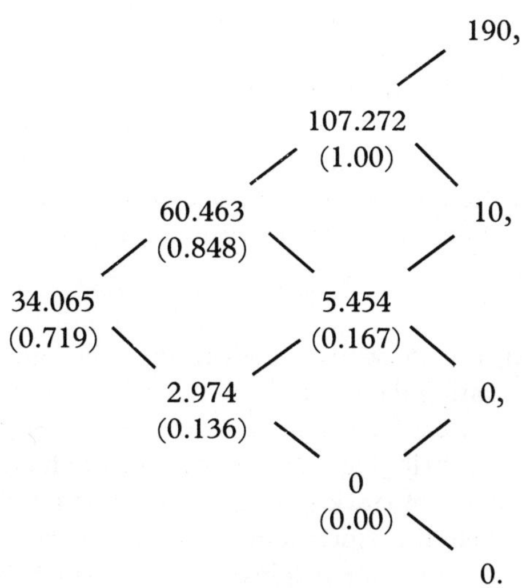

With this preliminary analysis, we are prepared to use the formula to take advantage of mispricing in the market. Suppose that when $n = 3$, the market price of the call is 36. Our formula tells us the call should be worth 34.065. The option is overpriced, so we could plan to sell it and assure ourselves of a profit equal to the mispricing differential. Here are the steps you could take for a typical path the stock might follow.

STEP 1 ($n = 3$)

Sell the call for 36. Take 34.065 of this and invest it in a portfolio containing $\Delta = 0.719$ shares of stock by borrowing $0.719(80) - 34.065 = 23.455$. Take the remainder, $36 - 34.065 = 1.935$, and put it in the bank.

STEP 2 ($n = 2$)

Suppose the stock goes to 120 so that the new Δ is 0.848. Buy $0.848 - 0.719 = 0.129$ more shares of stock at 120 per share for a total expenditure of 15.480. Borrow to pay the bill. With an interest rate of 0.1, you already owe $23.455(1.1) = 25.801$. Thus, your total current indebtedness is $25.801 + 15.480 = 41.281$.

STEP 3 ($n = 1$)

Suppose the stock price now goes to 60. The new Δ is 0.167. Sell $0.848 - 0.167 = 0.681$ shares at 60 per share, taking in $0.681(60) = 40.860$. Use this to pay back part of your borrowing. Since you now owe $41.281(1.1) = 45.409$, the repayment will reduce this to $45.409 - 40.860 = 4.549$.

STEP 4D ($n = 0$)

Suppose the stock price now goes to 30. The call you sell has expired worthless. You own 0.167 shares of stock selling at 30 per share, for a total value of $0.167(30) = 5$. Sell the stock and repay the $4.549(1.1) = 5$ that you now owe on the borrowing. Go back to the bank and withdraw your original deposit, which has now grown to $1.935(1.1)^3 = 2.575$.

STEP 4U ($n = 0$)

Suppose, instead, the stock price goes to 90. The call you sold is in the money at the expiration date. Buy back the call, or buy one share of stock and let it be exercised, incurring a loss of $90 - 80 = 10$ either way. Borrow to cover this, bringing your current indebtedness to $5 + 10 = 15$. You own 0.167 shares of stock selling at 90 per share, for a total value of $0.167(90) = 15$. Sell the stock and repay the borrowing. Go back to the bank and withdraw your original deposit, which has now grown to $1.935(1.1)^3 = 2.575$.

In summary, if we were correct in our original analysis about stock price movements (which did not involve the unenviable task of predicting whether the stock price would go up or down), and if we faithfully adjust our portfolio as described by the formula, then we can be assured of walking away in the clear at the expiration date, while still keeping the original differential and the interest it has accumulated. It is true that closing out the position before the expiration date, which involves buying back the option at its then current market price, might produce a loss which would more than offset our profit, but this loss could always be avoided by waiting until the expiration date. Moreover, if the market price comes into line with the formula value before the expiration date, we can close out the position then with no loss and be rid of the concern of keeping the portfolio adjusted.

It still might seem that we are depending on rational behavior by the person who bought the call we sold. If instead he behaves foolishly and exercises at the wrong time, could he make things worse for us as well as for himself? Fortunately, the answer is no. Mistakes on his part can only mean greater profits for us. Suppose that he exercises too soon. In that circumstance, the hedging portfolio will always be worth more than $S - K$, so we could close out the option then with an extra profit.

Suppose, instead, that he fails to exercise when it would be optimal to do so. Again there is no problem. Since exercise is now optimal, our hedging portfolio will be worth $S - K$.[9] If he had exercised, this would be exactly sufficient to meet the obligation and close out the position. Since he did not, the call will be held at least one more period, so we calculate the new values of C_u and C_d and revise our hedging portfolio accordingly. But now the amount required for the portfolio, $\Delta S + B$, is less than the amount we have available, $S - K$. We can withdraw these extra profits now and still maintain the hedging portfolio. The longer the holder of the call goes on making mistakes, the better off we will be.

Consequently, we can be confident that things will eventually work out right no matter what the other party does. The return on our total position, when evaluated at prevailing market prices at intermediate times, may be negative. But over a period ending no later than the expiration date, it will be positive.

In conducting the hedging operation, the essential thing was to maintain the proper proportional relationship: for each call we are short, we hold Δ shares of stock and the dollar amount B in bonds in the hedging portfolio. To emphasize this, we will refer to the number of shares held for each call at the hedge ratio. In our example, we kept the number of calls constant and made

[9] If we were reverse hedging by buying an undervalued call and selling the hedging portfolio, then we would ourselves want to exercise at this point. Since we will receive $S - K$ from exercising, this will be exactly enough money to buy back the hedging portfolio.

adjustments by buying or selling stock and bonds. As a result, our profit was independent of the market price of the call between the time we initiated the hedge and the expiration date. If things got worse before they got better, it did not matter to us.

Instead, we could have made the adjustments by keeping the number of shares of stock constant and buying or selling calls and bonds. However, this could be dangerous. Suppose that after initiating the position, we needed to increase the hedge ratio to maintain the proper proportions. This can be achieved in two ways:

(a) buy more stock, or

(b) buy back some of the calls.

If we adjust through the stock, there is no problem. If we insist on adjusting through the calls, not only is the hedge no longer riskless, but it could even end up losing money! This can happen if the call has become even more overpriced. We would then be closing out part of our position in calls at a loss. To remain hedged, the number of calls we would need to buy back depends on their value, not their price. Therefore, since we are uncertain about their price, we then become uncertain about the return from the hedge. Worse yet, if the call price gets high enough, the loss on the closed portion of our position could throw the hedge operation into an overall loss.

To see how this could happen, let us rerun the hedging operation, where we adjust the hedge ratio by buying and selling calls.

STEP 1 ($n = 3$)

Same as before.

STEP 2 ($n = 2$)

Suppose the stock goes to 120, so that the new $\Delta = 0.848$. The call price has gotten further out of line and is now selling for 75. Since its value is 60.463, it is now overpriced by 14.537. With 0.719 shares, you must buy back $1 - 0.848 = 0.152$ calls to produce a hedge ratio of $0.848 = 0.719/0.848$. This costs $75(0.152) = 11.40$. Borrow to pay the bill. With the interest rate of 0.1, you already owe $23.455(1.1) = 25.801$. Thus, your total current indebtedness is $25.801 + 11.40 = 37.201$.

STEP 3 ($n = 1$)

Suppose the stock goes to 60 and the call is selling for 5.454. Since the call is now fairly valued, no further excess profits can be made by continuing to hold the position. Therefore, liquidate by selling your 0.719 shares for

0.719(60) = 43.14 and close out the call position by buying back 0.848 calls for 0.848(5.454) = 4.625. This nets 43.14 − 4.625 = 38.515. Use this to pay back part of your borrowing. Since you now owe 37.20(1.1) = 40.921, after repayment you owe 2.406. Go back to the bank and withdraw your original deposit, which has now grown to $1.935(1.1)^2 = 2.341$. Unfortunately, after using this to repay your remaining borrowing, you still owe 0.065.

Since we adjusted our position at Step 2 by buying overpriced calls, our profit is reduced. Indeed, since the calls were considerably overpriced, we actually lost money despite apparent profitability of the position at Step 1. We can draw the following adjustment rule from our experiment: *To adjust a hedged position, never buy an overpriced option or sell an underpriced option.* As a corollary, whenever we can adjust a hedged position by buying more of an underpriced option or selling more of an overpriced option, our profit will be enhanced if we do so. For example, at Step 3 in the original hedging illustration, had the call still been overpriced, it would have been better to adjust the position by selling more calls rather than selling stock. In summary, by choosing the right side of the position to adjust at intermediate dates, *at a minimum* we can be assured of earning the original differential and its accumulated interest, and we may earn considerably more.

5. LIMITING CASES

In reading the previous sections, there is a natural tendency to associate with each period some particular length of calendar time, perhaps a day. With this in mind, you may have had two objections. In the first place, prices a day from now may take on many more than just two possible values. Furthermore, the market is not open for trading only once a day, but, instead, trading takes place almost continuously.

These objections are certainly valid. Fortunately, our option pricing approach has the flexibility to meet them. Although it might have been natural to think of a period as one day, there was nothing that forced us to do so. We could have taken it to be a much shorter interval—say an hour—or even a minute. By doing so, we have met both objections simultaneously. Trading would take place far more frequently, and the stock price could take on hundreds of values by the end of the day.

However, if we do this, we have to make some other adjustments to keep the probability small that the stock price will change by a large amount over a minute. We do not want the stock to have the same percentage up and down moves for one minute as it did before for one day. But again there is no need for us to have to use the same values. We could, for example, think of the price as making only a very small percentage change over each minute.

To make this more precise, suppose that h represents the elapsed time between successive stock price changes. That is, if t is the fixed length of calendar time to expiration, and n is the number of periods of length h prior to expiration, then

$$h \equiv t/n.$$

As trading takes place more and more frequently, h gets closer and closer to zero. We must then adjust the interval-dependent variables r, u, and d in such a way that we obtain empirically realistic results as h becomes smaller, or, equivalently, as $n \to \infty$.

When we were thinking of the periods as having a fixed length, r represented both the interest rate over a fixed length of calendar time and the interest rate over one period. Now we need to make a distinction between these two meanings. We will let r continue to mean one plus the interest rate over a fixed length of calendar time. When we have occasion to refer to one plus the interest rate over a period (trading interval) of length h, we will use the symbol $\hat{r}$.

Clearly, the size of $\hat{r}$ depends on the number of subintervals, n, into which t is divided. Over the n periods until expiration, the total return is $\hat{r}^n$, where $n = t/h$. Now not only do we want $\hat{r}$ to depend on n, but we want it to depend on n in a particular way—so that as n changes the total return $\hat{r}^n$ over the fixed time t remains the same. This is because the interest rate obtainable over some fixed length of calendar time should have nothing to do with how we choose to think of the length of the time interval h.

If r (without a "hat") denotes one plus the rate of interest over a *fixed* unit of calendar time, then over elapsed time t, r^t is the total return.[10] Observe that this measure of total return does not depend on n. As we have argued, we want to choose the dependence of $\hat{r}$ on n, so that

$$\hat{r}^n = r^t,$$

for any choice of n. Therefore, $\hat{r} = r^{t/n}$. This last equation shows how $\hat{r}$ must depend on n for the total return over elapsed time t to be independent of n.

We also need to define u and d in terms of n. At this point, there are two significantly different paths we can take. Depending on the definitions we choose, as $n \to \infty$ (or, equivalently, as $h \to 0$), we can have either a continuous or a jump stochastic process. In the first situation, very small random changes in the stock price will be occurring in each very small time interval. The stock price will fluctuate incessantly, but its path can be drawn without lifting pen from paper. In contrast, in the second case, the stock price will usually move in a smooth deterministic way, but will occasionally experience

[10]The scale of this unit (perhaps a day, or a year) is unimportant as long as r and t are expressed in the same scale.

sudden discontinuous changes. Both can be derived from our binomial process simply by choosing how u and d depend on n. We examine in detail only the continuous process which leads to the option pricing formula originally derived by Fischer Black and Myron Scholes. Subsequently, we indicate how to develop the jump process formula originally derived by John Cox and Stephen Ross.

Recall that we supposed that over each period the stock price would experience a one plus rate of return of u with probability q and d with probability $1 - q$. It will be easier and clearer to work, instead, with the natural logarithm of the one plus rate of return, $\log u$ or $\log d$. This gives the continuously compounded rate of return on the stock over each period. It is a random variable which, in each period, will be equal to $\log u$ with probability q and $\log d$ with probability $1 - q$.

Consider a typical sequence of five moves, say u, d, u, u, d. Then the final stock price will be $S^\star = uduudS$; $S^\star/S = u^3 d^2$, and $\log(S^\star/S) = 3\log u + 2\log d$. More generally, over n periods,

$$\log(S^\star/S) = j\log u + (n - j)\log d = j\log(u/d) + n\log d,$$

where j is the (random) number of upward moves occurring during the n periods of expiration. Therefore, the expected value of $\log(S^\star/S)$ is

$$E[\log(S^\star/S)] = \log(u/d)\cdot E(j) + n\log d,$$

and its variance is

$$\operatorname{var}[\log(S^\star/S)] = [\log(u/d)]^2\cdot\operatorname{var}(j).$$

Each of the n possible upward moves has probability q. Thus, $E(j) = nq$. Also, since the variance each period is $q(1 - q)^2 + (1 - q)(0 - q)^2 = q(1 - q)$, then $\operatorname{var}(j) = nq(1 - q)$. Combining all of this, we have

$$E[\log(S^\star/S)] = [q\log(u/d) + \log d]n \equiv \hat{\mu}n,$$
$$\operatorname{var}[\log(S^\star/S)] = q(1 - q)[\log(u/d)]^2 n \equiv \hat{\sigma}^2 n.$$

Let us go back to our discussion. We were considering dividing up our original longer time period (a day) into many shorter periods (a minute or even less). Our procedure calls for, over fixed length of calendar time t, making n larger and larger. Now if we held everything else constant while we let n become large, we would be faced with the problem we talked about earlier. In fact, we would certainly not reach a reasonable conclusion if either $\hat{\mu}n$ or $\hat{\sigma}^2 n$ went to zero or infinity as n became large. Since t is a fixed length of time, in searching for a realistic result, we must make the appropriate adjustments in u, d, and q. In doing that, we would at least want the mean and variance of the continuously compounded rate of return of the assumed stock price movement to coincide with that of the actual stock price as $n \to \infty$. Suppose we label the actual empirical values of $\hat{\mu}n$ and $\hat{\sigma}^2 n$ as μt and $\sigma^2 t$, respectively. Then we would want to choose u, d, and q, so that

$$\left.\begin{array}{l} [q \log(u/d) + \log d]n \to \mu t \\ q(1 - q)[\log(u/d)]^2 n \to \sigma^2 t \end{array}\right\} \quad \text{as } n \to \infty.$$

A little algebra shows we can accomplish this by letting

$$u = e^{\sigma\sqrt{t/n}}, \qquad d = e^{-\sigma\sqrt{t/n}}, \qquad q = \tfrac{1}{2} + \tfrac{1}{2}(\mu/\sigma)\sqrt{t/n}.$$

In this case, for any n,

$$\hat{\mu}n = \mu t \quad \text{and} \quad \hat{\sigma}^2 n = [\sigma^2 - \mu^2(t/n)]t.$$

Clearly, as $n \to \infty$, $\hat{\sigma}^2 n \to \sigma^2 t$, while $\hat{\mu}n = \mu t$ for all values of n.

Alternatively, we could have chosen u, d, and q so that the mean and variance of the future stock price for the discrete binomial process approach the prespecified mean and variance of the actual stock price as $n \to \infty$. However, just as we would expect, the same values will accomplish this as well. Since this would not change our conclusions, and it is computationally more convenient to work with the continuously compounded rates of return, we will proceed in that way.

This satisfies our initial requirement that the limiting means and variances coincide, but we still need to verify that we are arriving at a sensible limiting probability distribution of the continuously compounded rate of return. The mean and variance only describe certain aspects of that distribution.

For our model, the random continuously compounded rate of return over a period of length t is the sum of n independent random variables, each of which can take the value $\log u$ with probability q and $\log d$ with probability $1 - q$. We wish to know about the distribution of this sum as n becomes large and q, u, and d are chosen in the way described. We need to remember that as we change n, we are not simply adding one more random variable to the previous sum, but instead are changing the probabilities and possible outcomes for every member of the sum. At this point, we can rely on a form of the central limit theorem which, when applied to our problem, says that, as $n \to \infty$, if

$$\frac{q|\log u - \hat{\mu}|^3 + (1 - q)|\log d - \hat{\mu}|^3}{\hat{\sigma}^3\sqrt{n}} \to 0,$$

then

$$\text{Prob}\left[\left(\frac{\log(S^\star/S) - \hat{\mu}n}{\hat{\sigma}\sqrt{n}}\right) \leqq z\right] \rightarrow N(z),$$

where $N(z)$ is the standard normal distribution function. Putting this into words, as the number of periods into which the fixed length of time to expiration is divided approaches infinity, the probability that the standardized continuously compounded rate of return of the stock through the expiration date is not greater than the number z approaches the probability under a standard normal distribution.

The initial condition says roughly that higher-order properties of the distribution, such as how it is skewed, become less and less important, relative to its standard deviation, as $n \rightarrow \infty$. We can verify that the condition is satisfied by making the appropriate substitutions and finding

$$\frac{q|\log u - \hat{\mu}|^3 + (1 - q)|\log d - \hat{\mu}|^3}{\hat{\sigma}^3\sqrt{n}} = \frac{(1 - q)^2 + q^2}{\sqrt{nq(1 - q)}},$$

which goes to zero as $n \rightarrow \infty$ since $q = \frac{1}{2} + \frac{1}{2}(\mu/\sigma)\sqrt{t/n}$. Thus, the multiplicative binomial model for stock prices includes the lognormal distribution as a limiting case.

Black and Scholes began directly with continuous trading and the assumption of a lognormal distribution for stock prices. Their approach relied on some quite advanced mathematics. However, since our approach contains continuous trading and lognormal distribution as a limiting case, the two resulting formulas should then coincide. We will see shortly that this is indeed true, and we will have the advantage of using a much simpler method. It is important to remember, however, that the economic arguments we used to link the option value and the stock price are exactly the same as those advanced by Black and Scholes (1973) and Merton (1973, 1977).

The formula derived by Black and Scholes, rewritten in terms of our notation, is

Black–Scholes Option Pricing Formula

$$C = SN(x) - Kr^{-t}N(x - \sigma\sqrt{t}),$$

where

$$x \equiv \frac{\log(S/Kr^{-t})}{\sigma\sqrt{t}} + \tfrac{1}{2}\sigma\sqrt{t}.$$

We now wish to confirm that our binomial formula converges to the Black–Scholes formula when t is divided into more and more subintervals, and

$\hat{r}$, u, d, and q are chosen in the way we described—that is, in a way such that the multiplicative binomial probability distribution of stock prices goes to the lognormal distribution.

For easy reference, let us recall our binomial option pricing formula:

$$C = S\Phi[a; n, p'] - K\hat{r}^{-n}\Phi[a; n, p].$$

The similarities are readily apparent. $\hat{r}^{-n}$ is, of course, always equal to r^{-t}. Therefore, to show the two formulas converge, we need only show that as $n \to \infty$,

$$\Phi[a; n, p'] \to N(x) \quad \text{and} \quad \Phi[a; n, p] \to N(x - \sigma\sqrt{t}).$$

We will consider only $\Phi[a; n, p]$, since the argument is exactly the same for $\Phi[a; n, p']$.

The complementary binomial distribution function $\Phi[a; n, p]$ is the probability that the sum of n random variables, each of which can take on the value 1 with probability p and 0 with probability $1 - p$, will be greater than or equal to a. We know that the random value of this sum, j, has mean np and standard deviation $\sqrt{np(1 - p)}$. Therefore,

$$\begin{aligned} 1 - \Phi[a; n, p] &= \text{Prob}[j \leqq a - 1] \\ &= \text{Prob}\left[\frac{j - np}{\sqrt{np(1 - p)}} \leqq \frac{a - 1 - np}{\sqrt{np(1 - p)}}\right]. \end{aligned}$$

Now we can make an analogy with our earlier discussion. If we consider a stock which in each period will move to uS with probability p and dS with probability $1 - p$, then $\log(S^*/S) = j\log(u/d) - n\log d$. The mean and variance of the continuously compounded rate of return of this stock are

$$\hat{\mu}_p = p\log(u/d) + \log d \quad \text{and} \quad \hat{\sigma}_p^2 = p(1 - p)[\log(u/d)]^2.$$

Using these equalities, we find that

$$\frac{j - np}{\sqrt{np(1 - p)}} = \frac{\log(S^*/S) - \hat{\mu}_p n}{\hat{\sigma}_p\sqrt{n}}.$$

Recall from the binomial formula that

$$\begin{aligned} a - 1 &= \log(K/Sd^n)/\log(u/d) - \varepsilon \\ &= [\log(K/S) - n\log d]/\log(u/d) - \varepsilon, \end{aligned}$$

where ε is a number between zero and one. Using this and the definitions of $\hat{\mu}_p$ and $\hat{\sigma}_p^2$, with a little algebra, we have

$$\frac{a - 1 - np}{\sqrt{np(1 - p)}} = \frac{\log(K/S) - \hat{\mu}_p n - \varepsilon\log(u/d)}{\hat{\sigma}_p\sqrt{n}}.$$

Putting these results together,

$$1 - \Phi[a; n, p]$$

$$= \text{Prob}\left[\frac{\log(S^\star/S) - \hat{\mu}_p n}{\hat{\sigma}_p\sqrt{n}} \leqq \frac{\log(K/S) - \hat{\mu}_p n - \varepsilon\log(u/d)}{\hat{\sigma}_p\sqrt{n}}\right].$$

We are now in a position to apply the central limit theorem. First, we must check if the initial condition,

$$\frac{p|\log u - \hat{\mu}_p|^3 + (1-p)|\log d - \hat{\mu}_p|^3}{\hat{\sigma}_p\sqrt{n}} = \frac{(1-p)^2 + p^2}{\sqrt{np(1-p)}} \to 0,$$

as $n \to \infty$, is satified. By first recalling that $p \equiv (\hat{r} - d)/(u - d)$, and then $\hat{r} = r^{t/n}$, $u = e^{\sigma\sqrt{t/n}}$, and $d = e^{-\sigma\sqrt{t/n}}$, it is possible to show that as $n \to \infty$,

$$p \to \tfrac{1}{2} + \tfrac{1}{2}\left(\frac{\log r - \frac{1}{2}\sigma^2}{\sigma}\right)\sqrt{\frac{t}{n}}.$$

As a result, the initial condition holds, and we are justified in applying the central limit theorem.

To do so, we need only evaluate $\hat{\mu}_p n$, $\hat{\sigma}_p^2 n$ and $\log(u/d)$ as $n \to \infty$.[11]

[11] A surprising feature of this evaluation is that although $p \neq q$ and thus $\hat{\mu}_p \neq \hat{\mu}$, and $\hat{\sigma}_p \neq \hat{\sigma}$, nonetheless $\hat{\sigma}_p\sqrt{n}$ and $\hat{\sigma}\sqrt{n}$ have the same limiting value as $n \to \infty$. By contrast, since $\mu \equiv \log r - (\frac{1}{2}\sigma^2)$, $\hat{\mu}_p n$ and $\hat{\mu} n$ do not. This results from the way we needed to specify u and d to obtain convergence to a lognormal distribution. Rewriting this as $\sigma\sqrt{t} = (\log u)\sqrt{n}$, it is clear that the limiting value of σ of the standard deviation does not depend on p or q, and hence must be the same for either. However, at any point before the limit, since

$$\hat{\sigma}^2 n = \left(\sigma^2 - \mu^2\frac{t}{n}\right)t \quad \text{and} \quad \hat{\sigma}_p^2 n = \left[\sigma^2 - (\log r - \tfrac{1}{2}\sigma^2)^2\frac{t}{n}\right]t,$$

$\hat{\sigma}$ and $\hat{\sigma}_p$ will generally have different values.

The fact that $\hat{\mu}_p n \to (\log r - \frac{1}{2}\sigma^2)t$ can also be derived from the property of the lognormal distribution that

$$\log E[S^\star/S] = \mu_p t + \tfrac{1}{2}\sigma^2 t,$$

where E and μ_p are measured with respect to probability p. Since $p = (\hat{r} - d)/(u - d)$, it follows that $\hat{r} = pu + (1-p)d$. For independently distributed random variables, the expectation of a product equals the product of their expectations. Therefore,

$$E[S^\star/S] = [pu + (1-p)d]^n = \hat{r}^n = r^t.$$

Substituting r^t for $E[S^\star/S]$ in the previous equation, we have

$$\mu_p = \log r - \tfrac{1}{2}\sigma^2.$$

Examination of our discussion for parameterizing q shows that as $n \to \infty$,

$$\hat{\mu}_p n \to (\log r - \tfrac{1}{2}\sigma^2)t \quad \text{and} \quad \hat{\sigma}_p \sqrt{n} \to \sigma \sqrt{t}.$$

Furthermore, $\log(u/d) \to 0$ as $n \to \infty$.

For this application of the central limit theorem, then, since

$$\frac{\log(K/S) - \hat{\mu}_p n - \varepsilon \log(u/d)}{\hat{\sigma}_p \sqrt{n}} \to z = \frac{\log(K/S) - (\log r - \tfrac{1}{2}\sigma^2)t}{\sigma\sqrt{t}},$$

we have

$$1 - \Phi[a; n, p] \to N(z) = N\left[\frac{\log(Kr^{-t}/S)}{\sigma\sqrt{t}} + \tfrac{1}{2}\sigma\sqrt{t}\right].$$

The final step in the argument is to use the symmetry property of the standard normal distribution that $1 - N(z) = N(-z)$. Therefore, as $n \to \infty$,

$$\Phi[a; n, p] \to N(-z) = N\left[\frac{\log(S/Kr^{-t})}{\sigma\sqrt{t}} - \tfrac{1}{2}\sigma\sqrt{t}\right] = N(x - \sigma\sqrt{t}).$$

Since a similar argument holds for $\Phi[a; n, p']$, this completes our demonstration that the binomial option pricing formula contains the Black–Scholes formula as a limiting case.[12,13]

[12] The only difference is that, as $n \to \infty$, $p' \to \frac{1}{2} + \frac{1}{2}[(\log r + \frac{1}{2}\sigma^2)/\sigma]\sqrt{t/n}$.

Further, it can be shown that as $n \to \infty$, $\Delta \to N(s)$. Therefore, for the Black–Scholes model, $\Delta S = SN(x)$ and $B = -Kr^{-t}N(x - \sigma\sqrt{t})$.

[13] In our original development, we obtained the following equation (somewhat rewritten) relating the call prices in successive periods:

$$\left(\frac{\hat{r} - d}{u - d}\right)C_u + \left(\frac{u - \hat{r}}{u - d}\right)C_d - \hat{r}C = 0.$$

By their more difficult methods, Black and Scholes obtained directly a partial differential equation analogous to our discrete-time difference equation. Their equation is

$$\tfrac{1}{2}\sigma^2 S^2 \frac{\partial^2 C}{\partial S^2} + (\log r)S\frac{\partial C}{\partial S} - \frac{\partial C}{\partial t} - (\log r)C = 0.$$

The value of the call, C, was then derived by solving this equation subject to the boundary condition $C^\star = \max[0, S^\star - K]$.

Based on our previous analysis, we would now suspect that, as $n \to \infty$, our difference equation would approach the Black–Scholes partial differential equation. This can be confirmed by substituting our definitions of $\hat{r}$, u, d in terms of n in the way described earlier, expanding C_u, C_d in a Taylor series around $(e^{\sigma\sqrt{h}}S, t - h)$ and $(e^{\sigma\sqrt{h}}S, t - h)$, respectively, and then expanding $e^{\sigma\sqrt{h}}$, $e^{-\sigma\sqrt{h}}$, and r^h in a Taylor series, substituting these in the equation and collecting terms. If we then divide by h and let $h = 0$, all terms of higher order than h go to zero. This yields the Black–Scholes equation.

As we have remarked, the seeds of both the Black–Scholes formula and a continuous-time jump process formula are both contained within the binomial formulation. At which end point we arrive depends on how we take limits. Suppose, in place of our former correspondence for u, d, and q, we instead set

$$u = u, \qquad d = e^{\zeta(t/n)}, \qquad q = \lambda(t/n).$$

This correspondence captures the essence of a pure jump process in which each successive stock price is almost always close to the previous price ($S \to dS$), but occasionally, with low but continuing probability, significantly different ($S \to uS$). Observe that, as $n \to \infty$, the probability of a change by d becomes larger and larger, while the probability of a change by u approaches zero.

With these specifications, the initial condition of the central limit theorem we used is no longer satisfied, and it can be shown the stock price movements converge to a log-Poisson rather than a lognormal distribution as $n \to \infty$. Let us define

$$\Psi[x; y] \equiv \sum_{i=x}^{\infty} \frac{e^{-y} y^i}{i!},$$

as the complementary Poisson distribution function. The limiting option pricing formula for the above specifications of u, d, and q is then

Jump Process Option Pricing Formula

$C = S\Psi[x; y] - Kr^{-t}\Psi[x; y/u]$,

where

$y \equiv (\log r - \zeta)ut/(u - 1)$,

and

$x \equiv$ the smallest non-negative integer greater than $(\log(K/S) - \zeta t)/\log u$.

A very similar formula holds if we let $u = e^{\zeta(t/n)}$, $d = d$, and $1 - q = \lambda(t/n)$.

6. DIVIDENDS AND PUT PRICING

So far we have been assuming that the stock pays no dividends. It is easy to do away with this restriction. We will illustrate this with a specific dividend policy: the stock maintains a constant yield, δ, on each ex-dividend date.

Suppose there is one period remaining before expiration and the current stock price is S. If the end of the period is an ex-dividend date, then an individual who owned the stock during the period will receive at that time a dividend of either δuS or δdS. Hence, the stock price at the end of the period will be either $u(1 - \delta)^v S$ or $d(1 - \delta)^v S$, where $v = 1$ if the end of the period is an ex-dividend date and $v = 0$ otherwise. Both δ and v are assumed to be known with certainty.

When the call expires, its contract and a rational exercise policy imply that its value must be either

$$C_u = \max[0, u(1 - \delta)^v S - K],$$

or

$$C_d = \max[0, d(1 - \delta)^v S - K].$$

Therefore,

$$C \begin{cases} C_u = \max[0, u(1 - \delta)^v S - K], \\ C_d = \max[0, d(1 - \delta)^v S - K]. \end{cases}$$

Now we can proceed exactly as before. Again we can select a portfolio of Δ shares of stock and the dollar amount B in bonds which will have the same end-of-period value as the call.[14] By retracing our previous steps, we can show that

$$C = [pC_u + (1 - p)C_d]/\hat{r},$$

if this is greater than $S - K$, and $C = S - K$ otherwise. Here, once again, $p = (\hat{r} - d)/(u - d)$ and $\Delta = (C_u - C_d)/(u - d)S$.

Thus far the only change is that $(1 - \delta)^v S$ has replaced S in the values for C_u and C_d. Now we come to the major difference: early exercise may be optimal. To see this, suppose that $v = 1$ and $d(1 - \delta)S > K$. Since $u > d$, then, also, $u(1 - \delta)S > K$. In this case, $C_u = u(1 - \delta)S - K$ and $C_d = d(1 - \delta)S - K$. Therefore, since $(u/\hat{r})p + (d/\hat{r})(1 - p) = 1$, $[pC_u + (1 - p)C_d]/\hat{r} = (1 - \delta)S - (K/\hat{r})$. For sufficiently high stock prices, this can obviously be less than $S - K$. Hence, there are definitely some circumstances in which no one would be willing to hold the call for one more period.

In fact, there will always be a critical stock price, $\hat{S}$, such that if $S > \hat{S}$, the call should be exercised immediately. $\hat{S}$ will be the stock price at which $[pC_u + (1 - p)C_d]/\hat{r} = S - K$.[15] That is, it is the lowest stock price at which the value of the hedging portfolio exactly equals $S - K$. This means

[14] Remember that if we are long the portfolio we will receive the dividend at the end of the period; if we are short, we will have to make restitution for the dividend.

[15] Actually solving for $\hat{S}$ explicitly is straightforward but rather tedious, so we will omit it.

$\hat{S}$ will, other things equal, be lower the higher the dividend yield, the lower the interest rate, and the lower the striking price.

We can extend the analysis to an arbitrary number of periods in the same way as before. There is only one additional difference, a minor modification in the hedging operation. Now the funds in the hedging portfolio will be increased by any dividends received, or decreased by the restitution required for dividends paid while the stock is held short.

Although the possibility of optimal exercise before the expiration date causes no conceptual difficulties, it does seem to prohibit a simple closed-form solution for the value of a call with many periods to go. However, our analysis suggests a sequential numerical procedure which will allow us to calculate the continuous-time value to any desired degree of accuracy.

Let C be the current value of a call with n periods remaining. Define

$$\bar{v}(n, i) \equiv \sum_{k=1}^{n-i} v_k,$$

so that $\bar{v}(n, i)$ is the number of ex-dividend dates occurring during the next $n - i$ periods. Let $C(n, i, j)$ be the value of the call $n - i$ periods from now, given that the current stock price S has changed to $u^j d^{n-i-j}(1 - \delta)^{\bar{v}(n,i)} S$, where $j = 0, 1, 2, \ldots, n - i$.

With this notation, we are prepared to solve for the current value of the call by working backward in time from the expiration date. At expiration, $i = 0$, so that

$$C(n, 0, j) = \max[0, u^j d^{n-j}(1 - \delta)^{\bar{v}(n,0)} S - K] \quad \text{for} \quad j = 0, 1, \ldots, n.$$

One period before the expiration date, $i = 1$ so that

$$\begin{aligned} C(n, 1, j) = \max[&u^j d^{n-1-j}(1 - \delta)^{\bar{v}(n,1)} S - K, \\ &[pC(n, 0, j + 1) + (1 - p)C(n, 0, j)]/\hat{r}] \\ &\text{for } j = 0, 1, \ldots, n - 1. \end{aligned}$$

More generally, i periods before expiration

$$\begin{aligned} C(n, i, j) = \max[&u^j d^{n-i-j}(1 - \delta)^{\bar{v}(n,i)} S - K, \\ &[pC(n, i - 1, j + 1) + (1 - p)C(n, i - 1, j)]/\hat{r}] \\ &\text{for } j = 0, 1, \ldots, n - i. \end{aligned}$$

Observe that each prior step provides the inputs needed to evaluate the right-hand arguments of each succeeding step. The number of calculations decreases as we move backward in time. Finally, with n periods before expiration, since $i = n$,

$$C = C(n, n, 0) = \max[S - K, [pC(n, n-1, 1) + (1-p)C(n, n-1, 0)]/\hat{r}],$$

and the hedge ratio is

$$\Delta = \frac{C(n, n-1, 1) - C(n, n-1, 0)}{(u-d)S}.$$

We could easily expand the analysis to include dividend policies in which the amount paid on any ex-dividend date depends on the stock price at that time in a more general way.[16] However, this will cause some minor complications. In our present example with a constant dividend yield, the possible stock prices $n - i$ periods from now are completely determined by the total number of upward moves (and ex-dividend dates) occurring during that interval. With other types of dividend policies, the enumeration will be more complicated, since then the terminal stock price will be affected by the timing of the upward moves as well as their total number. But the basic principle remains the same. We go to the expiration date and calculate the call value for all of the possible prices that the stock could have then. Using this information, we step back one period and calculate the call values for all possible stock prices at that time, and so forth.

We will now illustrate the use of the binomial numerical procedure in approximating continuous-time call values. In order to have an exact continuous-time formula to use for comparison, we will consider the case with no dividends. Suppose that we are given the inputs required for the Black–Scholes option pricing formula: S, K, t, σ, and r. To convert this information into the inputs d, u, and $\hat{r}$ required for the binomial numerical procedure, we use the relationships:

$$d = 1/u, \qquad u = e^{\sigma\sqrt{t/n}}, \qquad \hat{r} = r^{t/n}.$$

Table 2 gives us a feeling for how rapidly option values approximated by the binomial method approach the corresponding limiting Black–Scholes values given by $n = \infty$. At $n = 5$, the values differ by at most \$0.25, and at $n = 20$, they differ by at most \$0.07. Although not shown, at $n = 50$, the greatest difference is less than \$0.03, and at $n = 150$, the values are identical to the penny.

To derive a method for valuing puts, we again use the binomial formulation. Although it has been convenient to express the argument in terms of a

[16] We could also allow the amount to depend on previous stock prices.

TABLE 2. BINOMIAL APPROXIMATION OF CONTINUOUS-TIME CALL VALUES FOR (1) JANUARY, (2) APRIL, AND (3) JULY OPTIONS; $S = 40$ AND $r = 1.05$.[a]

		$n = 5$			$n = 20$			$n = \infty$		
σ	K	(1)	(2)	(3)	(1)	(2)	(3)	(1)	(2)	(3)
	35	5.14	5.77	6.45	5.15	5.77	6.39	5.15	5.76	6.40
0.2	40	1.05	2.26	3.12	0.99	2.14	2.97	1.00	2.17	3.00
	45	0.02	0.54	1.15	0.02	0.51	1.11	0.02	0.51	1.10
	35	5.21	6.30	7.14	5.22	6.26	7.19	5.22	6.25	7.17
0.3	40	1.53	3.21	4.36	1.44	3.04	4.14	1.46	3.07	4.19
	45	0.11	1.28	2.12	0.15	1.28	2.23	0.16	1.25	2.24
	35	5.40	6.87	7.92	5.39	6.91	8.05	5.39	6.89	8.09
0.4	40	2.01	4.16	5.61	1.90	3.93	5.31	1.92	3.98	5.37
	45	0.46	1.99	3.30	0.42	2.09	3.42	0.42	2.10	3.43

[a] The January options have one month to expiration, the Aprils, four months, and the Julys, seven months; r and σ are expressed in annual terms.

particular security, a call, this is not essential in any way. The same basic analysis can be applied to puts.

Letting P denote the current price of a put, with one period remaining before expiration, we have

$$P \begin{cases} P_u = \max[0, K - u(1 - \delta)^v S], \\ P_d = \max[0, K - d(1 - \delta)^v S]. \end{cases}$$

Once again, we can choose a portfolio with ΔS in stock and B in bonds which will have the same end-of-period values as the put. By a series of steps which are formally equivalent to the ones we followed in section 3, we can show that

$$P = [pP_u + (1 - p)P_d]/\hat{r},$$

if this is greater than $K - S$, and $P = K - S$ otherwise. As before, $p = (\hat{r} - d)/(u - d)$ and $\Delta = (P_u - P_d)/(u - d)S$. Note that for puts, since $P_u \leqq P_d$, then $\Delta \leqq 0$. This means that if we sell an overvalued put, the hedging portfolio which we buy will involve a short position in the stock.

We might hope that with puts we will be spared the complications caused by optimal exercise before the expiration date. Unfortunately, this is not the case. In fact, the situation is even worse in this regard. Now there are always some possible circumstances in which no one would be willing to hold the put for one more period.

To see this, suppose $K > u(1 - \delta)^v S$. Since $u > d$, then, also, $K > d(1 - \delta)^v S$. In this case, $P_u = K - u(1 - \delta)^v S$ and $P_d = K - d(1 - \delta)^v S$. Therefore, since $(u/\hat{r})p + (d/\hat{r})(1 - p) = 1$,

$$[pP_u + (1 - p)P_d]/\hat{r} = (K/\hat{r}) - (1 - \delta)^v S.$$

If there are no dividends (that is, $v = 0$), then this is certainly less than $K - S$. Even with $v = 1$, it will be less for a sufficiently low stock price.

Thus, there will now be a critical stock price, $\hat{S}$, such that if $S < \hat{S}$, the put should be exercised immediately. By analogy with our discussion for the call, we can see that this is the stock price at which $[pP_u + (1 - p)P_d]/\hat{r} = K - S$. Other things equal, $\hat{S}$ will be higher the lower the dividend yield, the higher the interest rate, and the higher the striking price. Optimal early exercise thus becomes more likely if the put is deep-in-the-money and the interest rate is high. The effect of dividends yet to be paid diminishes the advantages of immediate exercise, since the put buyer will be reluctant to sacrifice the forced declines in the stock price on future ex-dividend dates.

This argument can be extended in the same way as before to value puts with any number of periods to go. However, the chance for optimal exercise before the expiration date once again seems to preclude the possibility of expressing this value in a simple form. But our analysis also indicates that, with slight modification, we can value puts with the same numerical techniques we use for calls. Reversing the difference between the stock price and the striking price at each stage is the only change.[17]

The diagram presented in table 3 shows the stock prices, put values, and values of Δ obtained in this way for the example given in section 4. The values used there were $S = 80, K = 80, n = 3, u = 1.5, d = 0.5$, and $\hat{r} = 1.1$. To include dividends as well, we assume that a cash dividend of five percent ($\delta = 0.05$) will be paid at the end of the last period before the expiration date.

[17] Michael Parkinson (1977) has suggested a similar numerical procedure on a trinomial process, where the stock price can either increase, decrease, or remain unchanged. In fact, given the theoretical basis for the binomial numerical procedure provided, the numerical method can be generalized to permit $k + 1 \leq n$ jumps to new stock prices in each period. We can consider exercise only every k periods, using the binomial formula to leap across intermediate periods. In effect, this means permitting $k + 1$ possible new stock prices before exercise is again considered. That is, instead of considering exercise n times, we would only consider it about n/k times. For fixed t and k, as $n \to \infty$, option values will approach their continuous-time values.

This alternative procedure is interesting, since it may enhance computer efficiency. At one extreme, for calls on stocks which do not pay dividends, setting $k + 1 = n$ gives the most efficient results. However, when the effect of potential early exercise is important and greater accuracy is required, the most efficient results are achieved by setting $k = 1$, as in our description above.

Thus, $(1 - \delta)^{\nu(n,0)} = 0.95$, $(1 - \delta)^{\nu(n,1)} = 0.95$, and $(1 - \delta)^{\nu(n,2)} = 1.0$. Put values in italics indicate that immediate exercise is optimal.

TABLE 3

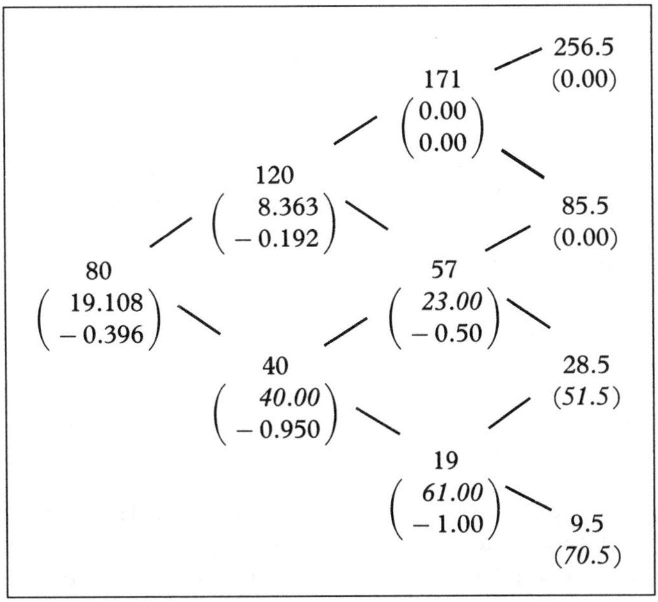

7. CONCLUSION

It should now be clear that whenever stock price movements conform to a discrete binomial process, or to a limiting form of such a process, options can be priced solely on the basis of arbitrage considerations. Indeed, we could have significantly complicated the simple binomial process while still retaining this property.

The probabilities of an upward or downward move did not enter into the valuation formula. Hence, we would obtain the same result if q depended on the current or past stock prices or on other random variables. In addition, u and d could have been deterministic functions of time. More significantly, the size of the percentage changes in the stock price over each period could have depended on the stock price at the beginning of each period or on previous stock prices.[18] However, if the size of the changes were to depend on any other random variable, not itself perfectly correlated with the stock price, then our

[18] Of course, different option pricing formulas would result from these more complex stochastic processes. See Cox and Ross (1976) and Geske (1979). Nonetheless, all option pricing formulas in these papers can be derived as limiting forms of a properly specified discrete two-state process.

argument will no longer hold. If any arbitrage result is then still possible, it will require the use of additional assets in the hedging portfolio.

We could also incorporate certain types of imperfections into the binomial option pricing approach, such as differential borrowing and lending rates and margin requirements. These can be shown to produce upper and lower bounds on option prices, outside of which riskless profitable arbitrage would be possible.

Since all existing preference-free option pricing results can be derived as limiting forms of a discrete two-state process, we might suspect that two-state stock price movements, with the qualifications mentioned above, must be in some sense necessary, as well as sufficient, to derive option pricing formulas based solely on arbitrage considerations. To price an option by arbitrage methods, there must exist a portfolio of other assets which exactly replicates in every state of nature the payoff received by an optimally exercised option. Our basic proposition is the following. Suppose, as we have, that markets are perfect, that changes in the interest rate are never random, and that changes in the stock price are always random. In a discrete time model, a necessary and sufficient condition for options of all maturities and striking prices to be priced by arbitrage using only the stock and bonds in the portfolio is that in each period,

(a) the stock price can change from its beginning-of-period value to only two ex-dividend values at the end of the period, and
(b) the dividends and the size of each of the two possible changes are presently known functions at most on: (i) current and past stock prices, (ii) current and past values of random variables whose changes in each period are perfectly correlated with the change in the stock price, and (iii) calendar time.

The sufficiency of the condition can be established by a straightforward application of the methods we have presented. Its necessity is implied by the discussion at the end of section 3.[19,20,21]

[19] Note that option values need not depend on the present stock price alone. In some cases, formal dependence on the entire series of past values of the stock price and other variables can be summarized in a small number of state variables.

[20] In some circumstances, it will be possible to value options by arbitrage when this condition does not hold by using additional assets in the hedging portfolio. The value of the option will then in general depend on the values of these other assets, although in certain cases only parameters describing their movement will be required.

[21] Merton's (1976) model, with both continuous and jumps components, is a good example of a stock price process for which no exact option pricing formula is obtainable purely from arbitrage considerations. To obtain an exact formula, it is necessary to impose restrictions on the stochastic movements of other securities, as Merton did, or on investor preferences. For example, Rubinstein (1976) has been able to derive the Black–Scholes option pricing formula, under circumstances that do not admit arbitrage, by suitably restricting investor preferences. Additional problems arise when interest rates are stochastic, although Merton (1973) has shown that some arbitrage results may still be obtained.

This rounds out the principal conclusion of this paper: the simple two-state process is really the essential ingredient of option pricing by arbitrage methods. This is surprising, perhaps, given the mathematical complexities of some of the current models in this field. But it is reassuring to find such simple economic arguments at the heart of this powerful theory.

REFERENCES

Black, F. and M. Scholes, 1973, The pricing of options and corporate liabilities, Journal of Political Economy 3, 637–654 (Chapter 19).

Brennan, M. J. and E. S. Schwartz, 1977, The valuation of American put options, Journal of Finance 32, 449–462.

Cox, J. C. and S. A. Ross, 1975, The pricing of options for jump processes, Rodney L. White Center Working Paper no. 2–75 (University of Pennsylvania, Philadelphia, PA).

Cox, J. C. and S. A. Ross, 1976, The valuation of options for alternative stochastic processes, Journal of Financial Economics 3, 145–166.

Geske, R., 1979, The valuation of compound options, Journal of Financial Economics 7, 63–81.

Harrison, J. M. and D. M. Kreps, 1979, Martingales and arbitrage in multiperiod securities markets, Journal of Economic Theory 20, 381–408.

Merton, R. C., 1973, The theory of rational option pricing, Bell Journal of Economics and Management Science 4, 141–183.

Merton, R. C., 1976, Option pricing when underlying stock returns are discontinuous, Journal of Financial Economics 3, 125–144.

Merton, R. C., 1977, On the pricing of contingent claims and the Modigliani–Miller theorem, Journal of Financial Economics 5, 241–250.

Parkinson, M., 1977, Option pricing: The American put, Journal of Business 50, 21–36.

Rendleman, R. J. and B. J. Bartter, 1978, Two-state option pricing, Unpublished paper (Graduate School of Management, Northwestern University, Evanston, IL).

Rubinstein, M., 1976, The valuation of uncertain income streams and the pricing of options, Bell Journal of Economics 7, 407–425.

Sharpe, W. F., 1978, Investments (Prentice-Hall, Englewood Cliffs, NJ).

21. WHO SHOULD BUY PORTFOLIO INSURANCE?

Hayne E. Leland

I. INTRODUCTION

The existence of options markets can generate new opportunities for portfolio management. As Ross [1976] has shown, a complete set of options markets on a reference stock or portfolio will enable investors to achieve any desired pattern of returns conditional on the terminal value of the reference asset. While "buy-and-hold" equity strategies allow investors to achieve returns *proportional* to the terminal value of a reference portfolio, buy-and-hold option strategies permit *nonproportional* returns to be achieved.

A nonproportional return of particular interest to some investors is that which provides portfolio insurance. Equivalent to a put option on the reference portfolio, portfolio insurance enables an investor to avoid losses, but capture gains, at the cost of a fixed "premium." Unfortunately, options markets do not currently exist for portfolios of securities, and a portfolio of options is *not* equivalent to an option on a portfolio.

Even when options markets do not exist, however, investors may be able to achieve nonproportional returns on terminal asset values by following *dynamic* investment strategies. If security returns are lognormally distributed at any future time, and continuous trading is possible, Black and Scholes [1973] show that the returns to any option on an asset can be duplicated by an appropriate trading strategy involving the asset and a riskless security. This

Reprinted from *The Journal of Finance*, May 1980

implies that, in a Black-Scholes world, there exists a dynamic investment strategy which can generate insured portfolio values. The investment strategy involves trading only in the securities of the portfolio and in the riskless asset; no options need exist to achieve insured values.

While the theory of option pricing suggests how to value options, and therefore how to value portfolio insurance, it does not suggest the nature of investors who would benefit from purchasing options or insurance. Unlike traditional insurance, in which everyone can benefit from a pooling of independent risks, portfolio insurance involves hedging against a common (market) risk. For every investor buying portfolio insurance, some other investor(s) must be selling it, either by writig the appropriate put option, or by following the inverse dynamic trading strategy. Who should buy, and who should sell?

In this paper, we provide a characterization of investors who will benefit from purchasing portfolio insurance. Indeed, our results are considerably more general: we characterize investors who demand arbitrary nonproportional patterns of returns on a reference portfolio, and thereby characterize the nature of investors who wish to buy (or sell) options. Since in the Black-Scholes environment there is a correspondence between options and dynamic strategies, our results also characterize the nature of investors who would wish to follow dynamic trading strategies. Some "rules of thumb," such as "run with your winners, cut your losses," and "sell at a new high, buy at a new low" will be shown to approximate the optimal dynamic trading strategies for certain types of investors.

The question we address is closely related to the theory of optimal risk sharing and insurance considered by Borch [1960], Wilson [1968], Ross [1973], and Leland [1978]. In an important recent paper, Brennan and Solanki [1979] have posed the question that we consider here. These studies, however, have all assumed identical expectations on the part of market participants. Besides extending results for this case, we consider the optimal behavior of investors whose expectations *differ* from those of the average investor. Since much of the demand for options is attributed to investors who are either more bullish or more bearish on the expected return of the underlying stocks, it seems important to include differing expectations as a possible source of demand for options or for portfolio insurance.

Our principal conclusions are:

1) Investors who have average expectations, but whose risk tolerance increases with wealth more rapidly than average, will wish to obtain portfolio insurance.
2) Investors who have average risk tolerance, but whose expectations of returns are more optimistic than average, will wish to obtain portfolio insurance.

Institutional investors falling in class (1) might include pension or endowment funds which at all costs must exceed a minimum value, but thereafer can accept reasonable risks. "Safety-first" investors would find portfolio insurance attractive on this basis.

Institutional investors falling in class (2) would include well-diversified funds which believe themselves to have positive "α's"—i.e., funds which expect on average to achieve excess returns by superior stock selection. In order to exploit these excess returns to equities, but at the same time keep risk within tolerable levels, insured-type strategies are optimal.

Given the connection between options and portfolio insurance, which is developed in detail in section II, classes (1) and (2) above also characterize the types of investors who would wish to buy call options on a reference portfolio. Since the dynamic trading strategy which yields call option returns (or insured returns) involves buying into the portfolio as its value goes up, but selling out as its value goes down, our results also suggest that investors in classes (1) and (2) would benefit from a "run with your winners, cut your losses" kind of dynamic strategy,[1] rather than a simply "buy and hold" policy. Investors with opposite characteristics would prefer the "buy low, sell high" strategy which is equivalent to writing a call (or selling insurance).

II. PORTFOLIO INSURANCE, PUTS, AND CALLS: A REVIEW

In this section, we show that purchasing portfolio insurance is equivalent to either:

1) holding the reference portfolio, and buying a put option on the portfolio with striking price equal to the initial portfolio value;
2) buying a call option on the reference portfolio with striking price equal to the initial portfolio value, plus holding cash equal to the initial portfolio value discounted by the riskless interest rate over the insured period.

These results have been derived elsewhere (see Brennan and Schwartz [1976], for example), but are reviewed here for completeness.

LEt W_0 and W_T represent the initial and terminal values, respectively, of a reference portfolio of stocks. If an investor obtains full portfolio insurance, he is assured of an end-of-period value Y given by

$$Y(W_T;\, W_0) \;=\; \mathrm{Max}[W_T,\, W_0].$$

[1] This is, of course, only a rough approximation of the exact trading strategy which reproduces insured returns. And it should be noted that "run with your winners" typically describes policies towards individual stocks in a portfolio, rather than the portfolio as a whole which is our focus here.

That is, the insured investor gets the larger of the reference portfolio's initial or terminal value. Of course, he must pay a premium to obtain insured values; the cost of insurance will be discussed later.

Now consider an investor who owns the reference portfolio, and who can buy a *put option* on the portfolio with striking price W_0. Such an option has end-period returns given by

$$P(W_T; W_0) = \text{Max}[W_0 - W_T, 0].$$

Holding the reference portfolio plus the put option will give terminal values

$$\begin{aligned} W_T + P(W_T; W_0) &= W_T + \text{Max}[W_0 - W_T, 0] \\ &= \text{Max}[W_T, W_0] \\ &= Y[W_T; W_0]. \end{aligned}$$

Therefore, holding the reference portfolio plus purchasing a put option with striking price W_0 gives insured returns. We now see that the price of insurance must equal the price of the put option with striking price W_0.

Finally, consider a portfolio consisting of a *call option* on the reference portfolio with striking price W_0, plus initial cash equal to $W_0/(1 + r)$, where r is the rate of interest paid on cash over the period of insurance. The call option will have terminal value

$$C[W_T; W_0] = \text{Max}[W_T - W_0, 0],$$

while the cash will have terminal value W_0. Together, the call option plus cash will have terminal value

$$\begin{aligned} W_0 + C[W_T; W_0] &= W_0 + \text{Max}[W_T - W_0, 0] \\ &= \text{Max}[W_T, W_0] \\ &= Y[W_T; W_0]. \end{aligned}$$

Thus we see a second way to obtain insured returns: buying a call option on the reference portfolio, plus holding cash. This implies that the dynamic trading strategy which creates portfolio insurance will be identical to the dynamic strategy which creates the equivalent call option. Rubinstein and Cox [1980] provide a full analysis of the strategy's properties. For our purpose, it is important to note that the dynamic trading strategy that creates insured portfolio values require higher investment in the reference portfolio as its value rises, and higher amounts in cash as its value falls. Thus anyone obtaining portfolio insurance via a dynamic trading strategy should follow a rule loosely described as "run with your winners, cut your losses." This is, of course, a crude approximation of the exact trading strategy.

III. GENERALIZED INSURANCE CONTRACTS AND CONVEX PAYOFF FUNCTIONS

In the previous section, we considered full portfolio insurance with zero deductible. But, as suggested by Brennan and Solanki [1979], in general it may not be optimal for an investor to have 100 percent protection of value below a certain level, and none above. Investors may simply wish increasing amounts of protection as the level of potential loss increases. Insurance policies with this property are termed *general insurance policies.*

General insurance policies can be created by insuring different fractions of the reference portfolio at different levels of deductible. For example, consider the terminal values of a portfolio with one-fifth of its value insured at zero deductible, and successive fifths insured at 5, 10, 15, and 20 percent deductible. These returns can be duplicated by holding the reference portfolio, plus buying a *portfolio* of put options on the reference fund with striking prices W_0, $.95\,W_0$, $.90\,W_0$, $.85\,W_0$, and $.80\,W_0$. Note that each put option is held in only one-fifth the quantity that was required for the full insurance discussed in the previous section.

The insured portfolio payoff schedule

$$Y(W_T;\cdot)$$

is a convex function of the reference portfolio's terminal value. Indeed, *we characterize general insurance policies as those that provide strictly convex payoff functions,* since convexity implies greater protection from loss at lower values of the reference portfolio.

Is there a relationship between convex payoff functions and portfolios that include the reference portfolio plus a further portfolio of put options on the reference portfolio? The answer is yes: a portfolio consisting of the reference portfolio plus put options will always provide a convex payoff function. Conversely, a (twice continuously differentiable) convex payoff function can always be generated by holding the reference portfolio and cash, plus a suitable portfolio of put options on the reference portfolio.[2]

[2] We are focusing on the twice continuously differentiable case here. However, our results could be extended to consider piecewise linear functions. Note also that Ross [1976] and Breeden and Litzenberger [1978] show any payoff function can be provided through a portfolio of options. The content of our result is that a convex function can be provided with a portfolio which contains only *long* positions in options.

To show this, consider an investor who holds a fraction α of some reference portfolio. In addition, he purchases put options at alternative striking prices. Let $\beta(K) \geqq 0$ denote the number of put options bought with striking price K. Then his insured returns will be given by

$$\begin{aligned} Y[W_T; \beta(\cdot)] &= \alpha W_T + \int_0^\infty \beta(K) P[W_T; K]\, dK \\ &= \alpha W_T + \int_9^\infty \beta(K) \text{Max}[K - W_T, 0]\, dK \\ &= \alpha W_T + \int_{W_T}^\infty \beta(K)[K - W_T]\, dK, \end{aligned}$$

from whence if follows that

$$Y''[W_T; \beta(\cdot)] = \beta(W_T) \geqq 0.$$

Thus, portfolios including the reference portfolio plus put options on that portfolio generate convex returns. Similarly, it can be seen that any twice-differentiable patterns of returns can be obtained by holding put options, a fraction of the reference portfolio, plus cash—a holding that includes portfolio insurance. As can be inferred from the preceding section, this pattern of returns also could be obtained by a suitable portfolio of call options, or by following the equivalent dynamic trading strategy.

Most of our future results will be aimed at characterizing investors who wish strictly convex payoff functions over the terminal value of the reference portfolio. The previous discussion indicates that these investors would demand a general portfolio insurance policy.

IV. THE MODEL

Consider a portfolio whose end-period value is given by W_T, a random variable, and whose initial value W_0 is normalized to one. Let

$p(W_T)$ denote the pricing function at the initial time period for \$1 delivered at the terminal time period, contingent on the value of the reference portfolio.

This pricing function, which reflects the market's expectations and attitudes towards risk, may be imputed from a number of possible environments:

a) A complete set of options markets on the reference portfolio exists, permitting computation of the $p(W_T)$ function.

b) The conditions for a risk-neutral valuation relationship[3] are satisfied.

c) The market behaves as if it were composed of representative or "average" investors, with utility function $V(W_{MT})$ over terminal period market wealth per capita, and with probability function $h(W_{MT}, W_T)$ giving the joint density of end-period market and portfolio values.[4]

These scenarios need not be mutually exclusive. We shall further assume that the prices $p(W_T)$ are competitive; that is, they are unaffected by the portfolio decision of any individual investor.

Now consider an individual whose terminal wealth is dependent upon the value W_T of a reference portfolio. While the reference portfolio is itself a choice variable, we shall not focus on this choice, but rather take it as given. Let

$Y(W_T)$ denote the individual's wealth given W_T.

The individual investor will choose an optimal $Y(\cdot)$ schedule to maximize his expected utility subject to his budget constraint:

$$\underset{Y(\cdot)}{\text{Maximize}} \int_{-\infty}^{\infty} U[Y(W_T)]f(W_T)\,dW_T \tag{1}$$

subject to

$$\int_{-\infty}^{\infty} Y(W_T)p(W_T)\,dW_T = I,$$

where

$f(W_T)$ denotes the investor's probability density function over terminal portfolio values,

and

I denotes the investor's initial wealth.

[3] A risk neutral valuation relationship exists if the relationship between the value of the payoff function and the value of the reference portfolio is the same as would exist if all market participants are risk neutral. Black and Scholes [1979] show that sufficient conditions for a risk neutral valuation relationship with continuous trading are that the value of the reference portfolio follow a Gauss-Wiener process and a riskless asset exists. Rubinstein [1976] and Brennan [1978] show that a necessary and sufficient condition for a risk neutral valuation relationship to exist in a discrete time model with lognormal returns is that the average investor exhibit constant relative risk aversion. Breeden and Litzenberger [1978] suggest this latter condition is also necessary with continuous trading when the value of the market portfolio is lognormally distributed.

[4] See Rubinstein [1974] for conditions sufficient for a representative or "average" investor to exist. These conditions are closely related to those consistent with risk-neutral valuation relationships existing for the market portfolio.

This problem is similar to that posed by the optimal risk-sharing literature, except that fixed market prices $p(W_T)$ substitute for the (variable) implicit contingency claim prices of the second party.

The solution to (1) is straightforward. For every level of wealth W_T,

$$f(W_T)U'[Y(W_T)] = \lambda p(W_T), \tag{2}$$

where primes denote derivatives, and λ is a positive constant whose level is determined through the budget constraint. Differentiating (2) with respect to W_T, solving for $Y'(W_T)$, and substituting from (2) for λ gives

$$Y' = -\frac{U'}{U''}\left(\frac{f'}{f} - \frac{p'}{p}\right) \tag{3}$$

for all W_T, where functions' arguments have been suppressed. Differentiating again with respect to W_T and simplifying gives

$$Y'' = \left[\frac{d}{dY}\left(\frac{-U'}{U''}\right) + \frac{d}{dW_T}\left(\frac{f'}{f} - \frac{p'}{p}\right)\Big/\left(\frac{f'}{f} - \frac{p'}{p}\right)\right]\left[\left(\frac{-U'}{U''}\right)\left(\frac{f'}{f} - \frac{p'}{p}\right)^2\right]. \tag{4}$$

Without further specification of the price, probability, and utility functions, little can be said at this stage. One rather weak result is, however, suggested by (4):

Proposition I: Other things being equal, investors whose risk tolerance increases with wealth more rapidly are more likely to desire portfolio insurance.

This can be verified by noting that the term in the right bracket of (4) is always positive. If the f and p functions are fixed, Y'' will more likely be positive if $d/dY\ (-U'/U'')$ is large—i.e., if the investor's risk tolerance is increasing rapidly with wealth. Of course $Y'' > 0$ implies the function is (locally) convex; if it is convex at all Y, generalized insurance is desirable.

Brennan and Solanki [1979] derive further results by assuming $f(\cdot)$ and $p(\cdot)$ are consistent with a risk-neutral valuation relationship. We pursue a somewhat different route; our results are compared in the conclusion.

V. CONTINGENCY CLAIM PRICES REFLECTING AN AGGREGATE INVESTOR

We now consider an environment where the contingency claim price function $p(W_T)$ reflects the preferences of an average (or aggregate) investor.[5] Then

[5] Again, see Rubinstein [1974]. Note that the individual investor we consider will in general differ in a significant way from the aggregate investor—either because of differing risk tolerance, differing expectations, or both. This could raise questions as to the consistency of our modelling unless the set of investors differing from the average is "small."

there exists an aggregate or market utility function $V(W_T)$ and a market probability density function $h(W_T)$, such that

$$p(W_T) = h(W_T)V'(W_T), \tag{5}$$

where $V'(W_T)$ is the (normalized) marginal utility of a dollar when the value of the reference portfolio is W_T.[6]

Given (5), we may now express (3) as

$$Y' = \frac{-U'}{U''}\left(\frac{-V''}{V'} + \frac{f'}{f} - \frac{h'}{H}\right). \tag{6}$$

a: Investor Has Same Expectations as the Market. We first consider the case examined by the optimal risk-sharing literature and by Brennan and Solanki [1979], where $f(W_T) \equiv h(W_T)$, i.e., the investor shares the market's expectations.

In this case, (6) reduces to

$$Y' = \frac{-U'}{U''}\Big/\frac{-V'}{V''}. \tag{7}$$

Note that $Y' > 0$ given risk aversion. We can now prove the following proposition, which is found in slightly different form in Leland [1978]:

Proposition II: if the investor shares the market's expectations, the optimal schedule $Y(\cdot)$ is strictly convex if and only if the risk tolerance of the individual is increasing more rapidly with Y than the aggregate investor's is increasing with W_T.

Proof: Differentiating (7) with respect to W_T gives

$$Y'' = \left(\frac{-V'}{V''}\left[\frac{d}{dY}\left(\frac{-U'}{U''}\right)Y'\right] + \frac{U'}{U''}\left[\frac{d}{dW_T}\left(\frac{-V'}{V''}\right)\right]\right)\Big/K, \tag{8}$$

[6] This equation holds as is when $W_T = W_{TM}$, i.e., the reference portfolio is the market portfolio, and $V(\cdot)$ is utility dependent upon the terminal value of the market portfolio. When $W_T \equiv W_{TM}$, we can define

$$V'(W_T) = \int V'(W_{MT})h(W_{MT}/W_T)\,dW_{MT},$$

where $h(W_{MT}/W_T)$ is the conditional probability function of W_{MT} given W_T. Equation (5) then holds with this newly defined $V'(W_T)$ function, interpreting $h(W_T)$ as the marginal density of W_T derived from the joint density function $h(W_{TM}, W_T)$. If $V(W_{MT})$ exhibits constant relative risk aversion, and W_{MT} and W_T are jointly lognormally distributed, then $V(W_T)$ will also exhibit constant relative risk aversion, although generally of a different degree.

where

$$K = (-V'/V'')^2 > 0.$$

Substituting for Y' from (7) yields

$$\text{sign } Y'' = \text{sign}\left(\frac{-U'}{U''}\right)\left[\frac{d}{dY}\left(\frac{-U'}{U''}\right) - \frac{d}{dW_T}\left(\frac{-V'}{V''}\right)\right]. \tag{9}$$

Since risk tolerance $(-U'/U'') > 0$, Y'' will be positive iff

$$\frac{d}{dY}\left(\frac{-U'}{U''}\right) > \frac{d}{dW_T}\left(\frac{-V'}{V''}\right),$$

i.e., the risk tolerance of the investor at $Y(W_T)$ is increasing more rapidly than that of the market at W_T, for all W_T.

Remarks. Proposition II does not assume any specific form for investor and market utility functions or expectations. However, if investors are not identical, Rubinstein [1974] has shown that sufficient conditions on market participants for the market to reflect an aggregate or average investor are

(a) identical expectations
(b) linear risk tolerance functions with identical slopes,[7] implying an aggregate or market utility function

$$-V'/V'' = a_M + b_M W_{TM},$$

where W_{TM} is the end-period value of the market portfolio.

Thus, if we restrict our attention to the case where the reference or insured portfolio is the market portfolio, and where the investor also has a linear risk tolerance function

$$-U'/U'' = a_i + b_i Y,$$

then $Y(W_{TM})$ will be a strictly convex function if and only if

$$b_i > b_M. \tag{10}$$

Note that Proposition II does *not* imply that more risk averse investors necessarily demand portfolio insurance. Indeed, if $a_M = a_i = 0$, then $b_i > b_M$

[7] Linear risk tolerance is, of course, an alternative terminology for "HARA class" utility functions. These functions include the quadratic, logarithmic, exponential, and power utility functions.

implies that at equal levels of wealth, the investor demanding portfolio insurance is *less* risk averse than average. He will demand a more levered or "higher beta" portfolio, but take out insurance on his levered position.

If the reference portfolio is not the market portfolio, the technique suggested in footnote 6 could be used to compute an appropriate "b" for the market. The work of Brennan and Solanki [1979] suggests that if returns are lognormally distributed, the appropriate b_M will be given by $\sigma^2/\hat{a}$, where σ^2 is the variance of the logarithm of the return, and $\hat{a}$ is the "risk premium" commanded by the portfolio in the market.[8]

b. Investors with Differing Expectations. We now examine cases where the investor's expectations differ from those of the market average. To derive specific results, we shall assume

(i) the individual investor has a linear risk tolerance

$$-U'/U'' = a_i + b_i Y;$$

(ii) the market utility function exhibits constant relative risk aversion, or proportional risk tolerance

$$-V'/V'' = b_M W_{TM};$$

(iii) the end-of-period market value W_{TM} is lognormally distributed, with

$$E[\ln W_{TM}] = \mu_M \text{ for the market, } \mu_i \text{ for the investor;}$$
$$\text{Var}[\ln W_{TM}] = \sigma_M^2 \text{ for the market, } \sigma_i^2 \text{ for the investor.}$$

These assumptions are similar to those of Brennan and Solanki [1979].[9] However, those authors assumed identical expectations. As before, we shall concentrate attention on where the individual investor's reference portfolio is the market portfolio, i.e., $W_T = W_{TM}$.

Recalling that we have set $W_0 = 1$, the lognormality assumption implies

$$h(W_T) = \frac{1}{\sqrt{2\pi}\sigma_m W_T} \exp\left[\frac{-1}{2\sigma_M^2}(\ln W_T - \mu_M)^2\right],$$

whereas the individual's density function is given by

$$f(W_T) = \frac{1}{\sqrt{2\pi}\sigma_i W_T} \exp\left[\frac{-1}{2\sigma_i^2}(\ln W_T - \mu_i)^2\right].$$

[8] $\hat{a}$ is the difference between the instantaneous rate of return $(\mu_M + 0.5\sigma_M^2)$ and the risk-free rate r.

[9] A fuller discussion of the relationship between the assumptions and Brennan/Solanki is contained in the final section.

Substituting these relationships into (6) gives

$$Y' = (a_i + b_i Y)\left[\frac{1}{B_M W_T} + \frac{1}{W_T}\left[\frac{\sigma_i^2(\ln W_T - \mu_M) - \sigma_M^2(\ln W_T - \mu_i)}{\sigma_M^2 \sigma_i^2}\right]\right] \tag{11}$$

which has solution

$$Y = c_0 W_{T[(b_i/b_M) + b_i k_1 + b_i k_2 \ln W_T]} - a_i/b_i, \tag{12}$$

where

c_0 is a constant of integration determined by the budget constraint;

$$k_i = \frac{\mu_i \sigma_M^2 - \mu_M \sigma_i^2}{\sigma_i^2 \sigma_M^2},$$

$$k_2 = \frac{\sigma_i^2 - \sigma_M^2}{2\sigma_i^2 \sigma_M^2}.$$

While (12) is a general solution to the case with differing expectations, we focus on the environment where the individual and market estimates of variance of $\ln W_T$ are identical, but the estimates of the mean return of $\ln W_T$ differ.[10] In this environment, $k_1 > 0$ if $\mu_i > \mu_M$, and $k_2 = 0$. From (12), the following proposition is immediate:

Proposition III: If the market and individual have identical risk tolerance behavior ($b_i = b_M$) and identical estimates of riskiness ($\sigma_i = \sigma_M$), the optimal schedule $Y(W_T)$ will be strictly convex if and only if $\mu_i > \mu_M$, i.e., if the investor has more optimistic expectations than the market.

Remarks. Proposition III implies that an investor with "average" risk tolerance behavior will demand portfolio insurance if he has a more optimistic expected return than the market. From the results of section II, such an investor could obtain insured returns either by (i) holding the reference portfolio (perhaps levered) and buying put options on the portfolio, (ii) investing in call options on the reference portfolio or (iii) following an appropriate dynamic trading strategy. An investor with less optimistic expectations would

[10] If the random terminal value W_T is created by a (continuous) logarithmic random walk over the period, and continuous trading is possible, the individual investor must have the same instantaneous estimate of the variance as the market has. Otherwise, a riskless arbitrage opportunity would be perceived, and equilibrium could not exist. Of course if continuous trading is not possible, equilibrium could support differences in variances.

be willing to provide insurance, or equivalently, to write put or call options, or follow the inverse dynamic trading strategy.

Portfolios managed with the expectation of excess returns, or "positive α's," will benefit from portfolio insurance. This may seem counterintuitive: why should an investor who is willing to seek out excess returns also wish to protect himself through insurance? The answer is that excess expected returns can more thoroughly be exploited, but risks controlled, through insured strategies. The investor can more fully exploit positive α situations through greater levels of risky investment. At the same time, risks can be kept within manageable bounds by the use of portfolio insurance.

Proposition III also indicates that the lessons of static portfolio theory must be broadened in the context where complete options markets do not exist, but continuous trading is possible. Static theory suggests that higher expected returns will lead to greater levels of investment in the risky portfolio. Our results indicate that not only is greater investment desirable, but that dynamic strategies may enable achievement of even high levels of expected utility. That is, *dynamic strategies should be an intrinsic part of any portfolio optimization.*

It should be stressed that the dynamic strategies considered here are not "market timing" strategies. They are not predicated on the idea that excess returns can be achieved by buying and selling at the "right" time. Rather, the dynamic strategies are used to create desirable nonproportional end-of-period values. Buying and selling are triggered only by changes in the value of the reference portfolio, according to the "informationless" hedging rules that recreate option returns. The resulting convexity of the end-of-period returns yield greater expected utility than any buy-and-hold strategy involving the reference portfolio, even though the trading strategy does not increase the α associated with that portfolio.

The result in Proposition III also applies to portfolios other than the market portfolio, with the recognition that the relevant b_M must be adjusted by the technique in footnote 6. For portfolios whose returns are highly correlated with the market's, as are many institutional portfolios, virtually no adjustment will be required.

c. Investors with Differing Expectations and Risk Tolerance Behavior. The following proposition also is an immediate consequence of (12) and generalizes Proposition III to the case where $b_i \neq b_M$:

Proposition IV: If the market and individual have identical estimates of the variance ($\sigma_i = \sigma_M$), the optimal schedule Y will be strictly convex if and only if

$$\frac{\mu_i - \mu_M}{\sigma_M^2} > \frac{1}{b_i} - \frac{1}{b_M}.$$

This follows from the convexity requirement that $(b_i/b_M) + b_i k_1 > 1$.

Thus, even if he has risk tolerance growing more slowly than the market average ($b_i < b_M$), the individual investor still may want a general insurance contract if his expectations are sufficiently positive. And not that the effects of more rapidly growing risk tolerance ($b_i > b_M$) and more optimistic expectations ($\mu_i > \mu_M$) on the demand for insurance are cumulative.

As either the risk tolerance of the investor increases more rapidly with Y, or his expectations become more optimistic, the optimal schedule $Y(\cdot)$ becomes increasingly steep and convex. Relative curvature (Y''/Y') also increases. The average steepness of the function can be associated with the exposure to risk—greater steepness implies a more leveled position in the reference portfolio. Convexity is associated with the amount of insurance purchased. Relative curvature is associated with the ratio of insurance purchased to exposure—loosely speaking, it measures the "fraction" of portfolio held that is insured. Thus, changes in either the risk tolerance parameter b_i or in expected returns μ_i (or both) lead to greater insurance coverage—or equivalently, greater purchases of call options on the portfolio. If insurance is provided by a dynamic trading strategy, greater insurance coverage implies more extensive trading as the value of the portfolio fluctuates.

VI. CONCLUSION AND RELATIONSHIP TO PREVIOUS WORK

Our objective has been to characterize the nature of investors who would benefit from portfolio insurance. Our conclusions, summarized by Propositions I to IV, indicate that investors (i) whose risk tolerance increases with wealth more rapidly than that of the average investor, and/or (ii) whose expectations are more optimistic than average, would benefit from portfolio insurance. Investors belonging to class (i) would include safety-first investors. Class (ii) investors would include institutions with portfolios managed with the expectation of above-average returns, or positive α.

We indicate that portfolio insurance can be obtained in a number of ways. If option markets exist on the reference portfolio, insurance can be achieved by purchasing appropriate put options in addition to holding the reference portfolio. It could also be achieved by purchasing appropriate call options, plus holding cash.

If (as is usually the case) options do not exist on the reference portfolio, insured returns can nonetheless be achieved when continuous trading is possible and portfolio returns are lognormally distributed. The dynamic trading strategy that reproduces the appropriate options' returns will provide the optimal portfolio insurance. This result has an important bearing on portfolio optimization strategies. Static portfolio theory suggests that more optimistic expectations should lead to greater investment in the risky portfolio. But our analysis suggests that in addition to greater investment, dynamic strategies should also be followed to produce the optimal pattern of returns. While current applied portfolio optimization techniques focus on static portfolios that minimize risk for a given level of return, further improvements in risk/return ratios can be achieved by following appropriate dynamic strategies. We noted that the dynamic strategy associated with portfolio insurance requires buying more of the reference portfolio as its value rises, and selling out as its value falls. The opposite strategy ("sell at a high, buy at a low") is appropriate for an investor wishing a concave payoff schedule.

Our results are related to a number of previous strands of research. Models of capital market equilibrium have focused on optimal portfolios and on valuation of risky assets. For analytical tractability, however, most of these models (including the CAPM) have assumed homogeneous expectations, and investors with linear risk tolerance utility functions with the same slope—precisely those assumptions that eliminate the demand for options! Thus these models are incapable of characterizing the nature of investors who demand options (or insured returns), since they make assumptions which in equilibrium preclude any investor from demanding them.

Our model is more closely related to the theory of insurance/agency/optimal risk sharing, which typically posits two parties sharing a random return, and examines the nature of the optimal sharing rule. By the assumption that an aggregate investor exists, we can examine the interaction between an individual investor and "the market." But a key difference between our study and the risk-sharing literature is that the market is perfectly competitive, and the portfolio choice of the individual investor does not affect the terms of trade. Nonetheless Proposition II is almost identical to the result derived by Leland [1978] in the optimal risk-sharing context.

The closest work to ours is Brennan and Solanki [1979], who formulate the general problem in the same manner as we do. In deriving specific results, however, they focus on the case where prices $p(W_T)$ are derived from "risk-neutral valuation relationships," and the portfolio returns are lognormally distributed. They do not consider differences between investor and market expectations. But it might appear that they avoid having to assume the existence of an aggregate investor, since a market utility function nowhere appears in their results. This is not the case, however. Brennan [1978] shows that risk-neutral valuation relationships and lognormality are consistent with a discrete time framework only if the market exhibits constant proportional risk aversion —i.e., has a utility function of the form $-V'/V'' = bW_T$, which is the special form assumed for our results in Propositions III and IV. Breeden and Litzenberger [1978] show that risk-neutral valuation and lognormality of market returns also requires constant proportional risk aversion for the market, when continuous trading is possible. Thus it appear that a market utility function with constant proportional risk aversion underlies the Brennan/Solanki results. Their key conclusion, that an individual investor will desire a convex payoff function if his index b_i of risk tolerance exceeds $\sigma^2/\hat{a}$, where $\hat{a}$ is the risk premium of the reference portfolio, is exactly the same as (10) when it is recognized that in equilibrium $\sigma^2/\hat{a} = b_M$. Note that (10) is a special case of Proposition II.

In sum, our results, would seem to extend Brennan/Solanki's results in the case of identical investor-market expectations. And we have derived results for the case with differing expectations, which are often held to be the principal source of the demand for options.

REFERENCES

Black, F., and Scholes, M. 1973. "The Pricing of Options and Corporate Liabilities." *Journal of Political Economy* 81: 637–654 (May–June); (Chapter 19).

Borch, K., 1960. "The Safety Loading of Insurance Premiums." *Skandinansk Aktuarietidskrift* 43: 163–184.

Breeden, D., and Litzenberger, R. 1978. "Prices of State Contingent Claims Implicit in Option Prices." *Journal of Business* 51: 621–652 (October).

Brennan, M. 1979. "The Pricing of Contingent Claims in Discrete Time Models." *Journal of Finance* 34: 53–68 (March).

Brennan, M., and Solanki, R. 1979. "Optimal Portfolio Insurance." Working Paper No. 666. Faculty of Commerce and Business Administration, University of British Columbia.

Friend, I., and Blume, M. 1975. "The Demand for Risky Assets." *American Economic Review* 65: 900–922 (December).

Ibbotson, R., and Sinquefield, R. 1976. "Stocks, Bonds, Bills, and Inflation: Year by Year Historical Returns." *Journal of Business* 49: 11–47 (Jan).

Leland, H. 1978. "Optimal Risk Sharing and the Leasing of Natural Resources, with Application to Oil and Gas Leasing on the OCS." *Quarterly Journal of Economics*: 413–437 (August).

Ross, S. 1973. "The Economic Theory of Agency." *American Economic Review* 63: 134–139 (May).

——. 1976. "Options and Efficiency." *Quarterly Journal of Economics* 90: 75–89 (February).

Rubinstein, M. 1974. "An Aggregation Theorem for Securities Markets." *Journal of Financial Economics* 1: 225–244 (September).

——. 1976. "The Valuation of Uncertain Income Streams and the Pricing of Options." *Journal of Economics* 7: 407–425 (Autumn).

Rubinstein, M., and Cox, J. 1980. *Options Markets*. Prentice-Hall, forthcoming.

Wilson, R. 1968. "The theory of syndicates." *Econometrica* 36 119–132 (Jan).

22. REPLICATING OPTIONS WITH POSITIONS IN STOCKS AND CASH

Hayne E. Leland and Mark Rubinstein

The volume of trading in exchange-traded puts and calls (in terms of share equivalents) now rivals share volume on the New York Stock Exchange.[1] Yet, for most investors, options remain an arcane or complex subject. One thing is obvious, however: An option provides a comparable alternative to a direct investment in its underlying stock. To decide between the two alternatives, we would like to know

— how to value an option,
— how to measure the expected return and risk of an option position,
— how the margin requirements and transaction costs of option positions compare with common stock,
— who should be buying and who should be selling options, and
— how to create an option position if options on a stock or on a portfolio do not exist.

Is is quixotic to hope that there is a single, simple principle that can provide satisfactory answers to all these questions? We think not. The key insight to modern option pricing theory is that, *in most situations of practical relevance, the price behavior of an option is very similar to a portfolio of the underlying stock and cash that is revised in a particular way over time.*[2] That

Reprinted from *Financial Analysts Journal*, July–August 1981

[1] Footnotes appear at end of chapter.

is, there exists a *replicating portfolio strategy*, involving stock and cash only, that creates returns identical to those of an option.

WHY THE PRINCIPLE MAKES SENSE

Suppose we want to replicate a *purchased call option* using only stock and cash. To succeed, our replicating strategy must satisfy three conditions:

1. for small changes in the stock price, the initial out-of-pocket investment must give the same absolute, *dollar return* as a call;
2. to equalize the *rate of return* as well, the initial out-of-pocket investment must equal the value of the call; and
3. thereafter, since a call requires no further investment, the replicating strategy must be self-financing.

If it satisfies these three conditions, we have reason to believe our strategy will resemble a purchased call at any time prior to expiration as well as at expiration.

A brief study of exchange-traded options and their underlying stocks shows that their respective daily price movements tend to parallel each other. In particular, (a) *call prices and stock prices change in the same direction*, but (b) *a one dollar change in the stock price causes a change of less than one dollar in the call price.* To satisfy Condition 1, the value of our stock-cash portfolio must, at a minimum, share these properties. This will be easy to achieve if we have a long position in less than one share of stock.

Further observation of call prices shows that they have additional important properties our replicating portfolio will have to match. More precisely, how a call option responds to a one dollar change in the stock depends largely on the relationship of its striking price to the stock price. (c) *When the stock price is much lower than the striking price (deep out of the money), a one dollar change in the stock price has little effect on the call price. If the stock price rises and becomes equal to the striking price (at the money), a one dollar change in the stock price produces about a half-dollar change in the call price. If the stock price rises further so the call becomes deep in the money, then a one dollar move in the stock price results in almost a one dollar change in the call price.*

Because the call price behaves this way, we will have to revise our replicating portfolio as the stock's price changes. We will hold almost no shares when the stock price is low, and we will buy more shares as the stock price rises. In particular, when the call is at the money, we will hold about half a share. As the stock price rises further and the call becomes deep in the money, we will gradually buy in until we hold almost one share. Conversely, whenever the stock price falls, we will reduce the number of shares held.

Exhibit A compares the value of a call with various positions in stock and cash. Both the striking price and current stock price are $30, so the call is currently at the money. The straight line from the origin with a slope of one shows how the value of an unlevered position in one share of stock depends on the stock price; in this very simple case, these values are identical. In contrast, the value of a fixed, fully levered position in the stock is represented by the straight line with a slope of one cutting the horizontal axis at 30.

The curve describing the call price as the stock price changes is positively sloped throughout (corresponding to property a). Although the slope of this curve is always lower than the unlevered stock line (property b), it increases continually as the stock price rises (property c).[3] Indeed, *the slope of the call price curve at the current stock price is equal to the number of shares in the replicating stock–cash portfolio.* At very low stock prices, the slope is almost zero; at a stock price of 30 the slope is one-half; and at very high stock prices the slope is almost one.

Equalizing dollar return is not enough. We must also equalize the rate of return (Condition 2). Observation of call prices shows that (d) *a one per cent change in the stock price cause a more than one per cent change in the call price.* Our stock–cash portfolio will share this property if the stock position is financed partly through borrowing.

For example, suppose the initial at-the-money call value equals three dollars and the stock price is $30. In this case, we will buy one-half share by investing three dollars and borrowing $12. The current value of our portfolio is thus three dollars – $15 worth of stock minus the $12 owed on borrowing. If the stock price then goes up by one dollar, the value of the portfolio will increase by only 50 cents. However, this represents a $16\frac{2}{3}$ per cent increase for our portfolio, compared with a $3\frac{1}{3}$ per cent increase for the stock.

Exhibit A shows that the amount of borrowing in the replicating portfolio ($12) can be read off the vertical axis by extending the dashed line tangent to the call price line at the current stock price ($30). The distance between the corresponding call price ($3) and the amount borrowed ($12) equals the dollar value of stock in the replicating portfolio ($15).

Finally, to satisfy Condition 3, our strategy must be self-financing from this point on. To accomplish this, we borrow more to buy more shares as the stock price rises and, as the stock price falls, we sell some of our shares and use the proceeds to retire a portion of our loan. Exhibit A shows what is happening. As the stock price rises, the dashed tangent line pivots counterclockwise, taking on increasing slope and an intercept farther from zero along the vertical axis. As the stock price falls, the tangent line pivots clockwise, with decreasing slope and an intercept closer to zero.

By the expiration date, if the call ends up in the money, we will find ourselves owning one share of stock and owing from our borrowing an amount exactly equal to the striking price. If the call finishes out of the money, we will

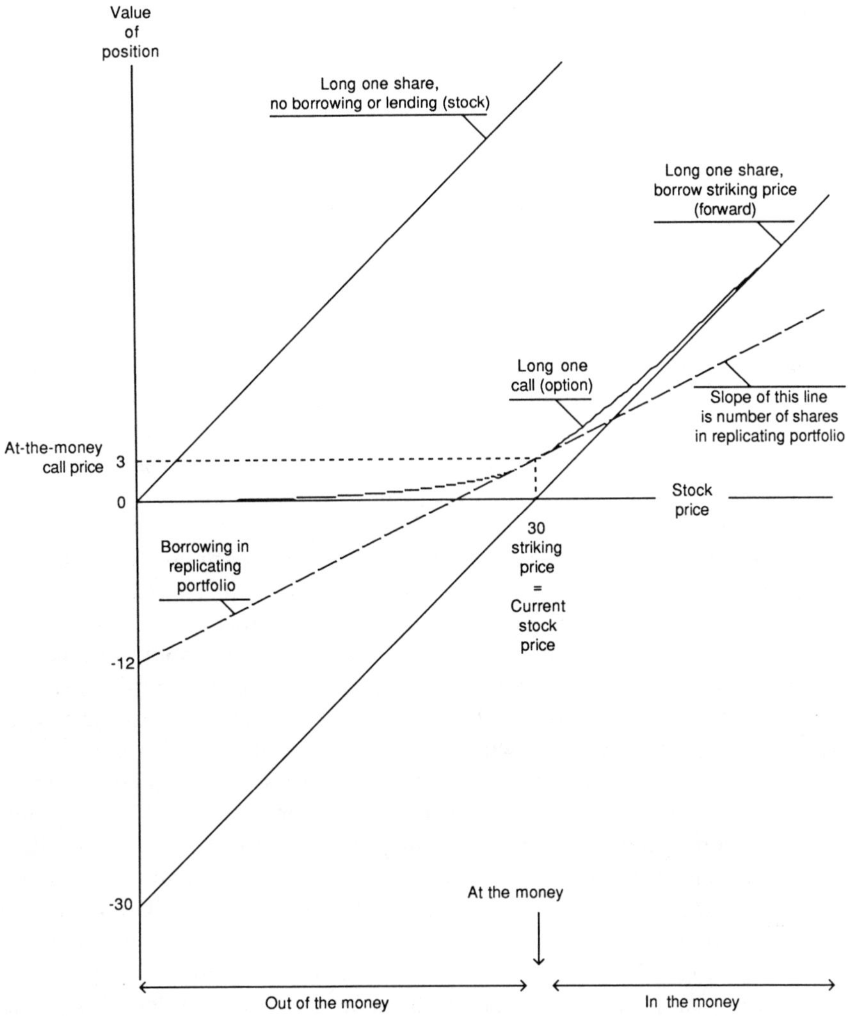

EXHIBIT A. Call Option vs. Positions in Stock and Cash

find ourselves fully disinvested with our borrowing fully repaid. This is, of course, equivalent to the position of the call buyer at expiration. In either case, since, prior to expiration, we were never fully invested when the stock price rose nor fully disinvested when the stock price fell, we will have depleted out initial out-of-pocket investment. It is a fact of modern option pricing theory that, subject to certain conditons, in either case this "shortfall" will always be the same and exactly equal to the initial value of the call.

SOME ADDITIONAL FACTORS

In conclusion, we can replicate a purchased call position by a strategy of *buying shares plus borrowing, where we buy (sell) shares and increase (decrease) our borrowing as the stock price rises (falls)*. Of course, the current level of the stock price and its relation to the striking price will affect how much stock we would be holding and how much we should be borrowing. In addition, the exact composition of our replicating portfolio will also depend on other factors. For example, if the call is sufficiently in the money, we should be holding more shares, the closer the option is to *expiration* or the lower the *stock volatility*, because profitable exercise is then more likely. Since we are borrowing against purchased shares, it should be obvious that we will also need to take account of *interest rates* and *cash dividends*. The appendix shows how a call option can be replicated exactly by a properly adjusted stock-cash portfolio.

The accuracy of the replicating strategy depends on four considerations. First, since the strategy may involve frequent trading, it is necessary that transaction costs be relatively insignificant. Second, if must be possible to borrow whatever is required to form the replicating stock–cash portfolio (or, in the case of other option positions, it must be possible to short the stock). Third, the possibility of gap opening or jump movements in the stock price means that a call can provide something that a levered stock position cannot. To take an extreme case, suppose a catastrophic event suddenly causes the stock price to collapse to zero. This may happen too fast for us to adjust our stock–cash position. A call, on the other hand, will pay off our borrowing even in such a catastrophe. Fourth, there may be significant uncertainty surrounding future rates of interest, the stock's volatility or cash dividends on the stock. For example, while an unanticipated increase in volatility will increase the value of a call, it is certainly conceivable that such a change could occur without affecting the price of the underlying stock. Consequently, the value of the call would change but the value of our stock–cash portfolio would not, no matter how we revised it.

Although it may be impossible to find a strategy that will allow a portfolio of stock and cash to duplicate exactly the returns of a call under all possible conditions, we nonetheless strongly believe that the concept of an option being equivalent to a carefully adjusted position in the underlying stock and cash is close enough to being true in most situations of practical interest to make it an invaluable tool for understanding options.

TRANSLATING OPTION POSITIONS INTO STOCK–CASH EQUIVALENTS

If we can replicate a call, we can replicate any other type of option position as well. Exhibit B, which translates the language of options into the more familiar language of stock and cash, shows what we would need to do. For each option position in the center of the table, the corresponding stock–cash portfolio is given at the top of its column and the appropriate adjustment strategy is given at the ends of its row. For example, the exhibit shows that buying a put is equivalent to a short position in the stock combined with lending, which will be revised by lending more and shorting more stock when the stock price falls and by lending less and buying back stock to reduce the short position when the stock price rises.

Some option positions are likened to "insurance." For example, an at-the-money put purchased against a long share of stock protects the investor against loss if the stock price falls. Our analysis implies that this insurance effect arises because the *protective put* is equivalent to a long stock-lending portfolio that is systematically shifted (1) away from stock and into cash as the stock price falls, providing a floor on losses, and (2) into stock and away from cash as the stock price rises, permitting future gains or losses to be realized.

To generalize, any hedged option position whose replicating portfolio involves shifting away from a long or short stock position toward no stock as the stock price falls implicitly involves the purchase of insurance. Conversely, any hedged option position whose replicating portfolio involves shifting further into a long or short stock position as the stock price falls implicitly involves the sale of insurance. Therefore, the far left and far right upper (lower) option positions in Exhibit B amount to buying (selling) insurance. For example, buying protective puts is similar to the purchase of insurance, while writing *covered calls* (buy one share and write one call) is similar to the sale of insurance.

Option positions have also been compared to forward contracts, which promise delivery of an underlying asset on a given date (delivery date) in the future at a currently agreed price (forward price). Like a call, a forward contract is equivalent to a levered position in the underlying asset. In contrast to a call, however, a forward contract requires unconditional delivery, rather than exercise at the option of the buyer. A forward contract could be replicated by borrowing to finance the *entire* holdings of the underlying asset and leaving this stock–cash position *unrevised* through the delivery date.[4] This is represented in Exhibit A by the straight line cutting the horizontal axis at 30.

Is there an option position that also has these two properties? If so, we can replicate forward contracts with options. Exhibit B shows that the replicating portfolios for both long calls and short puts involve long stock and borrowing. Moreover, the revision strategies for these two positions move in opposite directions. Therefore, we might suspect that the proper combination of the two positions would neutralize the required revisions. As the stock price changes we would find ourselves simply transferring stock between the two replicating positions with no net purchases or sales required. Indeed, as it turns out, we can replicate a purchased forward contract exactly by buying one call and shorting one put with a common expiration date equal to the delivery date and a common striking price equal to the forward price.[5]

We are now prepared to answer the questions posed at the beginning of the article. In each case, we simply need to examine the composition of the stock–cash portfolios that replicate option positions.

How To Value an Option. If we can exactly duplicate an option with a stock–cash position, we can also accomplish the reverse. If it turns out that the current market price of an option differs from that of the replicating portfolio, then we will have found an arbitrage opportunity, since both the option and its replicating portfolio (which is self-financing) are sure to have identical payoffs at expiration.[6] Thus the value of an option is equal to the value of its replicating stock–cash portfolio.

From this perspective, the problem of valuing an option is the same as the problem of determining the composition of its current replicating portfolio. The appendix provides an example where the current replicating portfolio consists of 5/7 shares of stock at $50 per share financed partially with $22.50 of borrowing. This implies that the current value of the call must be $13.20 ([$50 × 5/7] − $22.50).

The Black-Scholes option pricing model provides another way of determining the composition of the replicating portfolio. The Black-Scholes formula for a call takes the following form:

$$\text{call value} = (\text{stock price} \times \text{delta}) - \text{borrowing.}^{7}$$

The "delta" is the standard terminology used in the options market for the number of shares in the replicating portfolio. If the market price of the call exceeds this value, the call is overpriced; if it is less, the call is underpriced.

How to Measure the Expected Return and Risk of an Option Position. If we know how to measure the risk and return of stock–cash portfolios, we can easily measure these variables for option positions as well. The leverage of any stock–cash portfolio will be:

$$a \equiv \frac{\text{stock price} \times \text{number of shares}}{(\text{stock price} \times \text{number of shares}) - \text{borrowing}}$$

where the leverage a will exceed one if we are borrowing and be less than one if we are lending. From this formula we can derive the expected return, volatility and beta of any stock–cash portfolio:

$$\begin{aligned} \text{expected return} &= a \times \text{stock expected return} + (1 - a) \times \text{interest rate,} \\ \text{volatility} &= a \times \text{stock volatility,} \\ \text{beta} &= a \times \text{stock beta.} \end{aligned}$$

Measuring the return and risk of an option position (on a given underlying stock) entails three steps. First, we translate each option into its current replicating stock–cash portfolio; second, we aggregate across all the options to find their replicating net position as a group in stock and cash; third, we calculate the leverage parameter a for this netted position and apply the formulas for return and risk.[8]

For example, since a properly price purchased call is replicated by a margined long position in the stock, a will exceed one and the call will be both more risky and have greater expected return (provided the stock's expected return is greater than the interest rate) than the stock itself. Similarly, a covered call will have both lower risk and lower expected return than the stock, since a will be less than one.[9]

Moreover, observe that the leverage measure a of the option position's replicating portfolio will typically change continually through the future. Therefore, even if the expected return and risk of the underlying stock remain unchanged, the expected return and risk of the option position will typically change over time.

How the Margin Requirements and Transaction Costs of Option Positions Compare with Common Stock. Margin requirements on common stock involve (1) limits on borrowing against long positions, (2) limits on the use of proceeds of short sales snd (3) collateral to guarantee performance of short positions. An examination of their equivalent stock–cash positions shows how options can be used to relax each of these requirements.

For example, buying a call will often prove a way to relax the first requirement. Currently an investor can borrow only up to 50 per cent to initiate purchase of stock. In contrast, one of our previous examples, showed that one at-the-money call selling at three dollars was equivalent to the purchase of one-half share for $15, $12 of which was borrowed. In other words, the call implicitly allows borrowing 80 per cent (12/15) of the price of the stock.[10] Moreover, the call may implicitly permit borrowing at more favorable rates than otherwise obtainable. Indeed, this is likely to be the case for retail investors if it is the interest rates available to professionals that determine option prices. In this event, the lower borrowing rates available to professionals will be passed along to the public through lower call prices.

Buying puts may relax the second and third margin requirements. Remember that the replicating portfolio of a put consists of selling stock short and lending. Unlike many professionals, most retail investors cannot earn interest on the proceeds of short sales. Again, however, if these professionals determine option prices, then the interest they can earn on short sale proceeds will be passed along to the public in the form of lower put prices.[11] In addition, the lending contained in the replicating portfolios for many puts will be less than the collateral required to guarantee performance of short stock positions.

With respect to transaction costs, options and stock can be compared (1) dollar for dollar of investment, (2) option contract vs. round lot of stock or (3) option vs. replicating stock–cash portfolio. Under the first approach, options come out unfavorably; under the second, options look very good for holding periods not exceeding the life of the option. However, if we want to compare positions of similar expected returns and risks, then neither of these approaches is correct. The third approach, which will generally have implications intermediate between the first two, is what we want. An analysis of the commissions usually charged for exchange-traded options shows that options tend to dominate stock for short holding periods, but that the advantage shifts to stocks for longer term positions that exceed the life of the option.[12]

Who Should be Buying and Who Should be Selling Options. The most frequently given reason for trading options is that they offer *new desired patterns of returns*. Yet, as we have seen, much of what options offer can be replicated by properly adjusting a stock–cash position over time. There must be othe considerations that incline investors toward options.

As we have just seen, options may offer investors *more favorable implicit borrowing or lending opportunities, margin requirements, transaction costs or tax exposure*. Also, as we mentioned earlier, changes in stock volatility or dividends may very well leave the current stock price unchanged while affecting the option price.[13] Thus options can offer *opportunities either to take advantage of information about stock volatility or dividends or to hedge against their impact*.

The question remains, however, whether the investor who decides to hold an option position should be buying or selling. The correspondence between options and replicating stock–cash portfolios can help answer this question. For example, an average investor might want simply to buy and hold stock, with no borrowing or lending. But if he were more risk-averse than average, he might not want to assume the risk inherent in holding a typical stock. He can reduce his risk by investing only part of his money in the stock and lending the remainder. If the stock price subsequently rose, his risk would tend to increase as the relative dollar value of the stock–cash position shifted toward the stock. At the same time, as his position become more valuable, he might become willing to accept more risk. Indeed, if he were average in this respect, he would find that the increase in the stock price automatically injected just the desired amount of risk into the portfolio. He would then be content to buy and hold, and would have no need for options.

However, suppose that, as the stock price rose and he became wealthier, the investor's willingness to accept more risk were less than the average investor's. Then he would want to shift from stock to cash gradually as his position became more valuable, and into stock from cash as his position became less valuable. He could, of course, do this by continually revising his stock-cash position. On the other hand, he could let a fixed covered call position achieve

EXHIBIT B. STOCK-CASH PORTFOLIOS TO REPLICATE OPTION POSITIONS

		Long Stock (no more than one share) + Lending	Long Stock (no more than one share) + Borrowing	Short Stock (no more than one share) + Lending	Short Stock (no more than one share) + Borrowing		
As Stock Price Rises	Buy stock financed by borrowing	long stock (one share) + long one put*	long one call	long one put	short stock (one share) + long one call	Sell stock and lends proceeds	As Stock Price Falls
As Stock Price Rises	Sell stock and lend proceeds	long stock (one share) + short one call†	short one put	short one call	short stock (one share) + short one put	Buy stock financed by borrowing	As Stock Price Falls

NOTE: In all cases, any dividends received will be used to increase lending or reduce borrowing. Restitution for dividends paid while stock is held short will be financed by reduced lending or more borrowing.

*Protective put. †Covered call.

the same result automatically. Which strategy he prefers will typically depend on the comparative transaction costs.

In brief, covered call writers should typically be investors whose risk aversion *does not decrease as rapidly* as the average investor's as the value of their portfolios increases. Conversely, protective put buyers should typically be investors whose risk aversion *decreases more rapidly* than the average investor's as the value of their portfolios increases.[14] Similar reasoning applies to the other option positions in Exhibit B.

A completely separate reason for a preference between buying or selling options rests on certain technical theories of stock price behavior. If investors believe in trends, they may want to buy protective puts or buy uncovered calls. If they believe in reversals, they should prefer writing covered calls or writing puts.

What to Do When the Corresponding Option Doesn't Exist. If options on a particular stock or on a portfolio do not exist, we can create them by using the appropriate strategy for the underlying asset and cash. For example, we can effectively create an at-the-money protective put option on our equity portfolio. We would begin by placing part of our capital in the equity portfolio and part in cash and then, without changing the composition of the equity portfolio, shift between the portfolio and cash as the equity portfolio value changes and as the "expiration date" approaches. Such an investment strategy would be tantamount to insuring the equity portfolio against losses by paying a fixed premium to an insurance company.[15]

Even in the unlikely event that exchange-traded put options of synchronous maturity existed on all the stocks in a portfolio, a combination of put options could not match the above strategy in terms of cost. If we purchase put options against each stock in the portfolio, we would be insuring each individual stock, rather than the portfolio as a whole, against loss; even if our portfolio rose in value, as long as the price of at least one stock fell the insurance would pay off. The insurance provided by a stock–cash strategy would pay off if and only if the portfolio fell in value. As such, the implicit premium of the latter strategy will be less because only the portfolio as a whole, not every individual stock, is insured.

Total portfolio option replicating strategies, since they involve shifts between equities and cash, are similar to rebalancing strategies that seek to maintain the risk level by keeping the same relative amounts invested in equities and cash. In contrast, the total portfolio protective put option strategy systematically increases the risk of the overall position as the portfolio becomes more valuable and decreases exposure to risk as the portfolio falls in value.

For many financial institutions, the replicating strategies for protective puts and covered calls will be feasible because they do not require borrowing or short selling. However, replication of many other option positions will not be possible because they do require borrowing or short selling. ■

APPENDIX

A SIMPLE EXAMPLE OF REPLICATION OF OPTION RETURNS WITH A PORTFOLIO OF STOCK AND CASH

Suppose the current price of an underlying stock is \$50 and that, over the next period, it will either move up to \$70 or down to \$35. If it moves up to \$70 during the first period, then it will move to \$100 or \$50 during the second period. If it moves down to \$35 during the first period, then it will move to \$50 or \$25 during the second period. The tree diagram in Exhibit AA illustrates this behavior.

Suppose that we can borrow money at an 11 per cent rate of interest in each period. How can be replicate the returns of an at-the-money purchased call that expires at the end of the second period? First, les us see what we would do with just one period remaining when the stock price is at \$70. At expiration, the call will be worth \$50 (\$100–\$50) if the stock price goes up or zero if the stock price goes down (since we would then be indifferent to exercising it).

What mixture of stock and cash would produce these same returns? Suppose we let Δ stand for the number of shares we would need to buy and B for the number of dollars we would need to borrow. Then our problem is to find values of Δ and B such that:

$$(100 \times \Delta) - (1.11 \times B) = 100 - 50 = 50,$$

$$(50 \times \Delta) - (1.11 \times B) = 0.$$

EXHIBIT AA

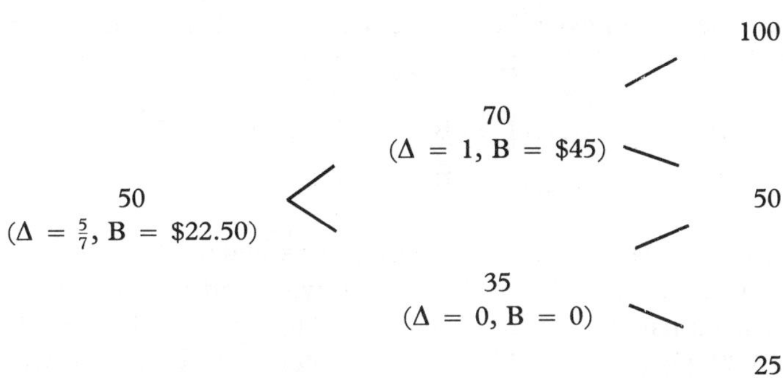

The first equation insures that our stock–cash portfolio has the same return as the option if the stock goes up and the second assures us the returns will also be equal if the stock goes down. It is easy to see that setting Δ equal to one and B approximately equal to \$45 will solve both these equations and therefore give us a stock–cash position with the same returns as a call.

On the other hand, suppose we have one period remaining and the stock price is at \$35, then our problem is to find values of Δ and B such that:

$$(50 \times \Delta) - (1.11 \times B) = 0,$$
$$(35 \times \Delta) - (1.11 \times B) = 0.$$

In this case the call has no chance of finishing in the money, so it makes sense that our solutions are Δ equals zero and B equals zero.

Finally, let us go back to the first period when the stock price was \$50. Now we must find a portfolio of stock and cash that will (1) provide us with just enough money to buy one share of stock, financed by \$45 of borrowing, if the stock price goes up over the first period to \$70, or (2) provide us with just enough money to buy zero shares of stock, financed with zero borrowing, if the stock price goes down over the first period to \$35. That is, in the first period we must choose Δ and B so that:

$$(70 \times \Delta) - (1.11 \times B) = (70 \times 1) - 45 = 25,$$
$$(35 \times \Delta) - (1.11 \times B) = 0.$$

In this case the call has no change of finishing in the money, so it makes sense that our solutions are Δ equals zero and B equals zero.

Finally, let us go back to the first period when the stock price was \$50. Now we must find a portfolio of stock and cash that will (1) provide us with just enough money to buy one share of stock, financed by \$45 of borrowing, if the stock price goes up over the first period to \$70, or (2) provide us with just enough money to buy zero shares of stock, financed with zero borrowing, if the stock price goes down over the first period to \$35. That is, in the first period we must choose Δ and B so that:

$$(70 \times \Delta) - (1.11 \times B) = (70 \times 1) - 45 = 25,$$
$$(35 \times \Delta) - (1.11 \times B) = 0.$$

In this case, Δ equals 5/7 and B equals approximately \$22.50.

To summarize, to replicate the call we will need to start by buying 5/7 shares financed partially by borrowing \$22.50. This implies we will have to put up \$13.20 ($[50 \times \frac{5}{7}] - 22\frac{1}{2}$) of our own money. If we do this, we will have just enough money to take the appropriate position during the second period, whether the stock price goes up or down. If the stock price goes up, we will find ourselves subsequently buying in, financing the additional 2/7 ($1 - \frac{5}{7}$) shares by additional borrowing. If the stock price goes down, we will find ourselves subsequently completely selling out and thereby raising just enough money to repay our borrowing. In either case, on the expiration date we will find that the value of our replicating portfolio is exactly equal to the value of the call. ■

FOOTNOTES

1. A *call* option is a contract giving its owner the right to buy a fixed number of shares of a specified common stock at a fixed price at any time on or before a fixed date. The act of making this transaction is referred to as *exercising* the option. The fixed price is termed the *striking price* and the given date, the *expiration date*. The individual who issues a call is termed the *writer* and the individual who purchases the call is termed the *buyer*. A *put* option is identical except it conveys the right to sell the stock.
2. The seminal articles developing the theory are Fischer Black and Myron Scholes, "The Pricing of Options and Corporate Liabilities," *Journal of Political Economy*, May–June 1973 (Chapter 19) and Robert C. Merton, "Theory of Rational Option Pricing," *Bell Journal of Economics and Management Science*, Spring 1973. A considerably simplified development of this theory appeared in John C. Cox, Stephen A. Ross and Mark Rubinstein, "Option Pricing: A Simplified Approach," *Journal of Financial Economics*, September 1979 (Chapter 20).
3. To simplify the figure, the interest rate on borrowing is assumed to be zero. If this were not the case, the call price curve would have the same zero vertical intercept, but be shifted somewhat to the left. The exact position and shape of the curve is also influenced by the time remaining to expiration and the stock volatility.
4. This conclusion presumes there are no carrying costs or cash payouts involved in holding the underlying asset. However, the conclusion of the next paragraph holds even with possibly uncertain carrying costs or cash payouts, as long as the replicating options are not protected against these costs or payoffs and cannot be exercised prior to expiration.
5. Readers may want to refer to Eugene Moriarty, Susan Phillips and Paula Tosini, "A Comparison of Options and Futures in the Management of Portfolio Risk," *Financial Analysts Journal*, January/February 1981. —Ed.
6. Indeed, many floor traders of options exchanges acting on their own account follow trading strategies based on this observation. They will almost simultaneously buy or sell an option and take an opposing position in the stock (or a related deep-in-the-money option that behaves like the stock). Over time, they will adjust the composition of this portfolio to keep its value insensitive to stock price movements, hoping to profit from mispricing of the option.
7. According to the original Black-Scholes formula, the current value of a call C depends only on its underlying stock price S, striking price K, time to expiration t, the interest rate $r - 1$, and the stock volatility σ. The composition of the replicating portfolio consists of N(x) shares of stock, where N(x) is the area under a standard normal distribution function to the left of x and

$$x \equiv \frac{\log(S/Kr^{-t})}{\sigma\sqrt{t}} + \frac{1}{2}\sigma\sqrt{t}.$$

The amount borrowed is $Kr^{-t}N(x - \sigma\sqrt{t})$ where $N(x - \sigma\sqrt{t})$ is the area to the left of $x - \sigma\sqrt{t}$. The value of a call is then

$$C = SN(x) - Kr^{-t}N(x - \sigma\sqrt{t}).$$

Although this formula applies only to stocks that do not pay dividends prior to the expiration date, it can be modified to include the effects of dividends.

8. This technique will only work exactly over the very short run, since the composition of the replicating portfolio changes as the expiration date approaches. However, as shown in John C. Cox and Mark Rubinstein, *Options Markets* (Prentice-Hall, 1981), these short-run measures of return and risk will usually be adequate approximations of the longer run exact measures. This makes sense intuitively, since if the chances are roughly equal that the stock price may rise or fall, then the chances are roughly equal that the short-run return and risk measures will increase or decrease in the future.
9. Note that the conclusions of this paragraph will hold exactly in the long run as well. For example, since a covered call *always* involves a replicating portfolio consisting of long no more than one share of stock and lending, it must always have less *expected* return and risk than the stock by itself, although for some stock price outcomes its *realized* return may be greater.
10. A full analysis of margin requirements should consider maintenance margins on stock and that the implicit leverage obtained through a call will change as the stock price changes.
11. Since the buyer of a put is implicitly lending, then the higher the interest rate he receives, the less he will need to lend to come up with the striking price on the expiration date if the put finishes in the money. Therefore, the lower the current value of the put. Since calls involve implicit borrowing, similar reasoning shows their values will be higher, the higher the interest rate, other things equal.
12. A complete analysis would also consider any differences in the bid-ask spread typically sacrificed or gained by various classes of investors in options and stock.
13. This will also be true of interest rates. But, in this case, interest rate futures would typically be superior to currently listed options for hedging or taking advantage of special information.
14. This correspondence was first discussed by Hayne Leland, "Who Should Buy Portfolio Insurance?" *Journal of Finance*, May 1980 (Chapter 21).
15. Remember that the analogy to insurance breaks down under a sudden catastrophic loss that does not leave sufficient time to adjust the replicating portfolio.

NEXT

23. AFTER THE FALL

Donald L. Luskin

On October 19, 1987, the stock market as represented by the Dow Jones Industrial Index fell by an unprecedented and horrifying 508 points, climaxing an eight-week decline of almost 1000 points. In the wake of the crash the need for portfolio protection strategies is clearer than ever. Yet as the need is greater, so must be the insistence that the strategy truly be able to deliver on its promises.

The purpose of this chapter is to ask three difficult questions:

First, *did portfolio insurance pass the test?* Portfolio insurance evolved in the sheltering updrafts of the five-year bull market beginning in 1982. The crash was its first true exposure to significant adversity.

Second, *did portfolio insurance cause the crash?* In the weeks following October 19 it was often said in the press that portfolio insurance exaggerated the crash, turning a would-be ordinary decline into a "market meltdown."

Third, *where do we go from here?* After the crash, investors will never again see equity investments as they used to. Certainly estimates of worst-case equity volatility will be permanently raised. This may well lead to a surge in demand for portfolio insurance, but investors may just as well be inhibited by a new appreciation of its high potential costs.

Until these questions are answered satisfactorily, the effectiveness of portfolio insurance, and its role in the marketplace, will be in serious doubt.

DID PORTFOLIO INSURANCE PASS THE TEST?

"It's never been tested in a bear market!" Before the crash, this oft-repeated statement seemed like a cheap shot for the critics and skeptics. In the crash's aftermath, they will never need to say it again.

The severe market decline that climaxed on October 19, 1987, presented three serious challenges to the effectiveness of portfolio insurance.

First, the volatility of the decline was greater than anyone had imagined to be possible. As Jeremy Evnine discusses in Chapter 14, estimating upcoming market volatility is a key input to most portfolio insurance programs. Needless to say, no one had accurately estimated the volatility of the crash or its aftermath. Because portfolio insurance managers had systematically *under*estimated volatility, their positions were systematically *under*hedged. When the crash came, their positions were more exposed to downside risk than they would have been with a higher estimate.

Second, the trading rules used by some portfolio insurance managers were overwhelmed by the sheer magnitude and rapidity of the decline. Ideally, managers would wish to trade continuously, updating their portfolio insurance positions whenever the market moved even slightly. But in the real world of transaction costs, managers have to set up arbitrary guidelines that establish a realistic frequency for trading. Guidelines that "lag" the market, by adjusting positions on the day following a market move, or adjusting only partially, were particularly deadly in the crash.

Third, the chaotic trading conditions that prevailed in the week of October 19 led to severe mispricings between stock index futures and their underlying indexes. Futures on the S&P 500 Index often traded at discounts of over 20 points below the index itself. To the extent that they had to sell these deeply underpriced futures, portfolio insurance programs were burdened with enormous unanticipated trading costs.

These three problems afflicted virtually all portfolio insurance managers to some extent. During the worst of the crash, some managers made the decision simply not to trade, to wait until the storm blew over.

Investment managers must often make difficult decisions with the best interests of their clients in mind. But as a result, some portfolio insurance programs failed to perform as planned. According to the *Wall Street Journal*, one major pension plan sponsor " . . . expected that a new hedging technique —portfolio insurance—would 'help us ride out the downturn.' Late last week, however, [he] pulled the plug. 'Portfolio insurance didn't work' at the $300 million pension plan he oversees . . . [He] had hoped to incur at most a 5% loss on stock-market holdings, no matter what the stock market did. Instead, he says, his fund felt the brunt of the stock market's 29% slump this month."[1]

Another large portfolio insurance manager, Wells Fargo Investment Advisors, made the difficult decision differently, and attempted to trade as closely as possible to the recommendations of the hedging program, despite adverse conditions. Their average account underperformed by 66 hundredths of one percent—in other words, an account with a maximum loss specified at 5% would have experienced an actual loss of 5.66%.

Did portfolio insurance pass the test? Yes, but not with flying colors. For the portfolio insurance managers who made the decision to singlemindedly follow the dictates of the model, market conditions of once-in-a-lifetime severity led to a certain degree of underperformance. While less than perfect, under the circumstances it was quite close—and a drastic improvement over the loss that would have been taken by an investor not using portfolio insurance at all.

DID PORTFOLIO INSURANCE CAUSE THE CRASH?

It has been argued that, if enough investors use portfolio insurance, it may exaggerate market volatility. The SEC's Division of Market Regulation has expressed the concern that " . . . dynamic hedging strategies, such as portfolio insurance, combined with other market events, could trigger selling that temporarily exceeds market liquidity . . . . The scenario begins with index futures prices moving to enough of a discount to trigger [arbitrage]. The resulting block sales of stocks depress the equity market to levels that trigger portfolio insurance programs. These programs, which involve futures sales, further depress futures prices and cause the cycle to repeat itself . . . finally leading to a market collapse."[2]

The key to portfolio insurance's role in this scenario is its tendency to systematically buy as the market goes higher and sell as the market goes lower —in other words, to "buy high and sell low." Portfolio insurance is a type of trend-following, the scientific embodiment of the all-too-human urge to reduce your risk when you appear to be suffering a loss, and to enlarge it when you are ahead of the game.

Because any action taken by an investor marginally moves prices in the direction of the investor's transaction, it is obvious that, to some extent, portfolio insurance trades must slightly "exaggerate" the very market moves that are being responded to. But this does not make a "market meltdown"; it is simply a small transaction cost no different than that paid by any transactor.

Neither portfolio insurance, nor any other strategy, can artificially move markets very far below their true fundamental levels. If they were to even begin to do so, value-oriented investors would quickly step in to hunt for bargains. Those who claim that portfolio insurance caused a "market meltdown" which would otherwise not have occurred completely fail to explain why the decline stopped when it did. The selling forces of portfolio insurance were present on Tuesday, October 20, and yet the market stabilized. Why didn't the "meltdown" continue indefinitely? Not because the portfolio insurers quit selling, but rather because the market had found a new and appropriate level of valuation.

If portfolio insurance had "artificially" caused a "meltdown" below true market value levels, we would expect to see a significant and immediate price recovery. Yet after the huge decline in the Dow from its August, 1987, peak, there was very little immediate retracement. As of the end of October, the highest closing price of the Dow had been only 289 points from the October 19 climax of the 983-point decline. 289 points seems like a big number, but it is only 29% of the 983 loss. On a scale with which we relate more easily, it is as if the market had declined 10 points and recovered 3.

Did portfolio insurance cause the crash? Of course not. Selling generated by portfolio insurance programs is no different from any other kind of selling, and cannot be held uniquely responsible. To explain away this momentous economic event by blaming it on portfolio insurance is to irresponsibly deny the deep global macroeconomic problems that are at its roots.

WHERE DO WE GO FROM HERE?

Does portfolio insurance have a future? Though many of its weaknesses emerged in high relief as the result of the stress-testing of the crash, portfolio insurance has shown itself to be a basically robust strategy. Nonetheless, after the crash, an investor contemplating a program of portfolio insurance has many uncertainties to face. These uncertainties have always been a part of portfolio insurance, but they can now no longer be ignored.

First, the investor must come to terms with the role of human trading judgment in its implementation. Does the investor wish to retain managers who will follow the model rigidly, or prefer to retain those who will override the program?

Second, the investor should ideally be willing to transact in the actual stock market and not just the futures market, which can become deeply mispriced. For many investors this will be a barrier to using portfolio insurance. While indexed portfolios can be traded fairly easily, trading actively managed portfolios can be cumbersome and expensive.

Third, the investor should understand that there is more uncertainty than ever about the *ex post* cost of insurance programs due to possible misestimation of volatility. Volatility has always been difficult to estimate, but never has the magnitude of misestimation been so great (Mr. Evnine remarked to me after the crash, "When quantitative methods are of no avail, punt!").

Fourth, the investor must realize that, however uncertain, the costs of portfolio insurance will be forever higher after the crash, precisely because portfolio insurance is now understood to be more valuable. Now that the marketplace has had a vivid lesson in the true possible magnitude of risk, it will not allow insurers to get away cheaply.

Where do we go from here? Those investors for whom portfolio insurance performed well in the crash will be adherents for life. Those who were disappointed will likely be bitter, and some will never use it again. For those who didn't use it at all, it may well provide a means of investing in an equity market seen suddenly as otherwise too risky.

Even if particular types of hedging goals are modified or abandoned, ultimately it is conceivable that portfolio insurance and dynamic hedging will not continue to expand their role in the world's markets. For in the broadest sense, these strategies are fundamental means by which investors seek to control their pattern of investment outcomes. Now that investors have been shown that they possess this control, they will never willingly give it up.

FOOTNOTES

1. George Anders, "Portfolio Insurance Proved Cold Comfort," *Wall Street Journal*, October 28, 1987; page 6.
2. U. S. Securities and Exchange Commission Division of Market Regulation, "The Role of Index-Related Trading in the Market Decline on September 11 and 12, 1986," March, 1987, pages 3, 21.

INDEX